TEXAS AND TEXANS
IN THE CIVIL WAR

By
Ralph A. Wooster

EAKIN PRESS ★ Austin, Texas

FIRST EDITION

Published in the United States of America
By Eakin Press
A Division of Sunbelt Media, Inc.
P.O. Drawer 90159 ★ Austin, Texas 78709

ISBN 1-57168-042-X

2   3   4   5   6   7   8   9

Library of Congress Cataloging-in-Publication Data:

Wooster, Ralph A.
    Texas and Texans in the Civil War / by Ralph A. Wooster. -- 1st ed.
        p.   cm.
    Includes bibliographical references and index.
    ISBN 1-57168-042-X
    1. Texas--History--Civil War. 1861-1865. I. Title.
    E580.W66   1995
    973.7'464--dc20   95-35743
                                                   CIP

Cover Illustration - *Victory at Sabine Pass*
By Gary S. Zaboly

Back Cover Photo - Private Hugh Cooke, Waller County, Texas
Archives Division, Texas State Library

Contents

Preface

Although a frontier state spared the devastation that took place in Virginia, Tennessee, and Georgia, Texas nevertheless played a major role in the American Civil War. Federal property was surrendered in the state two months prior to the firing upon Fort Sumter; the last battle of the war was fought in South Texas a month after Lee surrendered at Appomattox. Texans were involved in almost every great battle of the war. They fought and died from the deserts and mountains of New Mexico to the hills of Pennsylvania and Maryland. They battled in the mountains and valleys of Missouri and Arkansas, along the banks of the Mississippi, Tennessee, Cumberland, York, and James rivers, in the red clay of Georgia, in the bluegrass of Kentucky, and along the bayous and in the forests of Louisiana. They drove Federal invaders from Galveston, Port Lavaca, Corpus Christi, Sabine Pass, and Laredo, and helped defeat Nathaniel P. Banks in his attempt to invade East Texas. And, sadly, Texans fought Texans in the lower Rio Grande Valley.

This book represents an attempt to summarize the role Texas and Texans played in the war. There have been many scholarly works written in recent years about specific events and campaigns in which Texans participated. The late Harold B. Simpson eloquently described the achievements of Hood's Texas Brigade in Virginia and Tennessee, Martin H. Hall and Donald S. Frazier have narrated the story of Sibley's ill-fated New Mexico campaign, Jerry D. Thompson detailed the struggle along the Rio Grande, and Anne Bailey, Alwyn Barr, Norman Brown, and Stephen Oates have written and edited works describing the role of Texans in Arkansas, Missouri, and Louisiana. Others, particularly Walter Buenger, Randolph Campbell, James Marten, and Richard McCaslin, have shown the divisions among Texans over slavery, secession, and the war. Carefully researched dissertations by Robert P. Felgar (1935) and Allan Ashcraft (1960) provide broad coverage but have remained unpublished and not easily available to the average reader. The best published work that adequately summarizes the overall role of Texans in the war has remained O. M. Roberts' narrative in Volume XI of *Confederate Military History*, published in 1899.

I have written this book in an effort to fill the perceived need for a modern account of Texas' role in the war. Although I have researched both manuscript and printed sources, I have relied heavily upon the work of others as indicated in endnotes and bibliography. In doing so I hope to have provided a synthesis of modern scholarship relating to the subject. At the same time I have attempted to present an informative narrative for both the scholar and general reader seeking to learn more about the role Texans played in the conflict.

Many people have contributed to the completion of this work. The editors of the *Southwestern Historical Quarterly*, the *East Texas Historical Journal*, the *Texas Gulf Historical and Biographical Record*, and the University of Georgia Press have been kind enough to permit me to use portions of my articles that have appeared in their publications. In addition to thanking them and the numerous historians whose research forms the basis for this volume, I wish to thank a number of others who have helped along the way. The late Peter Wells, Beaumont attorney, historian, and collector of Texana, left a magnificent collection of books to the Mary and John Gray Library of Lamar University which has been indispensable to my work. To him and Charlotte Holliman, my former student who is now on the staff of the Lamar University library, I express my profound thanks. W. T. Block and W. D. "Bill" Quick of Nederland provided information concerning Sabine Pass and the upper Texas coast that was most helpful. Skipper Steely of Paris, Texas, furnished insights about the Ninth Texas Infantry from his exhaustive research concerning northeast Texas. Debra Clark of Beaumont was most generous of her time and expertise in helping a novice to understand (at least slightly) his new computer-word processor. Colleagues in the Lamar history department and close friends Karen and George Farrar, Sharon Pate, and Melissa Chesser were, as usual, encouraging as they learned more than they wished about Texas and the Civil War. My son, Robert Wooster of Texas A&M–Corpus Christi, an authority on the nineteenth century United States Army, was helpful in many ways and provided a Union perspective from his studies of Nelson Miles and John Schofield. As always his mother, my wife Edna, offered encouragement, inspiration, and assistance at every step of the way.

Ed Eakin, publisher and friend of Texas history and historians, expressed interest and support in the project from an early date and agreed to publish the work long before he saw a single page of copy. Special thanks go to Kevin Young, my editor at Eakin Press and author of *To the Tyrants Never Yield: A Texas Civil War Sampler* (1992). Kevin not only provided much encouragement and advice but also played a major role in obtaining photographs and maps. Kevin put me into contact with Gary Zaboly, an outstanding military artist, who painted the scene of Dick Dowling and other heroes of Sabine Pass for the cover of the book, and with Phil Ulbrich, who prepared the maps. Lawrence T. Jones III of the Confederate Calendar Works, John Anderson of the Texas State Archives, and the Forest View Historical Services were most helpful in locating photographs of Texas Confederates. Melissa Locke Roberts, editor at Eakin Press, did an outstanding job in editing the manuscript for publication. My thanks go to them all.

Finally, I would like to thank my students, friends, and colleagues at Lamar University who have listened to me talk about Texas and the Civil War for the past forty years. This book is dedicated to them.

— RALPH A. WOOSTER
Beaumont, Texas
September 1995

CHAPTER ONE

The Secession Crisis

The election of Republican Abraham Lincoln as president of the United States in November 1860 set off a chain of events that led to the outbreak of the American Civil War. For months prior to the election, political leaders in the Southern states had argued that Lincoln's election would be a direct threat to the Southern way of life. Although both the party platform and candidate Lincoln were pledged only to halt the expansion of slavery, many Southerners were convinced that a Republican victory would ultimately lead to the abolition of slavery.[1]

During the presidential campaign, many Southerners declared that if Lincoln was victorious they would withdraw from the Union. When it was apparent that Lincoln had been elected, seven states in the lower South, including Texas, seceded. South Carolina, the most radical slaveholding state, was the first to act. By a vote of 169–0 a convention of the people meeting in Columbia adopted an ordinance of separation on December 20, 1860. Five sister states of the deep South — Mississippi, Florida, Alabama, Georgia, and Louisiana — voted to secede in January.

Texas was the last state in the lower South to take action. The movement for separation in Texas was different from that in the other states of the region. In those states the governor was a leader in the movement for secession. In Texas, however, Governor Sam

Houston, was a staunch Unionist who refused to cooperate with those favoring secession. Secession was accomplished in spite of his determined opposition. Also, in Texas the state convention submitted its action to the voters for approval. Nowhere else in the lower South did this occur.[2]

Prior to Lincoln's election, a majority of Texans supported the Union which they had worked so hard to join only fifteen years earlier.[3] The sectional controversies which divided the North and the South in the late 1840s and 1850s caused concern to Texans but did not assume the importance felt in the older states. The war with Mexico, the New Mexico boundary dispute, settlement of the public debt, and frontier problems had absorbed the energies of the state's citizens in the fifteen years between annexation and Lincoln's election. The young state had enjoyed tremendous economic prosperity and expansion in those years. Assessable wealth increased over five-fold as thousands of new settlers, attracted by the generous land policy, fertile soil, and mild climate, cleared the land and established new farms, plantations, and towns. The number of improved acres devoted to farming increased from eleven million in 1850 to nearly twenty-three million in 1860. Production of cotton rose from less than 60,000 bales in 1850 to over 430,000 bales in 1860. Corn production increased from six million to over sixteen million bushels during the same period. The yield of wheat, confined mainly to North Texas, rose from 41,000 bushels in 1850 to nearly one and a half million bushels in 1860.[4]

In population, Texas was the most rapidly growing state in the South. The population of the state grew from 212,592 in 1850 to 604,215 in 1860, an increase of 184 percent. The majority of the newcomers migrated from the states of the Old South, especially Tennessee, Missouri, Mississippi, Alabama, and Georgia, but several thousand Northerners, primarily from Ohio, Indiana, and Illinois, settled in North Texas during the 1850s. Immigration from Europe and Mexico was also a contributing factor in the population expansion. In 1860 ten percent of the state's free residents were foreign born. Nearly half were Germans.[5]

The slave population was increasing even more rapidly than the free population. There were approximately 5,000 slaves in Texas at the time of the Texas Revolution. The number increased enormously during the years of the Republic. In 1845 tax rolls for thirty-two of Texas' thirty-six organized counties listed 27,555 slaves. The first United States census, taken in 1850, enumerated 58,161 slaves. By 1860 the figure was 182,566, an increase of 214 percent in the decade. Slaves constituted 27.4 percent of the state's total population in 1850. Ten years later they were 30.2 percent of the total.[6]

Historian Randolph Campbell pointed out that while slavery had a relatively brief history as an Anglo-American institution in Texas, it became increasingly important in the economic development of the state. In his book *An Empire for Slavery* (Baton Rouge: Louisiana State University Press, 1989), Campbell noted that while only one white Texas family in four owned slaves, slaveholders dominated the "state's economy, controlled its politics, and occupied the top rung on the social ladder." Slaveholders owned 73 percent of the state's real property, 71 percent of all improved acres, and 60 percent of all livestock. Over 90 percent of the state's cotton was grown by slaveholders in 1860. Nearly 70 percent of the state's political leaders were slaveholders.[7]

As slaveholders and slavery became more important to the political and economic life of the state, Texas interest and concern over the growing tensions between the North and the South heightened. John Brown's raid on the Federal arsenal at Harpers Ferry, Virginia, in the autumn of 1859 was, according to Walter Buenger, "the first of the psychological and physical shocks that would cause Texans to doubt the value of the Union."[8] Brown's raid occurred at the same time that Juan Cortina, a South Texas *ranchero* who championed the rights of Mexican citizens, seized control of Brownsville in South Texas. These events came at a time when Indian attacks along the Texas frontier were increasing. The failure of the Federal government to provide adequate security along their borders caused Texans to question the value of the Union and played into the hands of proslavery extremists who capitalized upon the emotional stress existing in the state.

Sam Houston, elected governor only two months prior to John Brown's raid, was determined to keep Southern extremists from taking any action that might take Texas out of the Union. In his inaugural address delivered on December 21, 1859, Houston called upon the people to remain faithful to the Union and the Constitution and warned against "the wild ravings of fanatics."[9] In a message to the state legislature on January 13, 1860, Houston reiterated his position that "Texas will maintain the Constitution and stand by the Union."[10] Several days later, when he received a communication

Sam Houston — Hero of San Jacinto and former president of the Republic of Texaswho was governor during secession crisis. Opposed secession; removed from office for refusing to take oath of allegiance to CSA.
     — Leib Image Archives,
York, PA

from the governor of South Carolina transmitting resolutions of that state's legislature asserting the right of secession and inviting Texas to participate in discussions relating to the subject, Houston again defended the Union and upheld the Constitution. "The Union was intended to be a perpetuity," he declared.[11]

Through skillful maneuvering the pro-Houston minority in the legislature was able to prevent Texas from accepting South Carolina's invitation. This was something of an empty victory for Unionists, however, because a majority of legislators expressed themselves in support of the right of secession. They preferred to await the outcome of the presidential election process before taking any precipitate action.[12]

Texas sent a states' rights, proslavery delegation to the National Democratic Convention held in Charleston, South Carolina, in April 1860. Headed by Guy M. Bryan, a nephew of Stephen F. Austin and a leading spokesman for Southern extremists, and including former governor and lieutenant governor Hardin R. Runnels and Francis R. Lubbock, the Texas delegation supported a platform guaranteeing protection of slavery in the national territories. When it became apparent that friends of Stephen A. Douglas would not accept such a platform guarantee, the Texans joined other delegates from the deep South in withdrawing from the convention. The

Texas delegates later participated in a meeting of Southern delegates at Richmond, Virginia, where they nominated John C. Breckinridge of Kentucky for president on a platform calling for the protection of slavery in the territories. The National Democratic Party, or what was left of it, nominated Stephen A. Douglas of Illinois as its candidate. The Douglas Democrats adopted a platform calling for popular sovereignty on slavery in the territories. John Bell of Tennessee was nominated by the newly formed Constitutional Union Party, a group which favored a moderate position on the slave question. Governor Houston came in second in the balloting of this party for a nominee. Meanwhile, the Republican Party, a purely sectional group, meeting in Chicago, nominated Abraham Lincoln for president. The Republicans were opposed to any expansion of slavery in the United States.[13]

The presidential campaign of Texas took place in an atmosphere of tension and hysteria. In early July a series of mysterious fires broke out in several North Texas towns. A month of unusually hot and dry weather with temperatures above 100 degrees had left wooden buildings dangerously dry. Extensive damage was caused, particularly in Dallas, where property estimated at nearly half a million dollars was destroyed. Rumors, fanned by newspaper editorials, spread that the work was that of abolitionists. Stories of suspected slave uprisings, poisoned wells, bottles of strychnine, and attempted assassinations added to the existing suspicions. Vigilance committees were formed and suspects, black and white, were arrested. A number of hangings, estimated by some as high as fifty, took place.[14]

One of those hanged was Anthony Bewley, a minister of the Northern Methodist Episcopal Church. Bewley, a native Tennessean, first came to Texas as a missionary in 1855. Although neither he nor his church advocated a forceful end to slavery, he was suspected of involvement in what newspapers called "the Texas Troubles." Bewley fled from the state but was trailed by vigilantes who caught him near Cassville, Missouri. They returned him to Fort Worth, where a mob hanged him. His body was left hanging all night and much of the next day. Three weeks later his body was taken from the shallow grave where it was buried. The bones were stripped of remaining flesh and placed on the roof of a local grocery store.[15]

The events of the summer of 1860 promoted the revitalization of the Knights of the Golden Circle, a secret order desirous of promoting the institution of slavery. The Knights had been organized in Kentucky in 1854 under the leadership of George W. L. Bickley, an ambitious and volatile individual. The Knights were originally concerned with building a slave empire in Latin America. Chapters, or castles, were formed throughout the South, and Bickley talked of a possible invasion of Mexico. Organization and financial difficulties sapped the Knights of the Golden Circle of much of its support, however, and by the late 1850s the order was almost defunct. The events of 1859–60 brought renewed interest and activity. In the autumn of 1860 Bickley visited Texas, where he found new support. By November there were at least thirty-two castles established in twenty-seven Texas counties. Elkanah Greer, a planter, merchant, and former major general of the Mississippi militia, was grand commander of the Knights in Texas. Although the dreams of a slave empire still remained, the Knights were now promoting secession in the event of a Republican victory in the presidential election.[16]

The 1860 presidential campaign was like none other. Lincoln and Douglas were the only candidates who had a serious chance to carry Northern states, while Breckinridge and Bell were the only two capable of carrying Southern states. Most Southerners rejected Douglas because of his failure to defend slavery in the territories, but a few still faithful to the National Democratic Party urged support for Union, or Fusion, electors pledged to vote for whichever candidate had the best chance of defeating Lincoln. This had some appeal to the Bell group but little to the Breckinridge supporters, who believed the Kentuckian could carry enough states to insure victory. In Texas the Fusion ticket had the support of Governor Houston and other Unionist leaders. At a mass meeting in Austin in late September, the governor warned his listeners of demagogues who "convert the misfortunes of the people into political capital." Even if Lincoln should be elected "we have no excuse for dissolving the Union," stated Houston. "The Union," he declared, is "worth more than Mr. Lincoln."[17]

The majority of Texans were not persuaded by Houston's arguments. They saw Abraham Lincoln and the Republican Party as a real threat to slavery and the Southern way of life. The only hope, they believed, was that Breckinridge, who pledged himself to protect slavery, would win enough states to deny Lincoln the victory. Many Texans agreed with fellow Southerners that Lincoln's election would make secession necessary.

Breckinridge carried Texas and all the other states of the deep

South. His victory in Texas was impressive. He received 47,561 votes, or 75 percent of the total. He had a majority in every Texas county except three: Bandera, Gillespie, and Starr, all sparsely populated frontier counties. In only seven other counties did Breckinridge fail to receive over sixty percent of the popular vote. The Fusion, or Union, ticket, in Texas pledged to Bell, received 15,402 votes, or approximately twenty-five percent of the total. Stephen A. Douglas picked up a few scattered votes from loyal supporters who refused to endorse the Fusion ticket. Electors supporting Lincoln did not appear on the Texas ballot.[18]

Although Breckinridge carried most of the Southern states, Lincoln was victorious nationally, receiving 180 electoral votes compared to 123 for his three opponents combined. Almost immediately pro-slavery advocates throughout the deep South called for secession from the Union. South Carolina, which had a long tradition of radicalism, was the first state to act. The state legislature called for a convention of the people to meet in December to determine the state's relationship with the Federal government. Other states in the lower South soon followed South Carolina's lead. By the end of the year South Carolina had seceded and five other slave states (Mississippi, Florida, Alabama, Georgia, and Louisiana) had called conventions to meet in January.

Texans followed with interest these developments in neighboring states. Walter Buenger, author of *Secession and the Union in Texas* (Austin: University of Texas Press, 1984), noted that prior to Lincoln's election no widespread call for secession occurred in the Lone Star state. The situation changed quickly. Mass meetings were held in a number of Texas towns to discuss the need for action. Letters, resolutions, and petitions were drafted requesting Governor Houston to convene a special session of the legislature for the purpose of calling a convention of the people to consider secession. Houston continued to oppose such action. In a response to a letter from citizens seeking his views on the crisis, the governor once again expressed his support for the Union: "I cannot believe that we can find at present more safety out of the Union than in it." He urged Texans to wait and see if the Lincoln administration governed fairly.[19]

Houston was supported in his opposition of secession by several prominent Texans, including Galveston businessman-publisher Ferdinand Flake, Galveston attorney William Pitt Ballinger, Austin lawyer-editor George W. Paschal, Collin County state senator James W. Throckmorton, former governor Elisha M. Pease, Congressman Andrew J. Hamilton, and Austin attorney-legislator John Hancock. An equally impressive group of state leaders was determined that Texas should secede. Attorney General George M. Flournoy, Supreme Court Justice Oran M. Roberts, *Texas State Gazette* editor John Marshall, lawyer-editor-politician Williamson Simpson Oldham, former congressman and state Democratic Party leader Guy M. Bryan, explorer-soldier-lawyer John S. Ford, and Mexican War hero William P. Rogers were outspoken advocates of secession. Even Congressman John H. Reagan, who had been a Unionist earlier, began to support secession.[20]

In spite of increased pressure, Houston still refused to call a special session of the legislature. He continued to hope that delay might have a calming effect upon the secessionists. On December 3 he issued an "Address to the People of Texas" in which he stated his confidence in the people's good sense and reason. He informed Texans that several days earlier he had transmitted to the governor of each slave state a copy of resolutions adopted by the Texas legislature in February 1858. These resolutions, approved during the Kansas crisis, called for a Southern convention to find ways to preserve equal rights of the states and at the same time restore harmony between the nation's sections.[21]

On the very day that Houston issued his address, four secessionist leaders, George M. Flournoy, O. M. Roberts, John Ford, and William P. Rogers, decided to take the initiative and issue their own address to the people, calling for election of delegates to a state convention. Citing the Texas Bill of Rights, the secessionist address declared that all political power was inherent in the people who had at all times the right to alter, reform, or abolish their form of government. The address set January 8 as the date for election of delegates to the convention scheduled to open on January 28.[22]

The address issued by the secessionist leaders was printed in major Texas newspapers and generally received favorable response throughout the state. In late December, candidates for the proposed convention were nominated, usually at meetings arranged by the secessionists. In some areas Unionists were discouraged from running; in others, Unionists refused to participate in the nomination and election process. In most counties the election was held on January 8, but a few counties held their elections earlier. In some areas the vote for convention delegates was light, but ninety-two of the 122 organized counties did select delegates. Walter Buenger, in his *Secession and the Union in Texas*, noted that after the elections the Unionists charged that the election process was illegal and did not truly represent the will of the people. Buenger agreed that some of the Unionist charges were correct and that a less biased election might have resulted in closer votes. However, he believed that the overall outcome would probably have still resulted in victory for the secessionists.[23]

Governor Houston continued his delaying tactics. When it became apparent that a convention was going to be held with or without his approval, Houston issued a proclamation calling a special session of the legislature in the third week of January. Several days later he ordered elections held for seven delegates to represent Texas in the convention of Southern states as provided in the legislative resolutions of February 1858. When the legislature assembled in January, Houston repeated his view that while Lincoln's election was deplorable he saw no cause for immediate and separate secession by Texas. Both to the legislature and J. M. Calhoun, Alabama commissioner sent to Texas to urge secession, Houston expressed his hope that a Southern convention as called for in the 1858 resolutions would meet. By this time, however, Houston could see that a state convention rather than a Southern assembly was the vehicle favored by most Texans. He assured members of the legislature that he would not oppose them should they endorse the state convention. He did urge that any action by such a convention be referred to the people for their consideration. Even so, he concluded that he had not yet lost hope that Texas' rights could be maintained in the Union.[24]

The legislature quickly demonstrated its support for the state convention scheduled to meet the following week. It repealed the resolutions of February 1858, which had called for the Southern convention to consider relations with the Federal government. Then by joint resolution the two houses endorsed the state convention. Citing the Bill of Rights of the Texas Constitution as authority for the people to hold such a meeting, the legislators offered the use of the House chambers for the convention. The legislature did agree with the governor that the convention should submit its actions to a final vote of the people for approval.[25]

The Convention of Texas, called to consider Federal relations, opened on Monday, January 28. Some of the state's best known leaders were among the 177 delegates. Ex-governor Hardin R. Runnels, defeated by Houston in the bitter 1859 election, represented Bowie County. Congressman John H. Reagan and Supreme Court Justice Oran M. Roberts, also East Texans, were equally prominent political figures serving as delegates. Four members, Roberts, James W. Throckmorton, Richard Coke, and John Ireland, would later be elected governor. Calhoun attorney Fletcher Stockdale would serve as lieutenant governor of Texas in the last two years of the Civil War. George M. Flournoy of Travis County was currently serving as state attorney general. Three delegates, John A. Wharton, John Gregg, and Joseph L. Hogg, would become generals in the Confederate army. Two others, Benjamin F. Terry and William P. Rogers, would be killed while commanding their regiments in the Civil War. William Beck Ochlitree, former Whig candidate for governor, was one of the state's most highly respected attorneys. Goliad lawyer Pryor Lea had served as a United States congressman from Tennessee prior to moving to Texas. John Henry Brown, newspaperman, state legislator, and Mexican War veteran, would later serve as mayor of Dallas but would gain more lasting recognition as the author of several works of history, including *Indian Wars and Pioneers of Texas* (Austin: L. E. Daniell Publisher, 1880). Elijah Sterling Clack Robertson of Bell County was the son of empresario Sterling C. Robertson, and Haden H. Edwards of Nacogdoches was the son of Fredonian revolt empresario Haden Edwards. Delegate Edwin Waller of Austin County had signed the Texas Declaration of Independence from Mexico.[26]

The delegates to the Texas convention were, as a group, reflective of the upper class of Texas society. Twelve of them had more than $100,000 in property and were among the wealthiest citizens of the state.[27] Three of these, T. Jefferson Chambers, William F. Scott, and John A. Wharton, held more than $200,000 in property. Median holding for the entire convention was $16,000, while the mean average was slightly over $37,000, six times higher than that of the average head of household in the state. Nearly three-fourths of the delegates, 72 percent, owned slaves, but the majority owned fewer than ten slaves in number. Thirty-five delegates, or 19.8 percent, held twenty or more slaves. Three delegates, Scott, Wharton, and Benjamin F. Terry, owned more than 100 slaves.[28]

The convention delegates were a comparatively young group.

Average age of the delegates was forty years, the lowest of any of the secession conventions in the South. Ninety-one percent of the delegates were born in the slave states, primarily Tennessee, Virginia, Georgia, and Alabama. Seventy-seven members, or slightly over 40 percent of the convention, were lawyers. Sixty-two members, or 35.3 percent, listed themselves as farmers or planters. Physicians, merchants, ranchers, and county judges were also in attendance along with a minister, editor, and blacksmith. Two delegates gave their occupation as "gentleman."[29]

The convention organized itself quickly. Judge O. M. Roberts, one of the four secessionist leaders who had issued the call for the convention, was chosen president. On the second day he appointed several committees, two of which (Federal Relations and Public Safety) proved to be particularly important. Even before the committees could meet, John A. Wharton, a member of the Committee on Federal Relations and son of Texas Revolution leader William H. Wharton, offered a resolution stating the sense of the convention that "Texas should separately secede from the Union." On motion of George M. Flournoy, the resolution was adopted by a 152–6 vote. It was obvious that Governor Houston's hopes for delay would find little favor in the convention.[30]

On the following day, Wednesday, January 30, the Committee on Federal Relations submitted an ordinance of secession to the convention. Presented by the committee chairman, the colorful Thomas Jefferson Chambers, the ordinance consisted of two sections. Section I declared that the federal government was using its power as "a weapon with which to strike down the interests and prosperity of the southern people," instead of permitting it to be a shield against aggression as intended. The people of Texas were therefore repealing the annexation ordinance of 1845 and Texas was resuming her status as a separate, sovereign state. Section II of the ordinance provided for referring secession to the people for ratification or rejection on February 23. Unless rejected by the voters the ordinance would take effect on March 2, 1861, the twenty-fifth anniversary of the Texas Declaration of Independence from Mexico. Chambers noted that because of the urgency for action he and several other committee members opposed the second section and were entering a minority report.[31]

Discussion of the secession ordinance began that afternoon and continued in an adjourned session that evening. There was little disagreement over Section I, which was adopted with only minor changes. Most debate centered around Section II, submission of the ordinance to a popular vote of the people. Some of the more radical members expressed regret over any delay, but others argued for the proviso, citing voter approval of the 1845 annexation resolution, as well as the wishes of the governor and legislature. On the following afternoon, January 31, a motion by John Gregg to strike the second section was defeated by a 145–29 vote.[32]

After a few minor amendments the convention agreed to vote on the whole ordinance the next day at noon with no additional debate allowed. A select committee, headed by John H. Reagan, presented a letter from Governor Houston in response to their visit with him. Houston assured the committee that he would act in har-

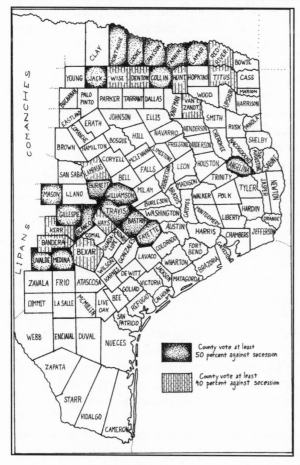

*Popular Referendum
on Secession,
February 23, 1861.*

mony with the convention in securing expression of the popular will on the matter of federal relations. "When the voice of the people of Texas has been declared through the ballot box, no citizen will be more ready to yield obedience to its will," wrote the governor.[33]

Convention president Roberts, who years earlier had handled some legal matters for Governor Houston, knew and respected the old hero of San Jacinto. Although Roberts disagreed with Houston on secession, he believed the governor would acquiesce with separation from the Union once he saw the tremendous support for secession among convention delegates. On the morning of the scheduled vote, Roberts sent two delegates, Joseph Hogg and William P. Rogers, to convince Houston to attend the convention when the vote was taken.[34]

The House galleries were crowded at midday on February 1 when Governor Houston, Lieutenant Governor Edward Clark, and state and district judges took their seats on the convention floor. Houston sat grim and motionless to the right of Roberts as the secession ordinance was read by the clerk. The roll was called alphabetically with each delegate responding "yes" or "no" to his name. Most members adhered to the rule of no public discussion before casting their ballot, but Thomas Jefferson Chambers shook his finger and shouted some words of abuse at Governor Houston.

Because earlier debates had indicated overwhelming support for secession, there was no great surprise as delegate after delegate voted "yes." Seventy members responded in the affirmative before Thomas Hughes of Williamson County, a longtime supporter of Houston, shouted "no" when his name was called. As the voting continued there was some applause and occasional hissing from the gallery. When James W. Throckmorton rose to vote he violated the no discussion rule by declaring, "Mr. President, in view of the responsibility, in the presence of God and my country — and unawed by the wild spirit of revolution around me, I vote 'no'." For the first time there was a great deal of noise from the galley, some cheering but more hissing. To this Throckmorton retorted, "Mr. President, when the rabble hiss, well may patriots tremble."[35]

The final vote on the secession ordinance was 166–8. W. H. Johnson, L. H. Williams, and George Wright from Lamar County, J. D. Rains and A. P. Shuford from Wood County, and Joshua Johnson from Titus County joined Hughes and Throckmorton in opposing secession. All except Hughes of Williamson County in Central Texas lived in northeast Texas, an area where secession was not popular. Six of the eight opposed to secession were slaveholders, but four of the six held fewer than twenty slaves. Five of the eight were lawyers, two were farmers, and one (Johnson of Titus) was a minister.[36]

After the final vote was announced there was much cheering and celebrating by delegates and spectators. A group of women moved down the aisle toward the speaker's platform. They presented a Lone Star flag to Attorney General Flournoy, who thanked them on behalf of the convention. The flag was then draped across the platform. Upon motion of John H. Reagan the convention agreed that the secession ordinance would be prepared for signing that evening. Governor Houston, who sat passively throughout most of the proceedings, exchanged a few words with President Roberts and then left the hall.[37]

Signing of the secession ordinance took place that evening. Edwin Waller, the only delegate who had signed the Texas Declaration of Independence, was given the honor of signing immediately after President Roberts. The signing then proceeded in alphabetical order. After this process was completed the convention went into executive session to discuss procedures for the February 23 popular referendum. In this session delegates agreed that each ballot would be marked "For Secession" and "Against Secession" so that there would be no confusion as to the voters' intent. The convention also stipulated that 1,000 copies of the secession ordinance be printed in Spanish and German to avoid any language difficulty.[38]

On the following day delegates approved a lengthy "Declaration of Causes which Impel the State of Texas to Secede from the Federal Union." This document, drafted by a committee chaired by John Henry Brown, was addressed to the people of Texas and offered reasons for Texas' secession. The declaration upheld the concept of white supremacy and criticized the North for supporting "the debasing doctrine of the equality of all men." Specific abuses which the state had suffered from the Federal government were cited, including failure to protect the frontier against Mexican and Indian raids, lack of protection of slave property in the national territories, and the election of a president and vice-president pledged to ruin the slaveholding states. The convention ordered the printing of 10,000 copies of the Declaration of Causes in English, 2,000 in Spanish, and 2,000 in German.[39]

The convention spent much of the time in the sessions of Saturday evening, February 2, and Monday, February 4, debating whether to send delegates to a convention of the six other seceding states then meeting in Montgomery, Alabama, for the purpose of forming a Southern Confederacy. Some delegates believed that such appointment exceeded the scope of their authority. They argued that they had been elected to consider the question of secession and nothing more. Others pointed out that it would be premature to send representatives prior to the popular referendum on February 23. The majority believed, however, that Texas should have some representation at such an important gathering and that any action taken would be contingent upon voter approval of secession. After much debate, the convention voted 102–38, with more than thirty abstentions, to elect seven delegates to represent Texas at the Montgomery meeting.[40]

On Monday evening the convention held its last session prior to an adjournment to await the vote of the people on the secession ordinance. Delegates John Gregg, W. S. Oldham, and John H. Reagan were elected to represent Texas at the Montgomery convention. The state's two United States senators, John Hemphill and Louis T. Wigfall, and Thomas N. Waul, prominent Central Texas lawyer and planter, were the other representatives chosen.[41]

Before adjournment the Texas convention authorized the Committee on Public Safety to remain in operation during the main body's recess. The committee, chaired by Harvard-educated lawyer John C. Robertson of Smith County, had instructions to provide for the defense of the state. This included authority to take control of Federal property in the state if deemed necessary.[42]

Even before the convention adjourned, the Committee on Public Safety sent a three-member commission consisting of Sam Maverick, Thomas Devine, and Philip Luckett to confer with Brig. Gen. David G. Twiggs, commander of the Department of Texas, at his headquarters in San Antonio relating to the surrender of all Federal arms, munitions, and stores in the state. Twiggs, seventy-year-old veteran of the War of 1812 and the Mexican War, had taken command of the Texas department in December. A native Georgian and supporter of states' rights, Twiggs was sympathetic to the Texas position. He had repeatedly asked Washington for instructions as he had no desire to begin a war in Texas.[43]

Twiggs expressed a willingness to surrender supplies and prop-

Texas militia in streets of San Antonio at time of Twiggs surrender.
— Archives Division, Texas State Library

erty in exchange for honorable withdrawal of his troops scattered throughout the state, but only after the secession ordinance had been ratified. He was reluctant to put the agreement in writing, however. The negotiations went on for several days when the commission learned that Twiggs was to be replaced as commander of the Texas department by Col. Carlos A. Waite, a New Yorker with strong Unionist beliefs. The commission decided to act at once. Ben McCulloch, famed Texas Ranger and hero of the Mexican War, had been instructed by the Committee on Public Safety to assemble several hundred Texans at his brother's ranch near Seguin. Late on February 15, McCulloch received orders from the commission to move on San Antonio. McCulloch was to allow Twiggs to surrender under honorable terms if he agreed to depart peacefully. If Twiggs declined to do so, McCulloch was to exercise his own judgment as to a course of action.[44]

Ben McCulloch was a man who needed little encouragement to take action. Before dawn on February 16 he moved his troops to San

This drawing in <u>Harper's Weekly</u> attempted to capture the Texans' seizure of the U.S. Army depot at the Alamo.

— Forest View Historical Services

Antonio, where they quickly occupied rooftops of buildings housing Federal men and supplies. McCulloch's men were joined by more than 100 Knights of the Golden Circle who had come to San Antonio to render assistance. By 7:00 A.M. the Texans controlled the main avenues of the city. Twiggs was taken captive as he was being driven into town from his quarters. He was taken to meet McCulloch and Texas commissioners on the main plaza. After some discussion Twiggs agreed to turn over all Federal property on the condition that he and his men be allowed to retain sidearms and march to the coast for passage out of Texas. Twiggs sent orders to other post commanders to turn over their property to Texas troops. They, too, were to be permitted safe passage to the coast for exit from the state.[45]

The manner in which McCulloch acted angered General Twiggs. Years later, J. K. P. Blackburn, one of the soldiers serving under McCulloch, wrote a description of the affair. According to Blackburn, Twiggs declared, "Ben McCulloch, you have treated me

HENRY McCULLOCH.

Ben McCulloch — Veteran of San Jacinto and Mexican War. Led Confederates in victory at Wilson's Creek in August 1861. Killed at Pea Ridge on March 7, 1862.
— Archives Division, Texas State Library

Henry McCulloch — Younger brother of Ben McCulloch. Veteran of Mexican War who commanded Texas troops in protecting frontier and stopping Federal advance in Arkansas and Louisiana.
— Archives Division, Texas State Library

shamefully, ruining my reputation as a military man and now I am too old to reestablish it." McCulloch responded, "I am serving my state, the State of Texas, sir." The older Georgian replied that if an old woman with a broomstick in hand had come to him having authority from the state of Texas demanding his surrender he would have yielded without a word of protest. "But you, sir," he added, "without papers, without any notice, have assembled a mob and forced me to terms." According to Blackburn, "General Twiggs in his humiliation wept like a child . . ."[46]

The sudden surrender of Federal property surprised many people. Lt. Col. Robert E. Lee, stationed in Texas but under orders to report to Washington, arrived in San Antonio that afternoon and was shocked to learn what had happened. Two days later, Colonel Waite arrived in San Antonio, but there was little he could do but acquiesce with what had taken place.[47]

The actual transfer of Federal property in other parts of Texas proceeded fairly smoothly. John S. Ford, veteran soldier and member of the secession convention, was ordered to the mouth of the Rio Grande, where he took possession of Fort Brown and other properties. Col. Henry McCulloch, younger brother of Ben, proceeded on orders to take surrender of Federal properties between the Red River and Fort Chadbourne in north central Texas. Lack of transportation delayed the departure of several hundred Federal troops. After the fighting at Fort Sumter in early April, Confederate President Jefferson Davis ordered Earl Van Dorn, the newly appointed Confederate commander of the Texas district, to prevent the movement of United States troops from Texas. One of his first acts was to capture the *Star of the West*, the side-wheel merchant ship being used to evacuate Federal troops from Texas. He also kept six companies, totaling nearly 400 men from Forts Bliss, Davis, Quitman, and Stockton, from leaving Texas until finally exchanged in April 1863.[48]

The Committee on Public Safety had been most successful. Without bloodshed and at little expense it had taken $3 million of Federal property and arranged the withdrawal of more than 2,000 Federal troops from the state. In addition, it took steps to acquire arms and supplies for state troops. Most of this occurred before the voters of the state gave their approval to secession.

The vote of the people on secession occurred as scheduled on February 23, six days after Twiggs had agreed to surrender. In the three weeks since adjournment of the state convention, active campaigning, both for and against secession, had gone on in earnest. Many of the convention delegates had returned to their homes to urge constituents to endorse their actions. As noted earlier, more than 10,000 copies of the Declaration of Causes had been printed for distribution. Influential newspaper editors, such as Charles DeMorse of the Clarksville *Northern Standard*, Charles Pryor of the *Dallas Herald*, and R. W. Loughery of the Marshall *Texas Republican*, urged voters to ratify secession. One of the state's most consistent supporters of secession, editor John Marshall of the Austin *Texas State Gazette*, was in Mississippi caring for his ill wife during the winter of 1860–61 but his paper continued to editorialize in sup-

port of separation. Even German editor-scientist Ferdinand Lindheimer of the *Neu Braunfelser Zeitung*, who had earlier supported
the Union, now accepted the necessity of secession.[49]

The secessionists were aided in the campaign by the momentum of events. The secession of the other six states of the lower
South, the quick and relatively easy passage of the secession ordinance by the state convention, the formation of the Southern Confederacy at Montgomery, and the surrender of Federal troops and
property built up the impression of an inevitable result. This, plus
coercion and intimidation by extremist groups such as the Knights
of the Golden Circle, better organization, and a definite plan of action, all worked to the advantage of the secessionists.[50]

Those opposed to separation did not give up easily. Some, such
as Congressman A. J. Hamilton, lawyer-state legislator Ben Epperson, editor James P. Newcomb of the *Alamo Express*, and Galveston
editor Ferdinand Flake of *Die Union*, continued to speak out
against secession. Four state senators, fourteen state representatives, and six secession convention delegates signed an "Address to
the People" urging fellow Texans to resist secession. In this address
the authors conceded that differences existed between the North
and South but argued that these could be solved by constitutional
amendments. Secession, they contended, would not preserve slavery
but would lead to its destruction. They also cited the highly un-
democratic and hasty procedures employed by the state convention
and called upon Texans to proceed in a careful and reasonable manner in resolving their differences.[51]

The election of February 23 was disappointing to Texas Unionists. The secessionists won a sweeping victory by a better than 3–1
margin, 46,154 to 14,747 votes.[52] In only eighteen of the 122 organized counties did voters reject secession. The secessionists were
victorious in 104 counties. In ninety-three of these, secession was
endorsed by over 60 percent of the voters. The vote for secession
was especially strong in the coastal counties, deep East Texas, and
the counties south of San Antonio. In this entire area only Angelina,
in the heart of East Texas, rejected secession. Voters in all twelve
Texas counties with a slave population in excess of 50 percent of the
total population endorsed secession. Travis was the only one of the
twenty-nine Texas counties with more than 35 percent slave population in which voters opposed separation.[53]

Opposition to secession was greatest in two clusters of counties in Central and North Texas. Ten of the eighteen counties opposing secession were in the cluster around Travis County. In part, this opposition was due to the German population. In the early days of statehood, most Germans had strongly supported the Union and many had opposed or been lukewarm toward slavery. In the 1850s, however, many Germans had become so assimilated into Texas society and identified with Southern institutions that their Unionist sympathies had moderated. As a result, Germans did not vote as a single bloc on the issue of secession. In Gillespie, a frontier county with Fredericksburg as its seat, citizens voted overwhelmingly, 398–16, against secession, but in Comal, another German county less exposed to the frontier and more influenced by Southern traditions, voters endorsed separation, 239–86. In fifteen of the twenty so-called German counties (those with a plurality of non-Texans born in the Germanic states) the voters endorsed the secession ordinance.[54]

The other center of opposition to secession was along the Red River of North Texas. Secession was rejected in seven counties of that area (Collin, Jack, Montague, Cooke, Grayson, Fannin, and Lamar) and nearly defeated in six others (Red River, Titus, Hunt, Wise, Denton, and Van Zandt). Several factors contributed to opposition in this area. Most of the inhabitants were nonslaveholding, small farmers from the upper South or Midwest, where support for slavery and other Southern insitutions was not strong. They were also concerned that they might be exposed to Indian attacks if Federal troops were removed from the string of forts north of the Red River. Too, this area was the home of James W. Throckmorton and Ben Epperson, both of whom campaigned vigorously against secession.[55]

The secession convention reassembled in early March. After the convention had canvassed the vote, Governor Houston issued a proclamation declaring that Texas had left the Union officially as of March 2. On March 5 the convention adopted an ordinance uniting Texas with the Confederate States of America by a vote of 109 to 2. Governor Houston regarded this action as beyond the jurisdiction of the convention. He informed a committee of the convention appointed to meet with him that the convention had completed the work for which it was empowered by the legislature. He told them that he would refer matters to the legislature scheduled to reconvene on March 18. [56]

According to convention president Roberts, Houston's plans caused "a storm of excitement." The convention delegates responded by unanimously declaring that they not only had the power to pass an ordinance of secession but also possessed power to do whatever necessary for protection of the state. The convention also expressed its intention to complete the union of Texas with the Confederacy as quickly as possible. This action was followed by adoption on March 14 of an ordinance requiring all state officers to take an oath to support the Confederate States of America.[57]

The convention required all state officers to take the oath before Monday, March 18, when the legislature would reconvene. Convention members and state officers took the oath on Friday, March 15. All responded except Governor Houston and his close friend and associate, Secretary of State E. W. Cave. On the evening of March 15, George W. Chilton, representing the convention, went to the executive mansion to inform Houston that he must take the oath by noon on the following day.

At noon the next day Governor Houston sat in the basement of the state capitol, whittling on a piece of soft pine. The secretary of the convention, R. P. Brownrigg, called his name three times but Houston did not respond. Secretary Cave's name was also called, but like his mentor he did not appear. The convention unanimously passed an ordinance declaring the offices of governor and secretary of state vacant. Lieutenant Governor Edward Clark, who had taken the oath, was instructed to assume the office of governor. Cave's successor would be named at a later date.[58]

On the day of his removal from office, Houston addressed a long letter to the people of Texas in which he protested the actions of the convention. "My worst anticipations as to the assumption of power by this Convention has been realized," he wrote. He cited what he believed to be various abuses of authority by the convention, including the creation of the Committee on Public Safety, the sending of delegates to the Montgomery convention, and the imposition of the "Test Oath" to the Confederacy. He concluded by declaring all actions of the convention null and void. He noted, however, that he "loved Texas too well to bring civil strife and bloodshed upon her," and stated that he would not endeavor to maintain his authority as chief executive. A similar message was sent to the legislature when it assembled on March 18. [59]

Some of Houston's friends encouraged him to use force to remain in office, but Houston refused. Twice during March and April, Houston was contacted by agents representing President Lincoln with offers of military assistance. The first offer was carried by Frederick West Lander, a prominent California engineer and politician who later became a brigadier general in the Union army. Lander, who described himself as a "confidential messenger," discussed with Houston a plan to use Federal troops still in Texas to aid and support Houston in defense of the Union. Houston declined the offer. In late March he wrote to Col. Carlos A. Waite, commander of the Federal troops in Texas, requesting withdrawal of all his forces.[60]

The second agent sent by Lincoln to Houston was George H. Giddings, San Antonio merchant and mail contractor. Giddings, who had just returned from a business trip to Washington, brought a confidential letter from the president to Houston. According to Giddings' account, the letter contained assurances of Federal military assistance if Houston would attempt to hold Texas in the Union. The exact nature of the assistance is unclear. Giddings later claimed Houston was offered a major generalship and authorized to recruit 100,000 troops. Other accounts say that 50,000 troops were offered; Houston himself later referred to an offer of 70,000 men. According to another account written some years later, Houston asked the advice of four Unionist friends, Ben Epperson, James W. Throckmorton, George W. Paschal, and David B. Culberson, whom he had invited to the Governor's Mansion. Epperson, the youngest of the group, favored acceptance of the offer. The other three opposed on the ground that secession could not be prevented. Houston thanked the group and agreed with the majority, declaring that if he were younger he might have accepted Lincoln's proposition. Then, in dramatic fashion, he threw Lincoln's offer into the fire.[61]

The Houston family left Austin the last day of March and headed for their farm home at Cedar Point on Galveston Bay. Although Houston would make occasional speeches during the next two years, he would never again hold public office. When the Union navy captured Galveston in October 1862, the family moved to Huntsville. Houston continued to see friends and from time to time criticized government policy. When Confederates recaptured Galveston on January 1, 1863, he congratulated Gen. John B. Magruder. His health gradually failed, and on July 26, 1863, Houston died in the family home at Huntsville.[62]

Houston's old nemesis, the secession convention, completed its work six days before the Houston family left Austin. Ratification of the Confederate Constitution, amendment of the state constitution to fit Texas' status as a Confederate state, and appointment of a three-man committee to prepare an address explaining and justifying the steps taken were the final actions of the convention. On March 26 the convention adjourned, and members headed home to await further developments.[63]

CHAPTER TWO

Early Phases of the War:
April 1861–August 1862

Texans did not have long to wait for events to unfold. In the early predawn hours of April 12, 1861, Confederate artillery opened fire upon Fort Sumter in the harbor of Charleston, South Carolina. After thirty-three hours of bombardment, the small Federal garrison surrendered. Three days later, on April 15, President Lincoln issued a proclamation calling 75,000 militiamen into Federal service to put down the rebellion of the seceded states. On April 19 Lincoln proclaimed a naval blockade of the Southern states from South Carolina to the mouth of the Rio Grande. A week later, after the secession of additional slave states, the blockade was extended to include Virginia and North Carolina.

The newly formed Confederate government headed by Mississippian Jefferson Davis had already taken steps to defend itself. Under an act passed by the Provisional Congress in March, President Davis was authorized to enlist 100,000 volunteers and to employ state militia for periods up to six months. Once the fighting began, the Confederate Congress granted Davis additional authority to enlist volunteers and militia. Similarly, the United States Congress gave President Houston's authorization for additional troops as the war expanded.[1]

Edward Clark, who assumed the duties as governor of Texas following Houston's failure to take the Confederate oath on March

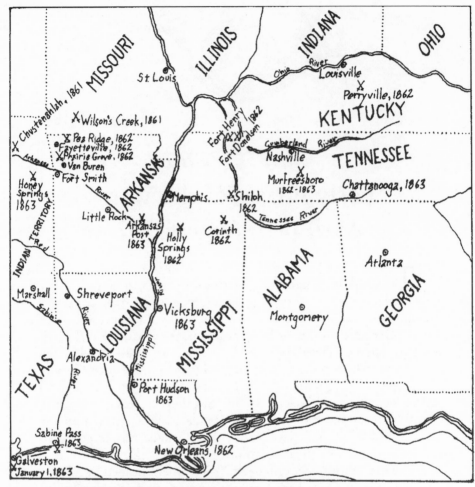

CAMPAIGNS in the MISSISSIPPI VALLEY
1861 - 1863

Campaigns in the Mississippi Valley, 1861–63.

Edward Clark — Became governor when secession convention declared office vacant following Houston's refusal to take oath. Later organized and commanded Fourteenth Texas Infantry in Walker's Division.
— Archives Division, Texas State Library

18, moved quickly to meet the state's military obligations. The Committee on Public Safety had already authorized John S. Ford and Ben and Henry McCulloch to raise cavalry units for the defense of Texas. They were brought into Confederate service and would play significant roles in military operations in the Southwest. In April, Confederate Secretary of War Leroy Pope Walker requested that Governor Clark raise 8,000 additional men for the infantry — not an easy task in Texas, where most volunteers preferred cavalry service.[2]

To assist in the task of recruiting and organizing these infantry units, Governor Clark divided the state into military districts and subdistricts. He appointed six prominent Texans to head the military districts: Hugh McLeod of Galveston, Joseph L. Hogg of Rusk, Matthew F. Locke of Gilmer, James H. Murray of Huntsville, Augustus Buchel of Indianola, and Tom Green of Austin. In May, Clark named Ebenezer B. Nichols, a successful Galveston merchant, as agent for the purchase of arms and ammunition. Nichols was directed to negotiate the sale of bonds authorized by the legislature to cover payment for the purchases. Later that summer Governor Clark appointed Samuel Maverick, Hamilton P. Bee, and Lemuel Evans as purchasing agents to assist in the procurement of arms. He also created four additional military districts to expedite recruiting.[3]

In the spring of 1861 it was often easier to recruit troops, even for the infantry, than it was to find arms and ammunition. By late spring military units were being formed in almost every community. Occasionally, youthful enthusiasm and impatience ran ahead of military organization. Twenty-one-year-old William A. Fletcher of Beaumont was working on the roof of a house when he heard that fighting had begun at Fort Sumter. Unable to find any local units being organized, he boarded a flatcar heading to Houston. Once in Houston he learned that no companies were being organized at the time, so he went to Galveston the next day. He found conditions similar in Galveston, so he boarded the first steamboat to Liberty, where he enlisted in a company being formed there.[4]

Most Texans had very little difficulty enlisting. Governor Clark worked with Brig. Gen. Earl Van Dorn, the newly appointed Confederate military commander for Texas, in recruiting, training, and equipping troops and in preparing for the defense of the state. Many of the recruits received military instruction, such as it was, in local encampments. Others were trained in camps of instruction set up by Governor Clark in each of the military districts. The training consisted largely of learning to obey commands and to march or ride in orderly fashion.

Oftentimes, military instruction, which was not popular with the men, was interrupted by public ceremonies featuring flag presentations by local women and speeches by local dignitaries or veterans of the Texas Revolution or Mexican War. Presentation of either the Confederate, Texas, or unit flag usually occurred when the company left for training camp or for the war theater and was the occasion for parades, food and drink, and speeches. In most instances the speaker praised Southern virtues, condemned northern abolitionists, and predicted speedy victory for Texas armies, but occasionally a more somber note was sounded. Ralph J. Smith, a member of the Second Texas Infantry, recalled that former governor Sam Houston spoke to his group. The hero of San Jacinto warned that the "resources of the north were almost exhaustless. . . . Time and money would wear us out." Such words had little effect, Smith stated: "[H]e might as well had been giving advice to the lunatic asylum. We knew no such word as fail."[5]

Most of these public ceremonies had the effect of building up enthusiasm for the war effort. Albert Blocker, who enlisted as a bugler in the Third Texas Cavalry at the age of sixteen, recalled that his company, known as the "Texas Hunters," received its flag in a public gathering at Jonesville on May 1, 1861. The speeches, parades, and barbecue that accompanied the affair made it a day that young Blocker would not forget. Sometimes the ceremonies resulted in additional recruits joining the army. Teenager David C. Nance and a friend attended an organizational meeting of a regiment being formed in Ellis County by lawyer-newspaper editor William H. Parsons. The whole affair was so impressive that both Nance and his friend joined the regiment, in spite of the wishes of Nance's father that the son not join the army.[6]

The Texans who enlisted in 1861 wore a wide variety of uniforms. Val C. Giles, who served in the Fourth Infantry, stated that no two companies had uniforms alike when his regiment was organized. "In my company we had about four different shades of gray, but the trimmings were all of black braid," he wrote. Jim Turner of the Sixth Texas Infantry noted that all the uniforms in his regiment were "a dark pepper and salt grey color, and were trimmed in green." The Reagan Guards of the First Texas Infantry had dark uniforms with bright red stripes. The Lavaca Guards of the Sixth Infantry wore linen jeans with red stripes and blue flannel frock coats trimmed with red braid.

Historian Stephen B. Oates, who chronicled Texas cavalry units, noted that cavalry uniforms were of all types. Most recruits wore gray woolen jeans, but Capt. Sam Richardson of the W. P. Lane Rangers wore exotic leopard skin pants. Coats were both single and double breasted, with a variety of color and style. Texans preferred wide-brimmed felt hats, but the gray French kepi was regulation attire. Some Texans, especially those from South Texas, preferred the Mexican sombrero.[7]

Texas Confederates carried an assortment of weapons. The first cavalry units formed in Texas were armed with weapons seized when the Federal forts in the state surrendered. Both state and Confederate governments appointed agents to purchase firearms wherever possible, and later some weapons were manufactured in the Confederacy. By late summer of 1861, however, most Texas soldiers were required to provide their own arms. Regulations called for the infantry to carry muskets or rifles and the cavalry to be armed with carbines, but there was much variation. Theophilus Noel stated that when Henry H. Sibley's brigade was formed in San Antonio in the fall of 1861, the men were "armed with squirrel-guns, bear guns, sportsmen's-guns, shot-guns, both single and double barrels, in fact guns of all sorts." Jim Turner of the Sixth Infantry observed that men of his company were armed with old flintlock muskets converted to rifles, which "presented quite a warlike and formidable appearance, but we soon learned that our guns were about as dangerous to the men behind them as they were to those who might be in front of them." When David C. Nance, the young volunteer in the Twelfth Cavalry, reached training camp at Simms Bayou near Houston, he found weapons of every type, from ancient fowling pieces to expensive, silverplated handguns. When the Eighth Texas Cavalry, better known as Terry's Texas Rangers, arrived at Bowling Green, Kentucky, in October 1861, they carried twenty different varieties and calibers of weapons (mostly six-shooters and shotguns). Bowie knives and Colt revolvers were weapons particularly favored by Texas Confederates. One regiment, commanded by Methodist minister George W. Carter, was scheduled to carry lances but the weapons failed to materialize. Three companies of Texas cavalry assigned to Sibley's Brigade were carrying lances in the New Mexico campaign of 1862 and took part in an ill-fated charge against Union infantry.[8]

Texans were often loaded down as they went off to war in 1861. C. C. Cox took two saddle horses, two wagon horses, a wagon, side arms, medicines, bedding, camp utensils, and a black lad when he left his South Texas ranch to join the army. David Nance in Parsons' cavalry carried various cooking utensils, a bag of food (including bread, a cured ham, pickled cucumbers, and honey), a double-breasted stormcoat, spare bedding, various toilet articles, a new Whitney pistol, and a double-barreled shotgun. A. W. Sparks of the Titus Grays, who rode a black gelding valued at $100, carried a double-barreled shotgun, underclothing, four shirts, four trousers, coat, boots, canteen, pistol, and knife as he joined his regiment. William W. Heartsill of the W. P. Lane Rangers left a classic description of what his horse "Pet" carried as he left for war in April 1861:

> myself, saddle, bridle, saddle-blanket, curry comb, horse brush, coffee pot, tin cups, 20 lbs ham, 200 biscuit, 5 lbs ground coffee, 5 lbs sugar, one large pound cake presented to me by Mrs C E Talley, 6 shirts, 6 prs socks, 3 prs drawers, 2 prs pants, 2 jackets, 1 pr heavy mud boots, one Colt's revolver, one small dirk, four blankets, sixty feet of rope, with a twelve inch iron pin attached;

with all these, and divers and sundry little mementoes from friends.[9]

By the end of 1861, approximately 25,000 Texans had been recruited for the Confederate army. Two-thirds of these enlisted in the cavalry, as Texans showed a decided preference for mounted service. The British military observer Col. Arthur Fremantle of the Coldstream Guards, who came through Texas during the war, noted "it was found very difficult to raise infantry in Texas, as no Texan walks a yard if he can help it." In his November 1861 message to the legislature, Governor Clark described some of the difficulties in recruiting infantry soldiers: "The predilection of Texans for cavalry service, found as it is upon their peerless horsemanship, is so powerful that they are unwilling in many instances to engage in service of any other description unless required by actual necessity."[10]

Sixteen regiments, three battalions, and three independent companies of cavalry, totaling 17,338 men, were enrolled in Texas by the end of 1861. Four of the cavalry regiments, the Second Mounted Rifles, the Fourth Cavalry, the Fifth Cavalry, and the Seventh Cavalry, would participate in Henry H. Sibley's invasion of New Mexico territory in early 1862. Brazoria County sugar planter Benjamin F. Terry raised the most famous of all the mounted Texas units, the Eighth Cavalry, better known as Terry's Texas Rangers. The Rangers were originally scheduled for service in Virginia, but the need for additional troops in Kentucky resulted in their being assigned to join Albert Sidney Johnston in that state.[11]

Even though cavalry service was preferred, seven regiments and four battalions of Texas infantry were recruited in 1861. Three of these regiments, the First, Fourth, and Fifth, were ordered to Virginia in the autumn of that year and became part of the Texas Infantry Brigade, first commanded by Louis T. Wigfall and later by John Bell Hood. As Hood's Texas Brigade, the Texans would distinguish themselves at Gaines' Mill, Second Manassas, Sharpsburg, Gettysburg, and Chickamauga.[12]

Recruitment of soldiers became more difficult as early enthusiasm for military life waned. Governor Clark found that trying to meet repeated calls by the Confederate government for additional troops was a more serious problem each month. He was frustrated by the War Department's practice of authorizing individuals to raise military units without informing state authorities. Clark was also unhappy that independent recruiters were allowed to raise cavalry while state authorities were required to enlist infantry, a more difficult task. Passage of the first of several conscription laws by the Confederate Congress in April 1862 gave some impetus to volunteering, but the distaste for any form of military discipline, the desire to remain at home with loved ones, and the possibility of obtaining occupational exemption or hiring a substitute were all factors contributing to the problem of raising troops. Even so, the number of Texans in military service increased steadily as the war progressed.[13]

Because of duplications and errors in reporting, it is difficult to determine the exact number of Texans who served in the Civil War. Stephen B. Oates, who studied enrollment figures carefully, stated that 58,000 Texans joined the cavalry and 30,000 Texans served in the infantry and artillery, or a total of 88,000 men. Francis Lubbock, who succeeded Clark as governor in the fall of 1861, reported to the legislature in November 1863 that 90,000 Texans were in the military at that time. Since the white male population in Texas between ages eighteen and forty-five was 92,145 in 1860, Lubbock's figure seems high for Texans in Confederate service at one time.[14]

The majority of Texans in the army spent the war in the Trans-Mississippi, defending the area from Indian raids and Union invasion or participating in expansionistic moves to the West. As noted earlier, the Committee on Public Safety ordered Henry McCulloch to raise a volunteer regiment to defend the northwestern frontier of Texas. This unit, the First Regiment of Mounted Volunteers, was spread out from the Colorado to the Red River on patrol against Indian raiders in the spring of 1861. The Second Regiment of Mounted Rifles, commanded by John S. Ford, was assigned the task of guarding the thousand-mile line of the Rio Grande from Brownsville to El Paso. Ford himself remained on the lower Rio Grande, while Lt. John R. Baylor and Maj. Edwin Waller were assigned to the upper part of the Rio Grande. Much of Ford's energies would be devoted to dealing with raids by the Mexican outlaw-Robin Hood Juan Cortina, while Baylor and Waller would later occupy southern New Mexico.[15]

In May 1861, William Cocke Young, a former United States marshal, veteran of the Mexican War, and the largest slaveholder in Cooke County, led a regiment of state cavalry recruited in North Texas across the Red River into Indian Territory. Young and most of the men in his regiment had opposed secession but were determined to defend their families and homes from hostile Indian attacks. They occupied Forts Washita, Arbuckle, and Cobb, which had been abandoned by Federal troops. Aided by another Cooke County slaveholder, James G. Bourland, who had been appointed by the Texas secession convention, Young negotiated a series of treaties with various groups of the Caddo, Chickasaw, Comanche, and Wichita.[16]

In the latter part of 1861, Henry McCulloch shifted his attention away from North Texas to the Rio Grande and the Texas coast to meet anticipated Union moves there. Young's regiment, which had been transferred to Confederate service as the Eleventh Texas Cavalry, was ordered to join Ben McCulloch in defense of Arkansas in the autumn of 1861. To replace these units in meeting new disturbances in the form of Kiowa and Comanche raids, the state legislature authorized creation of a body of state troops known as the Frontier Regiment. Col. James M. Norris, a lawyer and merchant from Central Texas, was the first commander of the regiment but lacked experience and skill in dealing with the men under his command. He was replaced by Col. James E. McCord, a former Texas Ranger knowledgeable in frontier affairs. Under McCord's leadership the Frontier Regiment brought a measure of stability to the frontier.[17]

Several of the Confederate cavalry regiments recruited in Texas saw service in the Arkansas–Missouri sector in the summer and fall of 1861. In May, Ben McCulloch was appointed brigadier general in the Confederate army with orders to defend Arkansas and Indian Territory. The Third Texas Cavalry, recruited in East Texas and commanded by Elkanah Greer, former grand commander of the Texas Knights of the Golden Circle, was assigned to McCulloch's command, known as the Army of the West. In late summer McCulloch moved his army consisting of two cavalry regiments (the Third Texas and Fourth Arkansas) and one infantry regiment (the Third Louisiana) into southwestern Missouri to support Sterling Price's Confederate forces. In early August the combined forces of McCulloch and Price were attacked by a smaller but better armed and disciplined Union army commanded by Nathaniel Lyon. In fierce fighting on August 10, the Federals were defeated. Lyon was killed in a battle the Confederates called Oak Hill and the Federals called Wilson's Creek. In this engagement Greer's Texas cavalry saw heavy action while attacking the Union right flank. Although McCulloch's army suffered heavy casualties in the battle, the Third Texas came through the conflict with only six men killed. The battle greatly enhanced McCulloch's reputation and forced the Federals to fall back to central Missouri. Units of the Third Texas commanded by Lt. Col. W. P. Lane occupied Springfield, Missouri, as the Union troops retreated.[18]

Other Texas units, including the Sixth Cavalry commanded by Col. B. Warren Stone, the Eleventh Cavalry commanded by Col. William C. Young, and an independent cavalry battalion commanded by former Indian agent and Kansas territorial delegate Maj. John W. Whitfield, joined McCulloch's army in early autumn. McCulloch planned a move against Kansas Jayhawkers; however, lack of adequate supplies, a measles epidemic, and renewed Union activity in Missouri led him to abandon the Kansas move. In December McCulloch traveled to the Confederate capital at Richmond to discuss military affairs with the War Department. While McCulloch was away, Col. James McIntosh, who was commanding in McCulloch's absence, took 1,200 troops into Indian Territory to assist Col. Douglas H. Cooper in dealing with dissident Creek Indians led by Opotheleyahola. Units of the Third, Sixth, and Eleventh Texas Cavalry and Whitfield's cavalry battalion rode with McIntosh. In late December, McIntosh attacked the Indians in their stronghold at Chustenahlah, or Salt Creek. The Texas cavalry shattered the Indian defenders and drove them from the field. The Creeks lost 200 men, and 160 women and children were captured. In addition, the Texans captured twenty-one African Americans, thirty wagons, seventy yoke of oxen, 500 horses, and several hundred cattle and sheep. Confederate losses were fifteen men killed and twenty wounded.

With this victory achieved, Confederate forces in Arkansas went into winter quarters. The Arkansas–Indian Territory front remained relatively quiet for the next two months.[19]

While some Texans were fighting in Arkansas, Missouri, and Indian Territory, other Texans were attempting to wrest New Mexico from Union control. New Mexico had been of interest to Texans for many years. Indeed, the Congress of the Republic had fixed the Rio Grande as the western boundary of Texas, thus laying claim to the eastern half of present-day New Mexico. In an attempt to assert Texas control, President Mirabeau B. Lamar had sent an expedition of nearly 300 men toward Santa Fe in 1841. Although this expedition had been unsuccessful, Texans had continued to claim eastern New Mexico. After the Mexican War and the Treaty of Guadalupe Hidalgo assured American ownership, Texans again attempted to assert their rights to the area. New Mexicans were opposed to Texas control, however, and it appeared for a while that Texans might fight to maintain their claims to the territory. These claims were surrendered only after the Federal government agreed to compensate Texas $10 million as a part of the Compromise of 1850.

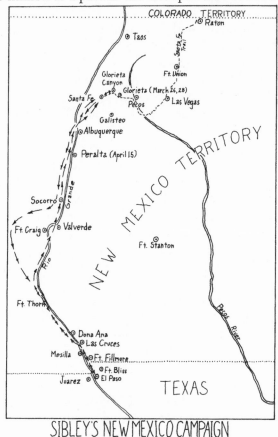

SIBLEY'S NEW MEXICO CAMPAIGN

The New Mexico Campaign

When the Civil War broke out, Texans and other Southerners were determined to add New Mexico to the Confederacy. Some considered the region a possibility for slave expansion; others saw New Mexico as a gateway to the Pacific. Southern influence in the region was considerable. The Santa Fe area had strong commercial ties with the slave state of Missouri, while Americans living in the Mesilla Valley in southern New Mexico had close connections with Texans in and around El Paso. The leading political figure of the region, Miguel A. Otero, territorial delegate to Congress, was married to a South Carolina native and was himself sympathetic to the South. The territorial governor, Abraham Rencher, and departmental military commander, Col. William W. Loring, were both Southerners.[20]

Sentiment in favor of the Confederacy was strongest in the southern half of the territory. Residents in this area had been agitating without success for separate recognition as the Territory of Arizona since 1854. Once the states of the lower South formed the Confederacy, citizen groups in Mesilla, largest town in the area and second largest in New Mexico Territory, and Tucson, located near rich silver mines, voted to repudiate Union authority and to seek admission to the Confederacy.[21]

Federal authorities in New Mexico were determined to hold the area for the Union. Col. Edward R. S. Canby, who succeeded Loring as departmental military commander when the latter resigned his commission, was particularly concerned about a possible threat to the Mesilla Valley from Texas. He ordered Maj. Isaac Lynde to move men and equipment to strengthen Fort Fillmore, located east of the Rio Grande across from the town of Mesilla and forty miles north of El Paso on the Texas border. Canby not only hoped that Lynde would overawe prosecessionists at Mesilla but also would reclaim abandoned Federal property at Fort Bliss near El Paso. Before Lynde moved against Bliss, however, several companies of the Second Texas Mounted Rifles under the command of veteran Indian fighter and frontiersman Lt. Col. John R. Baylor occupied the fort.[22]

Baylor, a large man weighing 230 pounds and standing 6'3, was a dynamic leader who had spent much of his life on the frontier. A firm believer in states' rights and secession, he was determined to liberate southern New Mexico, or Arizona as it was called, from Union control. In the third week of July he moved into New Mexico and occupied Mesilla. Major Lynde, commanding Union forces at Fort Fillmore, three miles southeast of Mesilla, made a halfhearted attempt to drive Baylor out of Mesilla but fell back to Fillmore after sustaining casualties. Convinced that he could not hold Fillmore against a determined attack because of its location in a basin over-looked by hills, Lynde attempted to withdraw to Fort Stanton, 140 miles to the northeast. Baylor pursued and overtook Lynde's troops, who were suffering from lack of water. In spite of opposition by some of his officers, Lynde surrendered his entire command of nearly 500 men to Baylor and his force of less than 300 Confederates.[23]

Following the capture of the Fillmore garrison, Baylor issued a proclamation on August 1, 1861, creating the Confederate Territory of Arizona. The territory consisted of all New Mexico Territory south of the thirty-fourth parallel, or roughly the southern half of Arizona and New Mexico. Baylor assumed power as civil governor and established his capital at Mesilla. Later the Confederate Congress and President Davis affirmed his actions.[24]

While Baylor was establishing the Territory of Arizona, Henry Hopkins Sibley was in Richmond, Virginia, discussing plans with President Davis for the conquest of all of New Mexico Territory. Sibley, a native of Louisiana and graduate of West Point, had a distinguished military record. He had served in the Seminole and Mexican wars, on the Kansas frontier, and more recently in campaigns against the Navajo in New Mexico. In addition, he had achieved recognition as the inventor of the Sibley tent, adopted by the United States Army. When the Civil War started, he was serving as captain in the Second Dragoons stationed at Taos, New Mexico. He was promoted to major on May 13, 1861, but resigned his commission to serve the Confederacy.[25]

Sibley outlined his plans for the conquest of New Mexico to President Davis. Based upon his extensive knowledge of New Mexico, Sibley believed that Union troops could be driven from the area without difficulty. Davis needed little convincing. On July 5 Sibley was appointed brigadier general with orders to proceed to Texas, where he was to organize such forces as he deemed necessary for the conquest of New Mexico.[26]

In early August, Sibley established his headquarters in San Antonio and there he began recruiting for the New Mexico campaign. By October, thirty companies had been formed and organized into three cavalry regiments: the Fourth Texas commanded by Col. James Reily, a native of Ohio who had settled in Texas shortly after independence and had experience as a soldier, politician, and diplomat; the Fifth Texas, commanded by the highly popular Tom Green, a graduate of the University of Tennessee and Princeton and a veteran of San Jacinto and the Mexican War; and the Seventh Texas, commanded by Col. William Steele, a native of New York, graduate of West Point, veteran of the Mexican War, and, like Sibley, a former officer in the U.S. Second Dragoons. Each regiment consisted of approximately 900 men, or a total of 2,700 for the entire brigade. Sibley himself appointed all the field grade officers. Unlike the usual procedure in which men in the ranks selected their officers, commissions were granted to captains who recruited companies for their local counties.[27]

In late October Sibley's Brigade began the long ride to El Paso, a journey of nearly 700 miles through rugged country. Because of the shortage of water and trail grass, Sibley sent his regiments forward one at a time. Reily's Fourth Regiment was the first to move out, followed several days later by Green's Fifth Regiment. William Steele's Seventh Cavalry came at the rear. Sibley did not leave San Antonio until November 18, but as he was traveling light he arrived at El Paso ahead of his troops on December 14. Sibley was suffering from ill health and was drinking heavily. Already there were signs that his overindulgence in alcohol, lack of physical stamina, and want of realistic planning would doom the campaign.[28]

Upon arrival in El Paso, Sibley assumed command of all Confederate forces in El Paso, New Mexico, and Arizona. John R. Baylor continued to function as the civil and military governor of Arizona Territory, but the troops formerly under his command and now led by Maj. Charles L. Pyron were placed under Sibley. Several days later Sibley issued a proclamation informing the people of New Mexico that he and his troops, now designated as the Army of New Mexico, came not to conquer but to throw off the yoke of Northern despotism.[29]

After dispatching Col. James Reily on a diplomatic mission to confer with the governors of the Mexican states of Chihuahua and Sonora and sending some detachments to Tucson and isolated posts, Sibley moved his forces up the Rio Grande to a camp near Fort Thorn, an abandoned Federal post between Fort Fillmore, now in Confederate hands, and Fort Craig, farther up the river under Union control. In early February Sibley's army, approximately 2,600 men strong, moved north toward Fort Craig.[30]

Col. Edward R. S. Canby, the Union commander of New Mexico, had 3,810 men concentrated at Fort Craig. Of these about 1,200 were Regulars. One company of Colorado volunteers had joined Canby. Most of his other troops were New Mexican militia and volunteers, including the First Regiment of Volunteers commanded by famed frontiersman Christopher "Kit" Carson. Canby himself was a steady, solid soldier, who, with the aid of newly appointed Union governor Henry Connelly, worked diligently to strengthen Federal defenses in the area. Canby knew Sibley well. The two had been classmates at West Point and they had campaigned together recently against the Navajo. Rumors, apparently untrue, circulated among troops in their command that the two men were related by marriage.[31]

As Sibley moved up from the south he attempted to draw Canby out of the defenses of Fort Craig into open terrain. When this failed, Sibley, believing the fort too strong to assault from the south, ordered his men to cross to the east bank of the Rio Grande, move north, and then swing back across the river at Valverde ford about five miles north of Fort Craig. When the Confederates attempted this on February 21, they found Union troops blocking the Valverde crossing. In the fierce fighting that followed the Texans led by Tom Green and William R. Scurry, commanding the Fourth Cavalry in Reily's absence, captured a Federal battery and drove Union forces back toward Fort Craig. Exhaustion, confusion over a Union flag of truce, and darkness prevented the Confederates from pursuing Canby's retreating forces.[32]

The battle at Valverde was a victory for the Confederates but at the cost of thirty-six killed, 150 wounded, and one missing. Canby's loss was even greater: 110 killed, 240 wounded, and thirty-five missing. But Canby still held Fort Craig and the Confederates were running low on commissary supplies. Morale among the Texans was poor. They had won the battle but accomplished little. The weather was cold, some of the soldiers no longer had horses, and criticism of Sibley, who had relinquished his command to Tom Green during the battle, was growing. Sibley claimed that poor health had necessitated the temporary transfer of command, but many of the Texans were convinced that Sibley was drunk. Now they suspected him of being a coward as well.[33]

Sibley, who resumed command, requested that Canby surrender, but the Union officer refused. Since Canby still held Fort Craig, Sibley decided to push north toward Albuquerque and Santa Fe, where he hoped to find needed supplies. The Confederate advance was slow, however, allowing the small Federal garrison at Albu-

querque time to remove or destroy most of the stores and provisions. The capture of a Union wagon train with supplies headed toward Fort Craig provided the Confederates with some relief. Confederate forces pushed on to Santa Fe, but when they entered the
city they found that most stores had been evacuated to Fort Union,
about eighty-five miles to the northeast. Those which could not be
moved had been burned. The Union territorial government had also
left the city, moving to Las Vegas near Fort Union.[34]

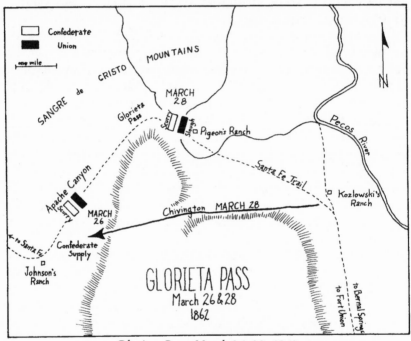

Glorieta Pass, March 26–28, 1862.

Following the occupation of Albuquerque and Santa Fe, Sibley
sent units of his army along the Santa Fe Trail toward Fort Union.
Sibley believed that capture of the fort, which was an important supply depot even before receiving stores from Albuquerque and Santa
Fe, would lead to Canby's surrender at Fort Craig. The Union garrison at Fort Union was small, but was receiving reinforcements from
Colorado. Led by Col. John P. Slough, Colorado volunteers reached
Fort Union on the night of March 11 after a forced march through
high winds and bitter cold. Instead of waiting for the Confederates
to attack, Slough, now in command of the fort's garrison as well as

his "Pike Peakers," moved southward along the Santa Fe Trail toward Santa Fe. On March 26, about 400 advancing Confederates led
by Maj. Charles Pyron clashed with a column of Slough's volunteers, commanded by Maj. John M. Chivington, a Methodist minister, in Apache Canyon at the western end of Glorieta Pass, about
twenty miles from Santa Fe. Pyron's Confederates were driven back
in the heavy fighting, but Chivington abandoned pursuit and fell
back through Glorieta Pass, first to Pigeon's Ranch on the eastern
slope of the mountains and then to Kozlowski's Ranch four miles to
the southwest, to await the arrival of Slough and the main body of
the Federal troops.[35]

Pyron sent a message to Col. William Scurry, who was with the
Fourth Regiment and a battalion of the Seventh Regiment some
twenty miles to the south, requesting support. Scurry quickly
moved his troops through the night to join Pyron's men at John-
son's Ranch at the west entrance of Apache Canyon. On March 28
Scurry, with 1,200 men, moved through Glorieta Pass to attack the
Federal forces commanded by Colonel Slough. In the battle of Glorieta Pass, known in New Mexico as the "Gettysburg of the West,"
the Texans drove Slough's "Pike Peakers" away from Pigeon's
Ranch. The Confederates had won a tactical victory in the battle of
Glorieta Pass but at a high price. While the battle had raged between
Scurry and Slough, Chivington had taken 430 troops along a mountain trail to the south of Glorieta Pass and swung around behind the
Confederate lines. They drove away a small force that Scurry had
left at Johnson's Ranch to guard the supply train and then destroyed
eighty Confederate wagons containing badly needed food, forage,
ammunition, and medical supplies.[36]

The loss of Scurry's supply train was a major blow to the Confederates. With little food and ammunition left, the Texans at Glorieta Pass were forced to fall back to Santa Fe. At first Sibley still
believed that the campaign could continue, but he learned that Canby was moving northward with troops from Fort Craig to link up
with the Colorodans. In addition, there were reports that Col.
James Carleton was leading several thousand Union troops from
California toward Arizona and the Mesilla Valley. Faced with the
prospect of being trapped between enemy forces and without
adequate food and ammunition, Sibley decided to retreat to Texas.
The withdrawal from Santa Fe and Albuquerque began on April 12.
Sibley still hoped to attack and destroy Fort Craig as he withdrew,

but after a skirmish with Federal troops at Peralta, just south of Albuquerque, Sibley decided to bypass Craig by moving west of the Rio Grande through the mountains and returning to the river south of the fort.[37]

The hundred-mile detour through uncharted wilderness was a nightmare. The mountainous terrain, covered with heavy brush and undergrowth, the lack of adequate food, water, and medicine, and the cold weather took a toll on the men and animals. Morale was completely shattered and confidence in Sibley totally disappeared. Fortunately for the retreating Confederates, Union pursuit was poorly coordinated and lacking in vigor. By early May, Sibley was back at Fort Bliss, where he issued a valedictory proclamation praising the men of the Army of New Mexico. In June, Sibley's army, now reduced by a thousand casualties, headed toward San Antonio. Additional hardships and suffering lay ahead as Sibley's exhausted troops struggled across West Texas in the heat of midsummer. In early August, the first units of the Army of New Mexico reached San Antonio. That same month the California column commanded by James Carleton occupied Fort Bliss and El Paso. The Californians remained in the area until relieved by other elements of the Union army in February 1865.[38]

Sibley's retreat ended Confederate and Texas military operations in New Mexico and Arizona and thus put an end to the Confederate Territory of Arizona. It did not, however, destroy all Southern interest in the area. John R. Baylor, who served as governor during the life span of the territory, was in Richmond, Virginia, conferring with Confederate officials when Sibley evacuated New Mexico. Although under a cloud of suspicion because of a letter he had written earlier which appeared to advocate extermination of hostile Indians, Baylor secured permission to recruit a brigade for military operations in the territory. Upon returning to Texas in the summer of 1862, he found little enthusiasm for the enterprise. His authority to recruit was subsequently revoked because of the extermination letter. But the war was not over, for Sibley, Baylor, or the Texans who served in the New Mexico campaign. All would see subsequent service in the struggle that lay ahead.[39]

Texans were more successful in defending their 400-mile coastline from enemy invasion than they were in securing New Mexico. Governor Clark and Brig. Gen. Earl Van Dorn, the Mississippian who commanded the Texas district from April to September of

1861, worked well together. They cooperated in recruiting and equipping military companies and obtaining heavy cannon for coastal defense. Twelve cannons taken from Federal forts in Texas were moved to Galveston, where Sidney Sherman, veteran of San Jacinto, and later John C. Moore, a West Point graduate and veteran of Indian wars, held command. The Third Battalion, Texas Artillery, commanded by Maj. Joseph C. Cook, a graduate of the United States Naval Academy, was organized to man batteries located at the extreme eastern part of the island (Fort Point), Bolivar Point (Fort Green), Pelican Spit (Fort Jackson), and San Luis Pass. The Fourth Texas Volunteer Regiment, commanded by Col. Joseph Bates, a former mayor of Galveston and U.S. marshal for eastern Texas, defended the coast from San Luis Pass to Caney Creek. This unit, which became the Thirteenth Texas Infantry when accepted for Confederate service, included four artillery batteries. Three additional companies of artillery provided defense for the Matagorda Bay-Corpus Christi area. On the upper coast, local citizens constructed Fort Sabine to defend Sabine Pass on the Texas-Louisiana border. The fort housed four cannon obtained from Houston and Galveston and was manned by Company B of the Sixth Texas Infantry.[40]

Although there were various rumors concerning an impending attack, the Texas coast was relatively quiet during the summer of 1861. The Union navy did make some efforts to enforce the blockade proclaimed in April by President Lincoln. A Federal warship, the *South Carolina*, commanded by James Alden, appeared off the Galveston coast in July. Within a few days the *South Carolina* captured ten Southern merchant vessels. Three of these Alden armed and used in the enforcement of the blockade. In early August, the Confederate battery at San Luis Pass hit the mainsail of one of these captured ships, the *Sam Houston*. In response the *South Carolina* opened fire upon the Confederate batteries on the island. This led to a general exchange of fire between the *South Carolina* and the coastal batteries. Hundreds of citizens rushed to the beaches to watch the exchange; one spectator was killed and three others wounded. Rebel gunners hit the *South Carolina* three times but with little apparent damage.[41]

As the war came closer to Texas in the autumn of 1861, changes occurred in the military and political leadership of the state. Earl Van Dorn, the dashing Mississippian who had gained the admiration and respect of Texans for his energy and boldness, was relieved of command of the district of Texas and ordered to report to Richmond for a new field command. His replacement in Texas was a former governor of Louisiana, Brig. Gen. Paul Octave Hebert. Hebert, who graduated at the top of his West Point class in 1840 and served with distinction in the Mexican War, was, in the words of historian Stephen B. Oates, "a superb example of the type of soldier Texans despised." He had the reputation of being a textbook soldier who, according to Northern visitor Thomas North, "preferred red-top boots, and a greased rat-tail moustache, with fine equipage, and suit of waiters, to the use of good, practical common sense." Such a reputation had little appeal to Texans, who admired military leaders not for their uniforms or administrative skills but for their fighting ability.[42]

At the same time that Van Dorn was being replaced as military commander of Texas, Edward Clark was completing his tenure as governor. Although Clark had managed state affairs reasonably well since taking office in March and had support in East Texas, where he was a highly respected lawyer, he was defeated in the gubernatorial election in August. Many former Unionists could not forgive him for taking office from the deposed Sam Houston. Staunch Confederates, on the other hand, believed Clark had been too lukewarm in the secession crisis. As usual the state Democratic Party was divided and could not agree upon a single candidate for the August election. As a result, three Democratic candidates — Clark, Francis R. Lubbock, former lieutenant governor, and Thomas Jefferson Chambers, wealthy early Texas pioneer and secessionist leader — entered the race.

The 1861 election contest was a spirited one. All three candidates pledged to prosecute the war with vigor and to cooperate with Confederate authorities. Most of the state's newspapers, including the *Texas State Gazette, Houston Telegraph*, and *Clarksville Standard*, supported Lubbock, the favorite of state Democratic Party leaders. Charles DeMorse, editor of the *Clarksville Standard*, was especially critical of Clark, whom he accused of being a Know-Nothing in the 1850s and riding Houston's coattails to victory as lieutenant governor in 1859, only to turn against Houston later.[43]

The election was extremely close. Lubbock received 21,854 votes, Clark 21,730, and Chambers 13,733. Thus Lubbock was chosen governor by a 124-vote margin. Although there were widespread rumors of fraud, particularly in San Antonio, where Lubbock polled over 65 percent of the total, Clark did not challenge the outcome of the election. He returned to East Texas, where he raised the Fourteenth Texas Infantry Regiment for Confederate service. As colonel of the unit he led the regiment in various battles later in the war.[44]

The election for Texas representatives to the first regular Confederate Congress was held that fall. John A. Wilcox of San Antonio, Claiborne C. Herbert of Eagle Lake, Peter W. Gray of Houston, Franklin B. Sexton of San Augustine, Malcolm Graham of Henderson, and William B. Wright of Paris were chosen to represent Texas in the Confederate House of Representatives. All six men had supported secession and all except Wilcox, who backed the Constitutional Unionists, were Democrats. All but Herbert would usually support the policies of President Davis in the Confederate Congress. The two Confederate senators, chosen by the state legislature, Louis T. Wigfall of Marshall and Williamson Simpson Oldham of Austin, were rabid secessionists. Both came to be critical of the Davis administration, especially as the war continued.[45]

The new governor, Francis R. Lubbock, took office in early November, just as General Hebert was becoming familiar with his duties as military district commander of Texas. The two men saw the defense of the Texas coastline in opposite manner. Lubbock believed the entire Texas coast could be defended, but Hebert was convinced that defense of Galveston island would be extremely difficult, given the military realities that existed. On October 24, 1861, he had written to Confederate Secretary of War Judah P. Benjamin that "it will be almost impossible to prevent a landing at some point upon this extensive and unprotected coast." As a consequence, he concluded, "I have settled upon it as a military necessity that he [the enemy] must be fought on shore or in the interior."[46]

General Hebert's apprehension was increased in early November, when Union vessels surprised and partially burned the Confederate patrol schooner *Royal Yacht*. Hebert now moved some of his artillery from the island to Virginia Point on the mainland. Lubbock, who took office in early November, wrote to Hebert urging that the island be defended. "Every effort should be made to prevent the enemy from effecting a landing," he wrote. The loss of Galveston, Lubbock believed, would be a serious blow; "it would dispirit the people from one end of the state to the other." Lubbock urged that every effort be made to defend the island. Should that be impossible, he said, the city should be destroyed rather than allow the enemy its control: "I would rather see the city one blackened ruin than that a miserable, fanatical abolition horde should be permitted to occupy it, gloating over their gains and laughing to scorn our abandonment of so important a strategic point."[47]

Lubbock's letter to General Hebert worried Galvestonians, who feared the governor intended to burn the city. Mayor Thomas M. Joseph wrote to Lubbock inquiring about the matter. Lubbock responded that only the most serious military necessity would cause him to recommend such action.[48]

In March 1862, Lubbock visited Galveston, hoping to reassure townspeople and at the same time convince them to resist the enemy. In a speech to a large group of citizens from the portico of the Tremont House, he urged Galvestonians to take whatever steps necessary to defend their city. The following month he authorized construction of additional fortifications and the conversion of several cargo ships into gunboats. At the same time, however, General Hebert was ordered by Confederate military authorities to forward all available troops except those necessary to man coastal batteries to Earl Van Dorn, who was then commanding Southern forces in Arkansas.[49]

Throughout the spring of 1862 the Federal navy harassed Confederates along the upper Texas coast, capturing or turning back ships trying to enter Galveston Bay. One such vessel was the *Wide Awake*, a schooner carrying Confederate minister William L. Yancey home from England. When the appearance of Union warships forced the schooner to run back, Yancey convinced the ship's captain to put him ashore near the mouth of Sabine Pass. There he was picked up by surprised Confederates from Spaight's Battalion and taken to local headquarters. Subsequently he made his way overland to New Orleans and finally on to Richmond.[50]

Capt. Henry Eagle, commanding the Union frigate *Santee*, demanded the surrender of Galveston in May. Hebert refused to surrender but did order civilians, livestock, and excessive provisions off the island. Governor Lubbock supported Hebert's actions, issuing a proclamation to organize the expected exodus, but many civilians refused to leave the island. There was some exchange of fire between Union ships and Confederate batteries, but Captain Eagle lacked army support to occupy the city.[51]

The Union navy continued to make raids along the Texas coast during the summer of 1862. Lt. John W. Kittredge, captain of the Federal bark *Arthur*, described as a "bold and daring officer," was active in the Aransas area, obstructing coastal trade and shelling several towns along the middle Texas coast. In August, Kittredge, commanding a five-ship flotilla, attempted to capture Corpus Christi. The Eighth Texas Infantry battalion, organized and commanded by Maj. Alfred M. Hobby, a merchant, state legislator, and Knight of the Golden Circle, beat back two attacks on August 16. After a lull on Sunday, Kittredge resumed the attack on August 18 but the Confederate defenders held the shoreline earthworks. In a final effort Kittredge landed some of his seamen and a field gun, only to be driven back to their ships by a charge of Hobby's infantry. Kittredge himself was captured the following month while ashore at Flour Bluff, south of Corpus, and the immediate threat to the city ended.[52]

While some Texans were defending the coastline from enemy attacks in the spring and summer of 1862, other Texans were fighting on battlefields from Arkansas to Virginia. In early spring Ben McCulloch and Albert Sidney Johnston, the state's two most highly respected military leaders, were killed on the field of battle — McCulloch in Arkansas and Johnston in Tennessee.

Ben McCulloch was killed on the afternoon of March 7, 1862, in the battle of Pea Ridge. At the time he was commanding one of two divisions in an army led by Earl Van Dorn. The other division was commanded by Sterling Price, former governor of Missouri and leader of the state's Confederate forces. Although McCulloch and Price had served together the previous year while defeating Lyon at Wilson's Creek, there was an uneasy relationship between the two. Price saw the war entirely in terms of freeing Missouri from Union control. McCulloch believed the defense of Arkansas and Indian Territory was his major concern. Too, the Texan considered Price to be overbearing, arrogant, and lacking in military skill. Van Dorn, recently promoted to major general, had been sent from Richmond to take command of their combined forces, then located in northern Arkansas. McCulloch's division was made up of Texans, Arkansans, Louisianians, and Cherokee, Choctaw, Chickasaw, and Creek Indians. Price's division consisted entirely of Missourians.[53]

Van Dorn planned to drive northward from Arkansas into Missouri. Opposing Van Dorn, who had 16,000 men in his army, was a smaller Federal army of some 11,000 men commanded by Brig. Gen.

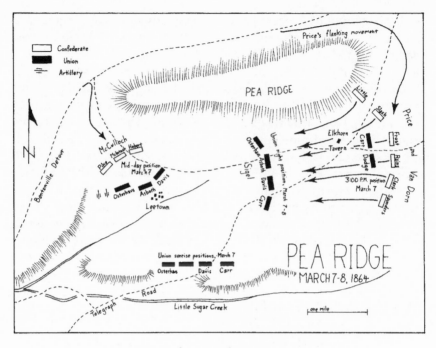

Pea Ridge, March 7–8, 1862.

Samuel R. Curtis. Van Dorn divided his army for the attack against Curtis' army, which was at that time camped near Pea Ridge in northwestern Arkansas. McCulloch's division opened the battle with an assault on the Union left near Leetown. Van Dorn and Price then followed with an attack on the Union right near Elkhorn Tavern, two miles to the northeast of Leetown. Although the Union left was driven back by McCulloch's attack that morning, enemy resistance stiffened by early afternoon. McCulloch was reconnoitering the enemy's position when a volley of enemy rifle fire killed him instantly.[54]

Brig. Gen. James M. McIntosh, the Arkansan who commanded McCulloch's cavalry, took command of the division when the Texan fell. McIntosh was killed a few minutes later when leading an attack on the enemy. The third ranking officer in the division, Col. Louis Hebert of Louisiana, was captured in the fighting that continued in the afternoon. Col. Elkanah Greer, commanding the Third Texas Cavalry, assumed temporary command of the division. The next morning fighting centered around Elkhorn Tavern with Confederates showing lack of coordination and leadership. After a spirited Union charge at midday, Van Dorn broke off the engagement and retreated.[55]

The defeat at Pea Ridge was a devasting blow to Confederate hopes of liberating Missouri from Federal control. Much criticism was focused around the Confederate commander, Earl Van Dorn. A bold and gallant soldier, Van Dorn made errors in planning the campaign and seemed to lack effective control of the army once the battle was under way. Many men in McCulloch's division were convinced that had McCulloch and McIntosh not been killed, the battle would have been won. Others believed that the Confederates should have continued the attack on the second day. Douglas Cater, a member of the Third Texas Cavalry, thought that Van Dorn "had given up the fight." Col. W. P. Lane, veteran of San Jacinto and the Mexican War, found it difficult to believe that Van Dorn had ended the fighting. "I was never so astonished in my life," he later recalled.[56]

Albert S. Johnston — Texan who became highest ranking field general in Confederate army. His death at Shiloh in April 1862 was a serious blow to Confederate cause. Painting by E. F. Andrews.
— Texas State Capitol, Austin, TX

One month after McCulloch's death at Pea Ridge, Texas' most distinguished soldier and the highest ranking field general in the Confederate army, Albert Sidney Johnston, was killed at Shiloh.

Johnston, former secretary of war of the Texas Republic and Mexican War hero, was one of the most highly regarded military men in America when the Civil War began. Although he had not favored secession, he resigned command of the Department of the Pacific and offered his services to the Confederacy when Texas left the Union. His former Transylvania and West Point classmate, President Jefferson Davis, appointed him to command Department No. 2 extending from the Appalachian Mountains westward to Indian Territory, with the rank of full general. Only Samuel Cooper, the venerable adjutant general of the Confederate army, outranked Johnston.

Much was expected of Sidney Johnston. His reputation was awesome; his biographer, Charles P. Roland, noted that "people expected miracles of him in the field." Lack of adequate manpower and equipment spread over the vast distances of his command proved too great even for Johnston. In February 1862, Brig. Gen. U. S. Grant boldly moved up the Tennessee and Cumberland rivers capturing Forts Henry and Donelson, with nearly 15,000 Confederates

Site of the Second Texas Infantry's famous but ill-fated charge in October 1862.

— Luanne Parish

including the Seventh Texas Infantry commanded by Col. John M. Gregg, former member of the Texas secession convention. The loss of Henry and Donelson opened middle Tennessee to Union gunboats, forcing Johnston to order withdrawal of his thinly spread forces from Kentucky and middle Tennessee.[57]

Johnston was determined not to repeat the mistake of dividing his forces, so he concentrated nearly 45,000 men at Corinth, Mississippi, including the Second Texas Infantry, commanded by Col. John C. Moore, the Ninth Texas Cavalry, commanded by Col. Wright A. Stanley, and the Eighth Texas Cavalry, now commanded by Col. John A. Wharton following the death of Col. Benjamin F. Terry at Woodsonville, Kentucky, the previous December. On April 3, Johnston moved his army northward toward Pittsburg Landing on the Tennessee River, where Grant's Union army was encamped. On April 6, Johnston launched a massive assault on Grant's army spread out around a small country church named Shiloh. In the bloody fighting that took place that Sunday, the Texans acquitted themselves well. John Moore's Second Infantry, which had just arrived at Corinth on April 1 after an exhausting march from Houston, was in the thick of fighting on the Confederate right around the Hornet's Nest that eventually led to the surrender of Union general Benjamin Prentiss. Among those wounded that day were Capt. Ashbel Smith, former surgeon general of the Texas Republic, diplomat, and scientist who commanded Company C of the Second Texas, and Sam Houston, Jr., a private in Smith's company.

The Ninth Texas, a small regiment made of men from northeast Texas, was to the left of the Second, as part of Patton Anderson's Second Brigade, Ruggles' Division. Like the Second, the Ninth helped push the enemy back under heavy fire. Colonel Stanley, commanding the Ninth, had a horse shot out from under him, and the regiment sustained sixty-seven casualties, or nearly 30 percent of those engaged, in fighting on Sunday and Monday. The Eighth Cavalry under Colonel Wharton was heavily engaged and fought both mounted and unmounted. On the second day of the battle Wharton's cavalry was ordered to ride around the Union right flank but encountered heavy enemy resistance. Wharton's horse was killed and Wharton himself was wounded but stayed on the field until the battle was over. In all, the Rangers suffered sixty-six casualties and fifty-six horses killed in the fighting.[58]

As was the case of McCulloch at Pea Ridge, Albert Sidney

Johnston Memorial at Shiloh.

—Forest View Historical Services

Johnston was killed in the early afternoon on the first day at Shiloh. Johnston was on the extreme Confederate right near the Peach Orchard, rallying an exhausted Tennessee regiment, when he was hit in the leg by a stray bullet. He was helped from his horse by Tennessee governor Isham G. Harris and lay on the ground. The bullet had severed an artery on the back of his right leg near the knee. Within fifteen minutes Johnston bled to death.[59]

Johnston's death left a momentary void in Confederate leadership. His second in command, Gen. P. G. T. Beauregard, assumed command of the army and continued the fighting until dusk. The Confederates resumed the attack the next morning, but Grant had received reinforcements during the night. Momentum gradually passed to Grant as the Confederates were slowly pushed back. On Monday evening Beauregard ordered a retreat. The Confederates fell back to Corinth, but under heavy enemy pressure were forced to surrender that city one month later.

Many Southerners believed that the battle of Shiloh would have

Texas Monument at Shiloh.
— Forest View Historical Services

been won if Albert Sidney Johnston had lived. Both Braxton Bragg and William J. Hardee, Confederate corps commanders in the battle, were convinced that only Johnston's death prevented the destruction of Grant's army on April 6. President Davis firmly believed this, as did Johnston's son, William Preston Johnston, who wrote a biography eulogizing his father.[60]

Although fighting on a limited scale continued in the western theater in the summer of 1862, major attention shifted to Virginia, where the Southern army fought to defend the Confederate capital against George B. McClellan's Union forces. McClellan had moved his army by water to the York Peninsula in March. After a successful landing, Federal forces slowly pushed the Confederates back up the peninsula toward Richmond. It was in the heavy fighting around Richmond in late May and June that Hood's Texas Brigade distinguished itself as one of the finest units in the Confederate army.

The Texas Brigade, consisting of the First, Fourth, and Fifth Texas Infantry, was organized in October 1861. Commanded initially by former U.S. Senator Louis T. Wigfall, the brigade was recruited primarily in East and Central Texas. The Eighteenth Georgia Infantry and several companies of Wade Hampton's South Carolina Legion were later added to the three Texas regiments to form a brigade of nearly 4,000 men. The brigade suffered severe losses during the fall and winter of 1861 due to disease and illness. Harold B. Simpson, who chronicled the story of the brigade in a series of books and articles, pointed out that the Texans were not acclimatized to the cold and damp weather they encountered in Virginia.

Many of them were poorly clothed and housed, and others were physically unfit when they enlisted. About 20 percent of the men in the three Texas regiments died or were discharged for disabilities related to illness between September 1861 and March 1862. Among those who died that first winter was Col. Hugh McLeod, commander of the First Texas. A graduate of West Point, McLeod was former adjutant general and inspector general of the army of the Texas Republic and commander of the ill-fated Santa Fe expedition in the Lamar administration. He died from pneumonia on January 3, 1862.[61]

When Wigfall left the Texas Brigade to take a seat in the Confederate Senate in February 1862, Col. James J. Archer, a Marylander who commanded the Fifth Texas Infantry, temporarily assumed command. In March Col. John Bell Hood of the Fourth Texas Infantry was promoted to brigadier general and took command of the brigade, soon to be known as Hood's Texas Brigade. Hood, a West Point graduate, was a native Kentuckian but had served as an officer in the United States Second Cavalry in Texas before the war and considered the state his adopted home.[62]

Gen. John Bell Hood, commander of Hood's Texas Brigade.
— Leib Image Archives, York, PA

Although Hood's Brigade was involved in some skirmishes with the enemy in the winter of 1861–62, the Texans first saw major action on the York Peninsula in May 1862.[63] Assigned to Brig. Gen. W. H. C. Whiting's division to cover the Confederate withdrawal from Yorktown, the Texans engaged Federal troops commanded by Brig. Gen. William B. Franklin near Eltham's Landing on the Pamunkey River. Franklin had moved his troops by water in an attempt to outflank the Confederates. Whiting ordered Hood's Brigade to drive the Federals back. The Fourth Infantry opened the assault, but the heaviest fighting was borne by the First Texas commanded by Palestine lawyer Alexis T. Rainey. At the cost of fifteen men killed and twenty-five wounded, the brigade drove the enemy back to the river, taking forty prisoners and securing eighty-four abandoned wagons.

The Texas Brigade received praise from Jefferson Davis and Maj. Gen. Gustavus Smith, commanding the left wing of the Confederate army, for its role in defeating Franklin's forces at Eltham's Landing. The victory prevented the Union army from outflanking the Confederates as they withdrew toward the Richmond defense lines.[64]

In the major battle near Richmond fought at Seven Pines and Fair Oaks the last of May and first of June, Hood's Texans saw only limited action as they formed part of the Confederate reserve. In the battle the Confederates halted McClellan's advance, but in the fighting Joseph E. Johnston, commander of the Southern forces defending Richmond, was wounded. President Davis appointed his military adviser, Gen. Robert E. Lee, to succeed Johnston.[65]

Robert E. Lee was a more aggressive general than his predecessor Joseph E. Johnston had been. While Johnston was content to fight a delaying campaign, Lee was more inclined to attack. In late June he launched a series of assaults aimed at driving McClellan away from Richmond. Lee's plan called for Confederate attacks on that portion of McClellan's army north of the Chickahominy River. In these battles, known as the Seven Days, the Texas Brigade served with Stonewall Jackson's command. The first battle at Mechanicsville on June 26 accomplished little as the Union lines held. On the following day the Confederates attacked again at Gaines' Mill. Union forces commanded by Fitz-John Porter held a strong position along Boatswain's Swamp. Earlier assaults against the Federal position failed, but in the late afternoon Hood led his brigade in a bayonet attack that broke the enemy line. The Fourth Texas, Hood's old regiment, which spearheaded the victorious assault, and the Eighteenth Georgia captured the enemy artillery. The Fifth Texas captured almost the entire Fourth New Jersey Regiment. The Union Fifth Cavalry attempted to stem the tide of the Confederate onslaught, but was driven back with heavy losses. Fitz-John Porter's corps retreated to the south of the Chickahominy River as dusk ended the fighting.[66]

The Confederate victory at Gaines' Mill resulted in praise for both the Texas Brigade and its commander. Because of their success McClellan was forced to retreat toward the James River. The victory was costly for the Texas Brigade, which suffered heavy losses: eighty-six killed, 481 wounded, and four missing, for a total of 571 casualties, or over 25 percent. The Fourth Texas, which led the attack, suffered the heaviest losses: 253 casualties, or about half of those who charged the enemy. Col. John Marshall, the fiery secessionist editor of the *State Gazette* and commander of the regiment, was killed; Lt. Col. Bradfute Warwick was mortally wounded; Maj. J. C. G. Key was wounded; nine other officers of the regiment killed or mortally wounded; and ten other officers wounded. Losses for the other regiments were not as high, although the Eighteenth Georgia had 146 casualties. Colonel Rainey of the First Texas and Col. Jerome Bonaparte Robertson of the Fifth Texas were both wounded.[67]

The Confederates continued to attack as McClellan fell back, but the Texas Brigade saw little action in the fighting at Savage Station and White Oak Swamp. In the last battle of the Seven Days fought at Malvern Hill on July 1, the brigade was held in reserve but suffered some casualties from Union artillery fire. Although Lee did not destroy McClellan's army as he had hoped, he had forced him to abandon his grip on Richmond. Ultimately, Lincoln would order McClellan to withdraw his army from the York Peninsula and return to the Washington area.

After the fighting on the peninsula, the Texas Brigade went into camp three miles northeast of Richmond. In August the brigade moved toward the old battlefield at Manassas Junction as a part of Longstreet's corps. In the Second Battle of Manassas fought in late August, the brigade again saw heavy action. General Whiting, the division commander, had taken medical leave, so Hood, the senior brigade commander, temporarily led the division as well as his own brigade.

The climax of the campaign came on the afternoon of August 30. During the previous day and the morning of the thirtieth, the Union army commanded by John Pope pounded away at Jackson's corps on the Union right. That afternoon Longstreet's corps launched a counterattack against the Union left flank. The Texas Brigade led the assault, scattering one New York infantry brigade, almost destroying a second one, and capturing an enemy artillery battery. Pope's army was driven from the field, and Second Manassas was another Confederate victory.[68]

Once again the Texas Brigade sustained heavy losses in battle: 628 killed, wounded, or missing. This time Jerome Robertson's Fifth Texas, which spearheaded the attack, suffered the most severe loss, 261 casualties. The Eighteenth Georgia had the second highest loss in the brigade, with 133 casualties.[69]

As August came to an end with the victory at Second Manassas, Texans could look back upon the first one and a half years of the war with mixed feelings. The failure of the New Mexico campaign and the defeats at Pea Ridge, Donelson, and Shiloh were bitter disappointments. The deaths of McCulloch, Johnston, Terry, McLeod, Marshall, and hundreds of others at Pea Ridge, Shiloh, Gaines' Mill, and Second Manassas were painful reminders of the horrors of war. So far, however, the Confederate army had the upper hand in Virginia, and Texas itself had been spared from enemy invasion. That was to change in the autumn of 1862.

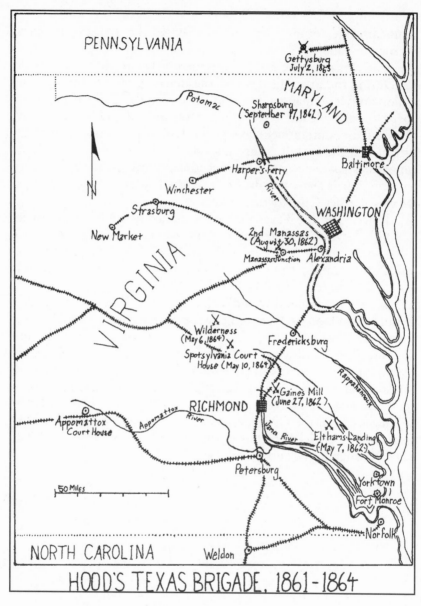

Major Actions, Hood's Brigade in the East, 1861–64.

CHAPTER THREE

The War Comes to Texas:
September 1862–December 1863

The Confederate cause looked bright in early September 1862. Robert E. Lee's Army of Northern Virginia defeated Pope's army in the Second Battle of Manassas in late August and was poised for a movement into Maryland. On the same day that Lee defeated Pope, a small Confederate army commanded by Edmund Kirby Smith routed Union forces at Richmond, Kentucky, opening the way to Lexington, Frankfort, and Louisville. In the battle four regiments of Texas dismounted cavalry (the Tenth, Eleventh, Fourteenth, and Thirty-second) serving in a brigade commanded by Arkansas Col. T. H. McCray made what Kirby Smith described as a "well-timed and dashing charge" through a corn field and a ravine to break the enemy line.[1]

On September 1, Kirby Smith's 15,000 troops crossed the Kentucky River and the following day entered Lexington. The state capitol at Frankfort was occupied on September 3. An even larger Confederate army, commanded by Braxton Bragg, was marching across Tennessee and would soon link up with Kirby Smith. Texan John A. Wharton commanded a cavalry brigade covering the right flank of Bragg's army as it moved north. Wharton's old regiment, the Eighth Texas Cavalry, was a part of this cavalry brigade. The Eighth Texas, or Terry's Texas Rangers, was now commanded by Col. Thomas Harrison, a Waco attorney known to his men as "Old

59

Iron Sides." Because he had escaped serious injury while engaged in many battles, the Rangers reasoned he was protected by iron that prevented bullets from penetrating his body. [2]

At the same time that Kirby Smith and Braxton Bragg moved to liberate Kentucky, Lee's army crossed the Potomac River and headed into western Maryland. The Texas Brigade, reduced in size due to losses at Gaines' Mill and Second Manassas, marched with Lee's army as a part of Longstreet's corps.

What appeared so promising in early September changed quickly. Lee's advance into Maryland was halted at the small town of Sharpsburg. There, in mid-September, along the banks of Antietam Creek, one of the bloodiest battles of the Civil War was fought. George B. McClellan, back in command of the Army of the Potomac, launched a massive attack on Lee's smaller army on September 17. In the morning fighting, Hood's Texas Brigade took the brunt of the main Union assault in Miller's corn field between the Hagerstown Pike and the East Woods. For two hours the Texas Brigade fought tenaciously to hold the corn field that was turned red with blood. The brigade slowly gave ground under heavy enemy infantry assaults and artillery fire and fell back across the Pike toward the West Woods. With most of their ammunition gone and casualties high, the brigade was shattered, but held until relieved by Lafayette McLaw's division. [3]

Texas Monument at Sharpsburg.
— Forest View Historical Services

The Texas Brigade saw no major action after 10:00 that morning. Unable to break through on the north, McClellan shifted the main attack to the center of Lee's line. For several hours heavy fighting went on there. In the afternoon the battle moved to the south as Union Gen. Ambrose Burnside's corps fought to cross the Rohrbach bridge. Al-

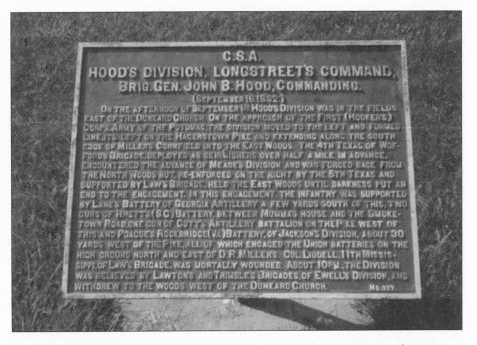

*Hood's Brigade Marker (corn field) — Marker indicating spot where
Hood's Texas Brigade suffered heaviest casualties in war in stopping
advance of Union army on morning of battle of Sharpsburg.*
— Forest View Historical Services

though the Confederates eventually fell back, their lines never broke. The battle was tactically a draw, but strategically it was a Union victory as Lee was forced to withdraw his battered army back across the Potomac to Virginia.

The battle of Sharpsburg, or Antietam as the Federals called it, was indeed the bloodiest day of the war. Nearly 23,000 Americans were killed, wounded, captured, or missing when the fighting ended that day. McClellan's army sustained 12,401 casualties, or 25 percent of those engaged. Lee's army had 10,318 casualties, or 31 percent. The casualty rate for the Texas Brigade, 64 percent, was twice as high as the rest of the Confederate army. The First Texas had the highest percentage of casualties for any regiment, North or South, for one day in the war. Col. Philip A. Work led 226 men into battle; 186, or 82.3 percent, were killed, wounded, or missing. The Fourth Texas sustained 107 casualties, or 53.5 percent, and the Fifth Texas had 86 casualties, or 49.1 percent.[4]

The Kentucky campaign of Braxton Bragg and Edmund Kirby Smith also ended in disappointment. Bragg and Smith briefly occupied the Kentucky state capital but withdrew from Kentucky in mid-October and returned to Tennessee. Except for Smith's victory at Richmond in late August, the only major battle fought was at Perryville, Kentucky, where part of Bragg's army clashed with three corps of Don Carlos Buell's Federals. In this engagement, fought on October 8, the Ninth Texas Infantry commanded by Col. William H. Young, a twenty-four-year-old resident of Grayson County, served in the Confederate right wing under Maj. Gen. Leonidas Polk. Wharton's cavalry brigade, which included Terry's Rangers, led the attack, charging the enemy with what Polk described as "great fury." Although the Confederates won a tactical victory by driving Union troops from the field, Bragg elected to pull back to Bardstown. Facing supply problems and a larger enemy force, Bragg and Smith subsequently withdrew to East Tennessee.[5]

The war came into Texas in the autumn of 1862. In late September Federal forces off the upper Texas coast took advantage of the weakness in Confederate defenses, exacerbated by a yellow fever epidemic at Sabine Pass, to stage a raid near the Louisiana border. On September 24 three Union ships commanded by Lt. Frederick Crocker crossed the bar at Sabine Pass and began shelling Fort Sabine. After a brief exchange of artillery fire, Maj. Josephus S. Irvine, a veteran of San Jacinto who commanded the Confederate defenders, determined to spike his guns and evacuate the fort. On September 26, Crocker's men came ashore, destroyed Fort Sabine, and burned the railway bridge over Taylor's Bayou and the railway depot near Sabine City.[6]

Although there continued to be some clashes in the Sabine area between Confederate defenders commanded by Col. Ashley W. Spaight and Capt. K. D. Keith and Crocker's naval units during October, the main Union thrust was directed at Galveston. General Hebert, convinced that defense of the city was futile, began constructing a Confederate fort across the bay on the mainland at Virginia Point. All but one of the heavy cannons were moved from Fort Point on the island and placed on the mainland. Galvestonians were bitterly opposed to the move and accused Hebert of loving his cannon more than the city.[7]

In September 1862, Union Rear Adm. David Farragut, commanding the West Gulf Blockading Squadron, ordered William B.

Renshaw, commanding a naval flotilla off the Texas coast, to move his ships into Galveston harbor if conditions seemed favorable. On October 4 the Union gunboat *Harriet Lane* steamed into the harbor with the demand that the city and the harbor be surrendered. After some delay and confusion, Renshaw brought his other seven ships into the harbor. The Confederate battery at Fort Point fired a warning shot at the Union fleet but was quickly knocked out of action by the larger guns of the Union warship *Owasco*. Renshaw repeated his demand for immediate surrender. After discussion with the defenders of the city, Renshaw agreed to a four-day truce to give civilians time to evacuate the island.[8]

During the truce the Confederates withdrew men and materials from the island. Renshaw protested the removal of machinery and weapons but could do little to prevent it. When the truce ended several hundred men and almost 2,000 women and children remained on the island. Many of them were ill, too poor to move, or fearful of fever on the mainland. They watched helplessly as Union forces occupied the island on October 8. William Pitt Ballinger, prominent Galveston attorney, described the Union occupation as "a bleak day in our history."[9]

Admiral Farragut was pleased to learn that Galveston had been taken without resistance. Commander Renshaw, however, remained uneasy. He had only 150 men with which to occupy the island. Food was needed for both Federal military personnel and the civilian population, so Renshaw allowed the railroad bridge connecting the island with the mainland to stand. Confederate authorities on the mainland attempted to seal off the island. Governor Lubbock issued a proclamation placing all trade and communications with Galveston under the military district commander. Steps were taken to make a Federal landing on the mainland more difficult.[10]

Later that month Commander Renshaw turned his attention to the middle Texas coast. On October 31, Renshaw took two of his ships, *Clifton* and *Westfield*, into Matagorda Bay and demanded the surrender of Port Lavaca. Maj. Daniel D. Shea refused the demand but requested time to evacuate women and children. Determined not to repeat his mistake at Galveston, Renshaw granted only ninety minutes for residents to depart. His ships then opened fire upon the town. Local batteries commanded by Captains John A. Vernon and Joseph Reuss returned the fire with some success. The Union ships pulled out of range but returned the next day to resume the shelling.

Once again the shore batteries opened fire. After this exchange Renshaw withdrew his ships and terminated the operation.[11]

Renshaw continued to have difficulties in the Galveston area. A Union foraging party that ventured onto the Bolivar Peninsula was attacked by Confederate cavalry and several Federals were captured. Later a small boat and crew from a Union schooner were captured while engaged in foraging on the mainland. Lacking sufficient forces and supplies, Renshaw wanted to withdraw from Galveston, but Admiral Farragut would not approve.[12]

On Christmas Day, 1862, Renshaw received reinforcements. Three companies of the Forty-second Massachusetts Volunteers, numbering 260 men commanded by Col. Isaac S. Burrell, arrived from New Orleans. The remaining members of the regiment, totaling over 700, were scheduled to arrive in the next several days.[13]

At that very moment Confederates were preparing an attack which would result in the recapture of Galveston. Maj. Gen. John Bankhead Magruder, a veteran officer who had served with Robert

Maj. Gen. John Bankhead Magruder
— Archives Division, Texas State Library

E. Lee in the fighting around Richmond, was transferred to Texas a few days after Galveston was captured. Magruder replaced General Hebert as district commander. As noted earlier, Hebert was never liked by the Texans. The loss of Galveston without a fight had increased his unpopularity.

The appointment of the colorful and flamboyant Magruder, known in the Old Army as "Prince John" because of his fondness for good food and drink, elegant furnishing, and sartorial elegance, was popular with Texans who had served with him in Indian campaigns and the

Mexican War. Although Magruder's performance in the Seven Days around Richmond had been disappointing to Robert E. Lee, Texans regarded him as a fighter and man of action. Texas Ranger-soldier John S. "Rip" Ford, himself a highly respected officer, believed "the advent of General Magruder was equal to the addition of 50,000 men to the forces of Texas." Too, Magruder was related to prominent Texans, including Jane Long, the "Anglo mother of Texas," Jared Groce, the largest slaveholder in Stephen F. Austin's colony, and Mrs. Thomas Affleck, wife of wealthy agricultural reformer and planter Thomas Affleck.[14]

Magruder assumed command of the Texas military district in late November 1862. He immediately began planning for the recapture of Galveston before additional enemy troops were landed. Among the forces at his disposal were elements of the Twenty-sixth Texas Cavalry, commanded by Col. Xavier Blanchard Debray, French-born graduate of St. Cyr Military Academy; several cavalry units of Sibley's Brigade commanded by Colonels Tom Green and Arthur P. Bagby, veterans of the ill-fated New Mexico campaign; and assorted state militia units assembled under order of Governor Lubbock. Magruder also had several artillery batteries and two river steamers, *Bayou City* and *Neptune*, which had been converted into gunboats. *Bayou City* was armed with a thirty-two-pounder cannon. Two twenty-four-pounder howitzers were placed on the *Neptune*. Bales of cotton were on the decks of both vessels to protect sharpshooters on board. Oversized gangplanks, to be used for boarding the enemy ships, were suspended on either side of the hurricane deck by guy ropes which could be cut so as to drop on any vessel alongside. Anchors were to be used for grappling the enemy ships. Two other vessels, the *John F. Carr* and *Lucy Gwinn*, were to serve as tenders. Leon Smith, an experienced steamboat captain whom Magruder had met years earlier in California, was named commander of the flotilla. William R. Scurry, who had commanded Texans in the battle of Glorieta Pass and had recently been promoted to brigadier general, was designated as commander of land forces in the attack.[15]

Magruder planned to move his land forces across the abandoned railroad bridge under cover of darkness while his naval flotilla descended from the upper part of Galveston Bay to attack the Union warships in the harbor. To gain better knowledge of the enemy's defenses, Magruder led a reconnaissance party on to the island at night. On this mission Magruder observed that the Union troops were stationed at the end of Kuhn's Wharf and were housed in buildings protected by guns of the warships anchored nearby. Two lines of barricades had been erected to block an approach from the landside. Part of the planking in front of the barricades had been removed to further impede any attackers. Magruder ordered the construction of fifty scaling ladders for the purpose of overcoming this obstacle in the attack.[16]

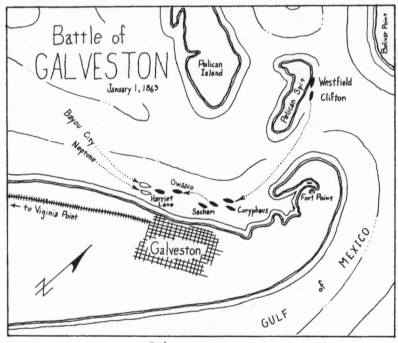

Galveston, 1862–63

The Confederate attack on Galveston began in the early morning hours of January 1, 1863. At 1:00 A.M., while Federal troops slept after an evening of celebration, Magruder and Scurry led Confederate troops from Virginia Point on the mainland across the railroad bridge to the island. Under cover of darkness they moved quietly five miles toward the marketplace in the center of town. Shortly before dawn, Confederate artillery opened fire upon Union positions along the waterfront. Union warships moored in the harbor returned the Confederate fire in a heavy exchange of artillery volleys.[17]

Meanwhile, Col. Joseph C. Cook led Confederate troops attempting to storm Union positions on Kuhn's Wharf. Cook's men advanced under heavy enemy fire but were unable to cross the dismantled portion of the wharf because the scaling ladders were not long enough. Fire from the Union gunboats *Sachem*, *Owasco*, and *Corypheus* forced Cook's men to withdraw to the safety of nearby buildings. Magruder instructed General Scurry to pull his artillery back to safe positions to avoid the hail of enemy fire. At that moment the Confederate cause looked bleak.[18]

Just as the Confederate assault on land appeared to be failing, the Confederate cotton-clad vessels *Bayou City* and *Neptune* came steaming into the harbor from Half Moon Shoals to the west. They moved toward the *Harriet Lane*, the most powerful of the enemy ships, which was to the east of the *Owasco*, *Corypheus*, and *Sachem*.[19] The two Confederate gunboats closed quickly so that sharpshooters could rake the *Lane* with rifle fire. In an exchange of cannon fire the *Bayou City's* heavy thirty-two-pound gun exploded, killing Capt. A. R. Weir and two of his men. As the ships were maneuvering in an attempt to ram one another, the *Neptune* was hit by a shell from the *Harriet Lane's* pivot gun and sank in shallow water.

Once again the Confederate attack seemed in danger of failing, but steady rifle fire from Tom Green's sharpshooters on the *Bayou City* forced Union seamen below deck on the *Lane*. The *Bayou City* managed to ram the *Lane*, locking the two vessels together. Capt. Leon Smith, cutlass in hand, leaped to the deck of the *Lane*, demanding surrender of the ship. The two senior officers of the *Lane*, Capt. Jonathan M. Wainwright and Lt. Cmdr. Edward Lea, were both mortally wounded in the fighting. Some believe that Smith, described by a contemporary officer as "a bluff sailor, more gallant than courteous," shot and killed Wainwright after the Union captain declined to surrender. The ship's surviving officers surrendered the *Harriet Lane* to Smith.[20]

The death of young Lt. Cmdr. Edward Lea, second in command of the *Harriet Lane*, provided one of the most poignant moments of the war. Lea was the son of Maj. Alfred Lea, a West Point graduate and an engineering officer under General Magruder. When the captured *Harriet Lane* was brought ashore the senior Lea found his son mortally wounded and dying. The younger Lea died shortly thereafter. His final words were, "My father is here."[21]

The loss of the *Harriet Lane* was a major blow to the Union defenders of the island. The *Owasco* attempted to aid the *Harriet*

Lane but pulled away to avoid hitting captured Union prisoners. Meanwhile, the other Union ships were having troubles of their own. The *Westfield*, the Federal flagship under Commodore W. B. Renshaw, ran aground on Pelican Spit near the harbor's mouth. Efforts by a sister ship, the *Clifton*, to move her were unsuccessful. The *Clifton* was then ordered to aid the other Union vessels attempting to silence the Confederate shore batteries, but the Federal efforts were poorly coordinated. Confederate Capt. Leon Smith sent word to Renshaw demanding surrender of the Union fleet. Renshaw was given three hours to comply.[22]

Not knowing the true Confederate strength or that the captured *Harriet Lane* was in no condition to continue the struggle, Renshaw decided to scuttle his grounded flagship and withdraw the other vessels from the harbor. He transferred most of his crew to the transport *Saxon*, set fire to the *Westfield*, and was preparing to leave by lifeboat when a premature explosion of the powder magazine blew up the ship, killing Renshaw and several crew members in the explosion. Lt. Cmdr. Richard L. Law of the *Clifton*, the ranking officer in the Union fleet, gave orders for the other Federal vessels to withdraw from the harbor. Confederate Captain Smith gave chase on the tender *John F. Carr*, but the enemy fleet escaped to New Orleans.[23]

More than 200 soldiers of the Forty-second Massachusetts watched helplessly as the Union fleet sailed away. Their commander, Col. Isaac S. Burrell, realized that further resistance was futile and surrendered to Brigadier General Scurry. The battle of Galveston was over. The city was once again in Confederate hands.[24]

Texans were elated at the news of Galveston's recapture. The *Houston Telegraph* proclaimed it "the most brilliant affair of the war." Northern visitor Thomas North reported that "news of the victory passed over the state with an electric thrill, and gave people an elevation of spirits, from which they never fully came down, even at the close of the war." Governor Lubbock congratulated Magruder for "the brilliant achievement," which he believed was "the most dashing of the war." President Jefferson Davis praised Magruder for the "brilliant exploit in the capture of Galveston" and "the boldness of the conception and the daring and skill of the execution" which "has been a heavy blow to the enemy's hopes." Former Governor Sam Houston wrote from his sick bed thanking Magruder for "driving from our soil a ruthless enemy. . . . You have breathed new life into everything."[25]

Union authorities viewed the Confederate recapture of Galveston with anger and chagrin. Assistant Secretary of Navy Gustavus V. Fox described the loss of Galveston as "the most melancholy affair ever recorded in the history of our gallant navy." From his headquarters at New Orleans, Maj. Gen. Nathaniel Banks, commander of the Department of the Gulf, wrote that the loss of Galveston was the "most unfortunate affair that occurred in the department during my command." He regarded "Galveston, as a military postion, . . . second in importance only to New Orleans or Mobile." Lieutenant Commander Law, who ordered the withdrawal of the Union fleet after Commander Renshaw's death, was court-martialed and found guilty of leaving before being properly relieved. Because of prior gallant service his sentence of dismissal from service was commuted to a three-year suspension.[26]

Rear Adm. David G. Farragut, directing the West Gulf Coast Blockading Squadron, was determined to recapture Galveston. On January 3 he ordered Commodore Henry H. Bell, captain of the powerful warship *Brooklyn*, to retake Galveston whenever the situation appeared favorable. In any event, Bell was instructed to recapture the *Harriet Lane* as soon as possible.[27]

Commodore Bell moved quickly to carry out his orders. On January 7, 1863, a Union flotilla under his command arrived off Galveston. In addition to his flagship, *Brooklyn*, Bell had the *Hatteras*, *Cayuga*, *New London*, *Sciota*, and *Owasco* under his command. The Union squadron could not enter the harbor, however, because the Confederates had removed the channel buoys. On January 10 the Federal ships opened fire on the city from long range. Over one hundred shells were fired, but with no appreciable success. Confederate batteries returned the fire but caused no major damage to the Union ships.[28]

Bell planned to resume the assault on Galveston the following day, but the appearance of the Confederate raider *Alabama* off the coast interrupted Union operations. The *Hatteras*, commanded by Lt. Cmdr. H. C. Blake, was directed to drive off the *Alabama*. In the ensuing battle the *Hatteras* was sunk before other Union ships could provide assistance.[29]

While Bell pondered what move to make against Galveston, Confederates at nearby Sabine Pass were assembling a small assault force to attack two Union vessels blockading the pass. Two river steamers, the *Josiah H. Bell* and *Uncle Ben*, were converted into gunboats. Artillerymen from Company B, Spaight's Battalion, commanded by Capt. K. D. Keith, were assigned to man both twelve-pounder guns on the *Uncle Ben,* while members of Company F, First Texas Heavy Artillery, commanded by Capt. Frederick Odlum, were assigned to the single sixty-four-pound rifled cannon on the *Josiah H. Bell.* Volunteers from Spaight's Battalion commanded by Captains George O'Brien and O. M. Marsh were placed on both vessels as sharpshooters. Maj. Oscar M. Watkins of Magruder's staff was named commander of the assault force.[30]

On the morning of January 21, the Confederate gunboats steamed out of Sabine Pass against the two Union blockaders, the *Morning Light* and *Velocity,* both sailing ships commanded by Capt. John Dillingham. The Federal ships withdrew before the attackers but were overtaken by the faster Confederate steamers. The Confederates opened fire at the range of two miles and scored several hits, first on the *Morning Light* and later on the smaller *Velocity.* As the ships closed, the Texas sharpshooters, protected by bales of cotton, forced the Federal gun crews from the decks. Captain Dillingham surrendered to avoid further casualties. With no losses, the Confederates took 109 prisoners, inflicted thirteen casualties, captured two enemy ships, and for the moment broke the Union blockade of the upper Texas coast. Prize crews brought the two Union ships to Sabine Pass; however, after attempts to float the *Morning Light* over the bar failed, she was scuttled and burned when other Federal warships appeared.[31]

Meanwhile, General Magruder utilized his theatrical skills to give the appearance of great Confederate defensive strength at Galveston. His engineers, Col. Valery Sulakowski and Maj. Julius G. Kellersberger, used slave labor to build fortifications which looked impressive from a distance. To compensate for the lack of artillery, the engineers moved two heavy cannon by rail from one fortification to another to create the impression of many weapons. They also placed improvised guns made of wood at strategic locations. These "Quaker guns" fooled Union observers for several weeks until a spring storm blew away one of the fake cannons. In early summer Magruder received some additional cannons from Houston and from the wrecked Union warship *Westfield,* leading Commodore Bell to report to Admiral Farragut that the Galveston fortifications were too strong for an assault without army support.[32]

While Texans were fighting to defend their coast against the enemy in the autumn and winter of 1862–63, the struggle between Federals and Confederates for control of Arkansas was continuing. After the Confederate defeat at Pea Ridge in March 1862, there had been a momentary lull in fighting in Arkansas. Earl Van Dorn's army, including four regiments of Texas cavalry, had been ordered to cross the Mississippi to join P. G. T. Beauregard's army at Corinth, Mississippi. Additional Texas regiments were originally scheduled to join Van Dorn but instead were ordered to Little Rock to defend the Arkansas capital from capture by Federal troops under the command of Maj. Gen. Samuel R. Curtis.

During the summer of 1862 these Texas units — the Twelfth, Fifteenth, Sixteenth, Seventeenth, and Eighteenth cavalry regiments — took part in a campaign to prevent Curtis from linking with Union naval forces ascending the White River east of Little Rock. In July these Texas regiments joined three Arkansas regiments commanded by Brig. Gen. Albert Rust in an effort to keep Federal troops from advancing southward along the Cache River. In bitter fighting on July 7 the Confederates were driven from the field near Cotton Plant, Arkansas, with heavy casualties. Fortunately for the Confederates, Curtis failed to take full advantage of the victory and missed connections with the Union fleet.[33]

The arrival of additional recruits from Texas in the autumn of 1862 assured the safety of Little Rock for the time being. Lt. Gen. Theophilus H. Holmes, the newly appointed Confederate commander of the Trans Mississippi Department, reorganized his forces to deal with any new Union threats. The First Corps, under the command of Maj. Gen. Thomas Hindman, a spirited Helena lawyer and former congressman, was scattered along the Arkansas River in the northwestern part of the state. The Second Corps, commanded by Holmes himself, held a narrow line along the west bank of the White River, forty-five miles east of Little Rock. Most of the Texas troops were assigned to Brigadier Generals Henry McCulloch and Allison Nelson in the Second Corps, but three Texas cavalry regiments were dismounted to form an infantry brigade under Col. William R. Bradfute in Hindman's First Corps.[34] The First Texas Cavalry Regiment, Partisan Rangers, now commanded by Lt. Col. P. R. Crump, was assigned to Hindman. The Rangers played a major role in the Cane Hill–Prairie Grove campaign of early December 1862, in which Hindman attempted to drive Union forces out of northwestern Arkansas. In the fighting at Prairie Grove, Crump's regiment and another Confederate regiment fought a running battle with two Union cavalry regiments. The Federals were routed and suffered 250 casualties. The Texans lost only twenty-one men out of 444 who took part in the battle. Unfortunately for Hindman, efforts elsewhere were less successful and the Confederates were forced to withdraw south of the Arkansas River, leaving the area between Fayetteville and Van Buren in enemy hands.[35]

Several of the Texas regiments assigned to Holmes' Second Corps were ordered to occupy a newly constructed defensive work named Fort Hindman near the small village of Arkansas Post, twenty-five miles from the mouth of the Arkansas River and slightly over 100 miles southeast of Little Rock. Confederate authorities were concerned about the massive buildup of Union forces commanded by Maj. Gen. U. S. Grant in northern Mississippi. At the time they were uncertain as to his intentions. Fort Hindman, an earthen work overlooking the Arkansas River, was designed to prevent Union gunboats from moving upriver. By late December nearly 5,000 Confederate troops, including the Sixth and Tenth Texas Infantry regiments, the Fifteenth, Seventeenth, Eighteenth,

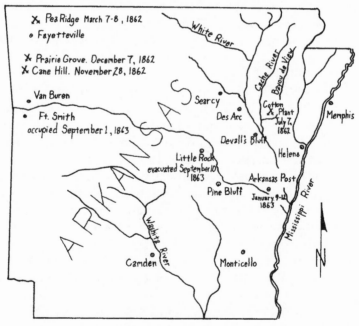

Arkansas, 1862–63

Twenty-fourth, and Twenty-fifth Texas Cavalry regiments (all dismounted), and Horace Haldeman's Texas artillery battery, occupied the fort under the command of Arkansas Brig. Gen. Thomas Churchill. A company of Texas mounted cavalry commanded by Capt. Sam Richardson served with Louisiana cavalry units assigned to Churchill's command.[36]

There were rumors of an impending Federal attack from the moment Fort Hindman was occupied. Rumors became reality on January 9, 1863, when Union gunboats under Rear Adm. David Porter anchored several miles below Arkansas Post and began disembarking nearly 30,000 troops commanded by Maj. Gen. John Mc-Clernand. On January 10 Porter's gunboats opened a massive bombardment of Fort Hindman and outlying Confederate positions. The next day McClernand's infantry and artillery, which had swung around Fort Hindman, opened fire on one side while Union gunboats continued fire from the river. Union infantry assaults were driven back, but by late afternoon all of the fort's heavy guns had been silenced. White flags appeared in the area held by the Twenty-fourth Texas, commanded by Methodist minister and colonel F. C. Wilkes. Soon white flags appeared elsewhere. Federal troops, taking advantage of the confusion among the defenders, breached the Southern lines. General Churchill, who blamed Wilkes and his brigade commander Col. Robert Garland for the white flags, was forced to surrender.[37]

A few of the Confederate defenders managed to escape from the fort in the confusion following surrender, but the majority (4,791) were prisoners of war. They were taken by steamboat and rail to Northern prisoner of war camps. Officers were confined at Camp Chase, near Columbus, Ohio, while enlisted personnel were sent either to Camp Butler, near Springfield, Illinois, or Camp Douglas in Chicago. The Texas prisoners had different opinions as to the treatment by their captors. Pvt. Franz Coller of the Sixth Infantry declared that the prisoners at Camp Butler "were treated very well." Ben Seaton of the Tenth Infantry later observed that the prisoners suffered because of the bitterly cold weather but "wer [sic] treated tolerable well[;] about as well as we cold [sic] exspect [sic] prisners [sic] of war to be treated." Capt. Samuel T. Foster of the Twenty-fourth Texas Cavalry admitted that "we get plenty to eat," but lamented that "we are treated just like so many beasts." W. W. Heartsill, confined to Camp Butler, complained that more than 200 men died in camp due to disease, poor medical care, and extremes of weather. Lt. Flavius W. Perry of the Seventeenth Texas Cavalry reported that members of his regiment were treated very poorly and that he was robbed of everything but one suit of clothes. Perry suffered from typhoid fever in prison and died shortly after his release. Jim Turner, on the other hand, stated that he and other officers of the Sixth Texas Infantry confined at Camp Chase were treated well by the guards and were supplied with good food.[38]

In April 1863, an exchange was arranged for the Arkansas Post prisoners, and by the first of May most were back in the Confederacy. Many of the Texans eventually served in the Army of Tennessee under Braxton Bragg and later Joseph E. Johnston.[39]

Those Texans still in Arkansas saw no other heavy fighting in the winter months of 1863. Bad weather and supply problems prevented any major operations in the area. Also, the Union army was shifting attention to the Mississippi River in a major effort to capture the Confederate stronghold at Vicksburg. Porter's Union gunboats and McClernand's army, which sustained over 1,000 casualties at Arkansas Post, were withdrawn to the mouth of the Arkansas River. Both would play signficant roles in U. S. Grant's Vicksburg campaign.[40]

Soon after the fall of Arkansas Post, the Confederates in the Trans Mississippi received new leadership. Edmund Kirby Smith, who had been successful as an army commander in East Tennessee, was appointed commander of the department, replacing the inept Theophilus Holmes. Smith set about immediately to take pressure off of Arkansas and Louisiana and to clear the Mississippi Valley of Union troops. In March he authorized a major cavalry raid from northern Arkansas into Missouri. More than 5,000 troopers, including a Texas cavalry brigade commanded by Methodist minister George W. Carter, took part in the raid led by Brig. Gen. John S. Marmaduke, a native of Missouri and recent graduate of West Point. Marmaduke's raid accomplished little. After riding a hundred miles through heavy rain, the Confederates were defeated by Federal troops at Cape Giradeau and forced to retreat back to Arkansas.[41]

Little additional fighting took place on the Arkansas–Missouri front in the spring of 1863. The division of Texas infantry formerly commanded by Henry McCulloch and now commanded by Maj. Gen. John G. Walker, a Missourian who had distinguished himself with Lee's army in Virginia and Maryland in 1862, was sent from

*John G. Walker — Missourian who commanded the largest all-Texas
division in the war, "Walker's Greyhounds."*
        — Lawrence T. Jones III Collection

Arkansas to Louisiana to assist Richard Taylor in his efforts to take
pressure off of Vicksburg and Port Hudson, another Confederate
post on the Mississippi River. Walker's troops, soon to be known as
"Walker's Greyhounds" because of their extensive and rapid
marches, consisted of three brigades of Texans commanded by Col.
Overton Young, a Brazoria planter, Col. Horace Randal, one of the
first Texas graduates from West Point, and Brig. Gen. Henry Mc-
Culloch, formerly the division commander. A battery of light artillery was attached to each brigade. The division, the largest all-Texas
unit (with the exception of Walker) in the war, numbered among its
members a former governor of the state, Col. Edward Clark of the
Fourteenth Texas Infantry, and two future governors, Col. O. M.
Roberts of the Eleventh Texas Infantry and Col. Richard B. Hubbard of the Twenty-second Texas Infantry. Col. William B. Ochiltree, prominent East Texas lawyer and judge, commanded the Eighteenth Texas Infantry in Young's Brigade. Lt. Col. George W.

Jones, later to be the leader of the Texas Greenback Party and a member of the United States Congress, was second in command of the Seventeenth Texas Infantry in McCulloch's Brigade.[42]

The Twelfth Texas Cavalry under Col. William H. Parsons, the Nineteenth Texas Cavalry under Lt. Col. Benjamin Watson, and a section of Joseph Pratt's artillery under Lt. Isaac A. Clare were ordered to join Walker's Division in the movement to Louisiana. Upon arriving in Louisiana, the Texans were joined by a Louisiana cavalry regiment and artillery batteries from Louisiana and Mississippi. Temporarily, all were under Parsons' command.[43]

In late May and early June of 1863, the Texans under the command of General Walker attacked various Federal units in Louisiana in an effort to impede Grant's movement around Vicksburg. In an assault on Milliken's Bend on the Mississippi west bank, Henry McCulloch's Brigade stormed a strong point held by an Iowa regiment and a small brigade of African-American troops. In a bayonet charge, the Texans, who outnumbered the defenders, drove the enemy back in hand-to-hand fighting. McCulloch's men gave no quarter to the former slaves, killing many wounded and defenseless blacks before being forced back by fire from Union gunboats. Three weeks later a number of blacks were killed by members of Parsons' Brigade in a raid along the Mississippi. Neither of these affairs succeeded in breaking the Union sieges of Vicksburg and Port Hudson, but they did illustrate the strong feelings many Texas troops had about the use of black troops. The conduct of the soldiers also raised a storm of protest in the North.[44]

During the late spring and summer of 1863, nearly 3,000 additional troops were sent from Texas to Louisiana in the effort to save Vicksburg and Port Hudson. These included three cavalry regiments commanded by Col. James P. Major and the three cavalry regiments of the old Sibley Brigade. Richard Taylor, commanding Confederate forces in Louisiana, hoped to use the Texans in a campaign along Bayou Teche and Bayou Lafourche to take pressure away from Port Hudson, then being attacked by Federals commanded by Nathaniel P. Banks. Unfortunately for the Confederates, superior Union strength in battles fought at Bisland and Irish Bend along the Teche prevented Taylor from achieving his objective. In the course of the fighting in the bayou country, Taylor removed General Sibley from command of his brigade on charges of incompetence and placed Texan Tom Green, promoted to brigadier general, in command. Although Green and Major won victories over Federal troops at Brashear City, and Bayou Boeuf in May and June, they were unable to relieve Port Hudson. In early July 1863, both Port Hudson and Vicksburg fell to the enemy.[45]

Texans played a part in the gallant but unsuccessful Confederate efforts to prevent Grant from taking Vicksburg. John W. Whitfield's brigade of Texas cavalry, consisting of the Third, Sixth, Ninth, and Twenty-seventh Texas regiments, saw extensive service in northern Mississippi in the winter and spring of 1862–63 in an attempt to impede Grant's move toward Vicksburg. The Texas brigade, which had served under Sterling Price and Earl Van Dorn in the battles at Iuka and Corinth the previous autumn, was one of three that took part in the highly successful raid on Grant's supply base at Holly Springs in December 1862. The brigade continued to serve with Van Dorn in cavalry raids into southern Tennessee in early 1863. After Van Dorn's death in May 1863, the brigade was part of the cavalry corps commanded by Tennessean Brig. Gen. William H. "Red" Jackson assigned by Gen. Joe Johnston to harass Grant in his siege operations at Vicksburg.[46]

Two Texas units, the Second Infantry regiment and Waul's Legion, were part of the 30,000 Confederate troops under siege at Vicksburg. The Second Infantry, originally commanded by Col. John C. Moore, had participated earlier in the battles of Shiloh and Corinth. In the fighting at Corinth, Col. William P. Rogers, who had assumed command of the regiment when Moore was promoted to brigadier general, was killed while leading an attack on a Union battery. After his death the distinguished physician-statesman Ashbel Smith was selected to command the regiment.[47] In the Vicksburg campaign the Second Texas continued to be a part of Moore's Brigade consisting of Alabama and Mississippi regiments in addition to the Second Texas. Occupying a position in the center of the Confederate line in front of Vicksburg, the regiment helped beat off five Union assaults against the Vicksburg defenses on May 19 and May 22.[48]

In the fighting on May 22, Waul's Texas Legion, consisting of two infantry battalions and small detachments of cavalry and artillery commanded by former Confederate congressman and planter Thomas N. Waul, distinguished itself in recapturing a redoubt taken in the initial Union assault. Of their action, their brigade com-

Thomas N. Waul — Wealthy plantation owner from Washington County who served in Confederate Provisional Congress. Formed Waul's Legion that fought in Vicksburg campaign.

— Archives Division, Texas State Library

mander Stephen D. Lee wrote "a more daring feat has not been performed during the war, and too much praise cannot be awarded to everyone engaged in it." Lee praised Colonel Waul "for his dashing gallantry and coolness" which "inspired every one around him with confidence . . ."[49]

After the failed assaults on May 19 and 22, Grant settled down to a six-week siege of Vicksburg. During this period constant artillery bombardment, sickness, hunger, and exposure took its toll among the Confederate defenders. Colonel Waul reported 245 casualties in his legion during the assault and siege. Ashbel Smith listed eighty-nine casualties from among the 468 men in the Second Texas during this period. Joseph E. Johnston, who had been appointed overall commander of the Mississippi–Tennessee Department, attempted to raise sufficient forces in central Mississippi to break the siege but was unsuccessful. On July 4, 1863, Lt. Gen. John C. Pem-

Texas Monument at Vicksburg.
— Forest View Historical Services

berton, commanding the Vicksburg defenders, surrendered to
Grant. The 30,000 Confederate soldiers, including the Second Texas
and Waul's Texas Legion, were paroled pending prisoner of war exchange.[50]

Port Hudson, slightly over 100 miles downriver from Vicksburg, surrendered to Union forces five days later. Several hundred
Texans, including the First Texas Battalion of Sharpshooters assigned to Samuel Maxey's brigade and the Seventh Texas Infantry
regiment of John Gregg's brigade, had been part of the Port Hudson
garrison during March and April but were ordered to Vicksburg in
early May. Due to the presence of Grant's army in western Mississippi, they had been unable to reach Vicksburg and joined Whitfield's Texas cavalry brigade with Joe Johnston in central Mississippi. After the fall of Vicksburg and the subsequent evacuation of

Jackson, Mississippi, they joined other Texans in Braxton Bragg's army in Tennessee.[51]

Even before the fall of Vicksburg and Port Hudson, Union efforts to expand control in northwestern Arkansas and northeastern Indian Territory resumed. In June Federal troops commanded by Maj. Gen. James Blunt pushed southward into Indian Territory, driving back Texas cavalry and Indian regiments commanded by Brig. Gen. Douglas Cooper. On July 17 Blunt's troops attacked Cooper's supply depot south of the Arkansas River near Honey Springs on Elk Creek. In the ensuing battle, the largest single engagement of the war in Indian Territory, Blunt's army, consisting of Union Indians, Kansas black troops, and Colorado infantry, launched a frontal assault on the Confederate lines. For nearly two hours the Texans and Confederate Indians held their ground, but a morning rainstorm dampened much of the low quality gunpowder with which the Confederates were equipped. This, plus superior Union artillery, enabled the Federals to break the center of the Southern line held by the Twenty-ninth Texas Cavalry and drive the Confederates from the field. The Confederates retreated southward across the Canadian River, leaving the northern half of Indian Territory in Union hands.[52]

In late summer Blunt resumed the offense, pushing Confederates under Cooper and Brig. Gen. William Steele farther southward into Choctaw country. Blunt then turned into Arkansas and on September 1 captured Fort Smith. Another Federal army commanded by Maj. Gen. Frederick Steele (Frederick Steele, a West Point classmate of William Steele) drove Confederate forces in eastern Arkansas back toward Little Rock. In the fighting to save the Arkansas capital, Carter's Texas cavalry brigade, temporarily commanded by Maj. Charles Morgan, and Joseph Pratt's Texas artillery battery served under Sterling Price, who directed the Confederate defense. In spite of all efforts, the Confederates were unable to hold the city. On September 10, Confederates evacuated Little Rock and withdrew to southwestern Arkansas.[53]

The war in the East was also going badly for the Confederates in the summer of 1863. In the same week the Vicksburg garrison surrendered to Grant, Lee's army met defeat at Gettysburg. The Texas Brigade, a part of Lee's army at Gettysburg, had done little fighting in the winter and spring of 1863. Now commanded by Washington County physician Jerome Bonaparte Robertson, who succeeded Hood when the latter was promoted to division commander after the battle of Sharpsburg, the Texas Brigade was in the center of the Confederate line at Fredericksburg in December 1862. Although heavy fighting took place on both sides of Hood's Division, the Texans and other soldiers in the division escaped major action in that battle. Then, after a winter of little activity other than snowball fights, Hood's Division, including the Texas Brigade, was detached to conduct foraging operations in the Suffolk region of Virginia. As a result the division did not participate in Lee's masterful triumph over Joe Hooker's army at Chancellorsville in May 1863.[54]

Hood's Division and the Texas Brigade rejoined Lee's army in time to participate in the invasion of Pennsylvania in June. The brigade crossed the Potomac River on June 26 and entered Chambersburg, Pennsylvania, on June 27. Lt. Col. Arthur Fremantle of the British Coldstream Guards was among those who watched the Texans as they entered Pennsylvania. They were "a queer lot to look at," he observed. He noted that the Texans carried less baggage than other military units and that many had discarded their shoes in the Pennsylvania mud. "All are ragged and dirty," he wrote, "but full of good humor and confidence in themselves and in their general, Hood."[55]

In the great battle that followed at Gettysburg in early July, the Texas Brigade was severely tested. As part of Longstreet's corps, Hood's Division led the assault against the Union left flank on the afternoon of June 2. In the attack along Plum Run the Texans encountered heavy enemy fire from Union batteries in the Devil's Den, a formation of rocks near a small mountain called Little Round Top. In the fighting General Hood was severely wounded by a shell fragment that shattered his left arm. Brigadier General Robertson and three of his four regimental commanders were wounded. Several other officers in the brigade were wounded, killed, or taken prisoner. Determined efforts by the Texas and Alabama regiments in the division failed to wrest control of Little Round Top from the enemy. The First Texas was able to drive Federal troops off an extension of Little Round Top known as Rocky Ridge, but was forced to break off fighting at dusk because of increasing Union strength on the left flank.[56]

Except for some skirmishing between the First Texas and Judson Kilpatrick's cavalry, the Texas Brigade did little fighting at Get-

Devil's Den and Little Round Top — Scene at Gettysburg where Hood's Texas Brigade fought to dislodge Union troops in bitter struggle on second day at Gettysburg.

— National Archives

Confederate dead, Gettysburg.

— National Archives

tysburg on July 3. Hood's troops were held in reserve as divisions commanded by George Pickett and James J. Pettigrew attacked the center of the Union line on Cemetery Ridge. Their failure to take the Ridge ended the battle of Gettysburg at great cost of lives. On July 4 the two armies watched one another like great wounded giants, neither attacking the other. That evening Lee began his withdrawal southward. Never again would he lead his army across the Potomac.[57]

Hood's Division moved back to Culpepper, Virginia, where it remained for several weeks. In August the division was ordered to the Rappahannock River near Fredericksburg, where most of the men expected to remain during the autumn and winter. In early September, however, the division was moved to Richmond, where it and other divisions in Longstreet's corps boarded trains for the longest Confederate troop movement of the war. Braxton Bragg's Army of Tennessee had been forced out of Chattanooga into the northwestern corner of Georgia. The Confederate War Department had decided to reinforce Bragg's army for a surprise attack against William Rosecrans' Union army along Chickamauga Creek south of Chattanooga.

Hood, his shattered left arm still in a sling from the fighting at Gettysburg, rejoined his division on the eve of the battle of Chickamauga on September 18. For the first time in the war, Hood and the Texas Brigade would be fighting alongside fellow Texans already with Bragg's army. Matthew D. Ector's brigade, which included the Ninth Texas Infantry and the dismounted cavalry of the Tenth, Fourteenth, and Thirty-second Texas regiments as well as North Carolina, Alabama and Mississippi units, had been with Bragg for nearly a year. The brigade commander, Matthew D. Ector, was like Nathan Bedford Forrest, a man who had risen from the ranks. A successful Rusk County lawyer and state legislator before the war, Ector enlisted in Hogg's Brigade as a private when the war began. His rise was rapid; by the autumn of 1862 he was a brigadier general. In the battle of Murfreesboro, or Stone's River, Ector's Brigade occupied the center of Bragg's army when it attacked the Union right flank on December 31, 1862. The Ninth Texas Infantry, a northeast Texas regiment commanded by Col. William H. Young, distinguished itself in heavy fighting that afternoon as a part of Cheatham's Division. The Eighth Texas Cavalry (Terry's Texas Rangers) was also in Bragg's army at Murfreesboro and along with the

Eleventh Texas Cavalry was part of John A. Wharton's cavalry division. The Seventh Texas Infantry, which had served at Fort Donelson and Port Hudson, was now part of Gregg's Brigade that joined Bragg's army in late summer of 1863. Another brigade, commanded by Alabama Brig. Gen. James Deshler, consisted of consolidated Texas and Arkansas cavalry regiments made up of Confederates captured at Arkansas Post. Capt. James P. Douglas' well-traveled artillery battery which had fought at Pea Ridge, Corinth, and Murfreesboro, was the only Texas artillery unit in Bragg's army. In all, nearly 4,000 Texans were in his army as Bragg prepared to attack the Federal forces. This constituted the largest number of Texans to participate in a Civil War battle east of the Mississippi River. The Texans would play a major part in the battle along Chickamauga Creek.[58]

There was some skirmishing on September 18, but the main fighting in the battle of Chickamauga took place on September 19 and 20. Bragg hoped to roll back the Union left flank in his assault on the nineteenth, but a delay by Leonidas Polk, commanding the Confederate right wing, gave Rosecrans time to reinforce that sector and prevent a breakthrough. Heavy fighting raged throughout the afternoon of the nineteenth, with both Confederates and Federals sustaining heavy casualties. Fighting continued the next day as each side looked for an opening. In the confusion of shifting troops, Rosecrans left a gap in his line on the right. Hood, leading his own and other divisions of Longstreet's corps, charged through the opening. Only the gallant efforts of Maj. Gen. George Thomas halted the Confederate advance in late afternoon and prevented a total Union collapse. Rosecrans and the Union army fell back toward Chattanooga. Longstreet and other Confederate commanders wanted to attack Chattanooga the following day, but Bragg determined to lay siege to the city.[59]

The Confederates had won a great victory, but the price was high. In the two-day battle the Confederates lost 18,000–20,000 men, approximately 30 percent of their army.[60] Robertson's Texas Brigade once again suffered among the highest casualties, 570 men killed, wounded, or missing, or almost 44 percent of its total strength. Ector's Brigade, which served in Polk's right wing, sustained almost as many casualties, 536. Texan John Gregg's brigade, which included the Seventh Texas Infantry, had 577 casualties including General Gregg, who was wounded in the neck and lay un-

John Gregg — One of the last commanders of Hood's Texas Brigade.
At the time of his death Gregg was considered by Robert E. Lee
as the best brigadier general in his army.
— Lawrence T. Jones III Collection

conscious on the battlefield until rescued by troops from Hood's Brigade. Three Texas regimental commanders were wounded and Alabamian James Deshler, commanding a brigade of Texas and Arkansas troops, was killed. General Hood, still suffering from the wound at Gettysburg, was hit in the right leg and the leg had to be amputated at the thigh.[61]

Following the battle of Chickamauga, the Army of Tennessee was reorganized and Texans in Bragg's army went in various directions. Ector's Brigade accompanied Leonidas Polk, when Polk was assigned to duty in Mississippi after quarreling with Bragg. Longstreet's corps, which included the Texas Brigade, moved to the Knoxville region and took part in unsuccessful operations there before going into winter quarters at Morristown in the Holston River valley. The Seventh Texas Infantry, commanded by Waco lawyer Col. Hiram Granbury, was transferred from Gregg's Brigade to the

Hiram Granbury — Waco lawyer who commanded the Texas Infantry Brigade in the Atlanta and Tennessee campaigns. One of six Confederate generals killed or mortally wounded at Franklin.
— Lawrence T. Jones III Collection

brigade formerly commanded by James Deshler and now led by Brig. Gen. James A. Smith. Smith's Brigade remained with Bragg's army, laying siege to Chattanooga, as did Douglas' Texas artillery battery and the Eighth and Eleventh Texas cavalry regiments.[62]

In late November 1863, the Union forces in Chattanooga, strengthened by the arrival of Grant's Vicksburg army, launched a major assault on Bragg's troops occupying Lookout Mountain and Missionary Ridge. Smith's Texas–Arkansas brigade, supported by Douglas' artillery battery, was posted near Tunnel Hill on the Confederate right flank as part of Patrick Cleburne's Division. In the heavy fighting that took place, both Brigadier General Smith and Col. Roger Q. Mills of the Tenth Texas Infantry were wounded. Temporary command of the brigade passed to Colonel Granbury. Although Cleburne's Division held its ground, Union troops broke through the center of the Confederate line on Missionary Ridge, necessitating a general withdrawal back into Georgia. The brigade commanded by Granbury played a major role in preventing the capture of Confederate wagons and artillery at Ringgold, Georgia, as Bragg's army retreated. For his gallantry Granbury was promoted to brigadier general and given permanent command of the brigade.[63]

While Texans under Ector, Granbury, Robertson, and Wharton

were fighting for control of Chattanooga and eastern Tennessee in the autumn of 1863, the struggle to prevent Union military occupation of the Texas coast was continuing. Texans were successful in beating off a Union attempt to occupy the upper coast at Sabine Pass in September, but were unable to prevent Federal troops from capturing Brownsville on the lower coast in November.

General Magruder had expected the Union attack upon the upper Texas coast for some time. In the spring of 1863 military engineer Maj. Julius Kellersberg had been dispatched to Sabine Pass with orders to construct a new fort to replace Fort Sabine, which had been destroyed the previous year. Kellersberg selected a point near the head of the channel several hundred yards above the original fort. The earthen and log fort built with slave labor was still not completely finished when the Federals attacked in September. The fortification, known locally as Fort Griffin for Col. W. H. Griffin, who commanded the post of Sabine Pass in the summer of 1863, was triangular in shape and about 100 feet long on each side. The fort had a sawtooth front where cannon were mounted, sloping walls ten feet high, and a parapet twenty feet wide. Underground arsenals and bombproofs were beneath the parapet. Six cannon were eventually in place: two thirty-pounder smoothbores dug up at old Fort Sabine and repaired at a Galveston foundry, two twenty-four-pounder smoothbores, and two thirty-two-pounder howitzers removed from forts on the Sabine and Neches rivers. Company F of Cook's Heavy Artillery, known as the Davis Guards, a company of Irishmen from Houston, garrisoned the fort. The Guards, commanded by Capt. Frederick Odlum, had participated in the successful capture of the Union vessels *Morning Light* and *Velocity* earlier in the year. Daily practice in sighting their guns on stakes driven into the Louisiana and Texas channels of the pass prepared the Guards for the coming battle.[64]

The Union attack on Sabine Pass came in early September. President Lincoln was anxious to create a counterweight to the presence of Maximilian and the French army in Mexico. In August the Federal War Department ordered Gen. Nathaniel P. Banks, commanding general of the Department of the Gulf with headquarters in New Orleans, to establish Union control at some point in Texas. Banks selected Sabine Pass as the place for the initial Union landing — in part because of its proximity to New Orleans, from where the expedition would originate, and in part because of the supposed weak defenses of Sabine Pass. Once Sabine Pass was in Federal hands the Union army could move against Beaumont and from there move along the railroad to capture Houston.[65]

Banks appointed the veteran general William B. Franklin as overall commander of the Sabine Pass expedition. Franklin, whose earlier encounter with Hood's Brigade at Eltham's Landing on the York Peninsula had been unsuccessful, was an experienced officer. He had commanded a corps in the Army of the Potomac in the 1862 campaigns, but a disagreement with Ambrose Burnside after the battle of Fredericksburg led to his transfer to the Department of the Gulf. Brig. Gen. Godfrey Weitzel was appointed to command the 5,000 troops of the Nineteenth Army Corps assigned to the Texas operation.[66] Navy Lt. Frederick Crocker, a veteran New Bedford

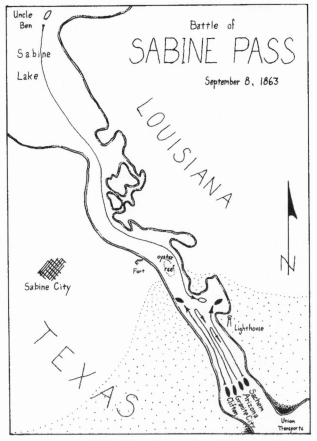

Sabine Pass, September 1863.

whaling captain, was appointed commander of the light draft gunboat flotilla (*Clifton, Sachem, Arizona*, and *Granite City*) that would accompany the twenty-two transport vessels carrying the Union troops to Texas. The expedition left New Orleans on September 4, but due to confusion and fear that the C.S.S. *Alabama* was in the area, the Federal fleet did not reach Sabine Pass until midnight on September 6. [67]

In the predawn hours of September 7 sentries at Fort Griffin reported seeing signal lights of the Union fleet. Lt. Richard W. Dowling, a Houston tavern owner who was in immediate command of Fort Griffin, notified Captain Odlum, who was in charge of headquarters at Sabine City in the absence of Colonel Griffin, of the enemy presence. Throughout the day couriers notified both Beaumont and Houston of the impending attack. [68]

The original Union plan called for landing troops on the sandy beaches west of Sabine Pass and then storming Fort Griffin by an artillery-supported infantry attack. Franklin decided, however, to have the gunboats shell the fort into submission before the infantry landed. On the early morning of September 8, Crocker's flagship, *Clifton*, a 210-foot, sidewheel steamer with eight guns, crossed the bar at Sabine Pass. When within 1,500 yards of the fort, she opened fire. Twenty-six shells were fired, most of which were misses. Two direct hits threw up mud and debris. Dowling kept his men under cover, waiting until the gunboat was within accurate range. [69]

The initial firing ceased at about 7:00 A.M. Using his spyglass, Crocker was impressed with the apparent strength of the fort. He steamed back to the mouth of the pass, where he convinced Franklin to change the plan again so that Union assault troops would storm ashore while the gunboat flotilla shelled the fort. With this agreed upon, the other Union gunboats and seven transports carrying 1,200 assault troops began crossing the bar. At 11:00 A.M. the *Uncle Ben*, a small Confederate gunboat, steamed down Sabine Lake to the upper end of the pass to observe the happenings. The more powerful Union gunboat *Sachem*, which had moved ahead of other Federal warships, lobbed several shells at the *Uncle Ben*, forcing her to pull back into the lake out of range of the heavier armed Federal ships. [70]

The main Union attack began at 3:30 in the afternoon. *Sachem* and *Arizona* steamed up the Louisiana channel of the pass, while the *Clifton* moved up the Texas channel nearest to the fort. [71] The *Granite City* came up the Texas channel behind *Clifton* and was to cover

Monument of Dick Dowling, Sabine Pass.
— Forest View Historical Services

the landing of Federal troops half a mile below the fort on the Texas side. *Sachem* and *Clifton* opened fire first, causing some damage but no injuries to the Confederate defenders. When the Union vessels reached the target stakes about 1,200 yards from the fort, the Confederate guns opened fire. The Davis Guards concentrated their fire first upon *Sachem*, which steamed ahead of the other Union gunboats. A Confederate shell tore through the steam drum of the *Sachem*, throwing scalding steam and water on the crew. Several additional rounds from the Confederate guns left *Sachem* in a helpless condition as she ran aground in the mud. Her captain requested aid from the *Arizona*, but the heavier and slower *Arizona* began backing down the channel. To avoid further casualties, the captain of the *Sachem* hoisted the white flag of surrender.

Confederate artillery now turned on the *Clifton* as she headed toward Fort Griffin with guns blazing. As the *Clifton* drew within 500 yards, a Confederate round destroyed her tiller ropes, throwing her out of control into the mud. Lieutenant Crocker continued to fight until most of his guns were disabled and the ship's boiler exploded from a direct hit. The *Granite City* joined the *Arizona* and the transport vessels in withdrawing from the pass, leaving *Sachem* and *Clifton* in Confederate hands. General Franklin, convinced that Confederate defenses were much stronger than they actually were, ordered withdrawal of his task force to New Orleans. Several hundred horses and mules, wagons, artillery, ammunition, and 200,000 rations were thrown overboard to lighten the vessels as they fled from the scene.[72]

The battle of Sabine Pass lasted less than an hour. In that time Dick Dowling and the forty-two men under his command damaged and captured two Union gunboats, killed or wounded nearly 100, captured 300 of the enemy including the gallant Lieutenant Crocker, and turned back an expedition of 5,000 troops. Amazingly, none of Dowling's men were wounded by enemy fire. Several had their hands or fingers burned from handling the hot guns, and others, including Dowling, had powder burns. One of the fort's six cannon

Dick Dowling — Irish-born saloonkeeper who commanded Davis Guards in the Battle of Sabine Pass.
— Lawrence T. Jones III Collection

had backed off its platform as the firing started, and two others were grazed by Federal shells. The five guns that Dowling had in action fired 107 times in thirty-five minutes, which was, according to historian Alwyn Barr, "an almost unheard of speed for heavy artillery."[73]

The defenders of Fort Griffin were highly praised for their victory. Two days after the battle General Magruder commended the Davis Guards in a special order and proclamation. On September 12 he made a visit to Fort Griffin, where he lauded the artillerymen as "the greatest heroes that history recorded." In a special order issued the following day, Magruder listed each of the Guards by name and conferred upon them the privilege of wearing the word "Sabine" embroidered in a wreath design on their hats. The Confederate Congress passed a congratulatory resolution and President Davis described the defense of Sabine Pass as "one of the most brilliant and heroic achievements in the history of the war." A special medal, attached to a green ribbon, was struck for each member of the garrison.[74]

General Magruder believed the enemy intended to return to southeast Texas. Accordingly, he ordered the improvement of fortifications in the area. A new fort, named Manhasset for a Union schooner that had beached nearby in a storm, was constructed at the mouth of Taylor's Bayou to guard the western land approaches to Sabine Pass. Several infantry regiments and artillery batteries were moved to the area from other parts of Texas. By the end of September more than 3,000 troops were in Jefferson County.[75]

General Banks, meanwhile, was considering ways to recover from the embarrassment at Sabine Pass and to satisfy President Lincoln's desire to see Federal control established at some point in Texas. He considered the possibility of an overland march from Brashear City in southern Louisiana to Sabine Pass, a move feared by General Magruder, but apparently decided that an advance up the Bayou Teche toward Alexandria and the Red River was a more likely way of getting at Texas. In late September General Franklin, given a chance to redeem himself, was ordered to move up the Teche. The Nineteenth Army Corps and elements of the Thirteenth Army Corps, seasoned veterans of the Vicksburg campaign, were assigned to Franklin.[76]

Franklin's movement in late September and October was slow. On September 29 Texas troops under Tom Green and Louisiana troops under Alfred Mouton took 480 Union prisoners at Morgan's

Ferry on Bayou Fordoche. Green's Texas cavalry harassed the Union army as it cautiously moved to occupy Opelousas on October 21. Three days later an attack by regiments of Walker's infantry division, supported by Major's cavalry brigade and six artillery batteries, led Franklin to withdraw below Opelousas to reconsider his forward move. There he received a message from Union headquarters in New Orleans advising him that General Banks had taken a large force by water to invade Texas. Franklin was instructed to keep pressure on the enemy.[77]

While Franklin puzzled over what he should do now, Tom Green took the offensive. On November 3 his cavalry and three regiments of Walker's infantry, the Eleventh, Fifteenth, and Eighteenth Texas, led by Colonel Roberts, attacked the rear guard of Franklin's army several miles south of Opelousas on Bayou Bourbeau. The surprised Union troops, mainly midwesterners, fought tenaciously but were driven back a mile and half. Green's units sustained 180 casual-

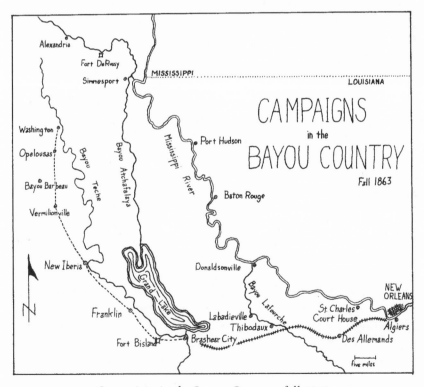

Campaigns in the Bayou Country, fall 1863.

ties, mainly in the infantry regiments, but captured over 500 enemy soldiers and killed or wounded 154 others. The Federals retreated back to New Iberia for the winter.[78]

The day before the battle of Bayou Bourbeau the first of Banks' 7,000 troops under the command of Maj. Gen. Napoleon Jackson Tecumseh Dana came ashore at Brazos Santiago, off the mouth of the Rio Grande. Three days later, on November 6, Brownsville, thirty miles inland, was occupied with no resistance. Confederate Brig. Gen. Hamilton P. Bee, former state legislator and Laredo merchant who succeeded John S. Ford as commander of the Rio Grande sub-district in 1862, ordered the evacuation of the city when it became apparent that with the few men available to him resistance would be futile. Under Bee's direction forty-five wagons of valuable supplies were taken into the interior. Cotton and other stores that could not be evacuated were set afire.[79]

Once Brownsville was secure, Federal troops moved against other points along the southern coast of Texas. Mustang, St. Joseph, and Matagorda islands were occupied in the last two weeks of November. On Christmas Day, a Union scouting party entered Corpus Christi. During the next several weeks, Federal troops visited the city several times. Confederate Fort Esperanza, near Saluria, on the northeastern tip of Matagorda Island, put up a token resistance but was abandoned by the Confederates on November 29 after the fort and magazines were set on fire. In December the Federals on Matagorda Island crossed over to Indianola, which they occupied during the winter months of 1863–64.[80]

Meanwhile, Col. Edmund J. Davis, commanding a brigade of Texas Union cavalry, moved up the Rio Grande to capture Ringgold Barracks, which had been held by a small Confederate force. From Ringgold Barracks Union troops under Col. John L. Haynes, another Texas Unionist, pushed upriver to the town of Roma. The interior of South Texas appeared open to military occupation. General Magruder was convinced that there was little he could do given the manpower available to him. He believed that the best he could do was to defend the area between the Sabine and Brazos rivers. He was particularly concerned about the mouth of the Brazos River. Accordingly, he concentrated his available forces in this region in anticipation of a major Federal invasion in early 1864.[81]

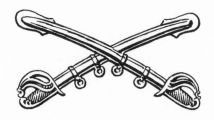

CHAPTER FOUR

Life on the Home Front

By the end of 1863 most Texas families had been touched by the war. Nearly all adult white males, 90,000 according to Governor Lubbock, were serving in the military, some far from Texas. Thousands of Texans had been killed or wounded in the bloody battles at Shiloh, Sharpsburg, Gettysburg, and Chickamauga. Some Texans, especially those who defended Fort Donelson and Arkansas Post, spent time in Federal prison camps. Residents of Galveston, Indianola, and Brownsville experienced military occupation by the enemy, while residents of Sabine Pass, Port Lavaca, and Corpus Christi had seen or heard the fighting. Trade and commerce had been disrupted by the Union naval blockade, and shortages of various commodities were becoming commonplace.

Francis Lubbock, who took office as governor in late 1861, coped with a multitude of problems that confronted the state as a result of the war. Like his predecessor, Edward Clark, and his successor, Pendleton Murrah, Lubbock expanded the powers of his office to deal with the requirements of the war. In addition to the usual concerns of public finance, transportation, education, and frontier defense, Lubbock and other war governors raised and equipped troops, purchased and sold raw materials, established factories, and dealt directly with Confederate military commanders in

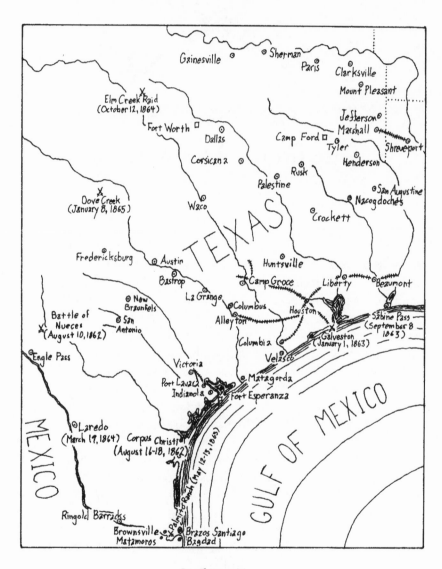

Civil War Texas

areas of conscription, impressment, martial law, and defense of the state against enemy invasion.[1]

In his inaugural message Lubbock praised the efforts that Texans had made in the first months of the war, but called for even greater sacrifices. The war, he declared, was for liberty, not slavery. He lauded the Confederate government for its ability, integrity, and patriotism, but called upon Texans to defend themselves against the "polluted tread of abolition hordes." He pointed to the need for frontier protection against hostile Indians and urged fellow Texans to pay both Confederate and state taxes so that government could operate efficiently.[2]

Francis R. Lubbock — Outstanding governor of Texas (1861–63) who worked closely with Davis administration in providing troops and supplies. Later became military aide to President Davis.
— Archives Division, Texas State Library

Lubbock considered finance the most serious problem facing the state. Although Governor Clark had recommended an increase in the ad valorem tax rate in order to bring in needed additional revenue, the legislature had failed to act. The state debt was nearly

$1 million when Lubbock took office. At his urging, the legislature in early January 1862 took steps to meet the growing revenue demands of the state. The ad valorem rate on general property was raised from sixteen and a half cents to twenty-five cents, the poll tax on adult males was increased from fifty cents to one dollar, and a license fee upon doctors, dentists, and lawyers was imposed. Under powers granted by the amended Constitution of 1861, the legislature also levied an income tax on those with a fixed annual salary at the rate of 25 cents on each $100 of salary above $500 annually.[3]

The January 1862 tax law brought in additional revenue but not enough to meet the needs placed upon the state by the war. In March 1863, the ad valorem tax rate was increased to fifty cents. In addition, a tax of $1,000 was placed upon distilleries, as much to discourage conversion of needed corn to liquor as to increase revenue. Later that year, the unpopular income tax on salaries was replaced by a tax of fifty cents per $100 of sales upon those selling alcoholic beverages.[4]

The 1863 legislation did not raise as much revenue as required by the mounting expenditures to support the war effort, so in November 1864 a tax of $300 and one percent of gross receipts was levied on wholesale merchants, and a tax of $100 and one percent of gross receipts was placed on retail merchants. The same measure levied a tax of $100 and two percent of gross sales upon billiard halls, nine and ten pin alleys, storage businesses, cotton compresses, and insurance companies. A two percent tax on gross receipts was placed on dentists and lawyers and a one percent tax on doctors. Railway officers and employees were singled out for taxation in the November 1864 legislation. Presidents, directors, engineers, conductors, secretaries, and clerks of railroad companies were required to pay a one percent tax. The 1864 tax was most productive, yielding over $300,000 in the first few months of 1865. Even so, expenses continued to outrun income. At the close of the war the state debt was $8 million.[5]

One of the most controversial steps taken by the Lubbock administration was the creation of the Texas State Military Board. Creation of the board was the result of a proposal from Confederate Acting Secretary of War Judah P. Benjamin to Governor Lubbock that Texas use United States five percent indemnity bonds held by the state to purchase arms and munitions for the army. The arms would then be sold to the Richmond government for eight percent

Confederate bonds. Governor Lubbock laid the issue before the legislature which, on January 11, 1862, passed two measures, one creating the Texas State Military Board with powers to purchase necessary war materials and the other authorizing the board to replace bonds held by the state with Confederate bonds. The board was instructed to use $500,000 of state bonds authorized in April 1861 for the purchase of military supplies and empowered to build an arms factory and munitions factories.[6]

The State Military Board, consisting of the governor, state comptroller, and state treasurer, went to work immediately. Efforts to exchange the United States indemnity bonds for war materials were largely unsuccessful, in part because of ineptness by agents employed by the board and in part because foreign investors feared that the United States government might not honor the bonds. The board was only slightly more successful in exchanging Texas cotton, which it purchased from citizens with state bonds, for war materials. Transportation problems, high prices, unrest along the Mexican border where the exchanges took place, and unreliable agents limited the success of the board in the cotton trade. By 1864, when reorganization occurred, the board had purchased 5,736 bales of cotton for $544,438 and sold 5,551 bales for $434,454. Historian Charles W. Ramsdell, who studied the work of the board, noted that because of the fluctuation of depreciated money and bonds it is impossible to know if the board made a profit or not. He also observed that this represented only about one-tenth of the Texas cotton produced in the early war years.[7]

The State Military Board carried on other activities. A cannon foundry was built in Austin, but only a few brass cannons were produced. A percussion cap factory was also established in Austin, and contracts were given several firms for the manufacture of rifles and pistols. The board was reorganized when Lubbock left office and continued to function under Governor Pendleton Murrah, but with even less success.[8]

Governor Lubbock was a firm supporter of the Davis administration and its efforts to carry the war to a successful conclusion. Like other governors of the states west of the Mississippi, however, Lubbock was concerned that the Richmond government might neglect the region. The loss of New Orleans and Memphis in early 1862 caused fear that the Trans Mississippi states might be abandoned, leading Governor Henry M. Rector of Arkansas to issue a statement that his state and Missouri might withdraw from the Confederacy and form their own government. Lubbock wrote to President Davis immediately, assuring him that Texas was loyal to the Confederacy and had no desire to take part in a separatist movement. Davis responded by sending Maj. Guy M. Bryan, a well-known Texan serving on Davis' staff, to confer with Lubbock. At Bryan's suggestion, Lubbock issued an invitation to the governors of Arkansas, Louisiana, and Confederate Missouri to meet with him at Marshall to discuss defense of the Trans Mississippi states.[9]

Neither Arkansas Governor Rector nor Louisiana Governor Thomas O. Moore were able to attend the Marshall conference held in late July. Lubbock and Confederate Missouri Governor Claiborne Jackson prepared a letter to President Davis and a proclamation to the people which both the Arkansas and Louisiana governors endorsed. In the letter the four governors urged that a commanding general for the states west of the Mississippi be appointed, that a branch of the Confederate treasury be established in the region, and that 20,000–30,000 small arms be provided for equipping soldiers in the Trans Mississippi states. In their proclamation to the people the chief executives stated their continued support for the Richmond administration and called upon their people to make even greater sacrifices.[10]

Lubbock believed that the Marshall conference had been helpful in providing an opportunity for the western governors to present their views to the administration. When Guy Bryan returned to Richmond with the letter to Davis, he also carried a letter from Lubbock to the Texas congressional delegation. In this document Lubbock spoke even more bluntly about the needs of the Trans Mississippi states and requested the aid of the Texas congressmen.[11]

In his reply to the western governors President Davis offered reassurance that the Trans Mississippi was not forgotten. He pointed out that steps had already been taken to create a new Department of the Trans Mississippi and that efforts were being made to provide more money and supplies for the department.[12]

The feeling of isolation on the part of the western governors was eased only slightly by Davis' reply. The occupation of Galveston in the autumn of 1862, the loss of Arkansas Post in early 1863, and the surrender of Vicksburg and Port Hudson in the summer of 1863 caused grave concern in Texas and the Southwest. The Mississippi River was now totally under Union control, and the Trans Mississippi was cut off from the rest of the Confederacy. The situation was so serious that Edmund Kirby Smith, who now commanded the Trans Mississippi Department, called a meeting of governmental leaders at Marshall in early August 1863.[13]

The second Marshall conference was better attended than the first. The Texas delegation included Governor Lubbock, Marshall attorney Pendleton Murrah, who had just been elected to succeed Lubbock, Maj. Guy M. Bryan, and Texas Confederate Senator Williamson Simpson Oldham. Governor Thomas O. Moore of Louisiana was accompanied by three representatives from his state. Arkansas was represented by Confederate Senator R. W. Johnson, serving as proxy for Governor Harris Flanagin, another senator, and a state judge. Thomas C. Reynolds, who had succeeded Claiborne Jackson as governor of Confederate Missouri when Jackson died in late 1862, was that state's sole representative at the meeting.[14]

The conference lasted several days. Kirby Smith presented a six-point agenda for consideration. These items were referred to committees appointed by Governor Lubbock, who was chosen chairman of the conference. The conference approved committee resolutions recommending the appointment of an agent to deal with the French and Mexican authorities in Mexico, calling upon General Smith to assume greater powers relating to the defense of the department, and expressing confidence in Smith's handling of departmental affairs. The Texas delegation favored a plan to pay for impressed cotton in certificates redeemable in Confederate bonds, but this proposal was defeated. In closing, the governors issued a proclamation to the people expressing their determination to remain a part of the Confederacy.[15]

Governor Lubbock was pleased with the work of the second Marshall conference. He had always supported cooperation with Confederate officials, and the conference endorsed support for the Confederacy and its representative in the Trans Mississippi, Gen. Kirby Smith. Lubbock returned to Austin, where he spent the last two months of his administration responding to various requests for money, men, and supplies. In his farewell message to the legislature in early November, Lubbock reiterated his support for the Confederacy and called upon Texas lawmakers to punish deserters, control extortioners and speculators, force shirkers into military service, and eliminate military exemptions. That evening Lubbock appeared at Governor Murrah's inaugural ball in the uniform of a Confederate officer. In December he joined General Magruder's staff. He was later reassigned to General Wharton's staff in Louisiana, and in August 1864 became aide-de-camp to President Davis.[16]

Lubbock had announced in early spring that he would not be a candidate for reelection, thus affording potential candidates ample time to decide whether they wished to run. At first it appeared there would be a wild contest for the post as various individuals including Pendleton Murrah, Thomas Jefferson Chambers, M. M. Potter, William Pitt Ballinger, John M. Crockett, Guy M. Bryan, Fletcher Stockdale, and Henry McCulloch were considered as possible contenders. Even former governor Sam Houston, then living in retirement in Huntsville, was mentioned as a possibility. Eventually, however, only Murrah and Chambers were candidates in the election.[17]

Thomas Jefferson Chambers was the better known of the two candidates. A native of Virginia, Chambers had participated in the Texas Revolution, obtaining a commission as a major general to raise volunteers in the United States for the Texas army. One of the state's wealthiest individuals, Chambers had been active in political and economic affairs of the Republic and state. An ardent Democrat and secessionist, he had been a candidate for governor on three previous occasions. He had the reputation of being a political maverick and an outspoken critic of the Davis administration, charges he denied during the campaign.[18]

Pendleton Murrah was little known outside of the town of Marshall, where he had practiced law since his arrival from Alabama in 1850. He served a term in the legislature during the late 1850s and was chosen as a member of the Democratic state executive committee in 1858. He announced as a candidate for the Confederate Congress in 1861, but withdrew due to ill health. He served briefly as an officer in the Fourteenth Texas Infantry, but poor health forced him to resign his commission. His announcement for governor in 1863 attracted little attention, but as other potential candidates dropped out he gradually emerged as a conservative alternative to the volatile Chambers. Although Murrah said little about the Richmond government, he came to be regarded as the pro-Davis candidate in the campaign.[19]

In the August elections, Murrah, who received 17,511 votes, defeated Chambers, who polled 12,455 votes. Murrah carried the coastal, western, and northern wheat counties in his victory. Chambers' strength, as in the 1861 election, was in Central Texas and surprisingly in northeast Texas where Murrah lived. Neither Murrah nor Chambers carried their home counties, and both ran poorly in counties neighboring their county of residence.[20] Nancy Head Bowen, who studied Civil War politics in some detail, concluded that in electing Murrah "the majority of Texas voters demonstrated their preference for a relatively unknown politican they judged to support the Confederate authorities rather than a well-known three-time loser they believed to oppose Administration policies."[21]

At the same time Murrah was chosen governor, Texas voters elected three new members to the Confederate Congress. John R. Baylor, Indian fighter and former governor of Confederate Arizona, defeated incumbent Malcolm Graham in a close contest in the fifth congressional district. In the campaign, Baylor, a colorful and dynamic personality, urged full support for the war effort but was highly critical of the leadership of Jefferson Davis. Graham, a former Texas attorney general, normally supported the Davis administration but condemned the imposition of martial law by military authorities. Simpson H. Morgan, a Clarksville lawyer and businessman, defeated Paris attorney, incumbent William B. Wright in a contest based on personalities rather than issues as both men generally approved the policies of the Richmond government. More surprising than either the Baylor or Morgan victories was the election of Huntsville lawyer A. M. Branch over incumbent Peter W. Gray of Houston. Gray, an outspoken Southern nationalist and supporter of the Davis administration, was considered one of the more able members of the Confederate Congress. His defeat was primarily a result of his support for conscription and overseer exemption from military service.[22]

Three incumbents were reelected to the Confederate House in the 1863 elections. John A. Wilcox of San Antonio, one of Jefferson Davis' strongest friends in Congress, and Franklin B. Sexton of San Augustine, another pro-Davis congressman, were both reelected. Wilcox died before Congress assembled, however, and Stephen H. Darden, who had served in Hood's Texas Brigade, was chosen as his replacement in a special election. Unlike Wilcox, Darden was opposed to the growth of presidential power. His views were similar to those of Claiborne Caleb Herbert, wealthy planter from Colorado County, who was reelected in 1863. Herbert was an outspoken opponent of the Davis administration who was described as "the most radical states' righter of all western congressmen."[23]

The newly elected congressmen joined incumbents Sexton, Herbet, and Senators Louis Trezevant Wigfall and Williamson Simpson Oldham in the Second Regular Confederate Congress that convened in May 1864. Wigfall and Oldham were veterans of congressional service, having participated in both the Provisional and First Regular Congresses, two of only twenty-eight individuals who served in all three Confederate Congresses. Both were staunch secessionists and supporters of the Confederacy; however, they were opponents of the Davis administration. Wigfall, one of the Old South's antebellum fire-eaters, had briefly held a brigadier's commission in the Confederate army and had preceded John B. Hood as commander of the Texas Brigade, but resigned to accept a seat in Congress. In the early days of the war he supported President Davis, but disagreement over military strategy in 1862 led Wigfall to become one of Davis' most vocal and persistent critics. Oldham, while not quite as outspoken as Wigfall, was equally opposed to administration policy, more so on states' rights issues than due to personal or military differences. Unlike Wigfall, who voted for conscription as a necessary military measure, Oldham opposed conscription and various other administration policies as violations of the rights of sovereign states.[24]

Oldham chaired the Senate Post Office and Roads Committee, while Representative Franklin B. Sexton sat on a similar committee in the House. As members of these committees they had occasion to oversee the work of the most influential Texan in Richmond during the Civil War, Postmaster General John H. Reagan. Reagan, a former member of the United States Congress and the Confederate Provisional Congress, accepted the position of postmaster general in the spring of 1861. He worked diligently to cut expenses and raise revenue of the newly established postal service so that the office became self-sufficient as required by the Confederate Constitution. In doing so he negotiated hard bargains with Confederate railroads and required newspapers and other publications to bear a greater share of the cost of delivering mail. He gained praise for his efforts, although many Confederates, especially in frontier areas such as Texas, complained of poor service. Even though he frequently disagreed with President Davis in cabinet meetings, Reagan maintained the confidence and respect of the chief executive. Reagan and

Secretary of Navy Stephen Mallory of Florida were the only two members of the cabinet to head their departments throughout the war. Reagan remained one of the president's most loyal supporters and was with Davis when the Mississippian was captured at the end of the war.[25]

Governor Murrah meanwhile was becoming involved in controversy with Confederate military authorities. In December 1863, General Magruder issued an appeal to planters and farmers for use of their slaves in building military fortifications in Texas. In a lengthy letter to Magruder, Murrah indicated that, unlike Governor Lubbock, he did not intend to allow the military a free hand in the matter of impressment. He advised Magruder to limit the number of slaves impressed and suggested that the military contract for slave labor rather than impress it.[26]

Murrah also quarreled with the Confederate military over the issue of whether individuals enrolled in the state militia were subject to the Confederate draft. Since November 1862, the state had enrolled individuals subject to Confederate conscription in the state militia, largely for frontier defense. The Conscript Bureau of the Trans Mississippi Department headed by the fiery Texan Elkanah Greer, formerly commander of the Third Texas Cavalry, objected to the practice but General Magruder did not intervene because several thousand state troops were turned over to him temporarily to help defend the Texas coast in 1863.[27]

The passage of new militia acts by the Texas legislature in December 1863, and Governor Murrah's implementation in January 1864, brought the matter to a head. For some time Texans had been dissatisfied with the inadequacy of frontier protection. One new law created what came to be known as the Frontier Organization. Under this act all persons liable for military service who were residents of frontier counties were to be organized into companies for border defense. Another act, entitled "An Act for the Defense of the State," provided that able-bodied men living elsewhere in the state would be retained in the state militia.[28]

The new Texas laws caused considerable confusion. Some Texas soldiers who were residents of frontier counties thought the laws applied to them and left their units to return home. Others believed the laws meant that they could serve only in state units. For the next two months Magruder and Murrah bickered over the matter. Magruder, whose patience was exhausted, argued that Confederate laws had superiority over state legislation. Murrah, increasingly irritated by what he considered Magruder's haughty attitude, was determined to uphold state sovereignty. A meeting between Murrah, Magruder, and Kirby Smith in February 1864 in Houston produced a temporary truce when the departmental commander proposed a compromise whereby the state retained those militiamen already under arms but with the proviso that all or part of the militia might be subordinated to Confederate authority in an emergency. Both Magruder and Murrah accepted the proposal, but neither with enthusiasm.[29]

The controversy over conscription was reopened in March, when it became evident that additional troops were needed to block Union military advances in Louisiana and Arkansas. General Magruder, under orders from Kirby Smith to send available troops from Texas to Louisiana and Arkansas, called upon Governor Murrah to transfer control of state troops to the Confederacy. Murrah agreed to do so, provided the militia remain in Texas and be permitted to keep their state officers and organization. Magruder, who intended to use the state troops to replace Confederate troops sent to Louisiana and Arkansas, accepted Murrah's request that the militia stay within the state, but informed the governor that under Confederate law he could not enroll organized state units into Confederate service. Murrah at first did not yield, but a second letter from Magruder finally convinced him to cooperate.[30]

Murrah's concession did not totally end the controversy between state and Confederate officials. The governor and the legislature refused to concede their claim over conscripts who resided in the frontier counties. In the summer of 1864 the Confederate Conscript Bureau attempted to gain control of conscripts in these counties, but state authorities held their ground. Kirby Smith finally agreed to submit the issue to Richmond to settle, but the war ended before the question was resolved.[31]

While Magruder and Murrah were arguing over the question of conscription, Kirby Smith was involved in his own controversy with the Texas governor over the issue of cotton purchasing. In an effort to obtain money and supplies for the department, Smith established a Cotton Bureau for the purpose of buying and selling cotton. Headquarters for the bureau was in Shreveport, but a branch, known as the Texas Cotton Office, was opened in Houston in early December 1863. The Cotton Office was authorized to purchase half of a planter's cotton with specie certificates which the Confederate government would later honor. The planter would also receive an exemption from impressment for the other half of his cotton and for the teams needed to transport it. Any planter declining to sell his cotton to the Cotton Office ran the risk of losing it to the government under the Impressment Act of 1863.[32]

Texas planters were quick to criticize Kirby Smith's cotton plan. Under procedures established by Col. William J. Hutchins, the wealthy Houston merchant-banker who was appointed to head the Cotton Office in Texas, owners of cotton were required to pay the cost of transporting the cotton to depots established by the office, a charge they considered unfair. In addition, many Texas planters had lost confidence in the Confederacy's ability to honor its financial commitments. Others resented the threat of impressment if they refused to cooperate.[33]

Governor Murrah and the state legislature responded to the planters' criticism with a "State Plan" for the purchase of cotton. Under this plan a new state organization called the Texas Loan Agency offered to purchase cotton at a fair market price payable in seven percent Texas bonds. The State Plan offered the planters a way to protect their cotton from Confederate impressment by agreeing to transport all cotton to the Rio Grande. Since the cotton in transit belonged to the state, it was safe from impressment. Once it reached the border half would be returned to the owner who could arrange sale and the other half would be purchased by the state with the bonds guaranteed by Texas land.[34]

The State Plan pleased Texas cotton planters. By March 1864, nearly half of all baled Texas cotton had been sold to the state. Kirby Smith and agents of the Cotton Bureau were most unhappy with what appeared to be an attempt to undermine their efforts. After repeated pleas failed to deter Governor Murrah, Smith issued new regulations for trade between his department and Mexico. Under these regulations Confederate military authorities would control the cotton trade. These regulations touched off another round of controversy between Texas and Confederate officials. Governor Murrah argued that the new regulations violated state sovereignty. General Smith contended that the State Plan weakened the department's capacity to defend itself and threatened the Confederacy.[35]

At Murrah's invitation, General Smith and the Texas governor met at Hempstead in the second week of July 1864 to discuss their differences. No record of the meeting has survived, but apparently Smith was most persuasive. On July 19 Murrah issued an address to the people in which he acceded to Smith's request. He informed Texans that their survival depended upon the army's ability to obtain supplies. He appealed to them to deliver their cotton to the Cotton Bureau's agents and announced the state would no longer protect shipments of privately owned cotton.[36]

Ironically, the complaints of Texas planters and Governor Murrah against practices of Smith's Cotton Bureau and Cotton Office led the Confederate government to transfer cotton transactions to the newly created Trans Mississippi Treasury Department two weeks after Governor Murrah's address to the people of Texas.[37]

While Governor Murrah was quarreling with Confederate authorities over conscription, cotton, and states' rights, he also had to contend with a growing opposition to the war effort within the state. Many Texans opposed secession and the Confederacy from the beginning. Some of these individuals became what historian James Marten has labeled "Confederate Unionists," individuals who initially opposed disunion but gave their support to the Confederacy once the people of Texas made the decision to secede. James W. Throckmorton of Collin County is perhaps the best example of such a Texan. One of eight delegates in the secession convention who voted against disunion, Throckmorton accepted the vote of the people in the secession referendum. He took an oath of allegiance to the Confederacy, helped raise a regiment of northeast Texas volunteers, fought in campaigns in Indian Territory and Arkansas, served in the wartime state senate, and in March 1864 was appointed commander of Brigade District No. 3 with the rank of brigadier general in state service.[38]

Throckmorton's good friend and political ally Ben H. Epperson was another Texas Unionist who came to support the Confederacy. A Red River County lawyer, Epperson was a railroad promoter, state representative, and former Whig candidate for governor. He was a confidant of Sam Houston and had urged Houston to accept Lincoln's offer of assistance in the secession crisis. Once the state seceded, however, he announced his loyalty to the Confederacy. A game leg kept him from military service, but he contributed time and money to raising and equipping troops. He ran for a seat in the Confederate Congress in the fall of 1861, but his opposition to secession made him suspect to many voters and he was defeated. He retired from public life for the remainder of the war but reentered the political arena during Reconstruction.[39]

Galveston attorney William Pitt Ballinger was another prewar Unionist who eventually supported the Confederacy. Although he continued to have reservations, he slowly accepted the Southern cause. He helped to acquire artillery for Galveston defense and was appointed receiver of confiscated enemy property. Thomas F. McKinney, one of Austin's Old Three Hundred and a leader in the Texas Revolution and Republic, Hamilton Stuart, editor of the *Galveston Civilian*, Reece Hughes, wealthy ironmaker in Cass County, and Col. William C. Young of Cooke County, commander of the Eleventh Cavalry in Indian Territory, were other Texas Unionists who, like Ballinger, came to support the Confederacy.[40]

Not all Texans who opposed secession became "Confederate Unionists" like Throckmorton, Epperson, and Ballinger. George Whitmore, a state representative from East Texas who signed the Unionist Address to the People of Texas condemning secession, remained quiet the first year of the war but in late 1862 became an open critic of the Confederacy. He was arrested the following year and held in prison for twelve months without being charged or tried for any crime. Dr. Richard Peebles, a prominent early Texan and one of the founders of Hempstead, was another Texas Unionist arrested on charges of impeding the Confederate war effort. After a controversy between military officials and the Texas Supreme Court over his arrest, Peebles and two other Texans were banished to Mexico.[41]

Some Texas Unionists left the state to escape criticism or possible punishment from Texas Confederates. Noah Smithwick, a pioneer Texas blacksmith and veteran of the Texas Revolution, headed to California, where he lived for the next thirty-eight years. Swen Magnus Swenson, pioneer Swedish merchant-banker and friend of Sam Houston, left the state in the autumn of 1863. He spent the remainder of the war in Mexico and New Orleans. A close friend of Swenson's, Federal Judge Thomas DuVal of Austin, also spent the latter part of the war as an exile in New Orleans. Melinda Rankin, Northern missionary-teacher, was another of those to leave the state. She returned to Brownsville during the Union occupation of 1863–64 but left again when the Federals abandoned South Texas several months later. Massachusetts-born William Marsh Rice, wealthy merchant, cotton broker, and railroad developer, transferred his business from Houston to Matamoros, Mexico, when the war broke out. He moved to New York City after the war but retained a business interest in Texas.[42]

Some Texas Unionists remained in the state but attempted to be neutral. Elisha M. Pease, Connecticut-born lawyer and former governor of the state, is an example of such an individual. Totally opposed to secession, Pease withdrew from public life when the war began and retired to his home near Austin. His friend and fellow Unionist George W. Paschal also stayed home during the war but found neutrality more difficult than did Pease. Although he claimed to accept the decision of the people on secession, Paschal opposed Confederate conscription laws leading to his imprisonment by local authorities. He was subsequently released from prison and retired to his home to codify and annotate the laws of Texas and the Constitution of the United States.[43]

Before his death in 1863, former Governor Sam Houston wrestled with the problems of conscience that faced Pease and Paschal. A month after his removal as governor in the spring of 1861, the old warrior had, in a speech at Independence, declared his fortunes with the South. When his son Sam Houston, Jr., went off to war with the Second Infantry, he traveled to Galveston to see the regiment depart. He never conceded that secession was right or legal, however, and opposed sending Texas troops out of the state. Houston followed the war closely, congratulating General Magruder for the victory at Galveston. He was quick to criticize his old nemesis Jefferson Davis, whom Houston regarded as "cold as a lizard and ambitious as Lucifer." In one of his last letters Houston wrote that "Davis deserves to be shot" for losing the war.[44]

Some Texas Unionists left the state to serve with Federal forces during the war. Historian Frank H. Smyrl estimated that 2,179 Texans, forty-seven of them African Americans, joined the Union army. Edmund Jackson Davis, a native of Florida and veteran of the Mexican War who had lived in Texas since 1848, was the leader of these Texans. Tall, graceful, and handsome, Davis was a successful attorney and public official in South Texas before the war. He was district judge at Corpus Christi when Lincoln was elected president. Although he opposed secession, Davis declared that he accepted the verdict of the people. Like Sam Houston, however, Davis declined to take the oath of allegiance to the Confederacy, and in May 1862 boarded a Federal ship at the mouth of the Rio Grande. After a visit to Washington he received a colonel's commission and began raising

*Edmund J. Davis — South Texas judge and Unionist leader who became
brigadier general commanding Texans in Union army.
Later Reconstruction governor of Texas.*
— Archives Division, Texas State Library

the First Texas Cavalry (Union) in New Orleans from Texans who
had left home rather than serve the Confederacy.[45]

Davis returned to the mouth of the Rio Grande in early 1863
for the purpose of recruiting additional troops and escorting his
wife and sons, who had also fled Texas, to New Orleans. While
awaiting embarkation near Matamoros, Mexico, Davis, William W.
Montgomery (a Texas rancher and fellow Unionist from Caldwell
County), and three other Unionists were seized by Confederate
raiders from Texas who had crossed the Rio Grande into Mexico.
Led by Maj. George W. Chilton, the raiders took the Unionist prisoners back into Texas. Several miles down the road, the Confederates lynched Montgomery, who had wounded two of the raiders
during his capture. Davis and the other three were taken to a camp
near Brownsville.

The Mexican government protested this violation of sovereignty, forcing Gen. Hamilton P. Bee to order their return to Mexico. Davis and his family eventually sailed on to New Orleans. Davis' regiment served briefly in the Louisiana campaign in 1863 and later returned to Texas with the Union army that occupied Brownsville.[46]

A second regiment of Texas Union cavalry was organized at Brownsville in December 1863, with John L. Haynes, a former state representative from Starr County, as commander. A native of Virginia and, like Davis, a Mexican War veteran, Haynes had lived in South Texas since the late 1840s. He had been very sympathetic to Mexican Texans. During the Cortina War of the late 1850s, Haynes angered some Anglo Texans by suggesting that the affair may have been caused by land frauds perpetrated upon Mexican Texans. Over half the recruits for the Second Texas regiment were Tejanos, the majority of them born in Mexico. Jerry Don Thompson, who studied the role of Tejanos in the war, pointed out that they did not join the Union army to preserve the Constitution or to end slavery, but rather to strike back at their old enemies and oppressors in Texas. The pay offered by the Union government was also quite attractive to these individuals, most of whom were poor laborers or herdsmen.[47]

In the spring of 1864 the First and Second Texas Cavalry (Union) were grouped together as a cavalry brigade, under command of Edmund J. Davis, who was promoted to brigadier general. They were joined by an independent company of Partisan Rangers commanded by Capt. Adrian J. Vidal, a young native of Mexico whose mother married wealthy Texas merchant-rancher Mifflin Kenedy. Vidal had served under Brig. Gen. Hamilton P. Bee in the Confederate army, but in late October 1863 he and his company mutinied and left Confederate service. After hiding out briefly, Vidal and his men, eighty to ninety in number, joined the Union army at Brownsville in December 1863. Vidal and his Rangers took part in several scouting missions for the Federal army in early 1864 but were unhappy with bureaucratic regulations and rampant prejudice within the Union army. Most of them, including Vidal, deserted from the Union army. Vidal later joined the forces of Benito Juarez in Mexico, but was captured and executed by Maximilian's Imperialists in 1865.[48]

Andrew Jackson Hamilton was perhaps the best known Texan to serve the Union cause. The Alabama native who became an Aus-

A. J. Hamilton — Former Texas congressman and prominent Unionist. Appointed military governor of Texas by Abraham Lincoln and later provisional governor of Texas by Andrew Johnson.
— Lawrence T. Jones III Collection

tin lawyer, acting attorney general, and state representative was elected to the United States Congress as an Independent Democrat in 1858. A political ally of Sam Houston, Hamilton opposed secession and worked in the Congress unsuccessfully to find a compromise satisfactory to both North and South. In the spring of 1862 he and several fellow Unionists made their way to Mexico. From there he traveled to Union-occupied New Orleans and then to the nation's capital. After a meeting with President Lincoln in October 1862, Hamilton was appointed brigadier general and military governor of Texas. He returned to the state with the Banks expedition in late 1863 and set up headquarters in Brownsville. When the Union army pulled out of South Texas in the spring of 1864, Hamilton went to New Orleans, where he remained until the end of the war.[49]

Historian Claude Elliott estimated that one-third of the Texas population actively or passively supported the Federal cause in the Civil War. Elliott believed that another one-third of the population remained neutral and only one-third actively supported the Confederacy. These ratios appear reasonable, particularly if the large slave population, consisting of one-third of the state's residents, is considered. While the majority of Texas slaves remained passive during the war, it is unlikely that they supported the Confederacy beyond performing those duties required of them by their masters.[50]

Unionist feeling in Texas was strongest in the German populated counties of Central Texas and in the northern counties along the Red River. As noted earlier, not all Germans opposed secession and the Confederacy. Several German counties, especially Comal, turned in heavy majorities for secession. Large numbers of German Texans served in Confederate military units during the war. Company G of the Fourth Texas Cavalry, Company B of the Seventh Texas Cavalry, and Company E of the First Texas Cavalry were almost entirely German. Waul's Legion, which served at Vicksburg, had a sizable number of Germans, as did Companies B and F of Terry's Rangers. The Third Texas Infantry, mustered in South Texas, included many Germans and Mexicans. Its executive officer was Lt. Col. Augustus Buchel, a native of the Rhineland and a veteran of the Mexican and Crimean wars.[51]

Many other Germans resisted serving in the Confederate army, some because of their opposition to secession and slavery, others because they were reluctant to leave their homes and families unprotected on the frontier. Several hundred Germans in Gillespie, Kerr, and Kendall counties organized a Union Loyal League, ostensibly to provide frontier protection. To counter this Unionist threat General Bee declared martial law in the region in April 1862. The following month General Hebert extended this to the entire state. Confederate authorities ordered the military companies organized by the Union League to disband. A detachment of Texas Partisan Rangers under the command of Capt. James Duff was sent to the Fredericksburg area to insure compliance. Several citizens were arrested for opposing the Confederacy and resisting military service. They were later tried in San Antonio by a military commission appointed by General Hebert. Some were imprisoned, others were released, and a few joined the army to avoid trial.[52]

The Unionist military companies in the Hill Country were disbanded, but approximately sixty men led by Maj. Fritz Tegener determined to leave the state. On August 1, 1862, they left the Kerrville area heading toward the Rio Grande. Captain Duff dispatched Lt. C. D. McRae with ninety-four Rangers in pursuit. On August 10, McRae and his men overtook the Germans on the west fork of the Nueces River, twenty miles from Fort Clark. In an early morning surprise attack the better armed Rangers killed approximately thirty Germans and wounded twenty others. Confederate losses were two killed and eighteen wounded. Several wounded German prisoners were later killed by the Rangers. At least eight of the Germans who escaped from the so-called Battle of the Nueces were killed two months later while attempting to cross the Rio Grande.

During the next several weeks numerous atrocities were committed against German Texans in the Fredericksburg area by Duff and his Rangers. Although passive resistance by German Unionists continued, open resistance ended in early 1864. The Germans killed on the Nueces were left unburied. Their remains were recovered after the war and enshrined at Comfort, where a monument inscribed *Treuer der Union* commemorates their devotion to the Union.[53]

Opposition to the Confederacy was also strong in a tier of counties north of Dallas and south of the Red River. These counties were settled largely by northern and border state farmers and mechanics with few slaves. Even so, the economy and local government of the area, including the militia, was dominated by a small minority of slaveholders, largely from the lower South. These pro-secessionists were determined to support the Confederacy in spite of the fact that the majority of citizens opposed secession. When the war came, some of the Union sympathizers formed a secret Peace Party or Loyal League, dedicated to resisting conscription and to restoring the Union. In the autumn of 1862 local authorities, who had learned of the existence of the organization centered in Gainesville, county seat of Cooke County, became convinced that the Unionists were planning some type of insurrection. On October 1, militia units moved into the county and arrested leaders of the movement. Twenty men were arrested the first night and more than a hundred were arrested during the next two weeks. A mob soon gathered in Gainesville and demanded immediate action against the Unionists. A citizens' jury of twelve men was selected to try the accused offenders. Within two weeks the citizens' tribunal found guilty and executed thirty individuals. Another fourteen were hanged by the mob without benefit of trial, and several others were murdered by individuals.[54]

Authorities in neighboring counties took action against Unionists suspected in the peace plot. Five men were hanged in Decatur (Wise County) for their alleged part in the conspiracy. Several arrests were made in Denton County, but only one man was executed. Forty arrests were made in Sherman (Grayson County), but James W. Throckmorton and other moderate leaders prevented any hangings.[55]

While the great hanging at Gainesville and action in other counties temporarily satisfied local concerns, unrest in North Texas continued in 1863. Opposition to conscription remained high and the number of deserters in the area grew. Confederate authorities, concerned that disaffection might interfere with wheat and beef production, ordered regular troops to the area. Brig. Gen. Henry E. McCulloch, placed in charge of the newly created Northern Sub-district, attempted to quiet the unrest. After efforts to bring in deserters were only partially successful, McCulloch was enjoined by departmental commander Kirby Smith to enlist the aid of William C. Quantrill and his raiders who made their winter camp in North Texas in late 1863. McCulloch was wary about using Quantrill, whom he regarded as little more than a bandit. The Texan admonished Quantrill that deserters be taken alive, but Quantrill took few prisoners. In addition, Quantrill's men created concern in Sherman and Bonham by their lawless activities. McCulloch ordered Quantrill's arrest, but the guerrilla chieftain fled the state.[56]

As the war went on and the Confederate cause looked more hopeless, evasion of conscription and desertion from the army became more common. John S. Ford, who served as Texas superintendent of conscription during 1862–63, regarded the conscription law as an "unfortunate enactment" that did great harm. He contended that it was an error to force Unionists into the Confederate army. Such men Ford believed would be of no value to the Confederacy and would desert at the first opportunity. Ford also believed the conscription act which exempted individuals with twenty or more slaves was a mistake, leading many to believe the conflict to be a "rich man's war and the poor man's fight."[57]

In some instances both state and Confederate troops rounded up conscript evaders and deserters. In many counties the Home Guard, consisting mainly of teenagers and old men, was used to arrest those suspected of evading conscription. John Warren Hunter, who with his son later published *Hunter's Magazine* and *Frontier Times*, reported that those not supporting the Confederacy referred to the Home Guards as "Heel-Flies" because, like the small insects that bite the ankles and heels of cattle, Home Guard units often harassed and annoyed those suspected of disloyalty.[58]

In her study of desertion in the Civil War, historian Ella Lonn found that 4,664 Texans were listed as deserters during the course of the war. She noted that nearly 3,000 of them were in the woods and brush of the Northern Sub-district in the autumn of 1863. Often deserters and draft dodgers hid out together. John Ford mentioned one such group that congregated in the Hill Country near Austin. According to Ford they formed camps and lived by hunting and the assistance of their friends. A correspondent for the *Houston Tri-Weekly Telegraph* described a community formed by deserters in Walker County. An area about sixty miles wide was controlled by the deserters before Confederate authorities raided the area and captured over twenty individuals. The Big Thicket of Hardin County was an ideal hideout for deserters, draft evaders, and opponents of the war. These individuals, generally referred to as "Jayhawkers," caused local authorities to call for assistance from the Confederate command at Galveston. In the spring of 1865 Capt. James Kaiser and a company of Confederates entered the Thicket and set fire to the Jayhawkers' hideout. Nearly 3,000 acres were burned in the region known even today as "Kaiser's Burnout."[59]

Some of the disaffected Texans turned to acts of terror and violence. Cullen Montgomery Baker was one of the most notorious of such individuals. A native of Tennessee, Baker moved to northeast Texas with his family as a child. During the 1850s he gained a reputation for lawlessness as he moved back and forth between Texas and Arkansas. He was conscripted as a private in the Confederate army in 1862 but deserted, spending much of the war hiding out in the swamps of the Sulphur River. He joined a group of partisans who robbed, murdered, and plundered indiscriminately in Texas and Arkansas. After the war he became something of a folk hero for his activities against the Reconstruction policies of the Federal government. Before he was murdered in 1869, Baker had killed more than twenty individuals.[60]

Martin D. Hart was another East Texan who turned to a life of crime after deserting from Confederate service. Hart's motives at first were more noble than those of Cullen Baker, although like Baker he, too, became the leader of a band of guerrillas who killed and plundered both Federals and Confederates. Hart was a responsible leader of his Greenville community in the antebellum period, serving first as a state representative and then a state senator in the late 1850s. A lawyer and businessman, Hart, a native of Indiana, opposed secession and signed the Unionist Address to the People of Texas in the spring of 1861. When the war came, however, Hart raised a company of men in Greenville for the Confederate army and received a captain's commission. In the fall of 1862 he switched sides and received a commission in the Union army. He formed a company of irregulars who at first tried to assist Northern troops in Arkansas but soon were murdering and plundering freely. He was captured by the Confederates, convicted of murder by a court-martial, and was hanged in January 1863.[61]

Although opposition to the Confederacy was strong, particularly in certain regions of the state, it must be remembered that the majority of white Texans continued to support the Southern cause. Texans suffered at home and on the battlefield for a way of life and a constitutional principal in which they believed. In sharp contrast to Cullen Baker and Martin Hart, who turned against the Confederacy, there is the example of two young Texans, both with the last name of Dodd but apparently unrelated, who gave their lives for the Confederacy. Not only did they have the same last name but also they were executed by the enemy on the same day, January 8, 1864, on the charge of spying for the Confederacy. One, Pvt. E. S. Dodd, was a soldier in Tennessee; the other, David O. Dodd, was a civilian store clerk and telegraph operator in Arkansas. The first, Private Dodd, was a native Kentuckian who came to Texas on the eve of the Civil War; the civilian David Dodd was born in Lavaca County but moved with his parents to their native state of Arkansas just before the war. Private Dodd was a member of Company D, Terry's Texas Rangers, who served in both the Murfreesboro and Chickamauga campaigns. He was captured in Tennessee during Wheeler's cavalry raid in December 1863, after being separated from his unit. Although he does not appear to have been a spy, he was convicted on the charges of wearing parts of a Union uniform while attempting to make his way back through Federal lines. He was sentenced to death by a court-martial on January 5 and was hanged on the morning of January 8.[62]

David O. Dodd was a spy in the more traditional sense. While working as a telegraph operator and store clerk in occupied Arkansas he gathered information for the Confederacy. Arresting Union authorities found a small notebook with Morse-coded military information in his possession. After brief confinement he was tried and found guilty of spying by a military court. According to some accounts, he was offered a pardon by Gen. Frederick Steele if he would name his accomplices but he refused to do so. Like Private Dodd he was executed by hanging on January 8, 1864. David Dodd was seventeen years old at the time of execution.[63]

As a frontier state far from the scene of major Civil War campaigns and battles, Texas escaped much of the suffering and physical devastation that occurred in sister states of the Confederacy. Even so, the war forced many adjustments in the social and economic life of Texas. Like the other cotton states of the deep South, Texas was affected by the Union naval blockade which interfered with the export of her principal agricultural commodity. While the Union naval blockade was never totally effective, it did impede the normal flow of cotton from Southern seaports. Unlike the other cotton states, Texas had the ability to ship a great deal of its cotton southward across the Rio Grande to Matamoros, Mexico and from there to waiting manufacturers in England and France.[64]

In an effort to force European intervention in the war the Confederate government in 1861 urged that Southern cotton be withheld from the world market. However, Confederate authorities exempted shipment into Mexico in the belief that Mexico offered an opportunity for exchanging Texas cotton for supplies that were desperately needed for the Southern war effort. Soon wagon trains were moving across Texas carrying thousands of bales of cotton gathered from all over the state as well as Arkansas and Louisiana. Almost overnight Matamoros, a sleepy Mexican town on the Rio Grande located about thirty miles upriver from the Gulf of Mexico, became a flourishing city with cotton buyers, speculators, agents, and merchants from all over the world.[65]

The journey from Central and East Texas to Mexico was a long and often difficult one. Two main routes were used by the teamsters in moving the cotton across Texas. Much of the East Texas and some Central Texas cotton came through Alleyton, the railroad terminus on the lower Colorado just east of Houston. From there the ox carts and wagons moved across the coastal prairie toward the King Ranch, which became a staging and refitting area before the final leg of the journey. From the King Ranch the teamsters had another 125 miles across rugged, semiarid land before reaching Brownsville. The second major route was from Central Texas through San Antonio. Cotton reaching San Antonio was sometimes carried to the King Ranch and then on to Brownsville; other times it was taken to Eagle Pass, Laredo, or Rio Grande City before movement across the Rio Grande. Cotton brought from northwestern Louisiana and Arkansas used this San Antonio route.[66]

The journey was not ended when the cotton reached Matamoros, as that city was thirty miles from the coast. The cotton was taken by small, shallow-draft river steamers down the winding Rio Grande to Bagdad, a small village on the coast, for transshipment to an oceangoing vessel. Because of the tides the steamboats were delayed in crossing the bar in the harbor, so it often took weeks before the larger ships were loaded. Similar delays were faced by vessels returning with cargoes of military supplies and consumer goods from Europe. In his memoirs, William Neale, a South Texas pioneer, noted that he had seen upward of 100 vessels ranging from thirty-ton schooners to 2,000-ton steamships anchored off the coast at Bagdad taking on or taking off cargo.[67]

Some of the cotton exported through Mexico was brought to Bagdad by shallow-draft schooners which sailed along the Texas coast. Carrying sixty to eighty bales of cotton, these small vessels stayed in coastal waters to avoid the Union blockade ships. Although most of the schooners got through, there were risks; occasionally such vessels were captured or sunk. Most Texas planters preferred the comparative safety of the long, overland wagon trip to the dangers of the coastal trade.[68]

Texas planters faced numerous obstacles in addition to the problem of transporting cotton to Mexico. Efforts by Confederate officials to control the cotton trade in order to assure acquisition of needed currency and war supplies led to orders and regulations that planters considered burdensome. The capture of Brownsville by the Union army in late 1863, bandit raids along the border, governmental instability inside Mexico, French intervention in support of Maximilian, and the dispute between Kirby Smith and Pendleton Murrah over cotton purchasing all caused difficulties. Even so, the rising prices for delivered cotton — from sixteen cents per pound in August 1862 to eighty cents in November 1863 — was an attractive incentive for cotton producers and cotton traders. By the time of the Federal occupation of Brownsville in December 1863, more than 150,000 bales of cotton passed through Matamoros. When the Federals occupied Brownsville, the trade simply moved upriver. By the end of the war approximately 320,000 bales of cotton had been shipped across the Rio Grande. Texas businessmen such as Richard King, Mifflin Kenedy, William Marsh Rice, and Charles Stillman made fortunes in the Civil War cotton trade.[69]

The embargo on the cotton trade elsewhere was slowly relaxed after the spring of 1862 until it completely ceased. Most Texas cotton continued to go through Mexico, but some cotton and other agricultural commodities were taken directly from Galveston, Sabine Pass, and other Texas ports by fast blockade runners to Havana, Cuba, over 800 miles away. Once in Cuba the commodities were transferred to larger, neutral flag vessels for journey to Europe, although some Texas cotton was shipped to New York and other northern ports. Returning vessels brought rifles, ammunition, and consumer goods back to Texas.[70]

It is impossible to determine the exact number of attempted runs through the Union blockade. Marcus W. Price, who made an exhaustive study of the subject, estimated that there were more than 8,000 violations of the blockade, including 2,960 attempted runs to and from the Gulf Coast. Price did not provide separate figures for the different regions of the Gulf, but Tuffly Ellis, who studied blockade running from Texas, believed that at least half of these attempts were in the far western Gulf. The majority of these runs were successful; Ellis estimated that captures and destructions were only 10 to 15 percent of the total attempts.[71]

Most of the Texas trade, other than through Mexico, came through Galveston. Much of the blockade running from Galveston was limited to sailing schooners which made quick profits for the owners but carried light cargo. One such vessel was the *Rob Roy*, a graceful seventy-eight-foot schooner owned by Capt. William Watson, a Scotsman who had lived in the South ten years before the outbreak of war. A businessman and engineer, Watson served in the Confederate army in Missouri and Arkansas before purchasing the *Rob Roy* in New Orleans. Determined to aid the Confederacy and at the same time increase his wealth, Watson attempted to engage in the Matamoros cotton trade, but the complexities of that trade determined him to move his operations first to the mouth of the Brazos and later to Galveston. Although he made several runs of the blockade in 1863, Watson sold the *Rob Roy* to new owners who shifted her run to the west coast of Florida.[72]

Even though Texans were more fortunate than most other Southerners in being able to trade with Mexico, their lives were greatly affected by the war. Shortages of various types existed in the state, perhaps none more acute in the towns than housing. Thousands of refugees came to Texas from Arkansas and Louisiana to escape invading Federal armies. Most of these refugees settled in East Texas, especially Tyler, Rusk, Marshall, Waco, and Corsicana, but some located in Houston and nearby coastal communities. Houston also received a number of refugees from Galveston. Thomas North, a visitor from the Midwest, reported that the evacuation from the island in 1862 resulted in a "general stampede of people and valuables up country." Hotels in the Bayou City were filled from attic to basement. Col. Arthur Fremantle of the Coldstream Guards noted that Houston was so crowded with refugees that all beds in his hotel had two occupants each; as a great favor to a foreign guest he was allowed a bed to himself.[73]

Many of the Louisiana refugees, including young Kate Stone of Brokenburn plantation in northern Louisiana, found life in East Texas to be harsh. They complained of the heat, dust, wind, reptiles, insects, and boorish neighbors. Indeed, Kate Stone believed that she had discovered "the dark corner of the Confederacy." Some who rented accommodations in Texas sight unseen were disappointed and moved about trying to find something suitable. A few, such as John Leigh, who first located in Wharton County but was forced to move to Robertson County in Central Texas because of the threat of military invasion, grew to like their new home and became Texas boosters. Even Kate Stone, who complained incessantly about poor accommodations, unsanitary conditions, and tasteless food and drink served in cracked or broken dishes, later admitted that her last twelve months in Civil War Texas "was the happiest year" of her life.[74]

The addition of hundreds of refugees and the effect of the Union naval blockade caused numerous other problems. Although cases of serious food shortages were rare, many commodities, especially those formerly imported, were difficult to obtain. The inability to acquire coffee in the quantities previously consumed created a particular hardship for many Southerners. Colonel Fremantle noted "the loss of coffee afflicts the Confederates even more than their loss of spirits." He observed that Southerners exercised their ingenuity in devising substitutes, most of which he believed were unsuccessful. While traveling in East Texas he was served a peculiar mixture called "Confederate coffee," made of rye, meal, Indian corn, and sweet potatoes. Mathilda Doebbler Gruen, a young German Texan, stated that her family used parched rye and wheat as a substitute for coffee. Others, she observed, used parched corn. The editor of the *Houston Weekly Telegraph* reported that okra was a suitable substitute for coffee. Eliza McHatton-Ripley, like Kate Stone a refugee from Louisiana, noted peanuts, sweet potatoes, rye, beans, peas, and cornmeal were used as coffee substitutes — "all of them wretched imitations, though gulped down, when chilly and tired, for lack of anything better."[75]

Ms. McHatton-Ripley commented that tea drinkers fared no better in Civil War Texas. She wrote that sage and orange leaves were used as substitutes. Some Texans substituted yaupon leaves for the imported Asian tea. Not all found the yaupon acceptable; one Union prisoner of war declared it produced "a burning sensation" in the stomach. Another observer referred to its "unpleasant medical effects."[76]

The shortage of salt was a matter of considerable concern. In this respect Texas was better off than some states as several local sources of salt were available, including the Steen and Brooks Saline in Smith County, the Grand Saline in Van Zandt County, the Palestine Salt Works in Anderson County, the Double Mountain Salt Works in Stonewall County, and an area of dry salt lakes west of Pecos. Even so, there were shortages of the badly needed preservative because much of commercial salt in antebellum Texas had come from Saltville, Virginia, which was overrun by the enemy early in the war. The discovery of a great salt mine on Avery Island in southern Louisiana provided a significant new source of salt, but Union military occupation of the area and the lack of adequate transportation prevented full utilization by the Confederacy. Texas and Confederate authorities attempted to increase production of salt on a state-owned lake in South Texas, but these works were destroyed by the Union army in late 1863. The price of salt increased from sixty-five cents per 200-pound sack in 1860 to seven or eight dollars a sack by autumn 1861. In some instances salt could not be secured at any price. Eliza McHatton-Ripley stated that she spent weeks with a family that could not secure salt to put up their meat. The family finally resorted "to the necessity of utilizing the dirt-floor of their smoke-house, which was rich in saline properties from the accumulation during a series of years of the waste salt and drippings."[77]

Texans used their ingenuity to find substitutes for many personal items that were formerly imported. The editor of the *Clarksville Standard* described a substitute for soda which could easily be produced. This consisted of adding ashes of corn cobs to boiling water, allowing that to stand a minute, then pouring off the liquid, which could be used at once with an acid such as sour milk or vin-

Amelia Barr — Englishwoman who lived with husband and children in Austin during Civil War. Later became one of America's most prolific authors.
— Archives Division, Texas State Library

egar. According to the editor it made "a bread as light almost as snow." Another editor noted that a homemade glue was "far superior to the common imported glue," but failed to describe how it could be made. Substitutes for ink were made of the bark of dogwood or oak, pomegranate rinds, elderberries, or green persimmons. Shoe blacking was also scarce during the war. One writer told of making blacking from chinaberries. Imported dye products were unavailable, so bark, herbs, and berries were used in coloring homemade cloth. Future novelist Amelia Barr, who resided in Austin during the war, reported that because pins and needles were so scarce, "some were compelled to use mesquite thorns for pins." One woman was so grateful for three needles that Barr gave her that she gave Barr a ham and two pounds of coffee.[78]

The shortage of goods grew as the war continued. Most manufactured items, especially clothing and shoes, were imported from

Europe or the North before the war. Now Texans had to produce their own goods. The largest cloth factory developed during the war was at the state penitentiary at Huntsville, where more than 200 convicts turned out nearly 6,000 yards of cloth daily. Part of the cloth made at the penitentiary was used to clothe the convicts and state troops. The rest was sold to the Confederate army, exchanged for supplies, distributed to soldiers' families, given to other state agencies, or sold to the general public. Most individual families, however, depended upon homespun cloth, a practice used earlier which had become less common in the 1850s. Newspaper editors and state leaders encouraged home weaving. In 1861 Governor Lubbock was inaugurated wearing a homespun suit.[79]

Wartime needs stimulated industries already established and encouraged development of new ones. A major ordnance works was built near Tyler for the manufacture of weapons and ammunition. After some initial delays caused by poor management and lack of skilled gunsmiths, the Tyler works was taken over by the Confederate government and produced thousands of rifles, cartridges, musket balls, ammunition boxes, and canteens. Although the Tyler works was the largest supplier of weapons in Texas, it was by no means the only such facility in the state. The ordnance works at San Antonio employed sixty-five operators and ten blacksmiths in the manufacture of carriages and recoil mechanisms for heavy cannon, small arms, cartridge boxes, Bowie knives, and cartridges. Other ordnance works were established in Anderson, Austin, Bastrop, Brazoria, Calhoun, Dallas, Galveston, Harris, Rusk, and Travis counties.[80]

The Confederate army established and maintained a number of shops and depots in Texas. One of the finest was the quartermaster depot at Mound Prairie in Anderson County. This facility included a sawmill, flour and grist mill, cotton spinning building, blacksmith shop, foundry, harness shop, tin shop, shoe shop, two large shortage warehouses, and fourteen dwelling places. The Trans Mississippi Department's Quartermaster Bureau sat up clothing and shoe shops and depots at Houston, Tyler, Austin, San Antonio, Jefferson, and Huntsville. The Field Transportation Bureau maintained wagon shops in Waco, Hempstead, Dallas, Tyler, Rusk, Mount Pleasant, and Paris. Shipyards were built on Goose Creek in east Harris County and at Beaumont in Jefferson County for the construction and repair of naval vessels.[81]

Efforts to supply the Confederate army with Texas beef were not too successful. There was an abundance of beef cattle in the state when the war began, nearly three million head, but transportational problems prevented the Confederacy from taking full advantage of Texas beef. Some early efforts were made to move cattle from Texas eastward, but with limited success. The closing of the Mississippi River with the loss of Vicksburg and Port Hudson in July 1863 ended major attempts to move Texas cattle to the areas of greatest need. The Trans Mississippi Commissary Department turned to the slaughter and packing of beef in Texas. A contract was signed with I. B. Dunn of Jefferson for delivery of canned beef, but the quality of the beef prepared was poor. Complaints came from troops to whom the meat was delivered. Efforts were made to correct the problem, but the war ended before appreciable improvement was made.[82]

The growing shortage of various goods, coupled with depreciation of Confederate currency, resulted in steadily rising prices. Butter, which sold for twenty-five cents per pound in 1861, cost $1.75 per pound in 1863 and $9.00 per pound in 1864. Sugar, priced at eight cents per pound in 1861, was valued at $7.00 per pound in 1864. Potatoes that sold for $1.75 per bushel in 1861 rose to $4.75 by 1863 and $20.00 in 1864. Corn, priced at sixty-seven cents in 1861, was selling at $25.00 a bushel in 1864. Eliza McHatton-Ripley reported that she paid $90.00 for one and a half yards of common cotton denim late in the war. Dr. Edward Pye, a Confederate surgeon stationed at Beaumont, paid $10.00 for a chicken and $12.00 for two sacks of flour in December 1864.[83]

The families of Texans in military service were particularly hard hit by the rising cost of commodities. The meager pay ($11.00 per month for privates) for servicemen was insufficient to support large families, which were common in the nineteenth century. Voluntary relief organizations were formed in most counties to provide some aid in money and goods, but it was soon evident that governmental assistance would be required. The state legislature passed several laws giving county courts the authority to levy special taxes for the purpose of relieving destitute families of those in military service. The legislature also appropriated money for such relief and authorized the distribution of 600,000 yards of cloth manufactured at the state penintentiary for distribution to soldier families. Even so, state and local appropriations proved to be inadequate. Difficulties in distribution, lack of sufficient money and materials, and the rising inflationary spiral all combined to prevent a completely satisfactory solution to this problem.[84]

Texas women, whether wives of soldiers or not, were affected by the war. Not only did they have to search for substitutes for many commodities and to set up looms in their houses to make clothing, but many had to manage farms and plantations while their husbands and sons were away. Mary Renfro, who was married just before the war, managed the 160-acre farm she and her husband Henry owned in Johnson County while he served in the army. Their wartime letters show that she planted corn, sowed oats, and cared for the domestic livestock during his absence. Rebecca Adams, daughter of wealthy planter Hamblin Bass, handled family affairs while her husband and oldest son served in the Confederate army. She had to care for nine children, supervise fifty slaves, and run an extensive plantation near Fairfield. Her letters written to her husband, an army physician, describe her concern about fattening and slaughtering hogs, trading corn for sugar, and paying for a teacher to instruct the children. Similarly, Sara Armour Munson of Bailey's Prairie kept Ridgley plantation operating while her husband was in the army. She saw that the cotton was planted at the proper time, cleared of weeds, harvested in the fall and shipped to Brownsville for sale. She did a great amount of sewing and making clothes for the family and slaves. She made shoes and hats, supervised the killing of hogs and making sausage, kept an extensive vegetable garden, and raised chickens, geese, ducks, and turkeys. In addition she cared for six children, including one born during the war.[85]

For some Texas women, widows or unmarried, the management of farms and plantations during the war was not a new experience. After her husband died in 1854, Martha Gaffney moved the family from South Carolina to Red River County, established a cotton plantation on land her husband had purchased, and successfully managed the plantation both before and during the war. Twice married and widowed, Rebecca McIntosh Hawkins Hagerty acquired an estate from her deceased husbands which she enlarged by sound management. By 1860 she was one of the wealthiest citizens in the state and owned or administered large plantations in Harrison and Marion counties. During the war she continued to manage the plantations. In addition, she and her son-in-law sold cattle and hogs to the Confederate Commissary Department. Similarly, Sarah Dev-

ereux, widow of Julien Sidney Devereux, continued to manage
Monte Verdi plantation, maintain a home, and raise four young sons
during the war. Another Texas widow, Mildred Satterwhite Littlefield, mother of George W. Littlefield (who was in Terry's Texas
Rangers), continued to operate a plantation in Gonzales County
during the conflict.[86]

Some Texas women entered professions formerly reserved for
men, such as teaching. Many visited hospitals and sick wards to minister to the needs of wounded servicemen, while others formed Ladies Aid Societies to make sheets, pillowcases, bandages, and other
hospital items. Others formed Soldier's Aid Societies to assist servicemen and their families with food, shelter, and clothing. A few
women even served in the army disguised as men. One Texas woman, Sophia Coffee Butts Porter of Glen Eden plantation in North
Texas, obtained information about troop movements from Federal
soldiers, forded the Red River, and rode twenty-five miles to warn
the Confederates, earning for herself the title "Paul Revere of the
Civil War." Another Texas woman, Sarah Livonia Crist Chaffin,
with the help of a slave, drove two ox-wagons loaded with food and
clothing from her farm in Limestone County to visit her husband
stationed at Galveston, a journey that took eight weeks. Sally Scull,
a successful horse trader before the war, became a gunrunner during
the conflict. She freighted cotton in wagons to the Rio Grande,
where she exchanged it for weapons and ammunition for the Confederacy.[87]

Many Texas women experienced the loneliness caused by
months of separation from their husbands and sweethearts as the
war went on. For those women living on the frontier there was the
added threat of an Indian raid or an attack by marauders or
Jayhawkers. James Nichols, a pioneer settler in Central Texas, noted
in his journal, for example, that an Indian raiding party in 1863 killed
a son and daughter of the Youngblood family and then tried to kill
Mrs. Youngblood. Although wounded by several Indian arrows,
Mrs. Youngblood drove off the attackers with a rifle and six-
shooters.

For some Texas women, such as residents of Galveston, Indianola, and Brownsville, there were changes brought about by Union
military occupation. And for many there was the sadness and des-
pair that came with news that a loved one had been killed on the field
of battle or died from wounds or disease in a hospital or enemy

prison camp. For those women whose husbands were Unionists there was the added concern for safety in a hostile environment. Mary Jane Hamilton, wife of Unionist congressman A. J. Hamilton, remained in Austin with her six children when her husband fled the state. She was under close surveillance from local authorities for months. When she visited some friends, her home was burned to the ground by Confederate sympathizers; the family's clothing, furniture, and possessions were all destroyed. She was eventually allowed to leave the state and join her husband in exile. Anne Elizabeth Davis, wife of Unionist Edmund J. Davis, had similar difficulties in South Texas, where she was treated as a prisoner before finally being allowed to leave the state.[88]

As noted earlier, many Texas women had the responsibility of directing the work of slaves during the Civil War. Although the Confederate conscription act provided an exemption for those individuals supervising twenty or more slaves, the majority of Texas white, adult males served in the army, leaving control of plantations and farms in the hands of Texas women and elderly men. Most Texas slaves continued to labor faithfully as before the war and caused little trouble for the women supervising them. Indeed, the body of contemporary evidence indicates that plantation mistresses and their children were able to carry on their tasks and sleep behind unlocked doors at night without fearing or experiencing harm from the slaves who lived around them. To be sure, there were some instances of insubordination and refusal to follow orders. Mrs. Lizzie Neblett of Grimes County wrote to her soldier husband Will in 1863 complaining that the family slaves "would not do anything until they were told." She agonized over the proper degrees of discipline to impose upon the slaves. When a hired overseer whipped the slaves, she intervened in behalf of the bondsmen. Slave insubordination continued, however, and in her frustration she began abusing her five children.[89]

Lizzie Neblett's concerns appear to be in the minority. James Marten in his study of loyalty and dissent in Civil War Texas cited numerous examples of slaves who continued working as usual while masters and overseers were in the army. He gave the example of a LaGrange planter who left his wife and four daughters alone with ninety-eight slaves without fear of harm. Similarly, slaves on Burke Simpson's plantation stayed on while the master was away in the army. When Union troops tried to entice slaves to run away from the King Ranch in South Texas they refused, choosing to remain loyal to their mistress. Kate Stone, who spent much of the war as a refugee in East Texas, noted that "the Negroes have behaved well, far better than anyone anticipated."[90]

The faithfulness of Texas slaves during the war may have been due in part to a sense of loyalty that many felt to individual families and in part because there was little opportunity to do otherwise. Texas escaped the disruptive effects of major enemy invasion which provided an opportunity to flee to Union lines. Although Galveston was occupied briefly, most slaveowners had already evacuated their slaves to the mainland. And the number of slaves in Union-occupied regions in South Texas was small. The comparative security of Texas caused dozens of planters in Louisiana, Arkansas, and Mississippi to "refugee" their slaves in Texas for the duration of the war. It is impossible to determine the exact number of such African-American refugees, but Randolph B. Campbell, who has to date written the most complete history of Texas slavery, conservatively estimated the number at 32,000.[91]

Campbell believed that Texas slaves did little to hinder the Confederate military effort or to contribute to Union success. He noted that there were no major rebellions during the war and that the number of runaways did not increase dramatically during the war. Of nearly 100,000 African-American soldiers recruited for the Union army in states of the Confederacy, only forty-seven came from Texas. Although some writers have suggested that slaves worked less efficiently and thus hurt the Confederate cause, Campbell found no evidence of reduced labor productivity in Civil War Texas.[92]

The most serious disruption of slave life in Civil War Texas came not from the Federal army or slave rebellion but from policies of the Confederate government. In March 1863, the Confederate Congress passed legislation authorizing military commanders to impress private propety, including slaves, for public service. Under this law slaves could be held for a maximum of sixty days and owners compensated at the rate of $15 per month. During the latter part of 1863, General Magruder, commanding the Texas district, made extensive use of this authority to impress slaves for building a stockade to enclose Federal prisoners of war near Tyler, in fortifying the Sabine Pass defenses including Fort Griffin, and in preparing defenses on the San Bernard River and Caney Creek on the middle Texas coast.[93]

While Magruder's actions were timely and necessary for the military defense of Texas, they were not popular with slaves or slaveowners. The slaves were needed at home, and their absence interfered with normal plantation routine. Also, the work they were required to perform in building fortifications was hard and oftentimes dangerous. Both slaves and planters complained that the impressed workers were not properly cared for while under military control, thus endangering valuable property. The money received from the government, raised to $30 per month in 1864, seemed inadequate to the owners. Complaints from Governor Murrah and other Texans led Kirby Smith to caution Magruder about the use of impressment in early 1864.[94]

Although the war caused disruptions in the lives of Texans, many social and cultural activities continued as before. John A. Edwards pointed out that most Texas families clung to their traditional forms of social activity during the war. Reading (especially newspapers), visiting and receiving neighbors, and celebrating holidays provided relief from the war. Christmas continued to be the holiday most enjoyed. Independence Day, the Fourth of July, had been a major holiday but was little observed during the war. Hunting and fishing remained the most common recreational pastimes for Texans. Theatrical performances, circuses, and horse racing, all popular in Texas before the war, were curtailed during the conflict. Musical concerts continued to be enjoyed, especially in areas where military regimental bands were stationed.[95]

Texas churches continued to play an important role in the religious, cultural, and social lives of Texans during the war. Various functions, such as Sunday services, camp meetings, and revivals, were carried on fairly much as usual, although associational meetings of some denominations, where men had provided the leadership, were limited. Many ministers served in the army during the conflict. Some, like Methodist minister and educator George W. Carter, president of Soule University at Chappell Hill, secured military commissions and commanded troops in the field. Others, like Henry Renfro, an ordained Baptist minister in Johnson County, became chaplains in the army. Renfro, who enlisted as a private in the Twenty-first Texas Infantry in May 1862, served for sixteen months as a regular soldier before he received his chaplain's appointment with the Fifteenth Texas Infantry in Louisiana. Renfro replaced Rufus Burleson, former president of Baylor University, who had been serving as chaplain of the Fifteenth Texas. Perhaps the best known Texas chaplains were Robert F. Bunting of Terry's Texas Rangers and Nicholas A. Davis of the Fourth Infantry Regiment, Hood's Texas Brigade. Both were Presbyterians who had settled in Texas after annexation, Bunting from Pennsylvania in 1851 and Davis from Alabama in 1857. Both were active not only in providing for the spiritual needs of the soldiers but also in seeking better food, clothing, and medical care for them. Bunting also served as a war correspondent for two Texas newspapers and operated a private courier service for Texas soldiers. Davis, who was concerned that the Texans were not receiving sufficient praise for their contributions to the war effort, published an account of the Fourth Infantry during the middle of the war: *The Campaign From Texas to Richmond* (Richmond and Houston, 1863). Both men were devoted to the Southern cause and convinced of the justice of the struggle for independence from Northern domination.[96]

Many churches assumed a major role in defending and supporting the Confederacy. Participation in special days of prayer called by President Davis, fund-raising drives to assist the war effort and families of servicemen, and sermons in support of the Confederacy were among the ways Texas churches contributed to the Southern cause.[97]

The war had a negative impact upon education in Texas. The number of students, teachers, and schools declined as adult males went off to war, children took on more duties at home leaving less time for school, and less money was available for tuition. Female education, limited in nineteeth-century Texas, continued without much difficulty. The number of female teachers increased during the war as women replaced male teachers serving in the army.[98]

Although Texas escaped most of the physical devastation caused by the war, the lives of all Texans were affected in one way or another. Texans supporting the Confederacy longed for victory and the return of husbands, fathers, and friends to their homes. Texas Unionists continued to hope for Northern victories and the restoration of the Federal Union. As 1863 came to a close, many Texans believed the end of the war was near and that 1864 would be a decisive year.[99]

CHAPTER FIVE

The End Draws Near: 1864

Many of the hopes for Southern independence that Texas Confederates held early in the war had disappeared by 1864. The defeats at Gettysburg, Vicksburg, and Chattanooga in 1863 had a sobering effect upon most Texans.

A prolonged drought that resulted in a poor harvest in 1863 was followed by an unusually cold and hard winter that brought freezing weather as far south as Brownsville. In late December more than a dozen Texans were killed and another dozen women and children were taken captive by the Comanches in a major Indian raid into Montague and Cooke counties in North Texas. At least ten homes were burned and many horses were taken by the Indians. State and Confederate authorities organized a pursuit, but the raiders recrossed the Red River before they could be overtaken.

The Union army held Brownsville and various points along the middle coast and was threatening Rio Grande City and Laredo. Union cavalry, including the Second Texas regiment (Union), was raiding ranches between the Nueces and Rio Grande.[1] Rumors were widespread that the Union army was preparing for a major invasion of the middle Texas coast. Rudolf Coreth, a young German Texan stationed on Caney Creek near the mouth of the Brazos, wrote to his parents that an attack was expected but he had little confidence that the Confederates would be successful in resisting it. Pvt.

Dunbar Affleck, attached to Magruder's staff at Bryan's plantation, was more optimistic. He reported to his parents that the enemy was shelling the Confederate works at the mouth of the Caney regularly but that everyone was ready and eager to fight. Confederate General Magruder gathered several thousand Confederate and state troops near the Brazos to meet the anticipated Federal attack. By early 1864 over 5,000 Confederates, including the Second Texas Infantry commanded by Col. Ashbel Smith, the First Texas Cavalry commanded by Col. Augustus Buchel, and the Third Texas Infantry commanded by Col. Philip Luckett, were camped along the lower Brazos and San Bernard rivers. Exchanges of artillery fire between the Confederates and the Union gunboats off the coast occurred regularly. Tensions mounted as a Union assault appeared imminent.[2]

Red River and Arkansas Campaigns, 1864.

Suddenly, the Union threat to the middle coast evaporated. Unknown to Magruder and the defenders, the Union high command shifted its main attention in the Trans Mississippi to a movement up the Red River of Louisiana toward northeast Texas. On March 10, 1864, Union forces evacuated Indianola and the Matagorda mainland, as most of the Federal troops were transferred to Louisiana. Union troops continued to hold Matagorda Island and Aransas Pass, but in early June withdrew from those areas as well.[3]

Meanwhile, General Magruder had ordered John S. Ford, who had been serving as superintendent of conscripts for Texas, to form an expeditionary force to drive Union troops from the lower Rio Grande Valley. Magruder was convinced Ford was the ideal man for the difficult assignment. Ford, a former Texas Ranger and Mexican War veteran, was highly respected in South Texas. He set about immediately to create a staff, recruit troops, and obtain supplies for what he called his "Cavalry of the West." This was no small task

John S. Ford — Colorful Texas Ranger, explorer, soldier, and political leader. Defeated Federal troops in last battle of Civil War at Palmito Ranch in South Texas.

— Lawrence T. Jones III Collection

given the scarcity of resources and the difficulty of moving troops across the barren country between the Nueces and the Rio Grande. In addition, there was confusion over Ford's rank and standing. Although he had orders from Magruder, the Confederate district commander for Texas, Ford held no commission in the Confederate army in spite of numerous petitions on his behalf by leading state officials. He had earlier held a state appointment as colonel, and in May 1864 Governor Murrah appointed him brigadier general of state troops.[4]

In mid-March, 1864, Ford and his cavalry left San Antonio heading for the mouth of the Rio Grande. While camped near the King Ranch, Ford received a report from Col. Santos Benavides describing an unsuccessful Federal attack on Laredo. The attack occurred on the afternoon of March 19. Approximately 200 Federals, attached to John L. Haynes' Second Texas Union cavalry, evaded Benavides' scouts by crossing into Mexico and then recrossing the Rio Grande within a few miles of Laredo. With only brief notice of the impending attack Benavides, who was seriously ill at the time, and seventy-two defenders beat off three Union assaults before darkness ended the fighting. During the night Benavides received reinforcements, causing the Federal attackers to withdraw before daylight. Although the Confederates had won the battle, Benavides feared another Union assault on the town.[5]

Ford continued his movement southward. Because of concerns for forage and water he took an indirect approach to Brownsville, swinging over to Laredo and then moving down the river. He reached Laredo on April 15 and one week later occupied Ringgold Barracks on the edge of Rio Grande City. After a delay of six weeks at Ringgold Barracks, caused by supply and administrative problems, the Cavalry of the West resumed its march toward Brownsville. In late June, Ford and several hundred men overwhelmed a Union picket outpost at Los Rucias defended by companies of the First Texas Union cavalry commanded by Capt. Philip G. Temple.[6]

With only 1,800 men, Ford moved cautiously toward Brownsville, which was occupied by more than 6,000 Federal troops. He learned in early July that Maj. Gen. Francis J. Herron, the Union commander at Fort Brown, had been ordered to withdraw most of his troops to Louisiana. A small force of 1,200 men was left behind to hold Brazos Island near the mouth of the Rio Grande. Accordingly, Ford waited until the Federals withdrew before attempting to

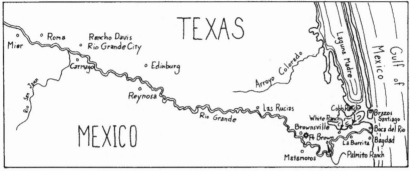

LOWER RIO GRANDE VALLEY in the CIVIL WAR

Brownsville and environs (Lower Rio Grande).

occupy Brownsville. On July 30, after Union forces had evacuated, Ford's troops rode into the town and raised the Confederate flag.[7]

The recapture of Brownsville and withdrawal of most Federal troops did not bring about immediate peace in South Texas. Ford's old antagonist, the Mexican Robin Hood-bandit Juan Cortina, now a general in the Mexican forces supporting Benito Juarez, was military governor of Tamaulipas, the Mexican state across from Brownsville. The United States consul at Matamoros, Leonard Pierce, urged Cortina to support the Federals against the Confederacy. Delighted to strike back at the Texans, Cortina suspended the cotton trade and moved artillery to the Rio Grande facing Texas. In early September 1864, Union troops on Brazos Island launched a surprise assault on Confederate outposts at Palmito Ranch while Cortina's artillery opened fire on the Confederates from across the Rio Grande. Although the Texans reeled from the attack at first, they fought back and repulsed the Federals with heavy losses. Among prisoners taken were Mexicans from Cortina's army who had crossed the river to support the Federal attack.[8]

Conditions along the lower Rio Grande stabilized after the September fighting. Cortina surrendered Matamoros to Mexican Imperialist and French forces in late September. Ford established cordial relations with Gen. Tomas Mejia, the Imperialist commander. The cotton trade was reopened and flourished. Although there were occasional skirmishes with the Federals still holding Brazos Island, there was relative calm in South Texas for the remainder of the year.[9]

As Union troops were withdrawn from the middle and south Texas coast in the spring and summer of 1864, attention shifted to the Red River of Louisiana. Henry W. Halleck, commanding general of the Union army until his replacement by U. S. Grant, had long been interested in a military movement into northern Louisiana and eastern Texas. He had urged such a campaign upon Nathaniel P. Banks in 1863, but Banks had chosen to attempt the invasion of Texas at Sabine Pass. That failing, Banks had sent troops to occupy Brownsville and points along the lower Texas coast. Although this latter move had satisfied President Lincoln's desire to establish a Federal presence in Texas, it had little real impact on the state's ability to carry on the war. Halleck continued to believe that northern Louisiana and eastern Texas should be Banks' major western military objective.[10]

Halleck felt that a campaign up the Red River would satisfy several purposes. First, occupation of northern Louisiana would give the Union control of the entire state. Second, numerous military warehouses, shops, factories, and administrative headquarters were located in the Shreveport-Marshall-Jefferson area. Their loss to the Confederacy would hurt Kirby Smith's efforts to continue the war in the Trans Mississippi. Finally, thousands of bales of cotton were stored in the region. The prospect of capturing this cotton, estimated at 150,000 bales, was a major factor in Banks' decision to accept Halleck's views regarding the Red River campaign. Acquisition of this cotton would enrich the Federal Treasury, relieve New England mill owners of their need for cotton, and deprive the Confederates of a commodity needed for the foreign arms trade.[11]

In late January 1864, Banks began serious preparations for the move up the Red River. Most of the Federal troops in Texas were recalled and ordered to join William B. Franklin's forces on the Bayou Teche. Naval support was assured when Rear Adm. David Porter agreed to provide transports and gunboats for the campaign.

William T. Sherman, who came to New Orleans to confer with Banks, agreed to send 10,000 of his veteran troops from Tennessee to participate in the initial move up the river to Shreveport. Frederick Steele, commanding Union forces in Arkansas, was ordered to move southward with 13,000 men in cooperation with Banks' movement.[12]

Kirby Smith, commanding the Confederate Trans Mississippi Department, and Richard Taylor, in charge of the western Louisiana district, took steps to meet the impending Union attack. Smith called upon General Magruder to rush cavalry reinforcements from Texas. Tom Green's veteran cavalry division, which had served in Louisiana under Taylor the previous autumn but was now foraging along the upper Sabine River, and a newly formed cavalry brigade commanded by Hamilton P. Bee were directed to join Taylor in Louisiana. Sterling Price, now commanding the Arkansas district, was instructed to send 5,000 Arkansas and Missouri troops to Shreveport while the remainder of his command opposed Steele's movement from Little Rock.

Meanwhile, Taylor himself began to concentrate his widely scattered troops north of Alexandria on the Red River. He had approximately 7,000 troops under his immediate command. These were organized into two divisions. The larger unit, consisting of three Texas infantry brigades, was Maj. Gen. John G. Walker's veteran division. The other division, commanded by Alfred Mouton, son of former Louisiana governor Alexander Mouton, was newly formed and consisted of two brigades, one made up of Louisianians commanded by Henry Gray and the other made up of Texas regiments commanded by a dapper French aristocrat, Camille Armand Jules Marie, Prince de Polignac. Polignac's Brigade, formed the previous autumn, consisted of the Fifteenth Texas Infantry, the Seventeenth Texas Consolidated Cavalry (dismounted), and the Twenty-second, Thirty-first, and Thirty-fourth Texas Cavalry (all dismounted). At first the Texans were suspicious of Polignac, a veteran of the Crimean War who offered his services to the Confederacy, but gradually came to admire his ability and referred to him affectionately as their "Polecat."[13]

Walker's Division was the first Confederate unit to encounter the Union forces as they attempted to move north. Heavily outnumbered, Walker fell back toward Fort DeRussy, a hastily built fortification on the Red River between Simmesport and Alexandria.

Mistakenly called by some "the Gibraltar on the Red River," the fort was incomplete when Union gunboats and infantry attacked. After brief skirmishing the small garrison surrendered the fort to superior Union forces on the afternoon of March 14 as Walker withdrew his division farther northward. On the next day lead vessels of the Union fleet reached Alexandria, which the Confederates evacuated.[14]

General Taylor, with Walker's and Mouton's divisions, continued to fall back while he awaited the arrival of Tom Green's Texas cavalry. In late March Taylor moved to Pleasant Hill, a small town north of Natchitoches about fifteen miles from the Red River. The Confederates had a small supply depot there where Taylor picked up arms for some of his men. From there he fell back to Mansfield, a crossroads town fifteen miles to the northwest of Pleasant Hill. At Mansfield he was joined by Green's cavalry and visited by his departmental commander, Edmund Kirby Smith. According to Taylor's account of the meeting, Smith suggested either concentrating Confederate forces at Shreveport or withdrawing into Texas. Taylor was opposed to both suggestions. He was embittered by the long retreat and favored fighting as soon as possible.[15]

On the afternoon of April 8, Taylor launched a full-scale attack on advanced elements of Banks' army three miles south of Mansfield along Sabine crossroads, a road leading west toward the Sabine River. In his move northward Banks made a number of errors. His troops were scattered along a twenty-mile stretch of road leading from Grand Ecore toward Pleasant Hill and Mansfield. Not familiar with the geography of northern Louisiana, Banks was moving his army along the stagecoach road from Grand Ecore, just north of Natchitoches, toward Shreveport, rather than taking a more direct route along the river. The road taken by Banks veered westward toward Mansfield and away from the Red River and the support of Porter's gunboats. Taylor, with 8,800 men in his immediate command, was determined to take advantage of Banks' error and strike a blow at the enemy before he could concentrate his entire army.[16]

In the Confederate attack Walker's Division was on the Confederate right. William R. Scurry's brigade was on the extreme right of the division, Thomas N. Waul's brigade to the left of Scurry, and Horace Randal's to the left of Waul. Alfred Mouton's Division was to the left of Walker's Division, with Gray's Louisiana Brigade next to Randal's Brigade and Polignac's Texas Brigade on the Confeder-

ate left. Hamilton Bee's cavalry, consisting of regiments commanded by Colonels Augustus Buchel and A. W. Terrell, was on the
extreme right side of the Confederate line just beyond Scurry's
Brigade. Xavier B. Debray's Twenty-sixth Texas Cavalry, also a part
of Bee's Brigade, was in front of Walker's Division astride the
Mansfield road. Tom Green's cavalry, consisting of brigades led by
Brig. Gen. James P. Major and Col. William P. Hardeman, was on
the Confederate extreme left beside Polignac's Brigade.[17]

The initial assault on the Union line was led by Mouton's Division at 4:00 P. M. on the afternoon of April 8. In the heavy fighting
that occurred as Mouton's Texans and Louisianians rushed across
the open field, General Mouton and several senior officers were
killed. Polignac took over command of the division, with Col. James
R. Taylor of the Seventeenth Texas taking command of the Texas
Brigade. Meanwhile, Walker's Division began its attack against the
left side of the Union line. After being repulsed several times,
Scurry's Brigade broke through the Union line. At the same time
Bee's and Green's cavalry were moving around Union forces on
both flanks. To avoid encirclement, the Union commander, Brig.

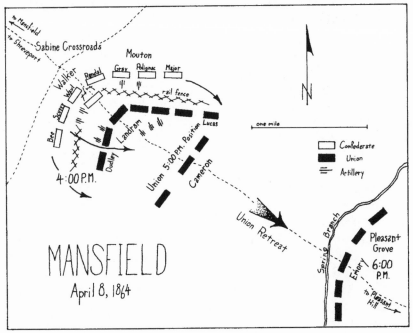

Mansfield

Gen. Thomas E. G. Ransom, ordered Federal troops to fall back to a second line of defense. Union reinforcements halted the Confederate advance for about an hour before the second line gave way. The Union forces broke and ran, with the yelling Confederates in pursuit through the woods. Darkness and the arrival of fresh Union troops stopped the Confederate advance in spirited fighting at a small orchard known as Pleasant Grove.[18]

The battle of Mansfield, or Sabine Cross Roads as the Federals called it, was a major Confederate victory. The Union advance toward Shreveport and Texas had been halted. The Union Thirteenth Corps was shattered, with 2,200 casualties out of about 12,000 engaged. Loss of materiel was particularly heavy: twenty pieces of artillery, over 150 wagons, and nearly 1,000 horses and mules. Taylor lost nearly 1,000 men out of 8,800 effectives. Two-thirds of these casualties were in Mouton's Division. Among those killed were Mouton, Col. James R. Taylor of the Seventeenth Texas (who assumed brigade command when Polignac succeeded Mouton), and Lt. Col. Sebron M. Noble, also of the Seventeenth Texas.[19]

Taylor was determined to resume the attack on Banks' army. He was convinced that Banks would retreat to the protection of Porter's gunboats on the river if given time. The troops of Sterling Price's army, commanded by Brig. Gen. Thomas J. Churchill, had reached Mansfield. Taylor planned to use them as the lead assault force against Banks' army.[20]

Banks withdrew his forces from Pleasant Grove during the night of April 8. Although he was personally inclined to give battle at Pleasant Grove the next day, he had been convinced by his senior officers that he should fall back to Pleasant Hill, fourteen miles away. Here he joined Maj. Gen. A. J. Smith and his veterans from Sherman's army.[21]

When Taylor learned of Banks' withdrawal he ordered his troops to give pursuit. He rode ahead with Green's cavalry, reaching the Pleasant Hill area at 9:00 A.M. Churchill and his Arkansas and Missouri divisions arrived at 1:00 P.M., followed by Walker's and Polignac's divisions. Taylor allowed his exhausted troops to rest before beginning the attack at 4:30 that afternoon. After an initial artillery barrage, Churchill's divisions drove back the Union forces on the south, or left, side of the Federal line. Walker's Division then made its attack to the north of Churchill's two divisions while Confederate cavalry charged from the extreme north, or Confederate left. Debray's troopers, leading the Confederate cavalry, were caught in a deadly flanking fire and suffered heavy casualties. Colonel Buchel pulled his regiment back to avoid a similar fate but was ordered by General Green to continue the attack. Dozens of men, including Buchel, were killed or mortally wounded in the futile charge.[22]

On the Confederate right, Churchill's two divisions overpowered the Union defenders and swept through the village of Pleasant Hill. As the Union left center was uncovered by the retreat of the Union left wing, Walker's and Polignac's divisions drove forward. At that moment it appeared that Taylor's army would triumph once again, but then A. J. Smith's veteran Federal regiments struck at Churchill on his right flank. In bitter fighting Churchill's troops gave ground. As they fell back, they left Walker's right flank, manned by Scurry's Brigade, unprotected. Only fierce fighting by Randal's and Waul's brigades stemmed the Federal onslaught. As darkness approached the Confederates slowly fell back. When some of Churchill's men fled in panic, Taylor ordered a general withdrawal to a point about six miles to the rear. The exhausted Federals made no attempt to pursue.[23]

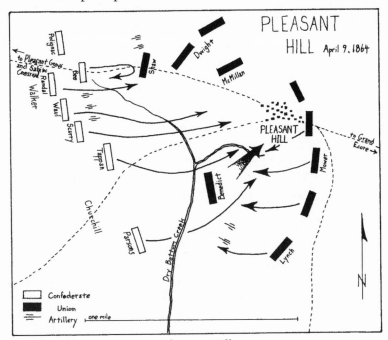

Pleasant Hill

The battle of Pleasant Hill was costly for both armies. In three hours of fighting Banks, with 12,200 men engaged, lost slightly over 1,000 killed and 495 captured. Taylor, with 12,500 men engaged, lost 1,200 killed and wounded. Confederate losses were especially heavy in Scurry's Brigade and Buchel's and Debray's cavalry.[24]

About 10:00 P.M. the night after the battle of Pleasant Hill, Taylor was visited by his departmental commander, Kirby Smith. Smith was worried about an attack by Banks, but stragglers from the battlefield reported that the Union army was withdrawing from Pleasant Hill and heading toward Grand Ecore on the Red River. Taylor favored an aggressive pursuit in strength but was overruled by Smith, who was more concerned about Frederick Steele's advance from Arkansas. In spite of Taylor's appeal that night and in subsequent conferences, Smith sent Churchill's and Walker's infantry divisions to Arkansas. Taylor was left with Polignac's battered division and Green's cavalry.[25]

Kirby Smith left Taylor to deal with Banks while he rode north to direct Confederate forces opposing Frederick Steele, who had advanced southward from Little Rock to Camden, Arkansas. In addition to Walker's and Churchill's divisions, Smith ordered Texan Samuel Bell Maxey, commanding Confederate forces in Indian Territory, to assist Sterling Price. Maxey, with two regiments of Tandy Walker's Indian Brigade and three regiments and an artillery battery of Richard Gano's Texas cavalry brigade commanded by Col. Charles DeMorse, joined Marmaduke's Missouri cavalry division near Washington, Arkansas, in mid-April. On the eighteenth the combined forces of Maxey and Marmaduke surprised Union troops protecting Steele's forage train at Poison Spring just west of Camden. The outnumbered Union defenders, half of them troops of the First Kansas Colored Infantry, were routed. The supply train of nearly 200 wagons was captured, along with 100 enemy prisoners and four guns.[26]

The loss at Poison Spring, followed by a similar Confederate capture of a Union supply train on April 25 at Mark's Mill between Camden and Pine Bluff to the north, convinced Steele to abandon Camden. On April 26 Union forces withdrew from the city with the Confederates, now under Kirby Smith's personal command, in pursuit. Heavy rain, deep mud, and lack of roads made movement difficult for both armies. The Confederate cavalry overtook the rear guard of Steele's army as it neared Jenkins' Ferry on the Saline River.

Steele's troops fought off the Confederate attackers while Federal engineers threw pontoon bridges across the flooded river. On a field of battle described as "a nightmare to both armies," Sterling Price's Missouri and Arkansas infantry made a series of disorganized attacks but were unable to stop the enemy's withdrawal. Kirby Smith then ordered Walker's Division to attack the Federal left flank. In the savage fighting that followed, all three of Walker's brigadiers were wounded, William Scurry and Horace Randal mortally. The Confederates suffered nearly 1,000 casualties but were unable to prevent the Federal withdrawal.[27]

Once across the river, Steele's troops destroyed their pontoon bridges and continued their weary retreat to Little Rock. The Confederates, having no pontoons, made no serious effort to pursue and fell back to Camden. Several days later Kirby Smith ordered General Walker to march his division back to Louisiana and report to General Taylor. Before Walker's "greyhounds" could reach the Red River, the campaign was over.[28]

Tom Green — Beloved Texas general who fought in New Mexico, Galveston, and Red River campaigns. Killed at Blair's Landing, April 12, 1864.
— Archives Division, Texas State Library

While the Confederates under Kirby Smith were forcing Steele's Union troops back to Little Rock, Richard Taylor and the Confederates left under his command attempted to prevent Banks' withdrawal down the Red River. On April 12 Texas cavalry regiments and a small artillery battery commanded by Tom Green opened fire on Porter's fleet at Blair's Landing, forty-five miles north of Grand Ecore. In a two-hour exchange of fire between Green's troops and the Union fleet, both sides suffered numerous casualties. Among the Confederate dead was Tom Green, hit by a cannon shell which tore away part of his skull, killing him instantly. As darkness fell the Confederates, now commanded by Brig. Gen. James Major, withdrew from the field.[29]

The death of Tom Green was a serious blow to the Confederates. A veteran of the Texas Revolution and the Mexican War, Green was much loved by his men, who referred to him affectionately as "Daddy" Green. A Texas infantryman noted that "[Green's] troops had unbounded confidence in him, and believed that whatever he did was right." General Taylor described Green's death as "a public calamity, and mourned as such by the people of Texas and Louisiana." At his funeral held in the state capitol, Governor Pendleton Murrah praised Green as the savior of Texas and compared his military victories to the battle of Tours in 732 A. D., in which Europe was saved from the Moors.[30]

After the fighting at Blair's Landing, Porter's fleet continued its movement down the Red River. Confederate troops harassed the Federal fleet from the shoreline with both rifle and artillery fire. At Grand Ecore, the powerful Federal ironclad *Eastport*, the pride of Porter's fleet, hit a Confederate torpedo and stalled in shallow water. Porter attempted to refloat the ship, but sharpshooters from Polignac's Fifteenth Texas Infantry drove off relief boats. To prevent her capture by the Confederates, Porter ordered the *Eastport* blown up. An encounter with the Thirty-fourth Texas Cavalry downriver resulted in the loss of two Federal transports and damage to several other vessels; however, by late April lead elements of the flotilla reached Alexandria.[31]

Banks' army, meanwhile, was marching southward in the open country between the Cane and Red rivers. Although outnumbered five to one, Taylor was determined to impede the Union withdrawal. He planned to attack Banks' army from all sides as it attempted to cross the Cane River at Monett's Ferry. He ordered Brig. Gen.

Hamilton P. Bee with 2,000 cavalry and four batteries of artillery to move downriver past Banks' larger and slower moving army and occupy a series of wooded bluffs on the south side of the Cane River commanding the crossing at Monett's Ferry. Taylor himself followed behind with Green's cavalry, now commanded by Texan John A. Wharton, who had recently arrived from Georgia. Polignac's infantry covered the flanks blocking Union escape on the right and the left.[32]

The vanguard of Banks' army reached Monett's Ferry on the morning of April 23. Seeing that Bee and his troops occupied a strong position, Brig. Gen. William H. Emory, the Federal commander, held his men out of range of Confederate artillery. A Union column led by Brig. Gen. Henry G. Birge crossed at a ford upriver and swung around to attack Bee's left flank held by Col. George W. Baylor and the Second Arizona Cavalry. In the heavy fighting which followed, the Union attackers on the left were repulsed. Federal artillery fire and the presence of massed Union infantry on the right, however, caused Bee to abandon his position. Thinking he was about to be outflanked, Bee ordered a retreat. Wharton's cavalry continued to attack the Federals vigorously from the rear, but with Bee out of the way there was little to stop the Union movement to Alexandria.[33]

Taylor blamed Bee for the escape of the Federal forces at Monett's Ferry. In May, Bee was relieved of his command and returned to Texas. He continued to believe that only by withdrawing had he saved his forces from being overrun by a much more powerful enemy. He sought vindication through a court of inquiry, but Kirby Smith, who generally supported him, believed such a court unnecessary and never called one. In December 1864, Bee was assigned command of a brigade in Indian Territory under his old friend Sam Maxey, but spent the rest of the war under a cloud of suspicion.[34]

When Banks' army reached Alexandria it found that Porter's fleet had been unable to cross the rapids near the town. Lack of rainfall had caused the river level to fall too low for the vessels to get across the rocks. Banks threw up a defensive ring around the city while the fleet waited for a rise in the river. One of Banks' engineers worked out a plan to free the fleet by damming the river and creating a chute of water to carry the ships over the rapids. This was slow, laborious work which took more than two weeks. During this time Taylor used his small army to attack the enemy wherever possible.

Wharton's cavalry skirmished with Union troops on all sides of Alexandria, while Polignac's infantry harassed Union troops along Bayou Boeuf, Bayou Robert, and Bayou des Glaize south of town.[35]

On May 13 Banks' fleet cleared the rapids at Alexandria and steamed southward toward the Mississippi. The Federal army moved out of Alexandria after setting fire to the town. Texas cavalry units commanded by Brigadier Generals James P. Major and Arthur P. Bagby harassed Union forces as they moved toward Simmesport. On May 16, General Taylor brought most of his forces together in an open field near the town of Mansura, just northwest of the Atchafalaya River, and temporarily blocked the Union withdrawal. After an artillery exchange for several hours, Taylor was forced to pull his troops back because of overwhelming enemy strength.[36]

The following day, Banks' army arrived at Simmesport and began crossing the Atchafalaya. Taylor's army continued harassing the Union rear in the hope of preventing all of the Federals from escaping. Brig. Gen. Joseph A. Mower, commanding the Union rear, turned his forces to strike back at the Confederates. In a heated battle fought along Yellow Bayou, both sides sustained heavy losses. John A. Wharton, commanding his cavalry and Poliganc's infantry, launched two separate assaults on the enemy in a desperate but unsuccessful bid to drive the Federals from the field. The Confederates sustained 608 casualties, many of them in Polignac's Texas Brigade. Losses were particularly heavy in the Fifteenth Texas Infantry and the Thirty-fourth Texas Cavalry. Union casualties at Yellow Bayou were estimated at 350 men.[37]

The battle of Yellow Bayou brought the Red River campaign to an end. While Mower held off the Confederates, Banks' troops crossed the Atchafalaya, using anchored transports and riverboats of Porter's fleet linked side by side as a bridge. By May 20 all of Banks' army had completed the crossing. Further pursuit by the Confederates was not undertaken. The Red River campaign was over.

Texans had played a prominent role in stopping Banks' army from occupying northern Louisiana and eastern Texas, but the price was high. Alwyn Barr estimated that 365 Texans, including the beloved Tom Green, were killed in the Red River campaign. An additional 1,677 Texans were wounded and 810 were missing, or a total of 2,852 Texas casualties for the campaign. Total Confederate losses were 4,300 men. An additional 2,300 Confederate casualties were sustained in the related Arkansas campaign. Union losses were slightly over 5,400 in Louisiana and 2,750 in Arkansas.[38]

Among the Union casualties in the Red River-Arkansas campaign were several thousand soldiers captured by the Confederates. Most of these prisoners of war were marched to Camp Ford, the Confederate prison compound about four miles northeast of Tyler, Texas. Established originally as a conscript training camp, the installation became a military prison in August 1863. At first Camp Ford housed only a few prisoners captured in the battle of Galveston and other coastal engagements. In November 1863, 450 Federal prisoners captured at Stirling's Plantation in Louisiana arrived. In late March 1864, the camp was enlarged to receive prisoners taken in Louisiana and Arkansas. The number confined increased rapidly, reaching slightly over 4,500 by the end of May 1864, making it the largest military prison in the Trans Mississippi.[39]

Life at Camp Ford was reasonably good until the arrival of the Louisiana-Arkansas prisoners in 1864 overtaxed the prison's facilities. From April 1864 until the beginning of a prisoner exchange in July, living conditions in the camp were poor due to lack of adequate shelter, food, and clothing. The situation eased as the prison population declined to less than 3,500 men by the autumn of 1864. Sickness, particularly scurvy, was common among the prisoners, but the death rate was held at a moderate level due to an abundance of pure spring water and good drainage. A total of 286 prisoners, or approximately five percent of those confined, died at Camp Ford. This compares favorably with the 15.5 percent death rate for all Federals held in Confederate prison camps and 12.1 percent for Confederates held in Union prison camps.[40]

Several hundred prisoners confined at Camp Ford were moved to Camp Groce, near Hempstead, in August 1864. Groce had been established in June 1863 to hold Federal soldiers and seamen captured along the Texas coast and in southern Louisiana. Life at Groce was similar to Camp Ford, although the death rate was slightly higher and living conditions a little more primitive.[41]

Although Banks' withdrawal down the Red River marked the end of major fighting in Louisiana in 1864, there were some smaller battles in which Texans participated. One such engagement took place at Calcasieu Pass in the southwestern corner of Louisiana. In late April two Union gunboats, the *Wave* and *Granite City*, entered the pass and put a small landing party ashore. The purpose of the expedition was to collect horses, cattle, and Unionist refugees in the area, but Confederate authorities in Texas feared a flanking movement against Sabine Pass. Lt. Col. William H. Griffin, commanding the Sabine Pass garrison, put together a mixed force of nearly 300 men, including infantry from Lt. Col. Ashley W. Spaight's battalion, a small troop of cavalry commanded by Lt. Col. Andrew Daly, and an artillery battery from Fayette County commanded by Capt. Edmund Creuzbaur. After a thirty-eight-mile march through the sand and mud of the coastal prairie, they launched a surprise attack on the Federal ships at dawn on May 6. In a spirited ninety-minute battle the Texans forced the surrender of the two Union gunboats. In addition to the boats the Texans captured fourteen cannon and 166 men. Texas losses included eight killed and fourteen wounded.[42]

Texans in Walker's and Polignac's infantry divisions continued to be active during the summer and autumn of 1864. In July both divisions were ordered to cross the Mississippi River under General Taylor's command and assist in the defense of Mobile. Such a move was unpopular with the Texans in the two divisions. The constant campaigning of the spring months, coupled with pay in arrears for nearly a year, poor rations, and lack of furloughs, resulted in low morale. In addition, the men of Walker's Division were unhappy with the appointment of Maj. Gen. John H. Forney, regarded as a martinet, to replace the popular Walker, who had been named district commander to succeed Richard Taylor, who was transferred to the Alabama, Mississippi, and East Louisiana district. As the two divisions approached the western bank of the Mississippi, hundreds of Texans deserted. The problem was so severe that Kirby Smith posted Wharton's cavalry along the Red River to intercept deserters heading for Texas. A full-scale mutiny was averted when Confederate authorities suspended the movement across the river.[43]

In late August 1864, Polignac's and Fortney's (formerly Walker's) infantry divisions and Wharton's cavalry were ordered to reinforce Gen. John B. Magruder, who had been appointed district commander for Arkansas.[44] A major cavalry raid into Missouri under the command of Sterling Price was being planned. The main purpose of the raid was to enlist Confederate recruits, seize weapons stored at St. Louis, and gather needed supplies. In addition Price hoped to occupy Jefferson City long enough to install a Confederate government. The Texas and Louisiana reinforcements were to be used by Magruder on the lower Arkansas River to keep Union general Frederick Steele from diverting troops to block Price's cavalry from achieving its Missouri objectives. By late September nearly 14,000 Confederate troops were concentrated between Camden and Monticello, Arkansas. At the same time Bee's Texas cavalry, now commanded by Arthur P. Bagby, joined Richard Gano's Texas Brigade under the divisional command of Sam Maxey in Indian Territory. These troops, along with the Indian brigades of Tandy Walker and Stand Watie, were to provide defense of the northern perimeter while Price was in Missouri and to protect Price's probable line of withdrawal from Missouri.[45]

In late September Sterling Price's cavalry left northeastern Arkansas heading into Missouri. With 12,000 Missouri and Arkansas troops organized into three cavalry divisions commanded by James F. Fagan, John Marmaduke, and Jo Shelby, Price's army moved slowly northward. The expedition was accompanied by Thomas C. Reynolds, the Confederate governor of Missouri who had been presiding over the Missouri government in exile in Marshall, Texas. Accompanying Price were the men of Maj. James H. Pratt's artillery battalion assigned to Marmaduke's Division. In addition to his own Texas battery, Pratt commanded one Arkansas and two Missouri batteries.[46]

Price's Missouri expedition did not achieve its objectives. Heavy enemy resistance prevented the Confederates from occupying either St. Louis or Jefferson City. Price's men rode across central Missouri, swung south along the Kansas-Missouri border, and retreated across Indian Territory, arriving in Bonham, Texas, in late November. Price claimed success for his expedition, pointing out that his army marched over 1,400 miles, fought forty-three battles, captured or paroled 3,000 Federals, and destroyed $10 million worth of property. But casualties were high. Price returned with a demoralized and bedraggled force of 6,000 men, half the number of troops who had ridden north with him.[47]

Pratt's artillery battalion, including the Texas battery commanded by Capt. H. C. Hynson, was actively engaged in many of the battles fought during Price's raid. On at least two occasions in the fighting along the Big and Little Blue rivers, Pratt's artillery checked Union advances that threatened to turn the Confederate flank. Pratt himself was seriously wounded in fighting along the Kansas-Missouri border on October 26 as his artillery covered the Confederate withdrawal.[48]

In his study of Trans Mississippi affairs in the Civil War, Robert L. Kerby pointed out that the suffering endured by Price's retreating army could have been relieved had the Confederate high command taken concerted action. He believed that if Magruder had used his infantry to make a feint toward Fayetteville or Fort Smith, pressure might have been eased on Price. Even a highly successful cavalry raid by Stand Watie's Indian troops and Richard Gano's Texas Brigade came too early to assist Price. In this raid the combined Indian and Texas troops swept through Union-held territory north of Fort Gibson, capturing supplies and destroying what they could not carry away. Their greatest success came at Cabin Creek on September 19, when they encountered a large Federal supply train. Encircling the enemy, the Confederates captured or destroyed more than 200 wagons, and captured or killed most of the 600 Union soldiers guarding the train. The raid was a brilliant success, but occurred a month too early to divert attention from Price's campaign.[49]

Price's retreat from Missouri marked the end of major activity along the Arkansas-Indian Territory front in 1864. The Indian and Texas troops under Sam Maxey went into winter quarters along the Red River in Indian Territory. Price's infantry and cavalry bivouacked in southern Arkansas, and both Polignac's and Forney's divisions returned to northern Louisiana. Wharton's Texas cavalry returned to East Texas, where the troopers would spend the remainder of the war.[50]

There was considerable unrest in the frontier counties of North Texas in 1864. Following the Cooke County raid of December 1863, Confederate and state authorities attempted to strengthen frontier defense but the transfer of Texas units to Louisiana and Arkansas in 1864 negated the efforts. In addition, the increased number of military deserters, evaders of conscription, jayhawkers, and other lawless elements made citizens of the region fearful of their safety. A suspected Unionist conspiracy in late spring resulted in the arrest of several suspects and the hanging of Capt. James M. Lackey, an officer in the First Frontier District who was involved in the plot, but rumors of other conspiracies continued to circulate. Col. James Bourland, commander of the Border Regiment, was particularly zealous in rounding up Unionists and deserters. Known as the "Hangman of Texas," Bourland was a tough-minded, strict disciplinarian who believed in quick action. Stories circulated throughout the region that his men frequently murdered suspected Unionists and deserters while holding them as prisoners. His superior, Brig. Gen. Henry E. McCulloch, was critical of Bourland's methods. In September he advised Bourland to concentrate on the Indian problem and leave internal security to others. A new rash of desertions in late autumn, however, caused McCulloch to modify his instructions and allow Bourland a free hand in dealing with the problem.[51]

Comanches and Kiowas took advantage of the weakened frontier defenses of Texas to stage a major raid in North Texas in October 1864. On the moonlit night of October 12, approximately 500–700 warriors crossed the Red River near present-day Burkburnett and rode southward into Young County. The Indians divided into several groups which attacked small ranches and farms along Elm Creek, a tributary of the Brazos River. Seven settlers and five Confederate troopers were killed, seven women and children were taken captive, and hundreds of horses and cattle were stolen. Several families took refuge in two small fortified stockades, Fort Bragg and Fort Murrah. There they and several troopers from a nearby garrison held out against repeated Indian attacks. Troops from Bourland's Border Regiment and Maj. William Quayle's Frontier District rode to the assistance of the besieged Texans but arrived after the Indians had withdrawn, taking their captives with them. Although the troopers gave pursuit, the Indians had too much of a head start to be overtaken.[52]

The Elm Creek raid caused great concern along the entire northwest Texas frontier. Citizens of counties along the upper Red and Brazos rivers feared and prepared for other attacks. The practice of "forting up," or drawing settlers and livestock into nearby fortified stockades or ranch houses, became common procedure for the remainder of the war.[53]

Confederate and state military authorities discussed ways to better insure the safety of the region. Plans were discussed for a preemptive strike upon Comanche and Kiowa camps in northwestern Indian Territory. James W. Throckmorton, who replaced the ailing William Quayle as commander of the First Frontier District in December, favored such a move; however, it was February 1865 before an expedition could be sent into Indian Territory. Bad weather and logistical problems cut short the campaign with little actually accomplished.[54]

While Texas Confederates in the Trans Mississippi were struggling with problems of invasion, Indian raids, and Unionist activity in 1864, other Texans were serving on distant fields far from home. Texans in Hood's old brigade spent a frustrating winter in 1863–64 chasing Federal cavalry and trying to stay warm in the bitter mountain cold of East Tennessee. They were not pleased when Jerome B. Robertson, the physician-soldier who had succeeded Hood as brigade commander in later 1862, was relieved of command. Robertson, a veteran soldier who had served in the army of the Texas Republic, incurred the displeasure of Brig. Gen. Micah Jenkins, who assumed command of the division after Hood was wounded at Chickamauga. Robertson disagreed with some of Jenkins' orders which he considered injurious to the welfare of his men. For this he was reprimanded and sent back to Texas. Most of the officers of the brigade sided with Robertson, who was highly regarded by his troops. Several of them signed petitions in Robertson's behalf but to no avail. Robertson returned to Texas, where he was given command of the Reserve Forces of the state. He was replaced as commander of the Texas Brigade by John Gregg, former colonel of the Seventh Texas Infantry who had been wounded while commanding a brigade at Chickamauga.[55]

In late March 1864, the Texas Brigade was ordered back to Virginia along with other units in Longstreet's corps. New issues of uniforms and shoes, along with additional food rations, improved morale in the brigade. John Gregg, the new commander, quickly won the respect if not the affection of the Texans under his command. A lawyer and judge in Freestone County before the war, Gregg was a rather stern and austere commander who held himself aloof from the troops. The division also had a new commander. Longstreet hoped to make Micah Jenkins the permanent commander of the division, but President Davis appointed Maj. Gen. Charles Field, a Kentuckian and West Point graduate, to the post. Like Gregg, Field was an experienced and highly competent officer, but also like Gregg was respected more than liked by the men in his command.[56]

In early May, Field's Division, including Gregg's Texas Brigade, was involved in the Wilderness campaign just to the west of the old battle site at Chancellorsville. U. S. Grant, now commanding all Union armies, attempted to move the Army of the Potomac through the heavily forested area as Joe Hooker had the previous May. Once again Robert E. Lee ordered an attack against his larger enemy. The corps of A. P. Hill and Richard Ewell were first engaged, with Longstreet's corps moving from the west to join the battle on May 6. The advanced elements of Longstreet's corps led by Gregg's Texans arrived on the scene as units of Hill's corps gave way and began to fall back under heavy enemy pressure.[57]

As General Gregg formed his brigade in line to enter the battle, General Lee arrived on the scene. Not familiar with Gregg, who had served in western armies, Lee inquired as to the identification of the brigade. When informed that it was the Texas Brigade, Lee expressed his pleasure and instructed Gregg to use cold steel in driving the enemy back. When Gregg gave the orders for the charge with the cry that "the eyes of General Lee are upon you," Lee waved his hat and exclaimed, "Texans always move them." As Lee's words were passed along the line, the Texans cheered and moved forward. Lee himself, apparently moved by the response, rode ahead to accompany Gregg's Brigade in the attack. When some of the men saw what was occurring they cried, "Lee to the rear," and "Lee, go back." According to some accounts one of the Texans seized the bridle of Lee's horse, Traveller, and with several staff officers escorted Lee to a safe spot where he could observe the attack.[58]

As Lee was taken to the rear, Gregg's Brigade moved across the field to engage Winfield Scott Hancock's Second Corps. The Third Arkansas, commanded by Col. Van H. Manning, was on the left, with the First Texas, led by Lt. Col. Frederick S. Bass on the right of the Arkansans. The Fourth Texas, commanded by Col. J. P. Bane, was to the right of the First Texas, while the Fifth Texas, commanded by Lt. Col. King Bryan, was to the right of the Fourth Texas. Two of the commanders, Bass and Bryan, were leading their regiments into battle for the first time.[59] The Arkansans and Texans swept across the open field and drove the enemy through the woods before heavy artillery fire forced them to fall back to regroup. After reforming and replacing ammunition, the Texas Brigade charged once again, stopping Hancock's corps as it attempted to move forward. After heavy fighting the Texans were relieved by other brigades from Field's Division. Hancock's advance was halted and some ground lost earlier by A. P. Hill's corps retaken in what historian Harold Simpson called "the [Texas] Brigade's finest hour."[60]

Casualties of the Texas Brigade in the Wilderness were high. Official lists for the brigade were either not reported or were lost, but various estimates placed the losses at between 450 and 550 out of the 700-800 engaged. Many men in the brigade suffered multiple wounds. One officer, Lt. Whit Randle of the Fifth Texas, was shot through the body five times and survived. Willis Watts, a soldier in the First Texas, was wounded three times. Watts also had been wounded three times at Chickamauga. Both Lieutenant Colonel Bryan of the Fifth Texas and Colonel Manning of the Third Arkansas were wounded, and Manning was also taken prisoner. General Gregg, the brigade commander, was not wounded but had three horses shot from under him in the morning attack.[61]

The success of the Texas Brigade in halting Hancock's corps shifted the initiative to the Confederates. Later that morning other brigades of Longstreet's corps rolled back the Union left flank. In the confusion of battle, Longstreet was wounded by his own men and the momentum of the attack was lost. That afternoon, Confederates on the other end of the line drove back the Union right flank. Instead of retreating, however, Grant swung the Union army around Lee's right and moved toward the crossroads town of Spotsylvania Court House.[62]

Lee quickly moved his army south to prevent the capture of Spotsylvania. Field's and Kershaw's divisions of Longstreet's corps, commanded by Dick Anderson while Longstreet was recuperating from his wound, were first on the scene at Spotsylvania and began entrenching in anticipation of the Federal attack. On May 10 the Federals launched several major assaults against the Texas Brigade. The first two charges were repulsed, but in the third attack the Federals broke the line held by the First Texas. Only after bloody hand-to-hand fighting was the enemy driven back.[63]

Fighting continued around Spotsylvania for nearly two weeks before Grant broke off and continued his sliding movement southward. In the vicinity of Cold Harbor, near the old battlefield at Gaines' Mill, both armies dug long lines of trenches supported by strong breastworks. Longstreet's corps was in the center of the Confederate line. On June 3 Grant launched a frontal assault against the Confederate center. The main Union attack was slightly to the right of Gregg's Texas Brigade, but the Texans poured heavy fire into the flank of the attacking Union troops. The brigade itself sustained few losses, but enemy casualties were extremely high.[64]

After the failure to break Lee's lines at Cold Harbor, Grant swung his army across the James River in an attempt to take Richmond from the south. Once again Lee moved his troops to meet

Grant. Both armies moved toward the town of Petersburg, twenty miles south of Richmond. The Texas Brigade crossed the James River on June 16 and two days later moved into trenches east of Petersburg and south of the Appomattox River. Here the brigade remained for five weeks, enduring heat, dust, and enemy fire. In late July the brigade moved back to a defense line north of the James and to the east of Richmond.[65]

The Texas Brigade spent the next nine months in the defense lines east of Richmond. During this time the brigade participated in six battles. Some were small affairs; others such as the battle of Darbytown Road on October 7 were larger engagements. In that battle the Texas Brigade was ordered to attack a strongly prepared enemy position. Unfortunately, the Texans were not properly supported by other brigades of Field's Division. Too, the enemy forces were equipped with repeating rifles which allowed them to put up a massive wall of fire. For once, the brigade failed to achieve its objective and was forced to fall back. Casualties, especially in the Fifth Texas, were high. General Gregg, by then regarded by Robert E. Lee as the best brigadier in the army, was among those killed. Col. Frederick Bass of the First Texas, who assumed command when Gregg fell, was also wounded in the battle.[66]

The fighting around Richmond in the autumn of 1864 reduced the brigade to less than 600 men present for duty. Colonel Bass, now commander of the Texans, proposed that the brigade be furloughed home to recruit additional troops, but this suggestion, similar to one earlier by Jerome Robertson, was not approved. There was fear that the brigade would be consolidated with another small brigade, but appeals from members of the brigade supported by General Lee convinced President Davis to allow the unit to remain a separate entity. The brigade would spend the winter of 1864–65 in the Richmond trenches awaiting the last campaign in the spring.[67]

Several thousand Texans were fighting in northern Georgia to prevent the Federal capture of Atlanta in the summer of 1864. The most prominent of these Texans was John Bell Hood, who had recovered sufficiently from the loss of his right leg at Chickamauga to resume his military duties. Now equipped with an artificial leg, Hood was promoted to the rank of lieutenant general and assigned command of a corps in the Army of Tennessee commanded by Gen. Joseph E. Johnston. Most of the men in the three divisions of Hood's corps were from Alabama, Georgia, Mississippi, Louisiana, and Tennessee. The only Texans serving in Hood's corps were the soldiers of Capt. James P. Douglas' Texas artillery battery. Recruited originally in the Dallas-Tyler area, the men of the Douglas battery were veterans who had seen action at Pea Ridge, Corinth, Richmond (Kentucky), Murfreesboro, Chickamauga, and Missionary Ridge.[68]

Several regiments of Texas infantry and cavalry served in Hardee's and Polk's corps of the Army of Tennessee. Five Texas regiments made up Granbury's Brigade in Cleburne's Division, Hardee's corps. This brigade, formerly commanded by James A. Deshler and briefly by James A. Smith, saw extensive action in the Tennessee campaign. Now led by Waco lawyer and county judge Hiram Granbury, the brigade continued to distinguish itself in northern Georgia. Granbury's Texans were in the battles at Resaca, Dug Gap, and New Hope Church as the Confederate army of Joe Johnston fell back under heavy enemy pressure. In the battle of Pickett's Mill, fought on May 27, the Texans prevented O. O. Howard's corps from turning the Confederate right flank. Later that evening in a rare night attack, Granbury led the brigade in a bayonet charge that resulted in the capture of nearly 300 enemy troops.[69]

The two armies continued to maneuver for position in northern Georgia. On June 27 at Kennesaw Mountain, Union general W. T. Sherman, apparently tired of the constant maneuvering and underestimating the strength of the Confederate defensive position, ordered a frontal assault against Johnston's army. Cheatham's and Cleburne's divisions of Hardee's corps and French's Division of Loring's (formerly Polk's) corps took the brunt of the Federal attack but drove the enemy back with heavy losses.[70]

Another brigade, two-thirds of whom were Texans, commanded by Matthew D. Ector, occupied the Confederate front line at Kennesaw Mountain. Like Granbury's Brigade, Ector's regiments (two North Carolina and four Texas) were veterans of Chickamauga and Missionary Ridge. They were serving in Leonidas Polk's army in Mississippi when ordered to northern Georgia. Although they were involved in fighting at Cassville and New Hope Church, their first major engagement in Georgia was at Kennesaw Mountain. In the battle Ector's Texans and North Carolinians, as part of Sam French's Division, helped hold the Confederate right flank against the enemy attack.[71]

Two brigades of Confederate cavalry taking part in the effort to

Matthew D. Ector — Rose from rank of private to brigadier general commanding brigade in Tennessee and Georgia campaigns. Leg amputated as result of wound received commanding brigade in battle of Atlanta.
— Archives Division, Texas State Library

stop Sherman's advance toward Atlanta were made up primarily of Texans. The first, an all-Texas brigade, was commanded by a twenty-six-year-old former Texas Ranger, Lawrence Sullivan ("Sul") Ross. Ross, previously commander of the brigade's Sixth Texas Cavalry, had distinguished himself in campaigning in Mississippi. He was appointed brigade commander in December 1863, replacing the generally ineffective John W. Whitfield, who returned to Texas. In addition to Ross' Sixth Cavalry, the brigade consisted of the Third, Ninth, and Twenty-seventh Texas Cavalry. After prolonged campaigning in the Yazoo River country in the winter of 1863–64, the brigade had been promised a furlough to Texas when it was ordered to join Johnston's army in northern Georgia. The brigade arrived in early May and during the next hundred days was involved in eighty-six battles. Most were small affairs, but in early July the brigade took part in major action along the Chattahoochee River, as the Confederates were forced to give ground to the stronger Union army.[72]

Wharton's cavalry brigade, half of whom were Texans, was also involved in fighting along the Chattahoochee. Made up of four regiments, the Third Arkansas, Fourth Tennessee, Eighth Texas and Eleventh Texas, this was a veteran unit that had served first under Nathan Bedford Forrest and then Joe Wheeler in the Tennessee and Kentucky campaigns of 1862 and 1863. The Eighth Texas, better known as Terry's Texas Rangers, had been with the Army of Tennessee since the late fall of 1861. John A. Wharton, a wealthy Brazoria County lawyer and planter, became commander of the Rangers following the deaths of Benjamin Terry and Tom Lubbock early in the war. When Wharton was promoted to brigade commander in 1862, Tom Harrison, a Waco lawyer, became regimental commander. When Wharton was transferred to the Trans Mississippi Department in early 1864, Harrison became brigade commander and Gustave Cooke, a lawyer and former judge from Fort Bend County, succeeded Harrison as commander of the Rangers.[73]

Terry's Rangers had established a reputation for boldness and daring before the northern Georgia campaign. Noted for their fearlessness in the attack, the Rangers preferred the six-shooter and the double-barreled shotgun to the saber. In his report of the Georgia campaign, General Wheeler cited the Eighth Texas for brilliant cavalry charges at Dug Gap and Varnell's Station. At Cass' Station the Rangers and two other Confederate cavalry regiments routed the enemy and took nearly 100 prisoners.[74]

The Eleventh Texas Cavalry, the other Texas regiment in Harrison's (formerly Wharton's) Brigade, was not as well known as Terry's Rangers, but was nevertheless a fine military unit. According to Harold B. Simpson, the Eleventh Texas "never received the acclaim due it." Recruited in North Texas in 1861 by Col. William Cocke Young, the Eleventh served in Indian Territory and Arkansas during 1861–62. Young resigned his commission in April 1862 due to ill health and returned to Cooke County. He was a moderating influence in the turmoil surrounding Unionist activities leading to the great hanging at Gainesville. While searching for renegades who were terrorizing the countryside he was murdered by a hidden assassin on October 16, 1862. The Eleventh Cavalry was transferred to Wheeler's cavalry brigade in Tennessee that autumn and under the command of Col. John C. Burks played an active part in the battle of Murfreesboro, or Stone's River. Burks was mortally wounded while leading an attack in that battle and command passed to Joseph M.

Bounds. Bounds led the regiment at Chickamauga, but was murdered by one of his own men during the siege of Chattanooga. George R. Reeves, former county sheriff and state representative from Grayson County, assumed command of the regiment following Bounds' death. Under his leadership the Eleventh Texas fought alongside Terry's Rangers in the campaigns in northern Georgia.[75]

In spite of the determined opposition by the Confederates, Sherman slowly pushed Johnston's army back toward Atlanta. On July 17 President Davis, exasperated by Johnston's refusal to communicate his plans for defending Atlanta, removed Johnston from command of the Army of Tennessee. In his place Davis appointed John Bell Hood. Southern reaction to Johnston's removal was generally unfavorable. Texas Confederate Senator Louis T. Wigfall, a confidant and champion of the deposed general, was highly critical of Davis' action. Most soldiers in Johnston's army were opposed to the move. Johnston, a mature, senior general in the Confederate army, was popular with his troops, who appreciated his careful, deliberate style of campaigning which emphasized maneuver and defense rather than aggressive attack. Hood, on the other hand, was young and inexperienced in army command. Although well liked and respected by members of his old Texas brigade, he was new to the Army of Tennessee. He was considered a bold and courageous fighter but was regarded by many as reckless.[76]

Most Texans in the Army of Tennessee were skeptical about Johnston's removal and Hood's appointment. Samuel T. Foster of Granbury's Brigade wrote in his diary that "Gen. Johnson [sic] has so endeared himself to his soldiers, that no man can take his place." Foster maintained that "Gen Joe Johnson [sic] has more military sense in one day than Hood ever did or ever will have." Samuel Alonzo Cooke in Granbury's Brigade declared the appointment of Hood "threw a damper on our army and most of us felt it was a death stroke to our entire army." Newton Keen, a private in Ross' Brigade, thought that as long as Johnston was in command things went well, but "when the army was put under hood [sic] all things went wrong." Another Texan, Capt. James P. Douglas, who commanded an artillery battery in Hood's corps, believed President Davis must have had good reasons for the change in command. "One thing certain," Douglas wrote his wife, "Gen'l Hood will fight the enemy, and I believe he can whip them."[77]

Douglas was correct in his assessment that Hood would fight.

Almost immediately upon assuming command, Hood ordered a major assault on the Federal army. Generals Hardee and A. P. Stewart, now commanding Polk's corps after Polk's death at Pine Mountain, were ordered to attack Union Gen. George Thomas' army as his troops crossed Peachtree Creek, five miles north of Atlanta. In the battle of Peachtree Creek fought on July 20, 1864, the Confederates lost more than 2,000 men in an uncoordinated and unsuccessful effort to halt the Union advance. Neither Ector's nor Granbury's brigades saw heavy action in the battle. Ector's Brigade held the extreme left flank of the Confederate line where the fighting was comparatively light, while Granbury's Brigade was part of the Confederate reserve on the right. On the following day, however, Granbury's Brigade, commanded temporarily again by Tennessean James A. Smith while Granbury was on sick leave, was under heavy enemy artillery fire near Bald Hill. Smith, a West Pointer and veteran of Shiloh, Murfreesboro, and Chickamauga, later reported that he had never before "witnessed such accurate and destructive cannonading." Seventeen of the eighteen men in a company of the Eighteenth Texas Cavalry were killed by one shell. Within a few minutes forty men were killed and more than 100 wounded by the artillery barrage. Once the shelling stopped the Union infantry advanced, pushing a Georgia cavalry brigade back and threatening the entire right flank of Cleburne's Division. Only a spirited counterattack by the Texans drove the enemy back and regained ground given up by the cavalry. The brigade lost forty-seven men killed, 120 wounded, and nineteen captured in the day's fighting.[78]

Hood did not give up with the failure at Peachtree Creek. He pulled his army back into the inner defenses around Atlanta with Stewart's Corps on the west, Hardee on the north and in the center, and Benjamin Cheatham's (formerly Hood's) corps on the east of the city. On July 22 he sent Hardee's corps on a sweeping move to the south that brought him around Cheatham for a flank attack on the Union right held by Maj. Gen. James McPherson. For several hours Hardee pounded away at the Union lines just east of Atlanta. In the bitter and often confused fighting General McPherson, commanding the Union Army of the Tennessee, was killed, probably by one of the men in Granbury's Brigade. Granbury's Brigade and Daniel Govan's Arkansas Brigade led the attack as the Union troops were forced to give ground. Enemy resistance stiffened, however, and first Govan's and then Granbury's Brigade was halted. General

Smith, commanding Granbury's Brigade, was wounded and many of the Texans in the Seventeenth-Eighteenth Consolidated regiment were captured in a Federal counterattack. Tennessee and Mississippi brigades took up the attack, but they, too, fell back under Union numerical superiority. Fighting continued until dusk but the Confederates failed to break the Union line. The battle of Atlanta came to an end with 5,500 Confederate and 4,000 Union casualties. Losses in Granbury's Brigade were nineteen killed, 107 wounded, 160 captured, and twenty-five missing, or a total of 311 casualties.[79]

Matthew Ector's Brigade of Texas and North Carolina infantry escaped heavy fighting in Hood's attacks at Peachtree Creek and Atlanta. As part of French's Division in Stewart's corps, Ector's men were stationed to the west of these battles and saw less action than Granbury's Texans. The brigade was involved in fighting in late July as the Union army swung to the west of Atlanta. On July 27 General Ector was wounded by a cannon ball, resulting in the amputation of his left leg above the knee. William H. Young of the Ninth Texas, the senior colonel in the brigade, assumed command and was later promoted to brigadier general.[80]

Texas cavalrymen in Harrison's and Ross' brigades saw limited fighting at Peachtree Creek and Atlanta. Harrison's Brigade, part of Wheeler's cavalry, was on the east side of Atlanta and was involved in some skirmishing on the Confederate right flank in the battle of Atlanta on July 22. Ross' Brigade, part of William H. "Red" Jackson's cavalry division, protected the left flank of the Confederate army west of Atlanta. Ross' troopers participated in the battle of Ezra Church on July 28, when Hood once again launched an attack on the Union army. Both Texas mounted brigades took part in cavalry operations south of Atlanta on July 29 as Jackson's and Wheeler's divisions were called upon to defend the railroad lines south of the city from attacks by Union cavalry. At Brown's Mill, near the town of Newnan, where the Confederates overtook Edward M. McCook's Union cavalry, hand-to-hand fighting occurred between Texas and Iowa troopers. General Ross himself was captured, but his men rescued him and drove the enemy fom the field. Soon the Confederates surrounded the embattled Union troopers. General McCook was able to slip through the Confederate lines but more than 500 of his men surrendered to the Confederates.[81]

At the same time McCook's men surrendered to the Texans, another Union cavalry commander, Gen. George Stoneman, surrendered himself and 700 troopers to Georgia cavalry near Macon, Georgia. The failure of the McCook and Stoneman raids convinced General Hood that the Union cavalry was not a threat to his supply lines. It also convinced him that he could send his own cavalry to destroy Sherman's railroad supply line. Accordingly, he ordered General Wheeler to take his entire cavalry corps consisting of 4,500 troopers, including the Eighth and Eleventh Texas Cavalry, on a massive raid into northern Georgia. Hood expected Wheeler to accomplish his mission in a few days and rejoin his army; it would be over a month before Wheeler returned.[82]

Wheeler's cavalry raid did little to stop Sherman's movement. Historian Richard McMurry believes that Hood's strategy was probably sound but failed due to Wheeler's ineptness and Sherman's careful planning, both in defending the railroad and in repairing damaged lines. Wheeler's raid resulted in some destruction but was not sufficient to interfere with Sherman's move around Atlanta.[83]

Wheeler's absence deprived Hood of several cavalry brigades at a critical moment and encouraged Sherman to launch another cavalry raid of his own. In mid-August Sherman sent Brig. Gen. Judson Kilpatrick with 4,700 cavalrymen, many armed with repeating Spencer carbines, on a raid to destroy the Macon and Western Railroad south of Atlanta. Sul Ross, with less than 400 troopers in his brigade, attempted to prevent Kilpatrick from taking Jonesboro on the Macon Railroad but was forced to withdraw before superior numbers. After destroying track and equipment at Jonesboro, Kilpatrick turned south to Lovejoy's Station, where he hoped to repeat the destruction. Ross' Brigade trailed behind while Confederate reinforcements were brought up from the south. Caught between Confederate infantry on one side and Ross' cavalry on the other, Kilpatrick ordered an assault on the Texans. In a rare saber charge, the Union cavalry swept across Ross' Brigade, capturing thirty Texans, killing two, and wounding twenty. The Third Texas Cavalry was hit the hardest, losing a regimental battle flag, three company commanders, four lieutenants, and sixteen enlisted men to the enemy.[84]

Although Kilpatrick escaped encirclement, he failed to cut the Confederate supply line. Sherman, growing impatient, decided to move his army south of Atlanta and destroy the railroads leading into the city. At first Hood believed Sherman was giving up the campaign for Atlanta, but when he determined the enemy's intent, he moved his army to meet him. In fighting near Jonesboro the

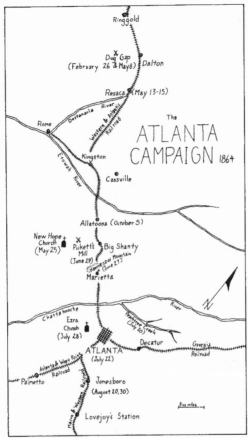

The Atlanta Campaign, 1864.

Texas infantry brigade, again commanded by Granbury as he had returned from sick leave, was on the front line. Union forces penetrated the Confederate defenses elsewhere, forcing General Hardee, commanding the Jonesboro sector, to order a withdrawal to Lovejoy's Station. On September 1, Hood, fearing encirclement, ordered withdrawal of Stewart's and Stephen D. Lee's (formerly Cheatham's) corps from Atlanta. On September 3 they joined Hardee at Lovejoy's Station. Sherman pulled back and moved into Atlanta.[85]

The battle for Atlanta was over. In mid-September Hood moved his army to the town of Palmetto, thirty miles southwest of Atlanta near the Chattahooche River. On September 25 he was visited by President Davis, who was accompanied by former Texas governor Francis R. Lubbock, now serving as his military aide. After some discussion, it was agreed that Hood should swing northwest to attack Sherman's railroad supply line in northern Georgia. In late September Hood moved his army to Lost Mountain near Marietta and began a series of attacks on the railroad leading into Atlanta. On October 5 Sam French's Division attacked the Union supply depot at Allatoona. In the attack on the Union position, Frances M. Cockrell's Missouri Brigade was on the Confederate right, Claudius W. Sears' Mississippi Brigade on the left, and Matthew Ector's brigade, commanded by Brig. Gen. William H. Young, in the center. In bitter fighting Ector's Brigade sustained heavy casualties in an unsuccessful assault on the Union position. General Young was wounded and captured by the enemy, and Col. John L. Camp, commanding the Fourteenth Texas Cavalry, was seriously wounded. Brigade losses were forty-three killed and 157 wounded.[86]

Although the attack at Allatoona failed, Hood continued to destroy rail track in northern Georgia. On October 8, Wheeler's cavalry, including the Eighth and Eleventh Texas regiments, rejoined Hood's army and took part in the process. Hood's plan seemed to be working as Sherman moved part of his army out of Atlanta to trail Hood. Additional rail track was destroyed near Tunnel Hill and Dalton, but Hood's corps commanders and division leaders believed they were not strong enough to defeat Sherman's army as it approached. Rather than take the defensive, Hood decided to take most of his army into northern Alabama, pick up supplies and reinforcements, and move northward against the major Union supply depot at Nashville. Such a move, Hood reasoned, would force Sherman to divert some troops to Tennessee and result in embarrassment to the enemy.[87]

Leaving Wheeler's cavalry behind to harass Sherman, Hood moved the rest of the army into northern Alabama. The move into Tennessee took much longer than Hood or his new departmental commander, Gen. Pierre Beauregard, anticipated. Extremely bad weather, Hood's poor health, and lack of proper planning delayed the advance into Tennessee. In late November Hood's army engaged Union forces commanded by Maj. Gen. John M. Schofield at Franklin, Tennessee, in a rash attack that proved to be a disaster for the Confederates. Schofield had slipped past Hood's army the previous night and formed a defensive line south of Franklin and the Harpeth River. The Confederates attacked with only part of their forces in place for the assault. A. P. Stewart's corps was on the Con-

Carter House — Franklin — Site of heaviest fighting in battle of Franklin. Granbury's Brigade made its attack between the Carter House and cotton gin.
— Forest View Historical Services

federate right and Ben Cheatham's corps on the left. Cleburne's Division of Cheatham's corps, which included Granbury's Texas Brigade, occupied the center of the Confederate line along the Columbia pike.

The initial Confederate assault drove the Federals back, but the Union center rallied and held. In bitter hand-to-hand fighting, described by Texas artillery captain James Douglas as "the bloodiest I have ever seen," the Confederates were forced back. General Cleburne, probably the best division commander in the Southern army, fell with a bullet through the heart. A few minutes earlier General Granbury, leading his Texans in the assault, was shot in the face and killed. In five hours of fighting the Confederates lost nearly 7,000 men, killed, wounded, and captured. In addition to Cleburne and Granbury, four other Confederate generals were killed and five others wounded. Union losses in the battle totaled slightly more than 2,000 men.[88]

Under cover of darkness that night Schofield withdrew his

troops to Nashville, where they joined the forces commanded by George H. Thomas. Hood had few options. His force of 25,000 men was too small to challenge Sherman in Georgia, so he moved on to Nashville. His only hope was that the army could take up strong positions near the city and wait for reinforcements from the Trans Mississippi.[89]

For nearly two weeks Hood's army camped outside Nashville in the bitter cold. Shortages of clothing, shoes, blankets, and shelter resulted in much suffering. A few reinforcements were brought up from Mississippi and Alabama but not in the numbers needed. On December 15, General Thomas' Union army struck. More than 60,000 troops, well equipped and ably led, hit the Confederates hard, first on the right flank held by Cheatham's corps and then in the main attack on the left flank held by Stewart's corps. In both instances Texans were heavily engaged. Granbury's Brigade, now reduced to 500 men and commanded by Capt. Edward T. Broughton of the Seventh Texas, was in the thick of fighting on Rains Hill, while Ector's Brigade, 700 men commanded by Col. David Coleman, occupied Shy's Hill on the left. For two days the Confederates held their thinly manned lines, but on the afternoon of December 16 they gave way. First Cheatham's and then Stewart's corps retreated in wild disarray. Only Stephen D. Lee's corps maintained some order as the army fled southward.[90]

As Hood's battered army made its way south, Confederate cavalry, including Ross' Brigade, carried on rear guard fighting against pursuing Federal cavalry. On Christmas Day the leading units of Hood's army reached the Tennessee River. As soon as a temporary bridge was constructed the army began crossing the river. The march continued on to Tupelo in northern Mississippi. Less than 19,000 men were present for duty on December 31. Granbury's Brigade had fewer than 350 men and Ector's Brigade had fewer than 575 effective for duty.[91]

For Texans in the Army of Tennessee, the year 1864 had been a bitter one. Hiram Granbury was dead, Matthew Ector had lost a leg, William H. Young was wounded again, captured, and sent to a northern prison, and John Bell Hood had destroyed his military reputation and the army under his command. Hundreds of Texans were killed, wounded, missing, or captured in the futile efforts to defend Atlanta and capture Nashville. Those Texans still with the army knew that the end of the war was near.

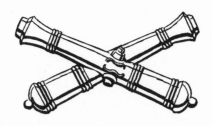

CHAPTER SIX

Defeat of the Confederacy

Nnews of the full extent of Hood's defeat in Tennessee gradually made its way to Texas. In early January, James Douglas, captain of the veteran artillery battery, in a letter which he cautioned not to be shown "out of our family," advised his wife that officers and men in the Army of Tennessee were demoralized by the disastrous Nashville campaign. "Unless something is done more than has yet been done, our great cause will fail," he warned. Carl Coerth, stationed at Camp San Augustine in East Texas, wrote to his parents on January 12 that he had heard that "Hood's Army is shot to pieces" and that Sherman had captured Savannah. Later that month O. C. Connor, a lieutenant in Walker's Division in Louisiana, admitted to his wife that he was depressed by the war news. "Evil forebodings" filled his mind, Connor wrote. He reported that troops in his unit had heard that Texas was preparing to secede from the Confederacy and form an alliance with France or Mexico. The following month he wrote that he was "low spirited" and had less hope for the success of the Confederacy than ever before.[1]

Rumors circulated freely in Texas and throughout the Confederacy in the winter of 1864–65. Amelia Barr, the future novelist who lived in Austin during the war, reported that at the first of the year there was "a great terror of negro insurrections," and that her husband, Robert, was often on guard most of the night. "Plots and

169

rumors of plots kept every one unhappy," she wrote in her autobiography. "It was a brave heart that kept any hope now for the Confederate cause."[2]

Along the Texas frontier, settlers were still "forted up" following the Elm Creek raid of the previous autumn. Fear over new Indian attacks led to an unfortunate and costly engagement with a band of migratory Kickapoos crossing Texas on their way to Mexico. The Indians were first reported in early December 1864 by Capt. N. W. Gillentine and scouts of the Second Frontier District. Although the Indians were unidentified, authorities feared a repeat of the Elm Creek raid. State militia of the Second Frontier District commanded by Capt. Silas Totten and Confederate troops of the Frontier Regiment commanded by Capt. Henry Fossett gave pursuit to the Indians. On January 7, 1865, scouts discovered the Indians, still unidentified, near Dove Creek, a tributary of the Middle Concho. Without further reconnaissance, Totten and Fossett decided to launch an attack on the morning of January 8. As planned, the militia would approach the camp from the north while Fossett's Confederates would swing southwest around the camp and attack from the west. The combined Texas forces numbered approximately 360 men. The exact number of Indians was undetermined, but was believed to be between 600 and 1,000 men, women, and children.[3]

Totten's militia opened the attack on the morning of the eighth. The Kickapoos, armed with Enfield rifles as well as bows and arrows, had taken a strong defensive position south of Dove Creek inside a dense brush thicket. When the Texans crossed the creek, the Indians opened fire with telling effect. After about an hour of fighting the state troops retreated with heavy losses.[4]

Just as the battered state forces were withdrawing from the battle site, the Confederates launched their attack from the west. Initially, the Confederates were successful. They drove off the Indians' herd of horses and began advancing on the camp. Here, too, the Indians' firepower was too great for the attackers. After several hours of fighting, Fossett's men attempted to disengage themselves from battle. As they did so they were caught in a murderous crossfire from Indians who had crept up the channels of the creek. The Confederates retreated northward in a state of panic and confusion. In late afternoon the Kickapoos rounded up their strayed horses and moved on toward Mexico.[5]

The Texans lost twenty-three men killed and nineteen wounded in the brave but foolish attack at Dove Creek. They estimated that at least 100 Indians were killed, but the Kickapoos reported their losses as only eleven killed and seven wounded. Stories circulated freely that the Indians tried several times to make the Texans aware of their peaceful intentions. Maj. George B. Erath, the veteran frontiersman who commanded the Second Frontier District, was away at the time of the Dove Creek affair. In his memoirs he criticized the failure to reconnoiter. He stated that had he been in command he would have allowed the Indians to pass on, "that is if I could have controlled the frontiersmen, always crazed at the sight of Indians and determined to kill." Texas historian William Pool perhaps best summarized the affair when he concluded "the Dove Creek expedition had traversed more than three hundred miles of the Texas frontier to catch a band of unknown Indians, after locating them, had been defeated in the unnecessary fight that followed."[6]

Elsewhere along the Texas frontier, state and Confederate troops continued to patrol against the possibility of new Indian incursions and to arrest army deserters. The last great roundup of deserters on the Texas frontier took place in the spring of 1865. A combined state and Confederate force of 134 men, commanded by Lt. Col. John R. Diamond of Bourland's regiment, captured nearly 100 deserters on the Little Wichita River in North Texas in early April. A similar foray into the area between the upper San Saba and Concho rivers led by Maj. John Henry Brown of the Third Frontier District resulted in the capture of thirty-two deserters.[7]

While Confederate and state forces guarded the northern and western frontiers of Texas in the closing months of the war, blockade runners continued to sail in and out of Galveston. Although the Union navy had more ships available for patrol duty than ever before, the volume of blockade running at Galveston increased during the last six months of the war. As other Confederate seaports were closed, ship captains risked capture in order to reap high profits in taking Texas cotton to Havana for transshipment to Europe. At least thirty-seven vessels, sixteen of which were steamships, were engaged in the Galveston trade during early 1865. The *Fox, Lark, Luna, Pelican, Zephine, and Denbigh* were the most successful blockade runners at Galveston in early 1865. The *Denbigh*, a small, iron-hulled sidewheeler built by Laird and Sons of Birkenhead, England, had a successful career as a blockade runner at Mobile before that port was closed to the Confederacy. In August 1864 she began voyages in and out of Galveston, carrying cotton to Havana and bringing small arms, ammunition, and other items to Galveston. Before she was burned by the Union navy after running aground on Bird Key Spit in May 1865, she had become the second most successful blockade runner in the Confederacy.[8]

Although the blockade runners brought out more than 10,000 bales of cotton in the closing months of the war, Galveston never reached the level of Wilmington, Charleston, or Mobile in volume of trade. Even so, the Texas blockade runners did help Confederate troops continue the struggle. Late in the war several thousand small arms, powder, cartridge paper, uniforms, and a battery of field artillery were brought in for the use of troops in Kirby Smith's department. The *Lark*, built by Laird and Sons in England, was the last steam blockade runner to clear a Confederate port, leaving Galveston for Havana on May 24, 1865.[9]

Farther down the Texas coast there was little military or naval action in the early months of 1865. Texas troops under John S. Ford attempted an assault on Union-held Brazos Island near the mouth of the Rio Grande in late November 1864, but unusually cold weather prevented more than a brief exchange of fire. In early March 1865, Union Maj. Gen. Lew Wallace, the future author of *Ben Hur* and governor of New Mexico Territory, arrived on the scene with a proposal concerning peace. Wallace met with Brig. Gen. James E. Slaughter, recently appointed commander of the Western Sub-district of Texas, and Colonel Ford under a flag of truce at Point Isabel on March 16. All parties agreed that further hostilities in South Texas would have little effect upon the outcome of the war. Although no formal agreement was signed, the three parties left the meeting with the feeling that fighting along the Rio Grande was over. Reports of the meeting were fowarded under seal of secrecy to Kirby Smith, commander of the Trans Mississippi Department. When they reached district headquarters at Houston they were opened by Maj. Gen. John Walker, then commanding the Texas district. Walker made the reports public and sent letters to Ford, Slaughter, and Wallace criticizing their actions. Walker made it clear that he did not approve of the agreement. Nevertheless, a virtual truce existed along the Rio Grande until the closing days of the war.[10]

Away from Texas, the war continued. In early January, John

Bell Hood, smarting from public criticism over the disastrous Tennessee campaign, asked to be relieved of command of the Army of Tennessee. Richard Taylor, departmental commander of Mississippi and Alabama, was initially selected to succeed Hood, but public pressure forced President Davis reluctantly to appoint Joseph E. Johnston to the post. Johnston's reappointment was pleasing to most Texans, particularly Senator Louis T. Wigfall, long a champion of the Virginian. On the floor of the Confederate Senate in early February, Wigfall called for Johnston's reappointment and criticized Davis for removing Johnston in the first place. Wigfall believed there was "a most remarkable magnimity of opinion amongst the people and the army that General Johnston should be restored." In his concluding remarks Wigfall, who was frequently interrupted by applause from fellow senators and spectators in the gallery, stated that in his opinion President Davis "had been an amalgum of malice and mediocrity."[11]

The army to which Joe Johnston returned was much smaller than it had been when he was removed from command in the summer of 1864. Even by pulling in scattered troops from the departments of South Carolina, Georgia, and Florida, Johnston had fewer than 25,000 men to oppose Sherman's army of over 60,000 as it advanced through the Carolinas. Three Texas regiments were still with the Army of Tennessee. What was left of Granbury's Texas Brigade was now the First Texas Consolidated Regiment. Commanded by Lt. Col. W. A. Ryan, the regiment was assigned to Govan's Brigade in Maj. Gen. John C. Brown's Division. The Eighth and Eleventh Texas Cavalry regiments were in the cavalry corps commanded by Lt. Gen. Wade Hampton. Two other Texas military units that had been part of the Army of Tennessee, Ector's Brigade and Ross' Brigade, were no longer with Johnston's army. Ector's Brigade, now commanded by Col. Julius A. Andrews, was assigned to the Mobile area, where it took part in the gallant but unsuccessful defense of Spanish Fort in March-April, 1865. Ross' Brigade was assigned to duty in central Mississippi, where it remained until the war's end.[12]

Texans in the Army of Tennessee were engaged in fighting in mid-March as Johnston attempted to block Sherman's army. On March 16 Hardee's corps fought a delaying action at Averasborough, North Carolina, which resulted in nearly 900 Confederate and 700 Union casualties before the Southerners were forced to give ground. Three days later the two armies fought a larger battle at

Bentonville. In this engagement Johnston, normally a cautious commander, launched a surprise attack on the left wing of Sherman's army that almost succeeded before Union reinforcements once again forced a Confederate retreat. In the closing stages of this battle an assault on the Confederate left by Joseph Mower's Union division nearly cut off the Confederates' escape route before the Eighth Texas Cavalry drove the Federals back in a spirited counterattack.

In the Texas charge sixteen-year-old Willie Hardee, only son of Gen. William Hardee, was mortally wounded. Young Hardee had joined the Texans only that morning, after overcoming his father's objections that he was too young for military service. In the same charge, William A. Fletcher of Beaumont, a veteran of Hood's Brigade now serving with Terry's Rangers, made an unsuccessful effort to capture an enemy squad by demanding that they surrender, "but two shots from the bunch made me think they were not a surrendering lot," Fletcher later wrote in his memoir *Rebel Private, Front and Rear*. In all, Johnston lost 2,606 men and Sherman 1,527 in what was the last major engagement in the Carolinas campaign.[13]

In the Confederate capital at Richmond, Congress continued to seek ways to carry on the war. A few congressmen talked of coming to terms with the enemy, but most Southern lawmakers, including the Texas delegation, supported continuation of the struggle. On January 19, A. M. Branch introduced resolutions in the House of Representatives passed by the Texas legislature stating that the Lone Star state did not want peace on any terms except independence. The resolutions declared that Texas would continue the war alone if necessary. Similar resolutions were presented in the Senate by Williamson Simpson Oldham later in the month. In early February, Oldham, who had opposed President Davis on many issues, wrote to the Confederate chief executive advocating the use of combustible materials to burn enemy vessels and to terrorize the Northern public.[14]

Senator Oldham, who had opposed conscription and similar measures as a violation of states' rights, was determined to carry on the war. On February 11 he and Representative Ethelbert Barksdale of Mississippi introduced bills in their respective houses for the recruitment of black troops. This controversial issue had been discussed both in and out of Congress for several months. Both President Davis and General Lee endorsed the plan, but numerous political leaders including Howell Cobb, R. M. T. Hunter, and Louis T. Wigfall denounced the concept. Oldham's bill called for raising 200,000 black troops, while Barksdale's measure left the number to the discretion of the president. Both bills left the question of freedom for military service to the individual states for action.[15]

As anticipated, the proposals to arm African Americans touched off spirited discussion. The issue was so sensitive that many of the legislative debates took place in executive session, much to the displeasure of Texas Senator Louis T. Wigfall. Wigfall favored the use of blacks for military labor but was totally opposed to arming or emancipating them. He believed the time had come "when it was to be settled whether this was a free Negro free country, or a free white man's free country." He stated that enlisting slaves as soldiers was the first step toward emancipation, which he opposed. Even the endorsement of his friend Joe Johnston for arming the slaves could not persuade Wigfall to support the measure.[16]

Wigfall's views were shared by the majority of Texans in Congress. In the final vote only John R. Baylor was among the forty representatives who voted for passage of the Barksdale bill. Texans A. M. Branch, Stephen Darden, Claiborne Herbert, and Franklin Sexton were among the thirty-seven House members opposing the bill. Oldham's version of the African-American soldier bill was rejected by the upper house, but in early March the Senate accepted an amended version of the Barksdale bill by a 9-8 vote, with Oldham supporting and Wigfall opposing the measure. The Confederate House accepted a Senate amendment, limiting to twenty-five the percentage of slaves who could be enrolled from any state, by a vote of 39–27. On this occasion Darden joined Baylor in supporting the measure. Branch, Herbert, and Sexton again voted in opposition.[17]

Passage of the bill to permit the arming of slaves came too late to have any practical effect on the outcome of the war. In late March, Lee made a last effort to prevent Grant's encirclement of Petersburg. On the night of March 24–25 he ordered John B. Gordon to make a bold attack on the enemy lines just east of Petersburg. Gordon captured a Federal strong point, Fort Stedman, but a Union counterattack forced him to fall back with heavy loss of life. On April 1 Union troops commanded by Phil Sheridan routed the Confederates at Five Forks to the west of Petersburg, sealing the doom of both Petersburg and Richmond. On the morning of April 2 Lee advised President Davis that he could no longer defend the Confederate capital. As Davis and the Confederate government evacuated the city, Lee ordered his men to pull out of the Petersburg and Richmond lines. He hoped to withdraw his army to the west and join forces with Johnston's army retreating north from the Carolinas.[18]

As Lee began his retreat, Field's Division, which included Hood's Texas Brigade, was ordered to withdraw from the Confederate line east of Richmond (which it had held since the autumn of 1864) and take a position along the Appomattox River near Petersburg. The Texas Brigade, now commanded by Col. Robert M. Powell, a lawyer and former state legislator from Montgomery County, was ordered to prevent the Federals from crossing the Appomattox River as the Confederate army pulled out of its lines. As the Confederates retreated westward the Texas Brigade formed the rear guard of Lee's army. For the next several days the Texans skirmished with the enemy as the Army of Northern Virginia retreated. The lack of adequate food was a major concern for the brigade and other Southern troops as they attempted to escape the enemy. Confusion and disorder abounded. Disabled artillery, overturned wagons, dead horses and mules, and scattered equipment marked the path of the retreating Confederates.[19]

Although they were hungry and exhausted, the veterans of the Texas Brigade continued to beat off probing attacks of the Union army. As they approached Appomattox Court House on April 8, the Texans learned that General Lee had opened negotiations with Grant for surrender of the army. When news of the surrender at Appomattox was confirmed, many Texans stood in disbelief. Some were angry and smashed their weapons against the rocks rather than surrender them to the enemy. Others accepted the decision as recognition of the hopeless situation they faced in confronting overwhelmingly superior enemy numbers.[20]

Formal surrender of the Texas Brigade and other units of the Army of Northern Virginia took place on Wednesday morning, April 12, 1865. Of the 5,300 men who had served in the three Texas and one Arkansas regiments that made up the brigade, only 617 were left to surrender on that day. The other 4,700 had been killed, died of disease or wounds, invalided home, discharged for being under or over age, or deserted. Some units were virtually decimated by the war. Company B of the First Texas had no survivors. Sgt. D. H. Hamilton of Company M of the First Texas reported that only six members of his old company remained on the day of surrender.[21]

One former Texan in Lee's army who did not surrender at Appomattox was Thomas Lafayette Rosser, a major general in the cavalry. Born in Virginia, Rosser spent most of the war commanding troops from the Old Dominion. As a result, Rosser is usually associated with Virginia rather than Texas. His family had moved to Panola County, Texas, in 1849, and he was appointed to West Point from Texas in 1856. He resigned from the United States Military Academy on April 22, 1861, two weeks before graduation, to accept a commission in the Confederate army. His advance in rank was steady as he saw action at First and Second Manassas, the Seven Days, Chancellorsville, and Gettysburg. He was promoted to brigadier general in September 1863, commanded a Virginia brigade in the Shenandoah campaigns of 1864, and was promoted to major general in November 1864. He commanded a cavalry division in Lee's army during the closing phases of the Petersburg campaign and the withdrawal toward Appomattox Court House. Rather than surrender at Appomattox, Rosser led his cavalry through Union lines. He hoped to carry on the struggle as part of Johnston's army but was captured in May 1865.[22]

Most of the men paroled at Appomattox were on their way back to Texas before Rosser was captured. General Grant ordered that all men paroled in Virginia be allowed to pass free on government transportation and military railroads. Some of the Texans made their way to Yorktown, Virginia, where they took water transportation to New Orleans or Galveston. A few, including Col. Robert Powell and Lt. Col. Clinton Winkler of the Fourth Texas, remained in Virginia temporarily to recuperate or take care of family matters before heading home. The majority of brigade members headed overland by the most direct route home. Most of the Arkansans took a route through Chattanooga, while the Texans traveled through the Carolinas, Georgia, and the Gulf states. More than 100 started out together under the leadership of Maj. William H. "Howdy" Martin, the gregarious executive officer of the Fourth Texas. Many of them, like Sgt. D. H. Hamilton of the First Texas, were "without rations and without a cent of money" as they headed home.[23]

As Major Martin and members of the Texas Brigade passed through North Carolina on their homeward journey, they joined veterans of the Army of Tennessee that surrendered to William T. Sherman in late April. They also met with fellow Texans John H.

Reagan, who served as postmaster general, former governor Francis R. Lubbock, and Col. William Preston Johnston as they accompanied President Davis on his flight from the Confederate capital. Davis hoped to reach Kirby Smith in the Trans Mississippi, where he could carry on the war. After a brief conversation, Martin and the paroled soldiers continued on their journey toward Texas. Davis and his party moved on through the Carolinas, conferring with various Confederate officials along the way. On May 10, 1865, the Davis party was captured by Union cavalry near Irwinsville, Georgia. Davis was subsequently imprisoned at Fortress Monroe, Virginia. Reagan was moved to Fort Warren in Boston harbor, and Lubbock and Johnston were confined in Fort Delaware on the Delaware River. Several months later the Texans were released from prison, but Davis was not freed until two years later.[24]

The Texans in Hood's Brigade and the Army of Tennessee slowly made their way across Alabama. The men with "Howdy" Martin took a boat from Montgomery down the Alabama River to Mobile and from there on to New Orleans and Texas, arriving at Galveston in early June. William Fletcher, formerly with Hood's Brigade but more recently with Terry's Rangers, made his way overland with a small group through Alabama and Mississippi to Alexandria, Louisiana. He stopped at his sister's house in central Louisiana for a month's visit before proceeding on home to Beaumont. Capt. Samuel T. Foster and other members of Granbury's Brigade made their way on foot from Greensboro, North Carolina, to eastern Tennessee, where they took the train to Nashville. From Nashville they traveled by steamboat down the Cumberland, Ohio, and Mississippi to New Orleans and from there by boat on to Galveston. For Captain Foster the trip home was a time for soul searching and thoughtful reflection. In eastern Tennessee he encountered black schoolchildren taught by Northern instructors. "I was never more surprised in my life," he wrote. "The idea was new to me." The more he thought of it, however, the more he approved and concluded, naively perhaps, "that color will not be so much in the future as knowledge."[25]

Williamson Oldham, the veteran Confederate senator, was another Texan who made his way home during April and May of 1865. Oldham left the Confederate capital by train after the close of Congress in late March, but did not arrive in Texas until early June. In the course of his journey Oldham witnessed the collapse of civil and military authority as various commands surrendered. He was forced to abandon the train in Alabama due to Union military operations but continued his odyssey by a combination of wagon, mule, and foot.[26]

Senator Oldham and returning soldiers found conditions in Texas chaotic in the late spring of 1865. Commodity prices were soaring, paper currency was virtually worthless, and rumors of all types circulated freely. Many soldiers stationed in the Trans Mississippi had not been paid for months, and discipline had deteriorated even in units noted for their valor. Desertion rates were high and lawlessness prevailed in many areas. Tempers often flared over the slightest provocation, real or imagined. A week before Lee's surrender an altercation between Maj. Gen. John A. Wharton and Col. George W. Baylor resulted in Wharton's death at Magruder's headquarters in Houston.[27]

The initial reaction of Texans to the news of Lee's surrender was one of disbelief followed by expressed determination by military and political leaders to fight on. Kirby Smith, commanding the Trans Mississippi Department, and John Bankhead Magruder, once again in command in the Texas district, both issued stirring appeals to their troops to stand firm and resist the enemy. Governor Murrah called upon the people of Texas to carry on the struggle. Col. Ashbel Smith, commanding the Galveston defenses, urged his soldiers to be of good cheer and not lose hope. George Lee Robertson, a Texas soldier in South Texas, vowed to continue fighting. "If I can't have a confederacy I don't want anything else," he wrote. W. W. Heartsill, stationed at Camp Waverly north of Houston, was convinced that the Trans Mississippi could hold out indefinitely if the people would truly unite. And E. H. Cushing, editor of the *Houston Daily Telegraph*, urged that Texans resort to guerrilla warfare if necessary to carry on the struggle.[28]

Determination to continue fighting soon began to evaporate. By the second week of May, Texans learned that Richard Taylor had surrendered his forces to Union General E. R. S. Canby at Citronelle, Alabama, on May 4. Many Texas soldiers were now convinced that the war was over and that it would be foolish to fight on. More and more troops began to leave their units in Texas and head home, some plundering public and private stores on their way. On May 8, Col. John T. Sprague, chief of staff for Union Gen. John Pope, commanding the Federal district of Missouri, was passed through Confederate lines to confer with Kirby Smith at Shreveport. He brought a letter from Pope stating that he had been authorized by General Grant to offer surrender terms to Smith similar to those accepted by General Lee at Appomattox. Smith called a conference of Trans Mississippi governors to meet at Marshall to discuss the Pope proposal. At this conference attended by Governors Henry W. Allen of Louisiana, Harris Flanagin of Arkansas, Thomas C. Reynolds of Missouri, and Col. Guy M. Bryan (representing Texas Governor Murrah, who was ill), the state executives drafted a set of proposals for peace without formal surrender. Adopted on May 13, these proposals provided that the army would disband without parole, United States citizenship would be restored to officers and men, state governments would continue to function until state conventions established new governments, and states would retain sufficient troops under arms to keep order.[29]

The resolutions drafted by the Trans Mississippi governors were unrealistic under the existing military conditions. Colonel Sprague explained that neither he nor General Pope could approve a political settlement along the lines requested. On May 15 Sprague returned to St. Louis, where he explained the failure of his mission to General Pope.[30]

On the day the governors adopted their resolutions, the last battle of the Civil War was being fought at Palmito Ranch in South Texas. For two months there had been an unwritten truce between Texas and Federal troops in the area. In early May a newly arrived and politically ambitious Union officer, Col. Theodore H. Barrett, commanding the Sixty-second Colored Infantry on Brazos Island, decided to attack the Texas mainland. On the night of May 11, approximately 800 Federal troops from the Sixty-second Infantry, the Thirty-fourth Indiana, and the Second Texas Cavalry (Union) crossed the Boca Chica pass over to the mainland in a blinding rainstorm. The next day they skirmished with Confederates commanded by Capt. W. N. Robinson near Palmito Ranch. On the afternoon of May 13 the Union troops made an assault on the Confederate line just as Colonel Ford arrived from Brownsville with 300 horsemen and a small artillery battery. After beating back two Federal attacks, the Texans launched a counterattack. The Union troops gave ground and fell back in disorder toward the Boca Chica. As dusk fell Colonel Ford called off the pursuit. His superior, General Slaughter, arrived on the scene just at that moment. Slaugh-

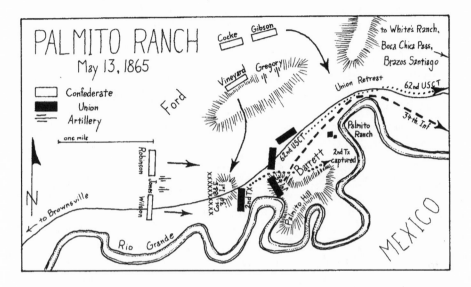

Palmito Ranch, May 1865.

ter ordered the attack to continue, but Ford insisted that his men were too tired to fight on. Union losses in the battle were between twenty-five and thirty killed and wounded and 113 taken prisoner. Although Ford reported only five men wounded, the number of Texans killed and wounded was probably about the same as the Federals.[31]

The Texas victory at Palmito Ranch ended the fighting in the Civil War. After the battle Ford learned from captured Union soldiers that Lee had surrendered at Appomattox Court House a month earlier. A few days later several Union officers rode into Brownsville to confer with General Slaughter and Colonel Ford. After some discussion Slaughter and Ford agreed that further resistance was futile. Ford released his cavalry, and he and his wife went to Matamoros. Slaughter rode up the river to Eagle Pass and from there eventually on into Mexico.[32]

Confederate military authority in the rest of Texas evaporated quickly. On the night of May 14, about 400 troops in Galveston attempted to desert but were persuaded by Col. Ashbel Smith to remain at their posts a while longer. Two days later General Magruder informed Kirby Smith that troops elsewhere were becoming unmanageable. In response Smith issued orders for the evacuation of Galveston and the concentration of troops at Houston, where he intended to make his new headquarters. Before he arrived in Houston, however, rioting occurred in Galveston and Houston as soldiers, whose pay was in arrears for over a year, broke into government buildings and warehouses to obtain supplies. Rioting spread to other towns, including Austin, San Antonio, Gonzales, La Grange, and Henderson.[33]

Meanwhile, Smith and Governor Murrah attempted to obtain favorable terms of surrender. Before he departed from Shreveport to Houston, Smith sent his deputy, Gen. Simon B. Buckner, to New Orleans to confer with Union Gen. E. R. S. Canby concerning surrender terms. Several days later Governor Murrah appointed Ashbel Smith and William Pitt Ballinger as special commissioners to meet with Canby to discuss terms. Canby received both Buckner and the Texas delegation but refused to discuss any political questions with them. He and Buckner did agree to a military convention providing for the surrender of all Confederate troops who would be paroled and allowed to return home. Under the convention all Confederate property would be turned over to officers of the United States government. The convention would take effect upon signature by Kirby Smith.[34]

When Kirby Smith arrived in Houston on May 27, he found that he had no army to command. Robert L. Kerby, who has chronicled the history of the Trans Mississippi Department, stated that Smith's reaction was a "mixture of bureaucratic habit, public concern, and personal justification." As a good bureaucrat Smith issued a special order convening a court of inquiry charged with investigating the causes for the disbandment of the army in Texas. On May 30 he wrote to Governor Murrah urging him to use state forces to maintain order and protect property. The same day he issued a final address to his soldiers in which he justified his actions and admonished them for disbanding, a step which he described as "unwise & unpatriotic." Then, on June 2, accompanied by General Magruder, Smith boarded the Union steamer *Fort Jackson* in Galveston harbor and signed the military convention negotiated by Generals Canby and Buckner.[35]

With Smith's surrender at Galveston, the Civil War ended. Two weeks later Union troops began to occupy the state, which marked the beginning of unsettled conditions in Texas. Looting of government stores continued and lawlessness prevailed in some areas. Rumors abounded that the Federal government intended to punish military and political leaders for their part in the war. Military trials and confiscation of property were expected. Many prominent Confederates decided to leave the state and seek refuge in Mexico.

In early June, Gen. Jo Shelby of Missouri led several hundred cavalrymen across the state on their way to Mexico. Joining the exodus were Governor Murrah, former Texas Governor Edward Clark, former Louisiana Governor Thomas O. Moore, Louisiana Governor Henry W. Allen, Missouri Governor Thomas C. Reynolds, and Generals Kirby Smith, John Magruder, Sterling Price, Cadmus Wilcox, and Alexander W. Terrell. In Mexico they joined Col. O. M. Roberts and Generals Hamilton P. Bee, James Slaughter, and Thomas Hindman. Eventually, more than 2,000 former Confederates located in Mexico, many in colonies of Southerners such as Carlota, seventy miles west of Vera Cruz, and Tuxpan, midway between San Luis Potosi and Tampico. Others, such as Frank McMullan and more than 100 emigrants mainly from Central Texas, migrated to Brazil and other Latin American countries.[36]

Meanwhile, the Union government proceeded with military occupation of Texas. Maj. Gen. Philip H. Sheridan was assigned to command the Military Division of the Southwest with headquarters at New Orleans. On June 10 he ordered Bvt. Maj. Gen. Gordon Granger and 1,800 men to Galveston as the advance party of Federal troops assigned to Texas. Granger arrived at Galveston on June 19 and assumed command of all Union forces in the state. He immediately issued orders declaring that the Emancipation Proclamation was in effect and that all slaves in Texas were free. He stated that all actions of the governor and legislature since secession were illegal, all offices and men of the Confederate army were paroled, and that all public property was to be turned over to officers of the United States.[37]

Two days before Granger arrived in Texas, President Andrew Johnson appointed Texas Unionist Andrew Jackson Hamilton provisional governor. Hamilton landed at Galveston on July 22. After a stopover in Houston, where he was honored by leading citizens at a banquet, Hamilton traveled on to the state capital, arriving on August 2. In speeches both at Houston and Austin, Hamilton criticized those who had supported secession and reaffirmed that slavery was ended. In a "Proclamation to the People of Texas," he declared all acts of the legislature passed during the war illegal and called for a new state constitution drafted by citizens loyal to the Union. The Civil War was over. Ahead lay the long months of Reconstruction.[38]

CHAPTER SEVEN
Aftermath

Many of the Texans who served in the Confederate army did not survive the war. Determining the exact number of casualties is probably impossible. In his highly acclaimed Pulitizer Prize-winning *Battle Cry of Freedom* (Oxford University Press, 1988), James M. McPherson pointed out that this is particularly true for the Confederacy, as many records were lost or destroyed. McPherson estimated that between 850,000 and 900,000 men served in the Confederate military and that approximately 260,000, or roughly twenty-eight percent, were killed, mortally wounded, or died from disease. If that percentage is applied to the number of Texans who served, slightly over 24,000 Texans lost their lives in Confederate or state military service during the war. Probably two-thirds of this number died from disease, as it is generally believed that twice as many Civil War soldiers died from disease as were killed or mortally wounded on the field of battle.[1]

Some of the better known Texans in Confederate service were killed or mortally wounded in combat: Ben McCulloch at Pea Ridge, Albert Sidney Johnston at Shiloh, Benjamin F. Terry at Woodsonville, Hiram Granbury at Franklin, Tom Green at Blair's Landing, John Gregg near Richmond, William P. Rogers at Corinth, John Marshall at Gaines' Mill, Augustus Buchel at Pleasant Hill, and William R. Scurry and Horace Randal at Jenkins' Ferry. John A. Wharton, the highly capable, young cavalry general, was killed by a fellow Texan, George W. Baylor, in an altercation at General Magruder's headquarters in Houston. Col. William Cocke Young, organizer and commander of the Eleventh Texas Cavalry, was killed by a hidden assassin in North Texas. His successor, Col. John C. Burks, was mortally wounded at Murfreesboro. Col. Joseph Bounds, who followed Burks as regimental commander, was murdered by one of his own men.

Several other prominent Texans died from disease while serving in the army. Among these were Col. Hugh McLeod, who died near Dumfries, Virginia, on January 3, 1862; Col. Tom Lubbock, who succeeded Benjamin Terry as commander of the Eighth Cavalry and died a month later; and Brig. Gen. Joseph L. Hogg, who died from dysentery near Corinth, Mississippi, in May 1862.[2] Practically all the Confederates were ill at one time or another during the war, with measles, mumps, malaria, diarrhea, pneumonia, colds, and bronchitis the most common ailments.

Twice as many Texans were wounded as died during the war. Some of these suffered serious injuries, such as John Bell Hood, who lost the use of an arm at Gettysburg and a leg at Chickamauga, William Hugh Young, who was wounded six times, and Matthew D. Ector, who lost a leg at Atlanta. For many others the wounds were less severe.

Many of the Texans who held leadership positions in the Confederate or state government or in the military recovered from the war to help rebuild Texas in the last third of the nineteenth century. John H. Reagan, former postmaster general of the Confederacy, was active in both state and national affairs after the war. In 1865, while a prisoner at Fort Warren in Boston harbor, he wrote a letter to President Andrew Johnson urging a lenient Reconstruction policy. He followed this with an open letter to the people of Texas, advising them to recognize Federal authority, renounce secession and slavery, and extend suffrage to former slaves who met educational and property requirements. Although this second Fort Warren letter alienated some former Confederates, Reagan believed that reason and necessity required an acceptance of the political reality that existed.[3]

Upon his return to Texas after release from prison, Reagan resumed a role in political affairs. He was a delegate to the constitutional convention of 1875 and was elected to Congress later that year. He served in the House of Representatives until he was chosen for the Senate in 1887. In 1891 he accepted appointment as the first chairman of the newly created Railroad Commission of Texas. After serving three appointive and one elective terms he retired to private life in 1903. He died of pneumonia on March 6, 1905, and was buried in Palestine. In recognition of his long service to the people of Texas, the entire state legislature attended his funeral.[4]

John H. Reagan was not the only Texas Confederate who served in the United States Congress after the war. Samuel Bell Maxey, former colonel of the Ninth Infantry and brigadier general in command of Indian Territory, served two terms in the U.S. Senate, from 1875 to 1887. William H. ("Howdy") Martin, the colorful major who led a contingent of Hood's Brigade veterans home to Texas following Lee's surrender, succeeded Reagan in the House when the latter took a seat in the Senate. Roger Q. Mills, who was wounded at Missionary Ridge and Atlanta while commanding the Tenth Texas Infantry, served in the House of Representatives for nearly twenty years (1873–92) prior to serving in the Senate, 1892-99. While in the House he was chairman of the powerful Ways and Means Committee and author of the Mills Tariff bill. George W. ("Wash") Jones, popular commander of the Seventeenth Texas Infantry when the war ended, became a leader of the Greenback Party, ran twice for governor, and served two terms in Congress, 1879–83. Tom Ochiltree, a sergeant in Hood's Brigade and later an officer on Sam Maxey's staff, was a member of the Forty-eighth Congress, 1883–85. In all, twenty-seven veterans of the Confederate army represented Texas in the Federal Congress after the Civil War.[5]

Four Texas former Confederates who sat in Congress also served as governor in the postbellum period. James W. Throckmorton, who opposed secession but came to support the Confederacy and became a brigadier general of state troops, was elected governor under the presidential Reconstruction plan in 1866, but was removed the following year by General Sheridan as "an impediment to Reconstruction." He later served several terms in the U.S. House of Representatives. Richard Coke, who entered military service as a private and rose in rank to captain, was elected to the U.S. Senate in 1876 while serving his second term as governor of Texas. Joseph D. Sayers, who distinguished himself as a young lieutenant in the battle of Valverde and became commander of the Valverde battery, represented Texas in Congress from 1885 to 1898 before becoming governor for two terms, 1899-1903. His successor as chief executive was a former House colleague, Samuel W. T. Lanham. Lanham, a sixteen-year-old private in a South Carolina regiment during the war, was the last Confederate veteran to be governor of Texas, 1903–07.[6]

Several other former Confederates served as governor. Richard B. Hubbard, former commander of the Twenty-second Infantry in Walker's Division, was lieutenant governor when Coke resigned to take a seat in the Senate. Hubbard completed Coke's unexpired term as governor. He was later appointed United States minister to Japan by President Grover Cleveland, serving from 1885 to 1889. Hubbard was succeeded as governor by another regimental commander from Walker's Division, O. M. Roberts. Roberts, who was a supreme court judge and president of the secesssion convention before the war, was the commander of the Eleventh Texas Infantry, who led the successful Confederate attack at Bayou Bourbeau in 1863. After two terms as governor (1879–83), Roberts became a professor of law at the newly established University of Texas. He published several historical and legal works and was an organizer and first president of the Texas State Historical Association. John Ireland, a former lieutenant colonel in the Eighth Texas Infantry, followed Roberts as governor (1883–87). He was succeeded by one of the most famous Civil War soldiers from Texas, Lawrence Sullivan ("Sul") Ross, former commander of Ross' Cavalry Brigade. After his tenure as governor, from 1887 to 1891, Ross became president of Texas Agricultural and Mechanical College.[7]

James Stephen Hogg (1891–95) and Charles A. Culberson (1895–99), two of the last Texas governors in the late nineteenth century, had been too young to serve in the Civil War but were sons of Confederate soldiers. Jim Hogg's father, Joseph Lewis Hogg, was a brigadier general at the time of his death near Corinth in 1862. Charles Culberson's father, David Browning Culberson, initially opposed secession. He was one of the four men who advised Sam Houston at the time of Lincoln's offer for military aid. Culberson later supported the Confederacy, however, and became a colonel of the Eighteenth Texas Infantry in Mississippi. When poor health forced him to return to Texas in 1863, he became the state adjutant general.[8] Edward Clark, who served as governor of Texas the first year of the war and as colonel of the Fourteenth Texas Infantry the latter part of the war, fled to Mexico with General Shelby's entourage in 1865 but remained only briefly. After engaging in several businesses he reopened his law practice in Marshall. He died on May 4, 1880.[9]

Francis R. Lubbock, the highly capable governor of Texas during 1861–63 and member of Jefferson Davis' staff (1864–65), spent several months imprisoned at Fort Delaware before returning to Texas. After an unsuccessful business venture he served briefly as tax collector in Galveston. In 1878 he was chosen state treasurer, a position he held for twelve years. He was a member of the Board of Pardons under Governor Hogg, retiring from public life at the age of eighty. He spent his last years writing his memoirs, which were published in 1900 as *Six Decades in Texas: The Memoirs of Francis R. Lubbock, Confederate Governor of Texas*. He died at the age of eighty-nine in 1905 and was buried in the state cemetery in a coffin draped with both Confederate and United States flags.[10]

Pendleton Murrah, who succeeded Lubbock in 1863, was governor of Texas when the war ended. He left Texas in the same group as former governor Clark and other prominent Confederates. The trip to Mexico was too much for Murrah, who suffered from tuberculosis. He was confined to bed upon reaching Monterrey and died on August 4, 1865. Thomas Jefferson Chambers, the veteran Texas politician and secessionist leader whom Murrah defeated for governor in 1863, preceded Murrah in death by six months. Chambers was killed by an unknown assassin while sitting with his family in the upstairs parlor of his home, Chambersia, at Anahuac on the night of March 15, 1865. Most assume the assassination was the result of one of the numerous land disputes in which Chambers was involved.[11]

Like Edward Clark and Pendleton Murrah, Texas' two Confederate senators, Louis T. Wigfall and Williamson Simpson Oldham, fled the country after the war ended. Wigfall, the stormy fire-eater and bitter critic of Jefferson Davis, feared that he would be arrested by Federal authorities. He returned to Texas disguised as a private soldier after Lee's surrender. From Galveston he fled to London, where he lived in humble circumstances for several years. He returned to the United States in 1872 and lived for two years in Baltimore. In January 1874, he returned to Texas. He planned to resume his law practice in Marshall, but died in Galveston on February 18, 1874, at the age of fifty-seven. He was preceded in death by his Senate colleague, Williamson Simpson Oldham. Like Wigfall, Oldham left the country in the summer of 1865. He spent time in Mexico and

Canada before returning to the United States in 1867. He remained an unreconstructed rebel, refusing a pardon for his activities during the war. He died from typhoid fever on May 8, 1868.[12]

John Hemphill and John Gregg, two of the Texans who served with Wigfall and Oldham in the Provisional Congress of the Confederacy, died before the war ended: Hemphill of natural causes and Gregg while leading Hood's Brigade in the defense of Richmond in October 1864. Like Gregg, Thomas N. Waul, another Texan in the Provisional Congress, had a successful military career after congressional service, first commanding Waul's Legion in the defense of Mississippi and later commanding a brigade in Walker's Division in Louisiana and Arkansas. After the war Waul served in the Texas constitutional convention of 1866, practiced law in Galveston, and retired to a farm near Greenville in Hunt County, where he died on July 18, 1903, in his ninety-first year. William Beck Ochiltree, also a Texan in the Provisional Congress, organized the Eighteenth Texas Infantry after congressional service. Due to poor health he was forced to resign from the army in 1863. He died at Jefferson in December 27, 1867. His son, Tom, mentioned earlier, was a member of the United States Congress, 1883–85.[13]

Two of the Texans who served in the Confederate House of Representatives in the regular Congress died in office, John A. Wilcox on February 7, 1864, and Simpson Morgan on December 15, 1864. Claiborne Herbert and A. M. Branch, also Texas Confederate congressmen, were elected to the United States Thirty-ninth Congress but were not seated because of their Civil War activities. Both died in 1867. Two other Texas Confederate congressmen, Peter W. Gray and Franklin B. Sexton, served briefly on the Texas Supreme Court after the war. William B. Wright of Paris was a delegate to the Texas constitutional convention of 1875. He moved to San Antonio several years later and died there in August 1895. Stephen H. Darden, who was elected to replace the deceased Wilcox in 1864, helped to reorganize the state Democratic Party after the war, and served as Texas comptroller of public accounts, 1877–81. John R. Baylor, former governor of Confederate Arizona and member of the Second Congress of the Confederacy, lived in San Antonio after the war. He continued to have an interest in politics and received support from frontier counties in an unsuccessful bid for governor in 1873. Later he became a rancher in the Nueces River canyon. He and his brother, George, became involved in a quarrel with the Gilcrease family of the region, in which John killed Chimm Gilcrease. Malcolm Graham, who served in the First Congress but was defeated by Baylor in his bid for reelection, returned to Alabama after the war and practiced law. [14]

Ten of the thirty-seven Texans who held the rank of general officer in the Confederate army died during the war: Hiram Granbury, Tom Green, John Gregg, Albert Sidney Johnston, Ben McCulloch, Horace Randal and William R. Scurry on field of battle; John A. Wharton in the quarrel with fellow Texan George W. Baylor; and Joseph L. Hogg and Allison Nelson of disease. [15]

Most of the twenty-seven who survived the war had active postwar careers, with Louis T. Wigfall, the brigadier general-Confederate senator discussed earlier, something of an exception. The highest ranking Texas officer to survive the war, John Bell Hood, returned to Texas only infrequently to attend veteran reunions. He settled in New Orleans, where he spent the next thirteen years as a commission merchant. He married the daughter of a prominent New Orleans attorney and fathered eleven children. His business interests prospered for a decade and the family lived a comfortable life. He spent much of his free time in gathering materials for his memoirs and answering criticisms, especially by Gen. Joseph E. Johnston, about the conduct of the Georgia and Tennessee campaigns. In 1878 he suffered economic reversals which wiped out his property holdings. In the summer of 1879, the general, his wife, and oldest daughter died from yellow fever in New Orleans. A memorial edition of his memoirs, *Advance and Retreat*, was published in 1880 for the Hood Orphan Memorial by his old comrade in arms, P. G. T. Beauregard. [16]

Thomas L. Rosser, more closely identified with his native Virginia than Texas, where he grew up, was second in rank only to Hood among Texans who survived the war. A major general in Lee's army, Rosser served as chief engineer for the Northern Pacific and Canadian Pacific railroads after the war before returning to Virginia to live. When the Spanish American War began, President William McKinley, himself a Union general of volunteers in the Civil War, appointed Rosser brigadier general of United States volunteers. Rosser donned the Federal uniform and helped train American soldiers near the old Chickamauga battlefield. Aftewards he retired to his farm at Charlottesville, Virginia, where he died March 29, 1910. [17]

Matthew D. Ector, whose brigade performed with credit in the

Tennessee and Georgia campaigns, settled in Marshall after the war. He was chosen district judge in 1866 but was removed from office by military authorities as an impediment to Reconstruction. In 1874 he was appointed judge of the Sixth District and in 1876 the first presiding judge of the Court of Appeals, a position he held until his death October 29, 1879. Thomas Harrison, commander of Texas cavalry in Tennessee and Georgia, was another former Confederate general officer who became a district judge after the war. Like his brother, James, a brigadier in Polignac's Division, Tom Harrison was active in Baptist affairs, serving as a trustee of Waco University (which was later consolidated with Baylor University). Both Harrison brothers died in Waco: James on February 23, 1875, and Tom on July 14, 1891.[18]

Alexander W. Terrell, commander of a Texas cavalry regiment whose appointment as brigadier general by Kirby Smith was never acted upon by President Davis, fled from Texas when the war ended. He served briefly with Maximilian's Imperial forces as "chief of battalion" before returning to Texas. He served four terms in the Texas Senate and three terms in the Texas House during the post-Reconstruction period. He was author of a number of important pieces of legislation, including the Terrell election law which created the Texas direct primary system for political party nominations to office. He also was appointed minister to Turkey by President Cleveland, 1893–97. Active in the creation of the Texas State Historical Association, Terrell was president of the association at the time of his death in Mineral Wells on September 9, 1912.[19]

Several former Confederate generals held administrative positions for the state of Texas after Reconstruction. William P. ("Gotch") Hardeman, veteran of the Texas Revolution and the Mexican War and a regimental and brigade commander in the Civil War, was state inspector of railroads and later superintendent of public buildings and grounds. Henry E. McCulloch, younger brother of Ben and a veteran of frontier service, was appointed the first superintendent of the Texas Deaf and Dumb School in 1876, a post he held for three years. William Steele, the West Point graduate who commanded Texas troops in New Mexico and Louisiana, engaged in mercantile business in San Antonio immediately after the war but later became state adjutant general under Governor Coke. In this capacity he helped reorganize the Texas Rangers, who had been replaced by the State Police during Reconstruction. Wilburn H. King, colonel of the Eighteenth Texas regiment, whose appointment by Kirby Smith as brigadier general was never approved by President Davis, was another Texas Confederate who served as state adjutant general, holding the post from 1881 to 1891.[20]

Richard Gano, the physician-general who commanded a brigade under Sam Maxey in Indian Territory, returned to Texas in 1866 after living a year in his native Kentucky. He became a minister for the Christian Church, a position he held for forty-four years, during which time he baptized 16,000 converts to Christianity. John C. Moore, who led the Second Texas at Shiloh and commanded a brigade in the Vicksburg and Chattanooga campaigns, became a schoolteacher after the war, residing in Mexia and Dallas. He was a prolific writer, contributing frequently to magazines and journals. Jerome B. Robertson, the popular commander of Hood's Brigade and, like Gano, a physician, returned to medical practice after the war. He also served as state superintendent of immigration under Governor Coke and was active in the Masonic Order and Hood's Texas Brigade Association, serving as president of that association eleven times. His son, Felix, also a Confederate brigadier, studied law after the war and practiced in Waco for many years. The only native Texas general in the Confederacy, Felix Robertson, was the last Confederate general to die, April 20, 1928. He was eighty-nine years old.[21]

Brig. Gen. Elkanah Greer, the former Texas head of the Knights of the Golden Circle, commander of the Third Texas Cavalry, and chief of the Trans Mississippi Conscript Bureau, returned to Marshall after the war but apparently was not active in public life. He died in March 1877 while visiting his sister in Arkansas. Richard Waterhouse, veteran of Mansfield and brigade commander in Indian Territory, preceded Greer in death by one year. He had lived in San Augustine and Jefferson since the war, engaging in land speculation. John W. Whitfield, cavalry brigade commander in Mississippi and Tennessee, died in Hallettsville, two years after Waterhouse. He had continued to be active in public affairs, serving in both the 1866 and 1875 constitutional conventions.[22]

Xavier Blanchard Debray, graduate of the French military academy who was promoted to brigadier for his part in the battle of Pleasant Hill, lived briefly in Houston and Galveston after the war before moving to Austin to resume his antebellum position as translator in the General Land Office. Hamilton P. Bee, the cavalry com-

mander who was removed from his command after the fighting at
Monett's Ferry in Louisiana, went to Mexico after the war but returned to Texas in 1876. He lived his last twenty-one years in the
Alamo city, where he died on October 2, 1897. Walter P. Lane, veteran of San Jacinto, the Mexican War, and Mansfield, returned to
Marshall after the war to resume his mercantile business. His memoirs, *Adventures and Recollections of General Walter P. Lane*, were
published in 1887. He died in Marshall on January 28, 1892.[23]

William Hugh Young, the often wounded brigadier general in
the Army of Tennessee, returned to San Antonio after his release
from Union prison camp at Johnson's Island. He practiced law, assisted his father in the freighting business, and organized the
Nueces River Irrigation Company. For a time he was owner of the
San Antonio Express. He died in San Antonio on November 28,
1901. Arthur P. Bagby, veteran of the New Mexico and Louisiana
campaigns, resumed his law practice after the war. He also served as
assistant editor of the *Victoria Advocate*. When he died in Hallettsville at the age of eighty-eight on February 21, 1921, he was one of
the last surviving Confederate general officers.[24]

John S. ("Rip") Ford, the old Texas Ranger who commanded
Texas troops in South Texas, had an active public career after the
war. He lived briefly in Matamoros but returned to Texas to serve as
United States parole commissioner. He was a delegate to the Democratic National Convention in Baltimore in 1872 and in the state
constitutional convention of 1875. A close friend and supporter of
Richard Coke, Ford was a member of the Texas Senate (1876–78).
He was appointed superintendent of the Deaf and Dumb School,
replacing Henry McCulloch. In later years he spent time in writing
his reminiscences and promoting the study of Texas history. He was
one of the organizers and charter members of the Texas State Historical Association. He died in San Antonio on November 3, 1897.[25]

Although not Texas residents, several Confederate general of-
ficers commanded Texas troops in significant military engagements.
One of these, John Bankhead Magruder, gained great favor with
Texans for the recapture of Galveston.

Like a number of other Confederates, Magruder fled to Mexico
when the war ended. There he became a major general in Maximilian's Imperial Army and chief of the Land Office of Colonization. For a few months Magruder lived in the grand style he so much
enjoyed. With Maximilian's defeat and subsequent death, the

dreams of imperial grandeur came crashing down and a crestfallen Magruder returned to the United States. Without adequate financial resources, Magruder lived his last days in humble circumstances. He died in Houston on February 18, 1871. He was buried there but was later reinterred in Galveston, the city where he achieved his greatest military success.[26]

Floridian Edmund Kirby Smith, Magruder's superior as head of the Trans Mississippi Department, had a successful career after the war. After signing the surrender agreement at Galveston, he joined the group of prominent Confederates who crossed the Rio Grande and entered Mexico. He returned to the United States after a brief sojourn in Mexico and Cuba. He organized and promoted the Atlantic and Pacific Telegraph Company in Louisville and headed an accident insurance company. Then he embarked on an academic career, first as president of a small military school and later as chancellor of the University of Nashville. In 1875 he joined the faculty of the University of the South at Sewanee, Tennessee, as professor of mathematics, a position he held until his death, March 28, 1893.[27]

Kirby Smith's unhappy subordinate, Lt. Gen. Richard Taylor of Louisiana, was financially ruined by the war and forced to file for bankruptcy. Nevertheless, Taylor resumed his aristocratic lifestyle and remained a leader in New Orleans social circles. He played an active role in the Democratic Party during the Reconstruction and Restoration periods and spent much time traveling in the North and in Europe. He moved to Virginia after his wife's death in 1875. His memoirs, *Destruction and Reconstruction: Personal Experiences of the Late War*, were published in early April 1879. Only a few days later, on April 12, Taylor died in the home of a New York friend.[28]

Henry Hopkins Sibley, the commander of Texas cavalry in the ill-fated New Mexico campaign who was later removed from brigade command in Louisiana by Richard Taylor, joined a group of Union and Confederate veterans who served on the Nile after the war. From 1869–73, Sibley held the rank of general of artillery in the Egyptian army. Apparently his old drinking habits continued to interfere with his performance, however, and in 1873 the Khedive discharged him from Egyptian service.

Sibley returned to the United States, spending his remaining years in poor health and comparative poverty. He died at Fredericksburg, Virginia, August 23, 1886.[29]

John G. Walker, the Missourian who led the largest division of

Texans during the war, was another Confederate general officer who spent some time abroad after the war. He left Texas for Mexico with a group of other Confederates in early June 1865. From Mexico he traveled to Cuba, and from there on to England, where he became the agent for a company promoting Confederate colonization in Venezuela. He returned to the United States in 1868 and was named United States consul general in Bogota, Columbia. Later, he became special commissioner to the South American republics on behalf of the Pan American Convention. Walker died in Washington, DC, on July 20, 1893.[30]

One of Walker's sub-district commanders in Texas, Virginian James E. Slaughter, went to Mexico when the Confederacy collapsed. Slaughter, who had disagreed with John S. Ford concerning military operations in South Texas, returned to the United States in 1870, living first in Mobile and later in New Orleans. He worked as a civil engineer and postmaster in the post-Reconstruction era. He died while on a visit to Mexico City, on January 1, 1901.[31]

Camille Armand Jules Marie, Prince de Polignac, the Texans' dapper "Polecat" who commanded a brigade and then a division in the Louisiana campaigns alongside John G. Walker, was sent on a mission to France for the Confederate government in early 1865 but arrived too late to accomplish anything. After the war he traveled to Central America, studied mathematics and music, and led a French division in the Franco-Prussian War. He was awarded the French Legion of Honor for his service during that conflict. He died in Paris, November 15, 1913, the last surviving Confederate major general.[32]

James P. Major, West Point graduate from Missouri who commanded a Texas cavalry brigade in the Louisiana campaigns of 1864, also left the country when the war ended. Major, who had been stationed in Texas before the war, had married the younger sister of Tom Green's wife. After a brief time in France, the Majors returned to Texas. He died in Austin on May 7, 1877.[33]

Paul Octave Hebert, the Acadian who commanded the district of Texas prior to Magruder, never lived up to prewar expectations as a general officer. Although he graduated first in his class at West Point and was decorated for gallantry in the Mexican War, Hebert had a mediocre Civil War career. After the loss of Galveston he was transferred to command of the Northern Sub-district of Louisiana. He was involved in only one major action in the war, at Milliken's

Bend in 1863. After the war he was active in the Louisiana Democratic Party. In 1873 he became state engineer of Louisiana, and he died on August 20, 1880.[34]

Santos Benavides, former mayor and victor over Federal forces in the battle of Laredo, was in the mercantile business with his brother after the war. He continued to be active in politics, serving two terms as alderman and three terms in the state legislature (1879-85). In 1884 he was Texas commissioner to the World's Cotton Exposition in New Orleans. He died on November 9, 1891.[35]

No Texas Civil War veteran had a more distinguished career, both before and after the war, than did Dr. Ashbel Smith, colonel of the Second Texas Infantry and last commander of Galveston during the Civil War. A staunch supporter of education, Smith was the first president of the board of trustees of the Texas Medical College and Hospital at Galveston and first president of the board of regents of the University of Texas at Austin. Indeed, his work for the state university was such that after his death the regents passed a resolution honoring him as the "Father of the University of Texas." Smith was also quite active in political affairs, serving two terms in the legislature and as a delegate to three national Democratic conventions in the postbellum period. The author of numerous scientific and historical treatises, Smith, who never married, died at his plantation home (Evergreen) on Galveston Bay, January 21, 1886.[36]

Like Ashbel Smith, Charles DeMorse, the fiery editor of the *Clarksville Northern Standard* who commanded the Twenty-ninth Texas Cavalry at Elk Creek and Poison Spring, was active in the Democratic Party after the war. He was a delegate to the Democratic National Convention in 1872, second to Richard Coke in the party nomination for governor in 1873, and mentioned seriously as a gubernatorial candidate in 1886. He was a delegate to the 1875 constitutional convention, a member of the Texas Grange, an organizer of the Texas Veterans Association, and a director of the Agricultural and Mechanical College of Texas. DeMorse was chosen as the first president of the Texas Press and Editorial Association and was later recognized as the "Father of Texas Journalism."[37]

Guy M. Bryan, the nephew of Stephen F. Austin and formerly a Texas congressman who served as liaison between President Davis, Kirby Smith, and Pendleton Murrah during the war, resumed his political activities after the war. A college classmate of Rutherford B. Hayes, Bryan visited his old friend when Hayes was governor and later when he was president of the United States. Bryan was elected to the state legislature in 1873 and reelected in 1879 and 1887. He served as Speaker of the Texas House in 1874. He was president of the Texas Veterans Association from 1892 until his death in 1901. Like a number of prominent Confederates, he was a charter member of the Texas State Historical Association. He was vice-president of that organization when he died.[38]

The hero of the battle of Sabine Pass, Richard W. ("Dick") Dowling, opened a coffee and amusement house in Houston following the end of the war. He was involved in a variety of business enterprises including a gas light company, a warehouse, a steamboat, streetcars, railroads, and oil leases. In late August 1867, he contracted yellow fever and died on September 23 at the age of twenty-nine. A native of County Galway, Ireland, who with a handful of Irishmen turned back a Union invasion fleet, Dowling is remembered today by statues at Sabine Pass and in Houston's Hermann Park.[39]

George W. Baylor, younger brother of John R. Baylor and colonel of a regiment in the Louisiana campaigns, was never convicted in the killing of John A. Wharton at Magruder's headquarters in April 1865. Baylor later became a Texas Ranger captain and served with distinction in driving Victorio's Apache band from West Texas. He commanded several Ranger companies in the Nolan County fence-cutting disturbances of 1882. He later represented El Paso in the state legislature and served as clerk of district and circuit courts for several years. He lived in Mexico from 1898 to 1913, and died in San Antonio, March 27, 1916.[40]

William H. Parsons, the Waco newspaper publisher who organized the Twelfth Texas Cavalry and later commanded his own cavalry brigade in the Trans Mississippi, left Texas for British Honduras after the war but soon returned. After serving in the Texas Senate he moved to New York. He held various governmental positions and lived in Virginia and Washington, DC. He died at the age of eighty-one in October 1907.[41]

Mariner Leon Smith, who commanded the Confederate naval forces in the battle of Galveston and at Sabine Pass, went to San Francisco after the war. He and his family later moved to Fort Wrangel, Alaska, where Smith operated a trading post. He was shot during a disagreement at the post and died on December 26, 1889.[42]

Artillery Capt. James P. Douglas of Tyler, whose letters to his young wife Sallie described the bitter fighting in Georgia and Tennessee, resumed his post as editor and part owner of the *Tyler Reporter* after the war. He served a term in the Texas Senate and later organized and served as first president of the Texas branch of the Cotton Belt Railroad, known as the Tyler Tap. He developed a keen interest in fruit trees, had the first peach orchards in East Texas, and built the first canning factory in Tyler. He died on November 27, 1901.[43]

Another Texas Civil War captain, Samuel T. Foster of Granbury's Brigade, returned to Live Oak County in South Texas after the war. After serving a term in the state legislature, he moved to Corpus Christi in 1868. He remained there twelve years, during which time he managed a merchandising and banking house, organized the first Baptist church in Corpus, and formed a militia company to guard the region against Mexican raiders. In 1880 he moved to Laredo, where he continued his business activities. In 1885 President Cleveland appointed him commissioner for the United States district court, a position he held until his death at the age of eighty-five on January 7, 1919.[44]

David Carey Nance, who enlisted in Parsons' Texas cavalry as a teenager in spite of his father's wishes and spent four years fighting in Arkansas and Louisiana, returned to farming in Dallas and Fannin counties after the war. He became moderately prosperous farming, teaching, carpentering, and buying and selling land. He married and raised four children and, in spite of crippling rheumatoid arthritis, lived a productive life. He died in the summer of 1925 at the age of eighty-two.[45]

W. W. Heartsill, another Confederate enlisted man whose war experiences were later published *(Fourteen Hundred and 91 Days in the Confederate Army)*, returned to Marshall after the war. He owned a small grocery business and served as a city alderman and mayor of Marshall before his death on July 28, 1916.[46]

William A. Fletcher of Beaumont, veteran of Hood's Texas Brigade and Terry's Texas Rangers, resumed his work as a carpenter about a hundred feet from where he had been working in 1861 when he heard of the firing on Fort Sumter. Unlike some Texas Confederates, Fletcher bore no grudge against his former enemies and associated freely with Federal occupation troops in Beaumont. He became a highly successful lumberman and formed the Texas Tram and Lumber Company, one of the largest yellow pine producing companies in the state. In 1902 he sold his lumber interests, purchased more than 2,000 acres, and became a gentleman farmer. He died on January 5, 1915, at the age of seventy-three.[47]

Kate Stone, the vivacious young Louisiana refugee who believed she had discovered the "dark corner of the Confederacy" in Texas, returned to her beloved Brokenburn plantation after the war only to find conditions quite changed. The destruction caused by the war led her to write in the last pages of her Civil War journal that "it does not seem the same place." Financial reverses resulted in the loss of Brokenburn in the postbellum period. In December 1869, she married Henry B. Holmes, the young Confederate officer mentioned often in her diary. They settled in Tallulah, Louisiana, where Kate was active in civic and cultural affairs. She helped organize a local United Daughters of the Confederacy chapter and was instrumental in having a Confederate memorial erected on the courthouse square. The mother of four children, Kate Stone died on December 28, 1907.[48]

Amelia Barr, the young Englishwoman who lived in Austin with her husband Robert and children during the war, became one of America's most prolific novelists in the postwar years. A year after the war ended the Barrs moved to Galveston, where tragedy struck. Robert and their three sons died during the yellow fever epidemic of 1867. For a while Mrs. Barr ran a boardinghouse, but eventually she moved with her three daughters to New York. After employment as a governess, Mrs. Barr turned to writing. She wrote over sixty books, including an account of her personal experiences in Texas entitled *All the Days of My Life*. She died in New York City, March 10, 1919.[49]

The emancipation of her slaves and an unfortunate second marriage had a disastrous financial impact upon Sarah Devereux, the mistress of Monte Verdi plantation in Rusk County. From real and personal property valued at over $130,000 when the Civil War began, Sarah saw her estate decline to $600 at the time of her death in April 1900. Rebecca Hagerty of Marion County suffered similar misfortune after the war. The holder of more than a hundred slaves and $125,000 in property in 1860, she owned less than $7,000 ten years later.[50]

Lizzie Neblett of Grimes County, whose difficulties in managing slaves were recounted in her wartime letters, welcomed the return of husband Will from the army once the war ended. The postwar years were difficult for the Nebletts. With emancipation, the problem of slave management was replaced by other concerns as Will struggled to run the farm with hired help. Personal property holding of the family, $14,500 in 1860, was almost wiped out when the eleven slaves owned were freed. Real property, enumerated at $12,500 in 1860, declined by 60 percent during the late 1860s. Will Neblett died from pneumonia in 1871, leaving Lizzie a widow at age thirty-eight and five months pregnant with a third daughter. Lizzie Neblett lived until 1917.[51]

Not all Texas Confederates suffered economic reversals as a result of the war. Richard King and Mifflin Kenedy, two Northerners who had a partnership in steamboating, merchandising, and ranching in South Texas, were highly successful in selling cotton to European buyers and providing supplies for the Confederacy. They expanded their ranching operations with proceeds acquired during the war. When their partnership was dissolved in 1868, they were two of the wealthiest men in the state. The 1870 census for Duval County listed Kenedy as the holder of $160,600 in property and King with $565,000 in property.[52]

Texans who supported the Union during secession and the Civil War followed various paths during the postbellum period. As noted earlier, several prominent Texans who opposed secession defected from the Unionist cause after the war began. Best known of these "Confederate Unionists" were James W. Throckmorton, Ben Epperson, and William Pitt Ballinger. Throckmorton, who had voted against secession, emerged from the war more popular than ever. His standing with former Confederates was enhanced when he was removed as governor in 1867 by General Sheridan. Throckmorton became one of the recognized leaders of Texas conservatives and served several terms in Congress. His friend and political ally, Ben Epperson, also supported the Confederacy after his initial opposition to secession. Like Throckmorton, Epperson reentered public life after the war. He was elected to Congress in 1866 but was not permitted to take his seat due to Radical opposition. He continued to be active in Democratic politics, serving as a delegate to the 1868 national convention, one term in the legislature, and as a presidential elector in 1876. He was involved in railroad promotion, and served for several years as president of the proposed Memphis and El Paso railroad. Galveston attorney William Pitt Ballinger, another reluctant Confederate, played the role of behind-the-scene political pragmatist in the postwar years working for the restoration of conservative government. He was twice offered a position on the state supreme court but declined. He was a delegate to the 1875 state constitutional convention.[53]

Those Texans who had continued to support the Union during the war welcomed the defeat of the Confederacy and the victory of Federal arms. A group of exiled Texas Unionists including A. J. Hamilton, Thomas DuVal, and S. M. Swenson celebrated in New Orleans when they learned of the evacuation of Richmond in the closing days of the war. Hamilton, a former Texas congressman, was appointed provisional governor of Texas by President Andrew Johnson. Hamilton returned to Texas in early summer, 1865, and took steps to restore civil government in the state. At the time Texas Unionists seemed united in the Republican Party, but divisions, particularly over the role to be played by ex-Confederates and former slaves, soon surfaced. Hamilton, Elisha M. Pease, Ferdinand Flake, and Thomas DuVal were moderate Republicans who opposed Radical Republican efforts to disfranchise former Confederates. While the moderates generally supported black suffrage, they favored some limitations upon the role former slaves would play.[54]

Edmund J. Davis, Edward Degener, George Whitmore, and Morgan Hamilton (brother of A. J. Hamilton) were the leaders of those Texas Unionists who favored more sweeping political and social changes than the moderates. These so-called Radical Republicans were much more supportive of efforts to encourage greater African-American participation in the political process. Led by Davis, former colonel of the First Texas Cavalry (Union), these Republicans were much opposed to the restoration to power by former secessionists. Davis' election as governor of Texas in 1869 came after a bitter political battle with A. J. Hamilton, supported by moderate Republicans and Democrats.[55]

John L. Haynes of Laredo, former colonel of the Second Texas Cavalry (Union), was one Texas Unionist who tried to work with both the moderate and radical factions of the party. Chosen as the first state chairman of the Texas Republican Party, Haynes was rewarded with appointment as customs collector at Galveston. His cooperation with the moderate faction of the party, however, led Edmund J. Davis, his old brigade commander, to use his influence with President Grant to secure Haynes' removal from the lucrative Galveston post. When the Hamilton faction fused with Democrats in a Horace Greeley presidential coalition, Haynes reversed himself and threw his support to the Davis faction of the party. Davis, in turn, personally worked to secure the appointment of Haynes as customs collector at Brownsville, a post he held for twelve years.[56]

Some Unionists who left Texas during the war chose not to remain in the state after the war. Swen Magnus Swenson, the highly successful Swedish-born merchant, fled from Texas in the autumn of 1863. He lived briefly in Mexico, then spent the remainder of the war in New Orleans. Unlike other exiles in New Orleans, Swenson chose not to return to Texas. He went to New York City, where he opened a bank and continued his business interests, both in Texas and elsewhere.[57] William Marsh Rice was another Texas Unionist who moved to New York City. One of the wealthiest men in Texas, Rice closed his business firm in Houston when the war began. In 1863 he moved to Matamoros, where he expanded his financial holdings through the sale of Texas cotton. He returned to Houston briefly in 1865, but soon thereafter moved to New Jersey and later New York. Through skillful business activities and investments he accumulated a small fortune of $3 million. He continued to have an interest in Texas and in 1891 endowed the William Marsh Rice Institute in Houston. Rice died in 1900, the victim of a bizarre murder plot involving a lawyer and Rice's valet.[58]

Pioneer settler Noah Smithwick was another Texan who did not return after the war. He remained in California until his death at the age of ninety-one in October 1899. Like Rice, he continued to have fond memories of Texas. When he closed his classic account titled *The Evolution of A State, or Recollections of Old Texas Days* (1900), written several months before his death, he stated, "I will cherish the memory of the long ago spent on her soil, and wish her a prosperous future." He told his daughter, who was transcribing his memoirs, this thought about Texas: "I am proud to note the progress she has made, though I can scarcely realize the transformation that progress has wrought."[59]

Notes

CHAPTER ONE

1. James G. Randall and David Donald, *The Civil War and Reconstruction* (2nd ed. rev., Lexington, MA: D. C. Heath, 1969), 166-167. For a discussion of the southern point of view, see J. G. deRoulac Hamilton, "Lincoln's Election an Immediate Menace to Slavery in the States?" *American Historical Review* 37 (July 1932): 700-711. For a different view, see A. C. Cole, *ibid.*, 36 (July 1931): 740-767.

2. Ralph A. Wooster, *The Secession Conventions of the South* (Princeton: Princeton University Press, 1962), 11-14, 20-22, 121-123, 149, 188-189. Tennessee and Virginia in the upper South both later submitted secession ordinances to the state's voters for approval.

3. Walter L. Buenger, *Secession and the Union in Texas* (Austin: University of Texas Press, 1984), 6-10.

4. Randolph B. Campbell and Richard G. Lowe, *Wealth and Power in Antebellum Texas* (College Station: Texas A&M University Press, 1977), 33-38, 67-81; Richard G. Lowe and Randolph B. Campbell, *Planters & Plain Folk: Agriculture in Antebellum Texas* (Dallas: Southern Methodist University Press, 1987), 19, 22-23, 69-79; Bureau of Census, *Agriculture of the United States in 1860; Compiled from Original Returns of the Eighth Census* (Washington: Government Printing Office, 1864), 140-151.

5. James D. B. DeBow, comp., *Statistical View of the United States . . . Being a Compendium of the Seventh Census* (Washington: Government Printing Office, 1854), 40, 82; Bureau of the Census, *Population of the United States in 1860; Compiled from the Original Returns of the Eighth Census* (Washington: Government Printing Office, 1864), 486-490, 598-599; Terry G. Jordan, "A Century and Half of Ethnic Change in Texas, 1836-1986," *Southwestern Historical Quarterly* (cited hereinafter as *SHQ*) 89 (April 1986): 385-393, 409-411.

6. Randolph B. Campbell, *An Empire for Slavery: The Peculiar Institution in Texas, 1821-1865* (Baton Rouge: Louisiana State University Press, 1989), 55-56.

7. Campbell, *ibid.*, 209; Campbell and Lowe, *Wealth and Power in Antebellum Texas*, 33-37, 110-119; Lowe and Campbell, *Planters & Plain Folk*, 157.

8. Buenger, *Secession and the Union in Texas*, 45.

9. Inaugural Address of Sam Houston, December 21, 1859, *Destiny By Choice: The Inaugural Addresses of the Governors of Texas*, ed. Marvin E. De Boer (Fayetteville, AR: University of Arkansas Press, 1992), 59.

10. Amelia W. Williams and Eugene C. Barker, eds., *The Writings of Sam Houston, 1813-1863*, 8 vols. (Austin: University of Texas Press, 1938-1943), 7:421.

11. *Ibid.*, 432.

12. Ernest Wallace, *Texas in Turmoil* (Austin: Steck-Vaughn Company, 1965), 52; M. K. Wisehart, *Sam Houston: An American Giant* (Washington: Luce Publishing, 1962), 584.

13. Buenger, *Secession and the Union in Texas*, 49-50; Francis R. Lubbock, *Six Decades in Texas, or Memoirs of Francis R. Lubbock, Governor of Texas in War Time, 1861-63*, ed. C. W. Rains (Austin: Ben Jones & Company, 1900), 259-294; James Alex Baggett, "The Constitutional Union Party in Texas," *SHQ* 82 (January 1979): 241-242.

14. On the Texas troubles of 1860 see Donald E. Reynolds, *Editors Make War: Southern Newspapers in the Secession Crisis* (Nashville: Vanderbilt University Press, 1970), 97-117; William W. White, "The Texas Slave Insurrection in 1860," *SHQ* 52 (January 1949): 259-285; Wendell G. Addington, "Slave Insurrections in Texas," *Journal of Negro History* 35 (October 1950): 419-424.

15. See Donald E. Reynolds, "Reluctant Martyr: Anthony Bewley and the Texas State Insurrection Panic of 1860," *SHQ* 96 (January 1993): 345-361; Wesley Norton, "The Methodist Episcopal Church and the Civil Disturbances in North Texas in 1859 and 1860," *ibid.*, 68 (January 1965): 317-341; Macum Phelan, *A History of Early Methodism in Texas, 1817-1866* (Nashville: Cokesbury Press, 1924), 452-458.

16. For the Knights of the Golden Circle, see C. A. Bridges, "The Knights of the Golden Circle: A Filibustering Fantasy," *SHQ* 44 (January 1941): 287-302; Roy Sylvan Dunn, "The KGC in Texas, 1860-1861," *ibid.*, 70 (April 1967): 543-573; and Linda S. Hudson, "Military Knights of the Golden Circle in Texas, 1854-1861" (M. A. thesis, Stephen F. Austin State University, 1990).

17. *Writings of Sam Houston*, 8:145-160; Baggett, "Constitutional Union Party in Texas," 243-251; Billy D. Ledbetter, "Politics and Society: The Popular Response to Political Rhetoric in Texas, 1857-1860," *East Texas Historical Journal* (hereinafter cited as *ETHJ*) 13 (Fall 1975): 16-20; Clyde J. Villemez, "Presidential Elections in Texas From Statehood to Secession" (M. A. thesis, Lamar State College of Technology, 1968), 102-111; Llerena B. Friend, *Sam Houston: The Great Designer* (Austin: University of Texas Press, 1954), 329-330.

18. W. Dean Burnham, *Presidential Ballots, 1836-1892* (Baltimore: Johns Hopkins University Press, 1955), 764-813. See the explanatory note, 947. For more on the Fusion ticket, see John V. Mering, "Allies or Opponents? The Douglas Democrats and the Constitutional Unionists," *Southern Studies* 23 (Winter 1984): 380-381; Baggett, "Constitutional Union Party in Texas," 247-250.

19. *Writings of Sam Houston*, 8:192-198; Buenger, *Secession and the Union in Texas*, 119; Friend, *Sam Houston*, 330-331; Anna Irene Sandbo, "First Session of the Secession Convention in Texas," *SHQ* 18 (October 1914): 169-172.

20. Earl W. Fornell, *The Galveston Era: The Texas Crescent on the Eve of Secession* (Austin: University of Texas Press, 1961), 288-289; John Moretta, "William

Pitt Ballinger and the Travail of Texas Secession," *Houston Review* 11, no. 1 (1989): 3-23; Buenger, *Secession and the Union in Texas*, 63-64, 120-126; Claude Elliott, *Leathercoat: The Life History of a Texas Patriot* (San Antonio: Standard Printing Co., 1938), 46-49, 56-59; Jane L. Scarborough "George W. Paschal, Texas Unionist and Scalawag Jurisprudent" (Ph.D. dissertation, Rice University, 1972), 58-60; Oran Lonnie Sinclair, "Crossroads of Conviction: A Study of the Texas Political Mind, 1856-1861" (Ph.D. dissertation, Rice University, 1975), 181-204; John L. Waller, *Colossal Hamilton of Texas: A Biography of Andrew Jackson Hamilton* (El Paso: Texas Western University Press, 1968), 26-29; Larry G. Gage, "The Texas Road to Secession and War: John Marshall and the *Texas State Gazette*, 1860-1861," *SHQ* 62 (October 1958): 198-210; Alma Dexta King, "The Political Career of Williamson Simpson Oldham," *ibid.*, 33 (October 1929): 112-131; John Salmon Ford, *Rip Ford's Texas*, ed. Stephen B. Oates (Austin: University of Texas Press, 1963), 315-318; Ben H. Procter, *Not Without Honor: The Life of John H. Reagan* (Austin: University of Texas Press, 1962), 118-124; and Philip J. Avillo, Jr., "John H. Reagan: Unionist or Secessionist? *ETHJ* 13 (Spring 1975): 23-33.

21. *Writings of Sam Houston*, 8:206-207. See also Edward R. Maher, Jr., "Sam Houston and Secession," *SHQ* 55 (April 1952): 453-454.

22. Sandbo, "First Session of the Secession Convention," *SHQ* 18:178-180; *Journal of the Secession Convention of Texas, 1861*, ed. E. W. Winkler (Austin: Austin Printing Co., 1912), 9-13.

23. Certificates of elections, *ibid.*, 409-452; Buenger, *Secession and the Union in Texas*, 143.

24. *Writings of Sam Houston*, 8:220-221, 225-231, 236-252.

25. Sandbo, "First Session of the Secession Convention," *SHQ* 18:179-184; *Dallas Herald*, January 30, 1861.

26. Wooster, *Secession Conventions*, 124-125; Wooster, "An Analysis of the Membership of the Texas Secession Convention," *SHQ* 62 (January 1959): 322-335; *Journal of Secession Convention*, Appendix III, 405-407; Austin *State Gazette*, February 9, 1861, and March 30, 1861; and Walter P. Webb, H. Bailey Carroll, and Eldon Branda, eds., *The Handbook of Texas*, 3 vols. (Austin: Texas State Historical Association, 1952, 1976).

27. See Ralph A. Wooster, "Wealthy Texans, 1860," *SHQ* 81 (October 1967): 163-180.

28. Wooster, "Analysis of Membership of Texas Secession Convention," 322-335.

29. The average age for heads of households in 1860 Texas was thirty-nine years. Campbell and Lowe, *Wealth and Power in Antebellum Texas*, 28. Age, occupational, and birthplace data taken from manuscript census returns, United States Eighth Census. See Wooster, "Analysis of Membership of Texas Secession Convention," 163-180. Average ages for other secession conventions may be found in Wooster, *Secession Conventions*.

30. *Journal of Secession Convention*, 25-26; Buenger, *Secession and the Union in Texas*, 145.

31. *Ibid.*, 35-36.

32. *Ibid.*, 42-44; Austin *State Gazette*, February 9, 1861.

33. *Journal of Secession Convention*, 45-48; *Writings of Sam Houston*, 8: 253-254; Procter, *Not Without Honor*, 126-127; John H. Reagan, "A Conversation

with Governor Houston," *Quarterly of Texas State Historical Association* 3 (April 1900): 279-281.

34. Friend, *Sam Houston*, 335-336; Wisehart, *Sam Houston*, 559-600.

35. Friend, *Sam Houston*, 336; Sandbo, "First Session of the Secession Convention," 191; Wisehart, *Sam Houston*, 600; Elliott, *Leathercoat*, 53-55.

36. Wooster, *Secession Conventions*, 131-132.

37. Buenger, *Secession and the Union in Texas*, 148-149; Wisehart, *Sam Houston*, 600; Randolph B. Campbell, *Sam Houston and the American Southwest* (New York: Harper Collins, 1993), 154. One recent Houston biographer, John Hoyt Williams, states that Houston "was visibly shaken by the lopsided vote" of the convention in passing the ordinance of secession. *Sam Houston: A Biography of the Father of Texas* (New York: Simon & Schuster, 1993), 340.

38. *Journal of Secession Convention*, 54-59.

39. *Ibid.*, 61-66. Charles W. Ramsdell, "The Frontier and Secession," *Studies in Southern History Inscribed to William Archibald Dunning* (New York: Columbia University Press, 1914), 63-79, stresses the importance of Indian raids in the secession movement in the western part of the state. See also Floyd F. Ewing, "Unionist Sentiment in the Northwest Texas Frontier," *West Texas Historical Association Year Book* (cited hereinafter as *WTHAYB*) 33 (October 1957): 58-70.

40. *Journal of Secession Convention*, 73-79; Sandbo, "First Session of Secession Convention," 192-194.

41. *Journal of Secession Convention*, 78-80. For brief biographical information on the Texas delegation to the Montgomery convention see Charles Robert Lee, Jr., *The Confederate Constitutions* (Chapel Hill: University of North Carolina Press, 1963), 45-47, 158.

42. *Journal of Secession Convention*, 70-78, 262-263; Julia Lee Hering, "The Secession Movement in Texas" (M. A. thesis, University of Texas, 1933), 117-134; Edward R. Maher, Jr., "Secession in Texas" (Ph.D. dissertation, Fordham University, 1960), 153-176.

43. Paula Mitchell Marks, *Turn Your Eyes Toward Texas: Pioneers Sam and Mary Maverick* (College Station: Texas A&M University Press, 1989), 220-222; Tom Cutrer, *Ben McCulloch and the Frontier Military Tradition* (Chapel Hill: University of North Carolina Press, 1993), 177; J. J. Bowden, *The Exodus of Federal Forces from Texas, 1861* (Austin: Eakin Press, 1986), 37-43. For more on Twiggs' career, see Jeanne Twiggs Heidler, "The Military Career of David Emanuel Twiggs" (Ph.D. dissertation, Auburn University, 1988).

44. *Journal of Secession Convention*, 262-308; Bowden, *Exodus of Federal Forces*, 44-48; Wallace, *Texas in Turmoil*, 64-66; Cutrer, *Ben McCulloch*, 176-180; Allan C. Ashcraft, "Texas: 1860-1866. The Lone Star State in the Civil War" (Ph. D. dissertation, Columbia University, 1960), 61-63.

45. *The War of the Rebellion: A Compilation of the Official Records of the Union and Confederate Armies*, 128 vols. (Washington, DC: Government Printing Office, 1880-1901) Series I, 1:503-516 (cited hereinafter as *Official Records*; unless indicated all citations are to Series I). See also Cutrer, *Ben McCulloch*, 180-184; Jack W. Gunn, "Ben McCulloch: A Big Captain," *SHQ* 58 (July 1954): 17-18; Kevin R. Young, *To The Tyrants Never Yield: A Texas Civil War Sampler* (Plano: Wordware Publishing Inc., 1992), 43-49; Bowden, *Exodus of Federal Forces*, 49-57.

46. J. K. P. Blackburn, "Reminiscences of the Terry Rangers," *SHQ* 22 (July 1918): 38-39, quoted in Cutrer, *Ben McCulloch*, 184-185. There are various schools of thought concerning Twiggs' surrender. J. J. Bowden, *Exodus of Federal Forces*, 39-43, 61-62, 119-120, believes Twiggs' advanced years, physical infirmities, and generally cautious nature explain his actions. Russell Brown, "An Old Woman with a Broomstick: General David E. Twiggs and the U.S. Surrender in Texas, 1861," *Military Affairs*, 48 (April 1984): 57-61, implies that Twiggs wanted to surrender the posts in order to strike back at both Winfield Scott and Robert E. Lee, whom he believed had previously wronged him. Jeanne T. Heidler, "'Embarrassing Situation': David E. Twiggs and the Surrender of United States Forces in Texas, 1861," *Military History of the Southwest* 21 (Fall 1991): 157-172, argues that Twiggs was a victim of circumstances brought about by the Federal government's lack of preparation to meet the crisis.

47. Cutrer, *Ben McCulloch*, 185-186; Carl Coke Rister, *Robert E. Lee in Texas* (Norman: University of Oklahoma Press, 1946), 158-161; Douglas Southall Freeman, *R. E. Lee: A Biography*, 4 vols. (New York: Charles Scribner's Sons, 1934), 1: 426-428; Caroline Baldwin Darrow, "Recollections of the Twiggs Surrender," *Battles and Leaders of the Civil War*, 4 vols. (1887, reprint; New York: Thoms Yoseloff, 1956), 1: 33-39; *Official Records*, 1: 521-522.

48. *Official Records*, 1:529-543, 587-599, 623; Robert G. Hartje, *Van Dorn: The Life and Times of A Confederate General* (Nashville: Vanderbilt University Press, 1967), 81-87; Bowden, *Exodus of Federal Forces*, 97-118; Robert Wooster, *Soldiers, Sutlers, and Settlers: Garrison Life on the Texas Frontier* (College Station: Texas A&M University Press, 1987), 202-203; Ford, *Rip Ford's Texas*, 318-321. For a critical view of the arrest of the Federal troops by a Union officer, see J. T. Sprague, *The Treachery in Texas, the Secession of Texas, and the Arrest of United States Officers and Soldiers Serving in Texas* (New York: New York Historical Society, 1862).

49. O. M. Roberts, "The Political, Legislative, and Judicial History of Texas For Its Fifty Years of Statehood, 1845-1895," in Dudley G. Wooten, *A Comprehensive History of Texas, 1685-1897*, 2 vols. (Dallas, 1898), 2:113; Buenger, *Secession and the Union in Texas*, 159-161; Walter L. Buenger, "Secession and the Texas German Community: Editor Lindheimer vs. Editor Flake," *SHQ* 82 (April 1979): 379-402; Gage, "The Texas Road to Secession and War," 191-226.

50. Walter L. Buenger, "Texas and the Riddle of Secession," *SHQ* 87 (October 1983): 174-175; Walter L. Buenger, "Secession Revisited: The Texas Experience," *Civil War History* 30 (December 1984): 298-300.

51. Buenger, *Secession and the Union in Texas*, 163-166; Fornell, *Galveston Era*, 288-289; Sinclair, "Crossroads of Conviction," 187-188; Ralph A. Wooster, "Ben H. Epperson: East Texas Lawyer, Legislator, and Civic Leader," *ETHJ* 5 (March 1967): 29-42; Dale A. Somers, "James P. Newcomb: The Making of a Radical," *SHQ* 72 (April 1969): 449-469; Frank H. Smyrl, "Unionism in Texas, 1856-1861," *ibid.*, 68 (October 1964): 191.

52. There has been confusion over the exact count in the February referendum. *The Journal of the Secession Convention*, 90, gives the total vote at 46,129 for secession and 14,697 against. Figures of 44,317 and 13,020 were reported in the *State Gazette*, March 23, 1861. The figures given here are from Joe T. Timmons, "The Referendum in Texas on the Ordinance of Secession, February 23, 1861: The

Vote," *ETHJ* 11 (Fall 1973): 12-28, based upon examination of the manuscript returns. As was true in many elections for convention delegates and in those two other states where a referendum was held, there were some claims of fraud in the Texas vote. For more on this, see Dale Baum, "Pinpointing Apparent Fraud in the 1861 Texas Secession Referendum," *Journal of Interdisciplinary History* 22 (Autumn 1991): 201-221.

53. Wooster, *Secession Conventions*, 132-134; Timmons, "Referendum on Secession," 15-16. For more on Angelina County and secession, see Teresa Kay York, "'Piney Woods' Dissidence: Angelina County in the 1850s and the Secession Crisis" (M. A. thesis, Stephen F. Austin State University, 1990).

54. Wooster, *Secession Conventions*, 133. For the German attitude on secession, see Terry G. Jordan, *German Seed in Texas Soil: Immigrant Farmers in Nineteenth Century Texas* (Austin: University of Texas Press, 1966), 182-185; and Buenger, *Secession and the Union in Texas*, 81-84. For a differing view see Rudolph L. Biesele, *The History of the German Settlements in Texas, 1831-1861* (Austin: privately printed, 1930), 206-207, and Ella Lonn, *Foreigners in the Confederacy* (Chapel Hill: University of North Carolina Press, 1940), 46-52.

55. Wooster, *Secession Conventions*, 133-134; Buenger, *Secession and the Union in Texas*, 64-70, 76-79, 173. For correlations and relationships between various factions in Texas, see Robin E. Baker and Dale Baum, "The Texas Voter and the Crisis of the Union, 1859-1861," *Journal of Southern History* 53 (August 1987): 395-420. The authors conclude that in the February referendum "the best single predictor of secessionist voting strength was the percentage of slaveholders in the electorate" (409). They also note that "counties with high percentages either of Lutherans or Disciples of Christ tended to support the Union" (410). Areas with large numbers of Methodists, Baptists, and Presbyterians were more likely to support secession. Walter L. Buenger, "Unionism on the Texas Frontier, 1859-1861," *Arizona and the West* 22 (Autumn 1980): 253-254, points out that while southwestern frontier counties tended to oppose secession, there was little opposition in northwestern frontier counties because of dissatisfaction with Indian policies of the Federal government. See also Floyd Ewing, "Origins of Unionist Sentiment on the West Texas Frontier," *WTHAYB* 33 (October 1956): 21-29.

56. *Writings of Sam Houston*, 8:265-266.

57. Roberts, "Political, Legislative, and Judicial History of Texas," 120-122; *Journal of Secession Convention*, 100-102, 119; Jimmie Hicks, "Texas and Separate Independence, 1860-1861," *ETHJ* 4 (October 1966): 93.

58. Roberts, "Political, Legislative, and Judicial History of Texas," 122-124; *Journal of Secession Convention*, 184-185. The various biographers of Houston describe his refusal to take the oath; see Friend, *Sam Houston*, 338-339; Campbell, *Sam Houston*, 155-156; Wisehart, *Sam Houston*, 609-610; Williams, *Sam Houston*, 344; Marshall De Bruhl, *Sword of San Jacinto: Life of Sam Houston* (New York: Random House, 1993), 392-394; Marquis James, *The Raven: A Biography of Sam Houston* (Indianapolis: Bobbs Merrill, 1929), 411-412.

59. *Writings of Sam Houston*, 8:271-292.

60. The most thorough account of the Lincoln offers is Howard C. Westwood, "President Lincoln's Overture to Sam Houston," *SHQ* 88 (October 1984): 125-144. For the Lander mission, see *Official Records*, 1:550-552; and O. M. Rob-

erts, "Texas," in Clement Evans, ed., *Confederate Military History*, 12 vols. (Atlanta: Confederate Publishing Company, 1899), 11:34.

61. Westwood, "President Lincoln's Overture to Sam Houston," 138-144; George W. Paschal, "The Last Years of Sam Houston," *Harper's New Monthly Magazine* 32 (1865-66): 663; Charles A. Culberson, "General Sam Houston and Secession," *Scribner's Magazine* 39 (May 1906): 586-587; Friend, *Sam Houston*, 345-346; De Bruhl, *Sword of San Jacinto*, 395-396.

62. Friend, *Sam Houston*, 347-353. See also David P. Smith, ed., "Civil War Letters of Sam Houston," *SHQ* 81 (April 1978): 417-426.

63. *Journal of Secession Convention*, 209-251; Wooster, *Secession Conventions*, 135.

CHAPTER TWO

1. Peter J. Parish, *The American Civil War* (New York: Holmes & Meier Publishers, 1975), 137; James M. McPherson, *Ordeal By Fire: The Civil War and Reconstruction* (New York: Alfred A. Knopf, 1982), 165.

2. Edward Clark to John S. Ford, March 22, 1861, in Executive Record Book, Texas State Archives, Austin; L. P. Walker to Edward Clark, April 16, 1861, in Governor's Letters, Texas State Archives, Austin; *Official Records*, 1:290-291, 609-610, 617-618; Stephen B. Oates, "Texas Under the Secessionists," *SHQ* 67 (October 1963): 184-186.

3. Appointment of Nicholas, Executive Record Book; Fredericka Ann Meiners, "The Texas Governorship, 1861-1865: Biography of an Office" (Ph.D. dissertation, Rice University, 1974), 48-50; Ralph A. Wooster, "Texas," in *The Confederate Governors*, ed. W. Buck Yearns (Athens, GA: University of Georgia Press, 1985), 196-197; Bill Winsor, *Texas in the Confederacy: Military Installations, Economy and People* (Hillsboro: Hill Junior College Press, 1978), 38.

4. William A. Fletcher, *Rebel Private, Front and Rear* (1908; reprint, Washington, DC: Zenger Publishing Company, 1985), 6-7.

5. Ralph J. Smith, *Reminiscences of the Civil War and Other Sketches* (reprint, Waco: Morrison, 1962), 2. For illustrations of some of these presentation flags, see the handsome volume by Alan K. Sumrall, *Battle Flags of Texans in the Confederacy* (Austin: Eakin Press, 1995).

6. Max S. Lale, "The Boy-Bugler of the Third Texas Cavalry: The A. B. Blocker Narrative," *Military History of Texas and the Southwest*, 14, no. 2 (1977): 73; B. P. Gallaway, *The Ragged Rebel: A Common Soldier in W. H. Parsons' Texas Cavalry, 1861-1865* (Austin: University of Texas Press, 1988), 13-14; B. P. Gallaway, "A Texas Farm Boy Enlists in the 12th Cavalry," *Texas Military History* 8, no. 2 (1970): 87. For descriptions of other ceremonies, see J. J. Faulk, *History of Henderson County, Texas* (Athens, TX: Athens Publishing Company, 1929), 129; Charles Spurlin, ed., *West of the Mississippi with Waller's 13th Texas Cavalry Battalion, C.S.A.* (Hillsboro: Hill Junior College Press, 1971), 28; Marshall *Texas Republican*, April 27, June 1, 1861; O. T. Hanks, "History of B. F. Benton's Company, or Account of Civil War Experiences," 2-3, O. T. Hanks Reminiscences, 1861-1862, Archives, University of Texas Library, Austin; Jim Turner, "Jim Turner, Co. G, 6th Texas Infantry, C.S.A., From 1861 to 1865," *Texana* 12, no. 2 (1974): 150; *Bellville Countryman*, July 17, 1861.

7. Ralph A. Wooster and Robert Wooster, "'Rarin' for a Fight': Texans in the

Confederate Army," *SHQ* 84 (April 1981): 390-391; Mary Lasswell, ed., *Rags and Hope: The Recollections of Val C. Giles, Four Years with Hood's Brigade, Fourth Texas Infantry* (New York: Coward-McCann Publisher, 1961), 23; Turner, "Co. G, 6th Texas Infantry," 150; Charles D. Spurlin, ed., *The Civil War Diary of Charles A. Leuschner* (Austin: Eakin Press, 1992), 4; Harold B. Simpson, *Hood's Texas Brigade: Lee's Grenadier Guard* (Waco: Texian Press, 1978), 16-18; Stephen B. Oates, *Confederate Cavalry West of the River* (Austin: University of Texas Press, 1961), 60-61.

8. Wooster and Wooster, "'Rarin' for a Fight'," 391; Oates, *Confederate Cavalry*, 62-65; Oates, "Texas Under the Secessionists," 191-192; Theo. Noel, *A Campaign from Santa Fe to the Mississippi* (Shreveport: Shreveport News Printing, 1865), 8; Turner, "Co. G, 6th Texas Infantry," 150; Anne J. Bailey, *Between the Enemy and Texas: Parsons' Texas Cavalry in the Civil War* (Fort Worth: Texas Christian University Press, 1989), 17-34; Anne J. Bailey, *Texans in the Confederate Cavalry* (Fort Worth: Ryan Place Publishers, 1995), 35-36; A. W. Sparks, *The War Between the States As I Saw It* (Tyler: Lee & Burnett, Printers, 1901), 14-15; Oscar Haas, trans., "The Diary of Julius Giesecke, 1861-1862," *Texas Military History* 3 (Winter 1963): 233; Larry J. Daniel, *Soldiering in the Army of Tennessee* (Chapel Hill: University of North Carolina Press, 1991), 40; Donald S. Frazier, *Blood and Treasure: Confederate Empire in the Southwest* (College Station: Texas A&M University Press, 1995), 167-168.

9. "Reminiscences of C. C. Cox, II," *SHQ* 6 (January 1903): 217; Gallaway, *Ragged Rebel*, 15; Sparks, *War Between the States*, 24; William W. Heartsill, *Fourteen Hundred and 90 Days in the Confederate Army; or, Camp Life, Day by Day, of the W. P. Lane Rangers from April 19, 1861, to May 20, 1865*, ed. Bell I. Wiley (1876; reprint, Jackson, TN: McCowat-Mercer, 1954), 5.

10. Arthur James L. Fremantle, *The Fremantle Diary: Being the Journal of Lieutenant Colonel Arthur James Lyon Fremantle, Coldstream Guards, on His Three Months in the Southern States*, ed. Walter Lord (1863; reprint, Boston: Little, Brown Company, 1954), 58; Edward Clark to the Legislature, November 7, 1861, in James M. Day, ed., *Senate Journal of the Ninth Legislature of the State of Texas, November 4, 1861-January 14, 1862* (Austin: Texas State Library, 1963), 12-14; "Message of Governor Clark to the Senate and House of Representatives, November 1, 1861," *Official Records*, Series IV, 1:717. Two authorities, Col. Charles C. Jones and Col. Henry Stone, who have made careful studies of Confederate military organization, believe that Texas provided more cavalry regiments for Confederate service than any other state. Thomas Livermore, *Numbers & Losses in the Civil War in America, 1861-65* (1901; reprint, Bloomington, IN: Indiana University Press, 1957), 16-29.

11. Oates, *Confederate Cavalry*, 5-29; Stephen B. Oates, "Recruiting Confederate Cavalry in Texas," *SHQ* 64 (April 1961): 463-477; Martin Hardwick Hall, "The Formation of Sibley's Brigade and the March to New Mexico," *ibid.*, 61 (January 1958): 383-405; Martin Hardwick Hall, *Sibley's New Mexico Campaign* (Austin: University of Texas Press, 1960), 29-58; Blackburn, "Reminiscences of the Terry Rangers," 41-42; Maury Darst, "Robert Hodges, Jr.: Confederate Soldier," *ETHJ* 9 (March 1971): 22-28.

12. The definite modern account of the Texas Brigade is by Col. Harold B. Simpson: *Hood's Texas Brigade in Poetry and Song* (Waco: Texian Press, 1968);

Hood's Texas Brigade: Lee's Grenadier Guard (Waco: Texian Press, 1970); *Hood's Texas Brigade in Reunion and Memory* (Waco: Texian Press, 1974); and *Hood's Texas Brigade: A Compendium* (Waco: Texian Press, 1977).

13. Meiners, "Texas Governorship," 32-38, 45-47, 59-65; Edward Clark to the Delegation of Texas in the Confederate Congress, August 22, 1861, in Executive Record Book.

14. Oates, "Texas Under the Secessionists," 187; Lubbock, *Six Decades in Texas*, 471; Evans, ed., *Confederate Military History*, 11:141. Robert P. Felgar, "Texas in the War for Southern Independence, 1861-1865" (Ph.D. dissertation, University of Texas, 1935), 106, estimates that only 50,000-60,000 Texans served in the Confederate army. Dudley G. Wooten, *A Comprehensive History of Texas, 1685 to 1897* (Dallas: William G. Scarff, 1898), 2:571, calculated that 89,500 Texans served in Confederate and state forces in the war. Texas' total free population in 1860 was 421,649. It may be noted that Louisiana, with a total free white population of 376,276 in 1860, provided between 56,000 and 65,000 men to the Confederate army. John D. Winters, *The Civil War in Louisiana* (Baton Rouge: Louisiana State University Press, 1963), 428. Carl Moneyhon, *The Impact of the Civil War and Reconstruction on Arkansas* (Baton Rouge: Louisiana State University Press, 1994), 114, notes that the number of Arkansans in service "cannot be known for sure," but estimates at least 60,000 Arkansans served in the Confederate army out of a male adult, free white population of nearly 100,000. North Carolina, with a free population of 661,563, furnished 111,000 soldiers to the Confederacy. John G. Barrett, *The Civil War in North Carolina* (Chapel Hill: University of North Carolina Press, 1963), 28.

15. David Paul Smith, *Frontier Defense in the Civil War: Texas' Rangers and Rebels* (College Station: Texas A&M University Press, 1992), 23-24; Ford, *Rip Ford's Texas*, 322-325; John Thomas Duncan, ed., "Some Civil War Letters of D. Port Smythe," *WTHAYB* 37 (October 1961): 147-176.

16. Smith, *Frontier Defense*, 32-37; William R. Geise, "Texas — The First Year of the War, April 1861-April 1862," *Military History of Texas and the Southwest* 13, no. 4 (1976): 32; Annie Heloise Abel, *The American Indian as Slaveholder and Secessionist* (Reprint, Lincoln, NE: University of Nebraska Press, 1992), 99-100; Richard B. McCaslin, "Conditional Confederates: The Eleventh Texas Cavalry West of the Mississippi River," *Military History of the Southwest* 21 (Spring 1991): 87-99; Richard B. McCaslin, *Tainted Breeze: The Great Hanging at Gainesville, Texas, 1862* (Baton Rouge: Louisiana State University Press, 1994), 41-46.

17. Smith, *Frontier Defense*, 41-56; W. C. Holden, "Frontier Defense in Texas During the Civil War," *WTHAYB* 4 (June 1928): 22-23.

18. *Official Records*, 3:104-107, 118-120; Cutrer, *Ben McCulloch*, 194-244; Victor M. Rose, *The Life and Services of Gen. Ben McCulloch* (1888; reprint, Austin: Steck Company, 1958), 136-142; Douglas John Cater, *As It Was: Reminiscences of A Soldier of the Third Texas Cavalry and the Nineteenth Louisiana Infantry* (1981; reprint, Austin: State House Press, 1990), 86-90; Douglas Hale, *The Third Texas Cavalry in the Civil War* (Norman: University of Oklahoma Press, 1993), 50-69; S. B. Barron, *The Lone Star Defenders: A Chronicle of the Third Texas Cavalry, Ross' Brigade* (New York: Neale Publishing Company, 1908), 49-51; Kel N. Pickens, "The Battle of Wilson's Creek, Missouri, August 10, 1861," *Journal of the*

West 19 (October 1980): 10-25; Carl Moneyhon, "1861: 'The Die Is Cast'," in *Rugged and Sublime: The Civil War in Arkansas*, ed. Mark F. Christ (Fayetteville: University of Arkansas Press, 1994), 14-17.

19. Walter P. Lane, *The Adventures and Recollections of General Walter P. Lane . . .* (1887; reprint, Austin: Pemberton Press, 1970), 85-89; Cutrer, *Ben McCulloch*, 245-273; Hale, *Third Texas Cavalry*, 79-83; Homer L. Kerr, ed., *Fighting with Ross' Texas Cavalry Brigade, C.S.A.: The Diary of George L. Griscom, Adjutant, 9th Texas Cavalry Regiment* (Hillsboro, TX: Hill Junior College Press, 1976), 10-11; Cater, *As It Was*, 100-105; Lary C. Rampp and Donald L. Rampp, "The Civil War in Indian Territory: The Confederate Advantage, 1861-1862," *Military History of Texas and the Southwest* 10, no. 1(1972): 35-36.

20. Hall, *Sibley's New Mexico Campaign*, 3-14; Stanley S. Graham, "Campaign for New Mexico, 1861-1862," *Military History of Texas and the Southwest* 10, no. 1 (1972): 5-12.

21. Hall, *Sibley's New Mexico Campaign*, 17-18; Alvin M. Josephy, *The Civil War in the American West* (New York: Alfred A. Knopf, 1991), 40.

22. Hall, *Sibley's New Mexico Campaign*, 24-26; Martin Hardwick Hall, *The Confederate Army of New Mexico* (Austin: Presidial Press, 1978), 18-21; Jerry Don Thompson, *Colonel John Robert Baylor: Texas Indian Fighter and Confederate Soldier* (Hillsboro, TX: Hill Junior College Press, 1971), 24-26.

23. *Official Records*, 4:5-20; Josephy, *Civil War in the American West*, 43-49; Martin Hardwick Hall, "The Skirmish at Mesilla," *Arizona and the West* 1 (Winter 1959): 343-351; Martin Hardwick Hall, "Planter vs. Frontiersman: Conflict in Confederate Indian Policy," in *Essays on the American Civil War*, ed. William F. Holmes and Harold M. Hollingsworth (Austin: Published for University of Texas at Arlington by University of Texas Press, 1968), 46-49.

24. Thompson, *Colonel John Robert Baylor*, 45-46; Hall, "Planter vs. Frontiersman," 49-50. Shortly after the capture of Lynde's forces, Albert Sidney Johnston, who had resigned his commission in the United States army and was making his way back to Virginia to accept appointment in the Confederate army, came through the area. Baylor turned over command to Johnston, whom he greatly admired. Johnston stayed at Mesilla only a week before continuing his journey. Baylor's younger brother, George, followed Johnston on east and became one of his staff officers. Jerry Don Thompson, in a note to Morgan Wolfe Merrick's Civil War journal, states that family legend holds that Johnston died in Baylor's arms after suffering a mortal wound at Shiloh in April 1862. *From Desert to Bayou: The Civil War Journal and Sketches of Morgan Wolfe Merrick* (San Antonio: Daughters of the Republic of Texas Library, 1991), 108-109. See also Charles P. Roland, *Albert Sidney Johnston: Soldier of Three Republics* (Austin: University of Texas Press, 1964), 255-258, for an account of Johnston's brief command in New Mexico.

25. Hall, *Sibley's New Mexico Campaign*, 29-30. For more on Sibley's career see Jerry Don Thompson, *Henry Hopkins Sibley, Confederate General of the West* (Natchitoches, LA: Northwestern University Press, 1978); Frazier, *Blood and Treasure*, 44-47.

26. There has been much speculation about Sibley's motives and plans. Capt. Trevanion T. Teel, an artillery officer with Sibley, later wrote that Sibley had told him that his ultimate goal was the conquest of California and annexation of northern Mexico. T. T. Teel, "Sibley's New Mexico Campaign — Its Objects and the

Cause of Its Failure," *Battles & Leaders*, 2:700. Martin Hall, *Sibley's New Mexico Campaign*, 32, in commenting on Teel's revelation, states that while California conquest may have been in Sibley's mind there is no record of it. For other views, see Frazier, *Blood and Treasure*, 3-4, 75; W. H. Watford, "Confederate Western Ambitions," *SHQ* 44 (October 1940): 161-187; and Jason H. Silverman, "Confederate Ambitions for the Southwest: A New Perspective," *Red River Valley Historical Review* 4 (Winter 1979): 63-71.

27. Hall, *Sibley's New Mexico Campaign*, 34-36; Marcus J. Wright, comp., *Texas in the War, 1861-1865*, ed. Harold B. Simpson (Hillsboro, TX: Hill Junior College Press, 1965), 78-79, 93, 112; Don E. Alberts, ed., *Rebels on the Rio Grande: The Civil War Journal of A. B. Peticolas* (Albuquerque, NM: Merit Press, 1993), 20-21; Frazier, *Blood and Treasure*, 78-83.

28. Hall, *Sibley's New Mexico Campaign*, 43, 54; Josephy, *Civil War in the American West*, 53. Drinking was not confined to Sibley. William Henry Smith, a private in the Fifth Cavalry, complained that the officers of the brigade were "drunk all the time, unfit for duty — incompetent to attend to duty." Walter A. Faulkner, ed., "With Sibley in New Mexico: The Journal of William Henry Smith," *WTHAYB* 27 (October 1951): 137. For more on Sibley's health see Jack D. Welsh, *Medical Histories of Confederate Generals* (Kent, OH: Kent State University Press, 1995), 196-197.

29. Roy C. Colton, *The Civil War in the Western Territories* (Norman: University of Oklahoma Press, 1959), 23-24; Hall, *Sibley's New Mexico Campaign*, 45-47.

30. *Ibid.*, 50-58; Arthur A. Wright, *The Civil War in the Southwest* (Denver: Big Mountain Press, 1964), 53-55.

31. William C. Whitford, *Colorado Volunteers in the Civil War: New Mexican Campaigns of 1862* (1906; reprint, Glorieta, NM: Rio Grande Press, 1971), 131, states that Canby was Sibley's brother-in-law, having married Sibley's sister. Max C. Heyman, Jr., *Prudent Soldier: A Biography of Major General E. R. S. Canby, 1817-1873* (Glendale, CA: The Arthur H. Clark Company, 1959), 178n, points out that this is incorrect. More recently Martin Hardwick Hall, *Confederate Army of New Mexico*, 35, and Alvin J. Josephy, Jr., *Civil War in the American West*, 38 (citing Hall), have written that Canby was married to a cousin of Sibley's wife. Ezra J. Warner, *Generals in Blue: Lives of Union Commanders* (Baton Rouge: Louisiana State University Press, 1964), 617n, states that after "exhaustive research" he found no connection by marriage between the Sibley and Canby families.

32. The most complete account of the battle is John M. Taylor, *Bloody Valverde: A Civil War Battle on the Rio Grande, February 21, 1862* (Albuquerque: University of New Mexico Press, 1985. The captured Union artillery pieces were organized into a new Confederate unit known as the Valverde battery. Hall, *Sibley's New Mexico Campaign*, 213n; *Official Records*, 9:490-521; Noel, *A Campaign from Santa Fe to the Mississippi*, 19-20; Alberts, ed., *Rebels on the Rio Grande*, 41-49; George H. Pettis, "The Confederate Invasion of New Mexico and Arizona," *Battles & Leaders*, 2:106-108; A. W. Evans, "Canby at Valverde," *ibid.*, 2:699-700; Heyman, *Prudent Soldier*, 166-170; David P. Perrine, "The Battle of Valverde, New Mexico Territory, February 21, 1862," *Journal of the West* 19 (October 1980): 26-38; Alwyn Barr, ed., *Charles Porter's Account of the Confederate Attempt to Seize Arizona and New Mexico* (Austin: Pemberton Press, 1964), 14-16.

33. Sibley's deputy, Texan Tom Green, also had a drinking problem, according to some witnesses. See Curtis M. Milburn, "Brigadier General Tom Green of Texas," *ETHJ* 32 (Spring 1994): 5, 10. Lt. Col. Arthur P. Bagby of the Seventh Cavalry was also accused of excessive drinking. See Martin Hardwick Hall, "The Court-Martial of Arthur Pendleton Bagby, C.S.A.," *ETHJ* 19 (Fall 1981): 60-67. For other views, see David B. Gracy, II, ed., "New Mexico Campaign Letters of Frank Starr, 1861-1862," *Military History of Texas and the Southwest* 4 (Fall 1964): 182; Michael L. Tate, ed., "A Johnny Reb in Sibley's New Mexico Campaign: Reminiscences of Pvt. Henry C. Wright, 1861-1862," *ETHJ* 25 (Fall 1987): Part I, 25-28; Martin Hardwick Hall, "An Appraisal of the 1862 New Mexico Campaign: A Confederate Officer's Letter to Nacogdoches," *New Mexico Historical Review* 51 (October 1976): 329-335.

34. Josephy, *Civil War in the American West*, 74-75; Jerry D. Thompson, ed., *Westward the Texans: The Civil War Journal of Private William Randolph Howell* (El Paso: Texas Western Press, 1990), 5; Alberts, ed., *Rebels on the Rio Grande*, 62-63.

35. Hall, *Sibley's New Mexico Campaign*, 131-140; Alberts, ed., *Rebels on the Rio Grande*, 75-76; Frazier, *Blood and Treasure*, 208-210.

36. Hall, *Sibley's New Mexico Campaign*, 140-160; Frazier, *Blood and Treasure*, 211-228; Josephy, *Civil War in the American West*, 75-85; J. F. Santee, "The Battle of La Glorieta Pass," *New Mexico Historical Review* 6 (January 1931): 66-75; *Official Records*, 9:530-545; Tate, ed., "Reminiscences of Private Henry C. Wright," *ETHJ* 26 (Spring 1988): Part II, 25; David Westphall, "The Battle of Glorieta Pass: Its Importance in the Civil War," *New Mexico Historical Review* 44 (April 1969): 144-150.

37. Alberts, ed., *Rebels on the Rio Grande*, 102-106. For more on the fighting at Peralta, see Don E. Alberts, "The Battle of Peralta," *New Mexico Historical Review* 58 (October 1983): 369-379.

38. Hall, *Sibley's New Mexico Campaign*, 161-214; Noel, *A Campaign from Santa Fe to the Mississippi*, 26-39; *Official Records*, 9:509-512; Thompson, ed., *Westward the Texans*, 7-9; Pettis, "The Confederate Invasion of New Mexico and Arizona," 110-111; Alberts, ed., *Rebels on the Rio Grande*, 107-152; Frazier, *Blood and Treasure*, 249-267.

39. Thompson, *Colonel John Robert Baylor*, 66-91; Hall, *Sibley's New Mexico Campaign*, 217-226; Hall, "Planter vs. Frontiersman," 61-72. For Baylor's defense of his letter see Thompson, *Colonel John Robert Baylor*, 99-103; Frazier, *Blood and Treasure*, 297, points out that Baylor continued to lobby for the conquest of the Southwest. In March 1865, he was reinstated in the army and was assigned to raise a regiment for that purpose. The war ended, however, before he could carry out the assignment.

40. Yearns, ed., *Confederate Governors*, 197; Hartje, *Van Dorn*, 88-89; Alwyn Barr, "Texas Coastal Defense, 1861-1865," *SHQ* 65 (July 1961): 3-4; Alwyn Barr, "Texas Confederate Artillery," *Texas Military History* 1 (August 1961): 1-8; Alwyn Barr, "Confederate Artillery in the Trans Mississippi," *Military Affairs* 27 (Summer 1963): 81; Lubbock, *Six Decades in Texas*, 317; *Handbook of Texas*, 3: 63-64; W. T. Block, *A History of Jefferson County, Texas From Wilderness to Reconstruction* (Nederland, TX: Nederland Printing, 1976), 98-99.

41. *Official Records of the Union and Confederate Navies in the War of Rebel-*

lion (Washington: Government Printing Office, 1894-1927), Series I, 16: 595-597, 605-609; cited hereinafter as *Official Records, Navies*; David G. McComb, *Galveston: A History* (Austin: University of Texas Press, 1981), 73-74; Ashcraft, "Texas: 1860-1866," 84.

42. Hartje, *Van Dorn*, 88-90; Oates, "Texas Under the Secessionists," 194-195; Thomas North, *Five Years in Texas; or, What You Did Not Hear During the War from January 1861, to January 1866* (Cincinnati: Elm Street Printing Company, 1971), 105-106.

43. Yearns, ed., *Confederate Governors*, 198; Nancy Head Bowen, "A Political Labyrinth: Texas in the Civil War — Questions in Continuity," (Ph.D. dissertation, Rice University, 1974), 27-36; *Texas State Gazette*, June 22, 1861; *Clarksville Standard*, July 20, 1861.

44. Lubbock, *Six Decades in Texas*, 324, 329. Lubbock's support was strongest in the upper Gulf Coast counties and in West Texas. He also carried the larger towns of the state (Houston, Galveston, San Antonio, and Austin). Clark ran well in east and north central Texas. Chambers, who was the gadfly in the election, had support in south central Texas, especially German counties where voters apparently were convinced that Clark was a Know-Nothing and considered Lubbock too supportive of secession and slavery. See Bowen, "Political Labyrinth," 36-39.

45. Lubbock, *Six Decades in Texas*, 329; Thomas B. Alexander and Richard E. Beringer, *The Anatomy of the Confederate Congress* (Nashville: Vanderbilt University Press, 1972), 354-405.

46. *Official Records*, 4:126-127.

47. Governor Lubbock to Gen. P. O. Hebert, December 7, 1861, Executive Record Book, Lubbock, *Six Decades in Texas*, 348-350. For more on the burning of the *Royal Yacht*, see Mitchell S. Goldberg, "A Federal Raid into Galveston Harbor, November 7-8, 1861: What Really Happened?" *SHQ* 76 (July 1972): 58-70.

48. Lubbock to Thomas M. Joseph, December 19, 1861, Executive Record Book; Meiners, "Texas Governorship," 160-161; Yearns, ed., *Confederate Governors*, 203.

49. Meiners, "Texas Governorship," 161-162; Governor Lubbock to B. Shepherd, W. J. Hutchins, and T. W. House, April 2, 1862, Executive Record Book; *Official Records*, 9:700.

50. The author wishes to thank Mr. W. D. (Bill) Quick of Nederland for providing this bit of information. See *Official Records, Navies*, 18:833, and "Confederate Minister to England Forced to Land Near Sabine After Federal Blockade," *Port Arthur News*, July 1, 1923.

51. Ashcraft, "Texas: 1860-1866," 115-117; Proclamation by the Governor, May 14, 1862, Executive Record Book.

52. Barr, "Texas Coastal Defense," 11-12; Lester N. Fitzhugh, "Saluria, Fort Esperanza, and Military Operations on the Texas Coast, 1861-1864," *SHQ* 61 (July 1957): 74-77; Norman Delaney, "Corpus Christi — The Vicksburg of Texas," *Civil War Times Illustrated* 16 (July 1977): 4-9, 44-48; Nueces County Historical Society, *The History of Nueces County* (Austin: Jenkins Publishing Company, 1972), 66-70.

53. Texas units under McCulloch at this time were the Third Cavalry (Elkanah Greer), Sixth Cavalry (B. Warren Stone), Ninth Cavalry (William B. Sims), Eleventh Cavalry (William C. Young), First Cavalry Battalion (Phillip

Crump), Fourth Cavalry Battalion, dismounted (John W. Whitfield), Good's Battery (John J. Good), and Welch's Cavalry Squadron (Otis G. Welch). William L. Shea and Earl J. Hess, *Pea Ridge: Civil War Campaign in the West* (Chapel Hill: University of North Carolina Press, 1992), 335-336. For more on the differences between McCulloch and Price, see William L. Shea, "The Road to Pea Ridge," *Arkansas Historical Quarterly* 52 (Autumn 1993): 209-210.

54. Shea and Hess, *Pea Ridge*, 110-112; Cutrer, *Ben McCulloch*, 303-304; William L. Shea, "1862: 'A Continual Thunder'," in *Rugged and Sublime: The Civil War in Arkansas*, 27-32.

55. Albert Pike, a brigadier general commanding two Confederate Indian regiments, was the ranking Confederate officer on the Leetown battlefield but was having difficulties controlling his own regiments. Shea and Hess, *Pea Ridge*, 113-260; Cutrer, *Ben McCulloch*, 305-309; Hale, *Third Texas Cavalry*, 97-99; Homer L. Kerr, "Battle of Elkhorn: The Gettysburg of the Trans-Mississippi West," in *Essays on the American Civil War*, 37-42; Edwin C. Bearss, "The Battle of Pea Ridge," *Arkansas Historical Quarterly* 20 (Spring 1961): 74-94; Walter L. Brown, "Pea Ridge: Gettysburg of the West," *ibid.*, 15 (Spring 1956): 3-16; Maynard J. Hanson, "The Battle of Pea Ridge, Arkansas, March 6-8, 1862," *Journal of the West* 19 (October 1980): 39-50. For more on Texas in the defense of Arkansas, see Robert T. Maberry, Jr., "Texans and the Defense of the Confederate Northwest, April 1861-April 1862: A Social and Military History" (Ph.D. dissertation, Texas Christian University, 1992).

56. Cater, *As It Was*, 119; Lane, *Adventures and Recollections*, 92; Cutrer, *Ben McCulloch*, 306-309; Shea and Hess, *Pea Ridge*, 311-313; Hartje, *Van Dorn*, 155-161; Lester Newton Fitzhugh, ed., *Cannon Smoke: The Letters of Captain John J. Good, Good-Douglas Texas Battery, C.S.A.* (Hillsboro: Hill Junior College Press, 1971), 162-166.

57. Roland, *Albert Sidney Johnston*, 261. Gregg and his troops were later exchanged. Gregg rejoined the army in Mississippi but was later transferred to Virginia, where he was placed in command of Hood's Texas Brigade. He was killed on October 7, 1864, near Fort Harrison. *Handbook of Texas*, 1:733; Wright and Simpson, *Texas in the War*, 80. For the Henry-Donelson campaigns, see Benjamin Franklin Cooling, *Forts Henry and Donelson: The Key to the Confederate Heartland* (Knoxville: University of Tennessee Press, 1987).

58. In his report of the battle, Maj. Gen. William J. Hardee was critical of the retreat of the Second Texas in the fighting on the second day at Shiloh. It was possible, however, that Hardee was using the Second Texas as a scapegoat for his own mistakes. Young, *To the Tyrants Never Yield*, 114-116. For more on the role of Texans at Shiloh, see *Official Records*, Pt. 1, 10: 494-504, 508-510, 560-571, 626; Evans, ed., *Confederate Military History*, 11:157-159; Eleanor Damon Pace, ed., "The Diary and Letters of William P. Rogers, 1846-1862," *SHQ* 32 (April 1929): 286-287; Wiley Sword, *Shiloh: Bloody April* (New York: William Morrow & Company, 1974), 230, 391, 406; James Lee McDonough, *Shiloh — in Hell before Night* (Knoxville: University of Tennessee Press, 1977), 177; Blackburn, "Reminiscences of the Terry Rangers," 55-61; Joseph E. Chance, *The Second Texas Infantry: From Shiloh to Vicksburg* (Austin: Eakin Press, 1984), 24-35; Elizabeth Silverthorne, *Ashbel Smith of Texas: Pioneer, Patriot, and Statesman, 1805-1886* (College

Station: Texas A&M University Press, 1982), 149-150; Sam Houston, Jr., "Shiloh Shadows," *SHQ* 34 (April 1931): 329-333.

59. Roland, *Albert Sidney Johnston*, 337-338. Roland notes that it is puzzling that Johnston's associates failed to care for the wound. There was a tourniquet on his person that could have been used to stop the flow of blood. Roland speculates that perhaps Harris and others were blinded by panic or may have been ignorant of the danger from bleeding. Johnston's physician was, by Johnston's order, attending wounded Confederates and Union prisoners in a nearby ravine. See also Appendix A, "The Death of Albert Sidney Johnston," Sword, *Shiloh: Bloody April,* 442-446. Sword believes that the bullet that killed Johnston may have been from his own men during the confused fighting. *Ibid.,* 444. Welsh, *Medical Histories of Confederate Generals*, 118-119, points out Johnston was struck three times in the lower limbs in addition to the fatal wound.

60. Charles P. Roland, *Albert Sidney Johnston*, 341, notes that today's students of the Civil War generally do not believe Johnston's death altered the outcome of the battle. Roland does agree that the Confederates lost momentum when Johnston fell. See also William Preston Johnston, "Albert Sidney Johnston at Shiloh," *Battles & Leaders*, 1:564-565.

61. Simpson, *Hood's Texas Brigade: Compendium*, viii - ix; and *Hood's Texas Brigade: Lee's Grenadier Guard* (hereinafter cited as *Lee's Grenadier Guard*), 82-84; Robert K. Krick, *Lee's Colonels: A Biographical Register of the Field Officers of the Army of Northern Virginia* (4th ed. rev., Dayton, OH: Morningside Press, 1992), 255-256.

62. *Ibid.,* 88-90; John Bell Hood, *Advance and Retreat: Personal Experiences in the United States and Confederate Armies* (New Orleans: G. T. Beauregard, 1880), 16.

63. For more on these early activities, and particularly their efforts in fighting their way out of an enemy abush on the night of January 28, 1862, see Judith N. McArthur, "'Those Texians Are Number One Men': A New Confederate Account of the Affair at Lee's House, Virginia," *SHQ* 95 (April 1992): 488-496; Simpson, *Lee's Grenadier Guard*, 75-78; J. B. Polley, *Hood's Texas Brigade: Its Marches, Its Battles, Its Achievements* (New York: Neale Publishing Company, 1910), 17.

64. Simpson, *Lee's Grenadier Guard*, 98-103; Donald E. Everett, ed., *Chaplain Davis and Hood's Texas Brigade* (San Antonio: Principia Press of Trinity University, 1962), 59-65; Richard M. McMurry, *John Bell Hood and the War for Southern Independence* (Lexington, KY: University Press of Kentucky, 1982), 37-40; Stephen W. Sears, *To the Gates of Richmond: The Peninsula Campaign* (New York: Ticknor & Fields, 1992), 85-86.

65. Everett, ed., *Chaplain Davis*, 65-70; Hood, *Advance and Retreat*, 21-23.

66. McMurry, *John Bell Hood*, 45-49; Simpson, *Lee's Grenadier Guard*, 112-122; Sears, *Gates of Richmond*, 239-244; Joseph P. Cullen, "The Battle of Gaines' Mill," *Civil War Times Illustrated* 3 (April 1964): 16-17.

67. Robertson, a Washington County physician and former state legislator, succeeded J. J. Archer in command of the Fifth Texas when Archer was promoted to brigadier general and given command of a Tennessee brigade. Simpson, *Lee's Grenadier Guard*, 122-124; McMurry, *John Bell Hood*, 49-50; *Official Records*, Pt. 2, 11:973; Everett, ed., *Chaplain Davis*, 74-92; Langston James Goree, V, ed., *The*

Thomas Jewett Goree Letters (Bryan: Family History Foundations, 1981), 1: 157-165; Krick, *Lee's Colonels*, 263, 387-388.

68. Simpson, *Lee's Grenadier Guard*, 135-154; *Official Records*, Pt. 2, 12:609-618; John J. Hennessy, *Return to Bull Run: The Campaign and Battle of Second Manassas* (New York: Simon & Schuster, 1991), 365-406; Mamie Yeary, comp., *Reminiscences of the Boys in Gray, 1861-65* (Dallas: Smith & Lamar, 1912), 816-817.

69. Simpson, *Lee's Grenadier Guard*, 156-157.

CHAPTER THREE

1. *Official Records,* Pt. 1, 16:934. See also Jon Harrison, "Tenth Texas Cavalry, C.S.A.," *Military History of Texas and the Southwest* 12, no. 2 (1975): 97-102; and James Lee McDonough, *War in Kentucky: From Shiloh to Perryville* (Knoxville: University of Tennessee Press, 1994), 134-145. The four Texas regiments, along with McCray's own Thirty-first Arkansas Infantry, made up the brigade. Because of consolidations, the Thirty-second Texas Cavalry was sometimes referred to as the Fifteenth Texas Cavalry. See Wright and Simpson, *Texas in the War*, 121, and *Official Records*, Pt. 1, 16:940-942.

2. Blackburn, "Reminiscences of the Terry Rangers," 68-71; Ralph A. Wooster, "With the Confederate Cavalry in the West: The Civil War Experiences of Isaac Dunbar Affleck," *SHQ* 83 (July 1979): 6-7; David B. Gracy II, "With Danger and Honor: George W. Littlefield, 1861-1864," *Texana* 1 (Winter 1963): 16-17.

3. *Official Records*, Pt. 1, 19:922-925, 927-937; Simpson, *Lee's Grenadier Guard*, 171-175; Hood, *Advance and Retreat*, 42-46; Stephen W. Sears, *Landscape Turned Red; The Battle of Antietam* (New Haven, CT: Ticknor & Fields, 1993), 197-210; William R. Hamby, "Hood's Texas Brigade at Sharpsburg," *Confederate Veteran* 16 (January 1908): 19-22; D. H. Hamilton, *History of Company M, First Texas Volunteer Infantry: Hood's Brigade* (Waco: W. M. Morrison, 1962), 22-24; John M. Priest, *Antietam: The Soldiers' Battle* (New York: Oxford University Press, 1989), 55, 60-67, 73, 83-99.

4. *Official Records*, 811, 922-925, 927-937; Simpson, *Lee's Grenadier Guard*, 176-177; Everett, *Chaplain Davis*, 192-193, 197-198, 228; Sears, *Landscape Turned Red*, 295-296. These figures vary slightly from those given in Priest,*Antietam*, 323.

5. *Official Records*, Pt. 1, 16:1088-1094, 1109-1112; Joseph Wheeler, "Bragg's Invasion of Kentucky," *Battles & Leaders*, 3:15-17; Evans, ed., *Confederate Military History*, 11:165; Robert W. Williams, Jr., and Ralph A. Wooster, eds., "With Terry's Texas Rangers: The Letters of Dunbar Affleck," *Civil War History* 9 (September 1963): 310-311; Ralph A. Wooster, "Confederate Success at Perryville," *Register of Kentucky Historical Society* 59 (October 1961): 318-323; Grady McWhiney, *Braxton Bragg and Confederate Defeat* (New York: Columbia University Press, 1969), 310-319; Grady McWhiney, "Controversy in Kentucky: Braxton Bragg's Campaign of 1862," *Civil War History* 6 (March 1960): 5-42; McDonough, *War in Kentucky*, 201-296.

6. Evans, ed., *Confederate Military History*, 11: 72-73; *Official Records*, 15: 143-147; *Official Records, Navies*, 19:227-229; W. T. Block, *History of Jefferson County*, 102-104; W. T. Block, "The Civil War Comes to Jefferson County, Texas," *Blue & Gray Magazine* 4 (September 1986): 14-15. Block, *History of Jeffer-*

son County, 104, notes that the compiler of the *Official Records* erroneously reported "the burning of the railway bridge and depot at Beaumont."

7. Barr, "Texas Coastal Defense," 13; *Galveston Weekly News*, October 15, 1862; Fornell, *Galveston Era*, 197-198.

8. *Official Records, Navies*, 19:213, 254-260; Charles C. Cumberland, "The Confederate Loss and Recapture of Galveston, 1862-1863," *SHQ* 51 (October 1947): 110-114.

9. *Official Records, Navies*, 19:256-258; Barr, "Texas Coastal Defense," 13; Ashcraft, "Texas: 1860-1866," 118-120; William Pitt Ballinger, Diary, Barker History Center, quoted in McComb, *Galveston*, 75.

10. Lubbock Proclamation, October 12, 1862, Executive Record Book, 118; Lubbock, *Six Decades in Texas*, 420-422.

11. Evans, ed., *Confederate Military History*, 9:76-77; Barr, "Texas Coastal Defense," 14; Young, *To the Tyrants Never Yield*, 123-127.

12. *Official Records, Navies*, 19:404; Cumberland, "Confederate Loss and Recapture of Galveston," 116-117.

13. *Ibid.*, 118; *Official Records, Navies*, 19:457.

14. Ford, *Rip Ford's Texas*, 343; Oates, "Texas Under the Secessionists," 194-195; Wooster, "With Confederate Cavalry in the West," 11-12, 18, 22. For more on Magruder's background, see Thomas M. Settles, "The Military Career of John Bankhead Magruder" (Ph.D. dissertation, Texas Christian University, 1972) and Timothy D. Spell, "John Bankhead Magruder: Defender of the Texas Coast, 1863" (M. A. thesis, Lamar University, 1981).

15. *Official Records*, 15:211-220, 884-886; Spell, "John Bankhead Magruder," 30-36; Ashcraft, "Texas: 1860-1866," 120-121; Faulk, *General Tom Green*, 48-50; Robert M. Franklin, *Battle of Galveston, January 1, 1863* (Reprint; Galveston: San Luis Press, 1975), 4-5; X. B. Debray, *A Sketch of the History of Debray's (26th) Regiment of Texas Cavalry* (Austin: Von Boeckmann, 1884), 6-7. For more on Capt. Leon Smith see James M. Day, "Leon Smith: Confederate Mariner," *ETHJ* 3 (March 1965): 34-49.

16. *Official Records, Navies*, 19:471-472; Spell, "John Bankhead Magruder," 36-37; Cumberland, "Confederate Loss and Recapture of Galveston," 123.

17. *Official Records, Navies*, 19:473; McComb, *Galveston*, 76-77; Spell, "John Bankhead Magruder," 39-41; Barr, "Texas Coastal Defense," 14-16.

18. *Official Records, Navies*, 19:473-474; McComb, *Galveston*, 76-77; Barr, "Texas Coastal Defense," 15-16; Evans, ed., *Confederate Military History*, 11:84-85.

19. The *Harriet Lane* carried a battery of two 32-pounders, three 9-inch Dahlgren guns, one 3-pounder Parrott gun, and two 24-pounder howitzers. Named for the niece of President James Buchanan, the *Harriet Lane* had been part of the naval squadron sent to relieve Fort Sumter in the spring of 1861. She had served as David Farragut's flagship in the capture of New Orleans in the spring of 1862. See Philip C. Tucker, III, "The United States Gunboat *Harriet Lane*," *SHQ* 21 (April 1918): 360-380; H. A. Trexler, "The *Harriet Lane* and the Blockade of Galveston," *ibid.*, 35 (October 1931): 109-123; and David P. Martin, "The *Harriet Lane*," *ibid.*, 39 (July 1935): 15-20.

20. Franklin, *Battle of Galveston*, 2; *Official Records, Navies*, 19:474; Cumberland, "Confederate Loss and Recapture of Galveston," 124-125. Controversy surrounds the death of Union Captain Wainwright. In his initial report of

the engagement, Magruder stated that Captain Smith killed Wainwright at close quarters. This was reported by both the *Galveston Weekly News* and the *New York Herald*. Smith defended himself from charges that he deliberately killed Wainwright, declaring that it was impossible to distinguish Wainwright from other officers because he wore no uniform or insignia of rank. See Day, "Leon Smith," 39, and Spell, "John Bankhead Magruder," 88.

21. Lubbock, *Six Decades in Texas*, 437; *Handbook of Texas*, 2:39-40; W. T. Block, "A Towering East Texas Pioneer: A Biographical Sketch of Colonel Albert Miller Lea," *ETHJ* 32 (Fall 1993): 27-28.

22. *Official Records, Navies*, 19:474; Cumberland, "Confederate Loss and Recapture of Galveston," 124-126; Evans, ed., *Confederate Military History*, 11: 85-86.

23. *Official Records, Navies*, 19:439; Cumberland, "Confederate Loss and Recapture of Galveston," 125-126; Virgil Carrington Jones, *The Civil War at Sea*, 3 vols. (New York: Holt, Rinehart, Winston, 1961), 2:323-325; Virgil Carrington Jones, "The Battle of Galveston Harbor," *Civil War Times Illustrated* 5 (February 1967): 33-38.

24. *Official Records, Navies*, 19:475.

25. *Houston Tri-Weekly Telegraph*, January 5, 1863; Thomas North, *Five Years in Texas*, 113; Lubbock, *Six Decades in Texas*, 451-453; *Writings of Sam Houston*, 8:324.

26. Edgar T. Welles, ed., *Diary of Gideon Welles*, 2 vols. (Cambridge: Riverside Press, 1911), 2:324; Lubbock, *Six Decades in Texas*, 453-454; *Official Records, Navies*, 19:463.

27. *Official Records, Navies*, 19:479.

28. *Ibid.*, 19:504; Lubbock, *Six Decades in Texas*, 454-455; Cumberland, "Confederate Loss and Recapture of Galveston," 127. Henry Renfro, a Texas soldier stationed on the island, reported that the Union fired 105 rounds but "there was nothing killed but a goat." William Clark Griggs, *Parson Henry Renfro: Free Thinking on the Texas Frontier* (Austin: University of Texas Press, 1994), 54.

29. Raphael Semmes, *Memoirs of Service Afloat, During the War Between the States* (Baltimore: Kelly, Piet, and Co., 1869), 542-550; Lubbock, *Six Decades in Texas*, 455-457; *Official Records, Navies*, 19:507-510.

30. W. T. Block, "The Swamp Angels: A History of Spaight's 11th Battalion, Texas Volunteers, Confederate States Army," *ETHJ* 30 (Spring 1992): 49; Block, *History of Jefferson County*, 106; *Official Records*, 19:564-565; K. D. Keith, "The Memoirs of Captain Kosciuszko D. Keith," *Texas Gulf Historical and Biographical Record* 10 (November 1974): 59-61.

31. Captain Keith and Capt. Peter D. Stockholm, the bar pilot on the *Bell*, blamed Major Watkins, who was intoxicated and knew nothing of navigation, with the loss of the *Morning Light*. Keith, "Memoirs," 62. See also Block, "Swamp Angels," 49-50; Block, *History of Jefferson County*, 106-107; Barr, "Texas Coastal Defense," 19; Charles A. Walker, "Spaight's Battalion, C.S.A.," *Texas Gulf Historical and Biographical Record* 8 (November 1972); J. Thomas Scharf, *History of the Confederate Navy From Its Organization to the Surrender of Its Last Vessel* (New York: Rogers & Sherwood, 1887), 515-516.

32. Barr, "Texas Coastal Defense," 20-21; *Official Records, Navies*, 20:183-184, 372; Maury Darst, "Artillery Defenses of Galveston, 1863," *Military History*

of Texas and the Southwest 12, no. 1 (1975): 63-67. See also a description by Lt. Col. Fremantle, *Diary*, 56.

33. William L. Shea, "The Confederate Defeat at Cache River," *Arkansas Historical Quarterly* 52 (Summer 1993): 129-155; Shea, "1862: 'A Continued Thunder'," in *Rugged and Sublime: The Civil War in Arkansas*, 42-44; Oates, *Confederate Cavalry West of the River*, 37-45; Bailey, *Between the Enemy and Texas*, 47-81; Robert W. Glover, ed., "War Letters of a Texas Conscript in Arkansas," *Arkansas Historical Quarterly* 20 (Winter 1961): 358-362; James M. McCaffrey, *This Band of Heroes: Granbury's Brigade, C.S.A.* (Austin: Eakin Press, 1985), 18-25.

34. Approximately half of the Texans in the Confederate army were in Arkansas in the autumn of 1862. Anne J. Bailey, "Henry McCulloch's Texans and the Defense of Arkansas in 1862," *Arkansas Historical Quarterly* 46 (Spring 1987): 46-49; *Official Records*, 13:883-884; Oates, *Confederate Cavalry West of the River*, 47-50, 88-89; Bailey, *Between the Enemy and Texas*, 83-87; Evans, ed., *Confederate Military History*, 11:193; Alwyn Barr, "Confederate Artillery in Arkansas," *Arkansas Historical Quarterly* 22 (Autumn 1963): 252.

35. For more on Cane Hill and Prairie Grove, see *Official Records*, Pt. 1, 22: 138-144, 154-157; Oates, *Confederate Cavalry West of the River*, 85-112; Stephen B. Oates, "The Prairie Grove Campaign, 1862," *Arkansas Historical Quarterly* 19 (Summer 1960): 119-141; Stephen B. Oates, "Cavalry Fight at Cane Hill," *ibid.*, 20 (Spring 1961): 65-73; Robert Logan, "The Battle of Prairie Grove," *ibid.*, 16 (Autumn 1957): 258-267; Ival L. Gregory, "The Battle of Prairie Grove, Arkansas, December 7, 1862," *Journal of the West* 19 (October 1980): 63-75; Robert S. Weddle, *Plow-Horse Cavalry: The Caney Creek Boys of the Thirty-fourth Texas* (Austin: Madrona Press, 1974), 81-84.

36. Norman D. Brown, ed., *One of Cleburne's Command: The Civil War Reminiscences and Diary of Capt. Samuel T. Foster, Granbury's Texas Brigade, C. S. A.* (Austin: University of Texas Press, 1980), xxxvii-xxxviii, 10; Spurlin, ed., *The Civil War Diary of Charles A. Leuschner*, 8-10; McCaffrey, *This Band of Heroes*, 27-28.

37. *Official Records*, Pt. 1, 17: 780-796; Brown, ed., *One of Cleburne's Command*, 8-21; Anne J. Bailey, "The Texas Cavalry's Race to Reinforce Arkansas Post, January, 1863," *ETHJ* 28 (Spring 1990): 45-56; Bailey, *Between the Enemy and Texas*, 100-108; John Q. Anderson, ed., *Campaigning with Parsons' Cavalry Brigade, C.S.A.: The War Journals and Letters of the Four Orr Brothers, 12th Texas Cavalry Regiment* (Hillsboro, TX: Hill Junior College Press, 1967), 87-89; Thomas L. Snead, "The Conquest of Arkansas," *Battles & Leaders*, 3:451-453; McCaffrey, *This Band of Heroes*, 34-43; Norman Delaney, ed., "The Diary and Memoirs of Marshall Samuel Pierson, Company C, 17th Reg., Texas Cavalry, 1862-1865," *Military History of Texas and the Southwest* 13, no. 3 (1976): 27-29.

38. Gilbert Cutherson, "Coller of the Sixth Texas: Correspondence of a Texas Infantry Man, 1861-1864, *Military History of Texas and the Southwest* 9, no. 2 (1972): 135; Harold B. Simpson, ed., *The Bugle Softly Blows: The Confederate Diary of Benjamin M. Seaton* (Waco: Texian Press, 1965), 32; Brown, ed., *One of Cleburne's Command*, 30; Heartsill, *Fourteen Hundred and 90 days in the Confederate Army*, 111-116; Joe R. Wise, ed., "The Letters of Lt. Flavius W. Perry, 17th Texas Infantry, 1862-1863," *Military History of Texas and the Southwest* 13, no. 2 (1976): 31-33; Turner, "Jim Turner, Co. G, 6th Texas Infantry," 159. Turner was

recaptured at the battle of Franklin in November 1864 and placed in Camp Douglas, where "our treatment was horrible and we almost starved to death." *Ibid.*, 177. Another Texan captured in 1864, Newton Asbury Keen, agreed with Turner that life at Camp Douglas was bad, with inadequate food, unsanitary conditions, and severe treatment by the guards. Keen, "'Such Is War': The Confederate Memoirs of Newton Asbury Keen," ed. William C. Billingsley, *Military History of Texas and the Southwest* 7 (Fall 1968): 179-183.

39. McCaffrey, *This Band of Heroes*, 58-59; Brown, ed., *One of Cleburne's Command*, 35-45; Bailey, *Between the Enemy and Texas*, 108-109. Larry J. Daniel, *Soldiering in the Army of Tennessee*, 3-4, points out that there was resentment in Bragg's army toward the Texans because of their surrender at Arkansas Post, but they were accepted into Patrick Cleburne's division and redeemed themselves in battle.

40. Samuel Carter, III, *The Final Fortress: The Campaign for Vicksburg, 1862-1863* (New York: St. Martin's Press, 1980), 106-107.

41. Oates, *Confederate Cavalry West of the River*, 121-131; Bailey, *Between the Enemy and Texas*, 113-131; Anne J. Bailey, "Texans Invade Missouri: The Cape Giradeau Raid, 1863," *Missouri Historical Review* 84 (January 1990): 166-187. The replacement of Holmes, known in the army as "Old Granny," as department commander was a popular move. See Norman D. Brown, ed., *Journey to Pleasant Hill: Civil War Letters of Captain Elijah P. Petty, Walker's Division, C.S.A.* (San Antonio: Institute of Texan Cultures, 1982), 150; Albert Castel, "Theophilus Holmes — Pallbearer of the Confederacy," *Civil War Times Illustrated* 17 (July 1977): 10-17; William R. Geise, "Holmes, Arkansas, and Defense of the Lower River, August 1862 - February 1863," *Military History of Texas and the Southwest* 14, no. 4 (1977), 234-236; Michael B. Dougan, *Confederate Arkansas: The People and Politics of a Frontier State in Wartime* (University, AL: University of Alabama Press, 1976), 92-93.

42. Robert L. Kerby, *Kirby Smith's Confederacy: The Trans-Mississippi South, 1863-1865* (New York: Columbia University Press, 1972), 98-121; J. P. Blessington, *The Campaigns of Walker's Division* (1875; reprint, Austin: State House Press, 1994), 45-59; Stewart Sifakis, *Compendium of the Confederate Armies: Texas* (New York: Facts on File, 1995), 113, 128-129. For a detailed account of one of the regiments in Walker's Division, see M. Jane Harris Johansson, "Peculiar Honor: A History of the 28th Texas Cavalry (dismounted), Walker's Texas Division, 1862-1865" (Ph.D. dissertation, University of North Texas, 1993).

43. Bailey, *Between the Enemy and Texas*, 136-138.

44. Brown, ed., *Journey to Pleasant Hill*, 234-236, 241-242; Blessington, *Campaigns of Walker's Texas Division*, 95-109; Terrence J. Winchel, "To Rescue Gibraltar: John Walker's Texas Division and Its Expedition to Relieve Fort Vicksburg," *Civil War Regiments*, Vol. 3, no. 3 (1994): 33-58; Bailey, *Between the Enemy and Texas*, 140-147; Anne J. Bailey, "A Texas Cavalry Raid: Reaction to Black Soldiers and Contrabands," *Civil War History* 35 (June 1989): 138-152; Joseph T. Glatthar, *Forged in Battle: The Civil War Alliance of Black Soldiers and White Officers* (New York: Free Press, 1990), 132-135; T. Michael Parrish, *Richard Taylor: Soldier Prince of Dixie* (Chapel Hill: University of North Carolina Press, 1992), 289-294.

45. James P. Major, a native of Missouri and a West Point graduate, served in

Texas with the United States Second Cavalry in the 1850s. During this time he married a sister-in-law of Tom Green. He was promoted to brigadier general in July 1863 as a result of his successes in Louisiana. Ezra J. Warner, *Generals in Gray: Lives of the Confederate Commanders* (Baton Rouge: Louisiana State University Press, 1959), 209-210; Parrish, *Richard Taylor*, 270-279; Thompson, *Henry Hopkins Sibley*, 327-331; Donald S. Frazier, "Texans on the Teche: The Texas Brigade at the Battles of Bisland and Irish Bend, April 12-14, 1863," *Louisiana History* 32 (Fall 1991): 417-435; Arthur W. Bergeron, Jr., *The Civil War Reminiscences of Major Silas T. Grisamore* (Baton Rouge: Louisiana State University Press, 1993), 111-124; Stephen S. Michot, "In Relief of Port Hudson: Richard Taylor's 1863 Lafourche Offensive," *Military History of the West* 23 (Fall 1993): 103-134.

46. *Official Records*, Pt. 1, 17:127-129, 392-393, 503; Barron, *Lone Star Defenders*, 96-155; Hale, *Third Texas Cavalry*, 120-173; Hartje, *Van Dorn*, 255-269.

47. Pace, ed., "The Diary and Letters of William P. Rogers," 298-299. For a full account of the Second Infantry's part in the battle of Corinth (October 3-4, 1862), see Joseph Chance, *The Second Texas Infantry: From Shiloh to Vicksburg* (Austin: Eakin Press, 1984), 63-81.

48. *Official Records*, Pt. 2, 24:381-388; Chance, *Second Texas Infantry*, 103-110.

49. *Official Records*, Pt. 2, 24:351; Evans, ed., *Confederate Military History*, 11:170-171; Herman Hattaway, *General Stephen D. Lee* (Jackson: University Press of Mississippi, 1976), 93-94; Laura Simmons, "Waul's Legion From Texas to Mississippi," *Texana* 7 (Spring 1969): 1-16; Wayne Flynt, "The Texas Legion at Vicksburg," *East Texas Historical Journal* 17 (Spring 1979): 60-67; Yeary, comp., *Reminiscences of the Boys in Gray*, 412.

50. *Official Records*, Pt. 2, 24:327-328, 384-394; Hattaway, *General Stephen D. Lee*, 97-98; Silverthorne, *Ashbel Smith*, 157-159; Walter H. Mays, ed., "The Vicksburg Diary of M. K. Simons, 1863," *Texas Military History* 5 (Spring 1965): 36; Chase, *Second Texas Infantry*, 112-119.

51. Lawrence Lee Hewitt, *Port Hudson: Confederate Bastion on the Mississippi River* (Baton Rouge: Louisiana State University Press, 1987), 40-45, 60, 122; Edward Cunningham, *The Port Hudson Campaign, 1862-1863* (Baton Rouge: Louisiana State University Press, 1963), 36-40; Louise Horton, *Samuel Bell Maxey: A Biography* (Austin: University of Texas Press, 1974), 32-34.

52. Col. Charles DeMorse, commander of the Twenty-ninth Texas Cavalry, blamed the defeat on the rain that dampened the gunpowder with which his troops were supplied. Ernest Wallace, *Charles DeMorse: Pioneer Statesman and Father of Texas Journalism* (Lubbock: Texas Tech Press, 1943), 146-147. See also Bradford K. Felmly, *Suffering to Silence: 29th Texas Cavalry, C.S.A., Regimental History* (Quanah, TX: Nortex Press, 1975), 82-95; Smith, *Frontier Defense in the Civil War*, 66-67.

53. Bailey, *Between the Enemy and Texas*, 149-153; Josephy, *Civil War in the American West*, 372-374; Albert Castel, *General Sterling Price and the Civil War in the West* (Baton Rouge: Louisiana State University Press, 1968), 153-170; Thomas A. DeBlack, "1863: 'We Must Stand or Fall Alone'," in *Rugged and Sublime: The Civil War in Arkansas*, 90-96.

54. Simpson, *Lee's Grenadier Guard*, 154-243; Hood, *Advance and Retreat*, 48-54; Fletcher, *Rebel Private, Front and Rear*, 47-58.

55. Fremantle, *Diary*, 191; Simpson, *Lee's Grenadier Guard*, 244-261.

56. *Official Records*, Pt. 2, 27:404-412; Simpson, *Lee's Grenadier Guard*, 268-282; Hood, *Advance and Retreat*, 54-59; Edwin B. Coddington, *The Gettysburg Campaign: A Study in Command* (New York: Charles Scribner's Sons, 1968), 385-410. Among those Texans captured on the second day at Gettysburg was Decimus et Ultimus Barziza, a captain in the Fourth Infantry. For his experiences as a prisoner see Decimus et Ultimus Barziza, *The Adventures of a Prisoner of War, 1863-1864*, ed. R. Henderson Shuffler (Austin: University of Texas Press, 1964).

57. Simpson, *Lee's Grenadier Guard*, 282-289. The Texas Brigade suffered 597 casualties, or 54.3 percent of those present for duty, in the Gettysburg campaign. *Official Records*, Pt. 2, 27:339-340.

58. James Lee McDonough, *Stone's River — Bloody Winter in Tennessee* (Knoxville: University of Tennessee Press, 1980), 90-91, 99-100, 248, 253-254; McCaffrey, *This Band of Heroes*, 65-68; Peter Cozzens, *No Better Place to Die: The Battle of Stone's River* (Chicago: University of Chicago Press, 1991), 85-86, 113-114, 144-146; Peter Cozzens, *This Terrible Sound: The Battle of Chickamauga* (Urbana: University of Illinois Press, 1992), 135, 544-553; Spurlin, ed., *Civil War Diary of Charles A. Leuschner*, 14-19; Simpson, *Lee's Grenadier Guard*, 290-312; *Official Records*, Pt. 2, 30:187-196; James P. Douglas, *Douglas's Texas Battery, C. S. A.*, ed. Lucia Rutherford Douglas (Waco: Smith County Historical Society, 1966), 44-46, 56-59; H. J. H. Rugeley, ed., *Batchelor-Turner Letters, 1861-1864, Written by Two of Terry's Texas Rangers* (Austin: Steck Company, 1961), 41-43.

59. *Official Records*, Pt. 2, 30:21-37, 287-292; Simpson, *Lee's Grenadier Guard*, 314-327; Hood, *Advance and Retreat*, 61-64; Evans, ed., *Confederate Military History*, 11:174-179; Cozzens, *This Terrible Sound*, 406-416.

60. James Lee McDonough, *Chattanooga — A Death Grip on the Confederacy* (Knoxville: University of Tennessee Press, 1984), 13-15, points out that determining exact figures for Chickamauga is difficult. Peter Cozzens, *This Terrible Sound*, 534, notes that "missing reports and contradictory estimates make it impossible to offer up with certainty any figures for the Confederacy." Thomas L. Livermore, *Numbers and Losses*, 105-106, estimates Confederate losses at 18,454. Glen Tucker, *Chickamauga: Bloody Battle in the West* (Indianapolis: Bobbs-Merrill, 1961), 388-389, gives 20,950 as the Confederate casualties.

61. *Official Records*, Pt. 2, 30:153-159, 187-191, 239-243, 287-292, 497, 510-519; Simpson, *Lee's Grenadier Guard*, 320-329; Turner, "Jim Turner, Co. G, 6th Texas Infantry," 162. Col. William Hugh Young, commander of the Ninth Texas, was one of the regimental commanders wounded at Chickamauga. Wright and Simpson, *Texas in the War, 1861-1865*, 97-98, point out that few officers in the Civil War received more wounds than Young, who was wounded in the shoulder at Murfreesboro, in the thigh at Jackson, in the chest at Chickamauga, in the neck and jaw at Kennesaw Mountain, and in the foot at Allatoona. He was captured at Allatoona in 1864 and imprisoned at Johnson's Island. For more on Young's injuries, see Welsh, *Medical Histories of Confederate Generals*, 242-243.

62. *Official Records*, Pt. 2, 30:239-243; Judy Watson McClure, ed., *Confederate From East Texas: The Civil War Letters of James Monroe Watson* (Quanah, TX: Nortex Press, 1976), 27-28; Simpson, *Lee's Grenadier Guard*, 333-381; Rugeley,

ed., *Batchelor-Turner Letters*, 71-72; Steven E. Woodworth, *Jefferson Davis and His Generals: The Failure of Confederate Command in the West* (Lawrence, KS: University Press of Kansas, 1990), 239-241.

63. *Official Records*, Pt. 2, 31:664-667, 772-775; Evans, ed., *Confederate Military Record*, 11:179-182, 227-228, 230-231; Douglas, ed., *Douglas' Texas Battery*, 77-78; Brown, ed., *One of Cleburne's Command*, 58-65; Spurlin, ed., *Civil War Diary of Charles A. Leuschner*, 23-27; McCaffrey, *This Band of Heroes*, 88-96. Wiley Sword, *Mountains Touched with Fire: Chattanooga Besieged, 1863* (New York: St. Martin's Press, 1995), 243-244, 246-247, 335-338, 343.

64. W. T. Block, "Sabine Pass in the Civil War," *ETHJ* 9 (October 1971): 132; Block, "Fort Griffin Myths Exploded," *ibid.*, 137-138; Block, "Legend of 2 Old Cannons," *ibid.*, 147-149; Block, *History of Jefferson County*, 108; Harold Simpson, "The Battle of Sabine Pass," in Seymour Connor, et. al., *Battles of Texas* (Waco: Texian Press, 1967), 139-140, 145-149. Major Kellersberg, a native of Switzerland, lived in California in the 1850s but returned to Texas on the eve of the war. The family spelled the name "Kellersberger," but he enlisted in the Confederate army as "Kellersberg." For more on Kellersberg, see W. T. Block, "The Ghostly-Silent Guns of Galveston: A Chronicle of Colonel J. G. Kellersberger, The Confederate Chief Engineer of East Texas," *East Texas Historical Journal* 33 (Fall 1995): 23-34.

65. *Official Records*, Pt. 1, 26:672-675; Block, *History of Jefferson County*, 113; Andrew Forest Muir, "Dick Dowling and the Battle of Sabine Pass," *Civil War History* 4 (December 1958): 412-413; H. L. Sandefer and Archie P. McDonald, "Sabine Pass: David and Goliath," *Texana* 7 (Fall 1969): 177-178; Jo Young, "The Battle of Sabine Pass," *SHQ* 52 (April 1979): 398-399.

66. There is some disagreement concerning the exact number of troops in the expedition. Sandefer and McDonald, *ibid.*, 179, point out that the *Official Records, Armies*, 26:288-289, gives 5,000 as the number of troops, whereas *Official Records, Navies*, 20:515, reports 4,000 as the number of troops.

67. Ernest Jones, "The Battle of Sabine Pass, September 8, 1863," *Blue & Gray Magazine* 4 (September 1986): 22, notes that Charles W. Lamson, captain of the lead ship *Granite City*, was obsessed with fear of the *Alabama*, which was thousands of miles away. See also Simpson, "Battle of Sabine Pass," 151-152, and Frank X. Tolbert, *Dick Dowling at Sabine Pass* (New York: McGraw-Hill, 1962), 55-65.

68. Muir, "Dick Dowling and the Battle of Sabine Pass," 414-415; Simpson, "Battle of Sabine Pass," 154-155.

69. *Official Records*, Pt. 1, 26:309-311; *Official Records, Navies*, 20:522; Simpson, "Battle of Sabine Pass," 152-155; Tolbert, *Dick Dowling at Sabine Pass*, 92.

70. Simpson, "Battle of Sabine Pass," 156-157; Tolbert, *Dick Dowling at Sabine Pass*, 93-94.

71. Sabine Pass was split into two channels by an oyster bed half a mile wide and a mile and a half long. The channel on the western side nearest the Texas shore was called the Texas channel; the eastern channel nearest to Louisiana was called the Louisiana channel. See Simpson, "Battle of Sabine Pass," 156, and Block, "Fort Griffin Myths Exploded," 137.

72. *Official Records*, Pt. 1, 26:294-297, 311-312; Barr, "Texas Coastal Defense," 25-27; Simpson, "Battle of Sabine Pass," 157-162; Sandefer and McDonald, "Sabine Pass," 183-187.

73. Barr, "Texas Coastal Defense," 27; Alwyn Barr, "Sabine Pass, September 1863," *Texas Military History* 2 (February 1962): 17-22. As in most Civil War battles, it is difficult to ascertain exact numbers of men involved. Andrew Forest Muir, "Dick Dowling and the Battle of Sabine Pass," 417n, points out that in his report Dowling referred to forty-seven men among the defenders, but he included several individuals such as Capt. Leon Smith and Capt. Frederick Odlum who were present only briefly. It appears there were three officers (including Dowling) and forty enlisted men who made up the Davis Guards that day.

74. Muir, "Dick Dowling and the Battle of Sabine Pass," 420-421; Simpson, "The Battle of Sabine Pass," 167-168.

75. Block, *History of Jefferson County*, 115-116; W. T. Block, "New Chapter in History of Sabine Pass Written," *ETHJ* 9 (Fall 1971): 145-147.

76. *Official Records*, Pt. 1, 26:695-698. There is no agreement as to the Union objective at this point. Winters, *Civil War in Louisiana*, 296, states that Banks planned to move up the Teche to Lafayette or Vermilionville, then over to Niblett's Bluff, and on to Texas. Kerby, *Kirby Smith's Confederacy*, 191, says Banks had ruled out an overland march as too hazardous. Parrish, *Richard Taylor*, 309, believes that Banks gave Franklin complete authority to decide the army's route.

77. Parrish, *Richard Taylor*, 310-312; Winters, *Civil War in Louisiana*, 197-198; Blessington, *Walker's Texas Division*, 132-133; Alwyn Barr, *Polignac's Texas Brigade*, Texas Gulf Historical Association Publication Series 8 (November 1964): 24-27; Cooper K. Ragan, ed., "The Diary of Captain George W. O'Brien, 1863," *SHQ* 67 (July 1963): 39-40. Carl A. Brasseaux, *Acadian to Cajun: Transformation of A People, 1803-1877* (Jackson, MS: University Press of Mississippi, 1992), 67-70, notes that the Acadians initially resented the presence of so many Texas troops. They greeted Federal soldiers as "liberators," but came to dislike the Union invaders even more than the Texans.

78. *Official Records*, Pt. 1, 26:354-359, 393-395; Alwyn Barr, ed., "The Battle of Bayou Bourbeau, November 3, 1863: Colonel Oran M. Roberts' Report," *Louisiana History* 6 (Winter 1965): 83-91; Barr, *Polignac's Texas Brigade*, 30-31; Thomas W. Cutrer, ed., "'Bully for Flournoy's Regiment, We Are Some Pumkins, You'll Bet': The Civil War Letters of Virgil Sillivan Rabb, Captain 'I', Sixteenth Texas Infantry, C.S.A.," *Military History of the Southwest*, Pt. 1, 19 (Fall 1989): 185-188; Blessington, *Walker's Texas Division*, 138-149; Block, "The Swamp Angels," 52; David C. Edmonds, "Surrender on the Bourbeux: Honorable Defeat or Incompetency Under Fire," *Louisiana History* 18 (Winter 1977): 63-86.

79. *Official Records*, Pt. 1, 26:396-401, 411-420, 434-435; Jerry Thompson, *Sabers on the Rio Grande* (Austin: Presidial Press, 1974), 206-207; Thompson, *Vaqueros in Blue & Gray* (Austin: Presidial Press, 1976), 75-76; James A. Irby, *Backdoor at Bagdad: The Civil War on the Rio Grande* (El Paso: Texas Western Press, 1977), 29-30; Nannie M. Tilley, ed., *Federals on the Frontier: The Diary of Benjamin F. McIntyre, 1862-1864* (Austin: University of Texas Press, 1963), 248-260; Allan C. Ashcraft, "The Union Occupation of the Lower Rio Grande Valley in the Civil War," *Texas Military History* 8, no. 4 (1970): 13-26.

80. *Official Records*, Pt. 1, 26:416-421; Lester N. Fitzhugh, "Saluria, Fort Esperanza, and Military Operations on the Texas Coast, 1861-1864," *SHQ* 61 (July 1957): 95-97; Eugenia Reynolds Briscoe, *City By the Sea: A History of Corpus Christi, Texas, 1519-1875* (New York: Vantage Press, 1985), 230-231; Nueces

County Historical Society, *History of Nueces County* (Austin: Jenkins Publishing Company, 1972), 73-74.

81. Fitzhugh, "Saluria, Fort Esperanza, and Military Operations on the Texas Coast," 98-99; Barr, "Texas Coastal Defense," 28-29; Jerry D. Thompson, *Mexican Texans in the Union Army* (El Paso: Texas Western Press, 1986), 15. Shelby Foote, *The Civil War, A Narrative: Fredericksburg to Meridian* (New York: Random House, 1963), 871-872, points out that neither President Lincoln nor the commanding general, Henry W. Halleck, were enthused about the occupation of the South Texas coast. Halleck favored the Red River approach to Texas and wanted Banks prepared for an invasion along that route when spring rains made the river passable for Union gunboats and transports.

CHAPTER FOUR

1. Ralph A. Wooster, "Texas," in W. Buck Yearns, ed., *Confederate Governors*, 195-215.

2. James M. Day, ed., *Senate Journal of the Ninth Legislature of the State of Texas, November 4, 1861-January 14, 1862* (Austin: Texas State Library, 1963), 14-17.

3. E. T. Miller, "The State Finances of Texas During the Civil War," *Quarterly of the Texas State Historical Association* 14 (July 1910): 6-8; Day, *Senate Journal of Ninth Legislature*, 49-59; Meiners, "Texas Governorship, 1861-1865," 95-98; James B. Warner, "A Legislative History of Texas During the Civil War" (M. A. thesis, Lamar State College of Technology, 1971), 54-58.

4. Miller, "State Finances of Texas During the Civil War," 8-9; Warner, "Legislative History of Texas," 81-82.

5. *Ibid.*, 9-11; Wallace, *Texas in Turmoil*, 124-125.

6. Yearns, ed., *Confederate Governors*, 200; Day, *Senate Journal of Ninth Legislature*, 238-239; Meiners, "Texas Governorship, 1861-1865," 99-101; Charles W. Ramsdell, "The Texas State Military Board, 1862-1865," *SHQ* 27 (April 1924): 257-259; Michael Robert Green, ". . . So Illy Provided . . . Events Leading to the Creation of the Texas Military Board," *Military History of Texas and the Southwest* 10, no. 2 (1972), 115-125.

7. Ramsdell, "Texas State Military Board," 259-267; Lubbock, *Six Decades in Texas*, 365-371; Ronnie C. Tyler, "Cotton on the Border," *SHQ* 73 (April 1970): 456-477; Fredericka Meiners, "The Texas Border Cotton Trade, 1862-1863," *Civil War History* 23 (December 1977): 293-306.

8. Ramsdell, "Texas State Military Board," 268-272. Of the general operations of the Board, Ramsdell concludes the first board (the one under Lubbock) "often showed a childlike simplicity in conducting business, but no worse than that can be lodged against it. . . . To exonerate the second or new board is not so easy." *Ibid.*, 274.

9. Lubbock, *Six Decades in Texas*, 388-390; Lubbock to Jefferson Davis, June 27, 1862, Lubbock to Governor Rector, June 27, 1862, Lubbock to Governor Jackson, June 27, 1862, and Lubbock to Governor Moore, June 27, 1862, all in Executive Record Book; George P. Garrison "Guy Morrison Bryan," *Quarterly of the Texas State Historical Association* 5 (October 1901): 126.

10. Lubbock, *Six Decades in Texas*, 391-394; Lubbock, Jackson, Moore, and Rector to Jefferson Davis, July 28, 1862, Executive Record Book.

11. Meiners, "Texas Governorship, 1861-1865," 166-167.

12. Davis to Governors Lubbock, Jackson, Moore, and Rector, September 12, 1862, in *Official Records*, 53:879-880.

13. Kerby, *Kirby Smith's Confederacy*, 137-138; *Official Records*, 22:935-936.

14. Lubbock, *Six Decades in Texas*, 493; Kerby, *Kirby Smith's Confederacy*, 139.

15. Kerby, *Kirby Smith's Confederacy*, 139-142; Lubbock, *Six Decades in Texas*, 493-501; Governors to the People of Louisiana, Texas, Arkansas, and Missouri, and the Allied Indian Nations, August 18, 1863, *Official Records*, 53:892-894.

16. Lubbock received two unusual requests during his last months in office. The first was from Benjamin Theron, French consul at Galveston, inquiring if Lubbock did not believe it would be beneficial if Texas resumed her status as an independent republic. The second, from a son of former President John Tyler, suggested that Texas, once part of the Louisiana Purchase, had the right to appeal to France for protection. The Theron letter Lubbock treated with scorn; the second he dismissed as "beautiful English" wasted to no purpose. See Carland Elaine Crook, "Benjamin Theron and French Designs in Texas During the Civil War," *SHQ* 68 (April 1965): 432-454; Charles W. Ramsdell, "Last Hope of the Confederacy — John Tyler to Governor and Authorities of Texas," *Quarterly of the Texas State Historical Association* 14 (October 1910): 129-145; Lubbock, *Six Decades in Texas*, 511-525.

17. Several of the prospective candidates decided against entering the race because they feared a wide open contest might work to the advantage of either Chambers or Houston, both of whom were distrusted by Confederate nationalists. Their fear of Houston bordered on the unreal. Seventy years old and in poor health, Houston died in July 1863. See Nancy Head Bowen, "A Political Labyrinth," 118-127; Williams, *Sam Houston*, 359-362; De Bruhl, *Sword of San Jacinto*, 400-401.

18. Bowen, "A Political Labyrinth," 119-120, 129-130. For more on Chambers, see Llerena B. Friend, "The Life of Thomas Jefferson Chambers" (M. A. thesis, University of Texas, 1928).

19. Benny E. Deuson, "Pendleton Murrah," in W. C. Nunn, ed., *Ten Texans in Gray* (Hillsboro, TX: Hill Junior College Press, 1968), 122-123; James T. DeShields, *They Sat in High Places* (San Antonio: Naylor Company, 1940), 247-248; Meiners, "Texas Governorship, 1861-1865," 258-262.

20. Bowen, "A Political Labyrinth," 137-139.

21. *Ibid.*, 137; George C. Rable, *The Confederate Republic: A Revolution Against Politics* (Chapel Hill: University of North Carolina Press, 1994), 219-220. The total vote of 31,045 (including 1,079 scattered votes) in the 1863 governor's race is less than half of that in the last prewar gubernatorial contest, when Sam Houston and Hardin Runnels polled 63,727 votes. It is much lower than the 57,402 votes cast in the first election held during the war, August 1861. This is not too surprising, however, when one considers that 60,000 or more Texans (many over age twenty-one and thus potential voters) were serving in the military at the time of the election.

22. Ezra J. Warner and W. Buck Yearns, *Biographical Register of the Confederate Congress* (Baton Rouge: Louisiana State University Press, 1975), 19-20,

30, 103-104, 106-107, 180-181, 264; W. Buck Yearns, *Confederate Congress* (Athens, GA: University of Georgia Press, 1960), 56, 236-294; Thomas B. Alexander and Richard E. Beringer, *The Anatomy of the Confederate Congress: A Study of the Influence of Member Characteristics on Legislative Voting Behavior, 1861-1865* (Nashville: Vanderbilt University Press, 1972), 354-419; Bowen, "A Political Labyrinth, 141, 144-147.

23. Warner and Yearns, *Biographical Register of Confederate Congress,* 117-118. See also *ibid.,* 69, 217-218, 257-258; Bowen, "A Political Labyrinth," 141-144, 147-148; and Mary S. Estill, ed., "Diary of a Confederate Congressman [Franklin B. Sexton], 1862-1863, *SHQ* 38 (April 1935): 270-301, and 29 (July 1935): 33-65.

24. Warner and Yearns, *Biographical Register of Confederate Congress,* 187-188, 256-257; Alexander and Beringer, *Anatomy of the Confederate Congress,* 14-15, 57-58, 106; Yearns, *Confederate Congress,* 234-235; Alvy L. King, *Louis T. Wigfall, Southern Fire-eater* (Baton Rouge: Louisiana State University Press, 1970), esp. 135-153; Eric H. Walther, *The Fire-Eaters* (Baton Rouge: Louisiana State University Press, 1992), 189-190; Alma Dexter King, "The Political Career of Williamson Simpson Oldham," *SHQ* 33 (October 1929): 121-124.

25. William C. Davis, *"A Government of Our Own": The Making of the Confederacy* (New York: Free Press, 1994), 182-184, points out that Reagan twice turned down the postmaster generalship but finally accepted when no one else would take the position. Clement Eaton, *Jefferson Davis* (New York: Free Press, 1977), 131-132; Ben H. Procter, *Not Without Honor: The Life of John H. Reagan* (Austin: University of Texas Press, 1962), 122-161; John H. Reagan, *Memoirs, With Special Reference to Secession and the Civil War,* ed. Walter McCaleb (New York: Neale Publishing, 1906), 109-135, 157-160, 219-220. Francis B. C. Bradlee, *Blockade Running During the Civil War and the Effect of Land and Water Transportation on the Confederacy* (Philadelphia: Porcupine Press, 1925), 277-290; Herman Hattaway, "Via Confederate Post," *Civil War Times Illustrated* 15 (April 1976): 22-29; and L. R. Garrison, "Administrative Problems of the Confederate Post Office," *SHQ* 19 (October-January 1915-1916): 111-141, 232-250, provide good discussions of Confederate postal operations.

26. Pendleton Murrah to Gen. John B. Magruder, January 17, 1864, in Governors' Letters, Texas State Archives, Austin, Texas.

27. Meiners, "Texas Governorship, 1861-1865," 293-294.

28. David P. Smith, "Conscription and Conflict on the Texas Frontier, 1863-1865," *Civil War History* 36 (September 1990): 252-254; Smith, *Frontier Defense in the Civil War,* 88-98; Kerby, *Kirby Smith's Confederacy,* 218-219.

29. Felgar, "Texas in the War for Southern Independence," 212; Kerby, *Kirby Smith's Confederacy,* 277; *Official Records,* 53:926-930; Albert Moore, *Conscription and Conflict in the Confederacy* (New York: Macmillan Company, 1924), 247-248.

30. *Official Records,* Pt. 2, 34:1093-1095, Pt. 3, 739-741, 747-750.

31. Meiners, "Texas Governorship, 1861-1865," 314-316; Felgar, "Texas in the War for Southern Independence," 210-225; Smith, "Conscription and Conflict on the Texas Frontier," 257-261.

32. Kerby, *Kirby Smith's Confederacy,* 138-139, 159-160; Meiners, "Texas Governorship, 1861-1865," 326-327; James L. Nichols, *The Confederate Quartermaster in the Trans-Mississippi* (Austin: University of Texas Press, 1964), 58-69.

33. Ashcraft, "Texas: 1860-1866," 179-180, 218-221; Nichols, *Confederate Quartermaster*, 69-75.

34. Meiners, "Texas Governorship, 1861-1865," 329-330.

35. *Official Records*, 53:979-980, 1008-1015; Smith to Murrah, March 1, 1864, Magruder to Smith, March 28, 1864, Murrah to Smith, June 17, 21, 24, 25, 28, 1864, in Governors' Letters, Texas State Archives; Kerby, *Kirby Smith's Confederacy*, 201-202.

36. Murrah to the People of Texas, July 19, 1864, in Governor's Proclamations, Texas State Archives; Joseph H. Parks, *General Edmund Kirby Smith, C.S.A.* (Baton Rouge: Louisiana State University Press, 1954), 364-365.

37. Kerby, *Kirby Smith's Confederacy*, 206-207.

38. James Marten, *Texas Divided: Loyalty and Dissent in the Lone Star State, 1856-1874* (Lexington, KY: University Presses of Kentucky, 1990), 32-38; Elliott, *Leathercoat: The Life of James W. Throckmorton*, 63-98; Smith, *Frontier Defense in the Civil War*, 129-130.

39. Ralph A. Wooster, "Ben H. Epperson: East Texas Lawyer, Legislator, and Civic Leader," *ETHJ* 5 (March 1967): 29-42.

40. Marten, *Texas Divided*, 40-49; John A. Moretta, "William Pitt Ballinger: Public Servant, Private Pragmatist" (Ph.D. dissertation, Rice University, 1985); Ben C. Stuart, "Hamilton Stuart: Pioneer Editor," *SHQ* 21 (April 1918): 386; McCaslin, *Tainted Breeze*, 42-48.

41. Randolph B. Campbell, "George W. Whitmore: East Texas Unionist," *ETHJ* 28 (Spring 1990): 20-21; Campbell, *A Southern Community in Crisis*, 187-191, 209-210; Marten, *Texas Divided*, 59-62; *Handbook of Texas*, 2:356, 901; William L. Richter, "Devil Take Them All: Military Rule in Texas, 1862-1870," *Southern Studies* 25 (Spring 1986): 12.

42. Marten, *Texas Divided*, 53-85; Noah Smithwick, *The Evolution of A State, or Recollections of Old Texas Days* (1900; reprint, Austin: Texas State Historical Association, 1983), 249-263; James Marten, "A Wearying Experience: Texas Refugees in New Orleans, 1862-1865," *Louisiana History* 28 (February 1987): 343-356; James Marten, ed., "The Diary of Thomas H. DuVal: The Civil War in Austin, Texas, February 26 to October 9, 1863," *SHQ* 94 (January 1991): 435-457; Ruthe Winegarten, *Texas Women: A Pictorial History from Indians to Astronauts* (Austin: Eakin Press, 1986), 46; *Handbook of Texas*, 2:440, 467, 697-698; Andrew Forest Muir, "William Marsh Rice, Houstonian," *ETHJ* 2 (Spring 1964): 32-39; Richard Moore, "A Smuggler's Exile: S. M. Swenson Flees Texas," *ibid.*, 25 (Spring 1987): 23-29.

43. Marten, *Texas Divided*, 72-74; *Handbook of Texas*, 2:343-344, 351-352; Claude Elliott, "Union Sentiment in Texas, 1861-1865," *SHQ* 50 (April 1947): 452. For more on Pease and Paschal, see Roger Allen Griffin, "Connecticut Yankee in Texas: A Biography of Elisha Marshall Pease" (Ph.D. dissertation, University of Texas, 1973), and Jane Lynn Scarborough, "George W. Paschal: Texas Unionist and Scalawag Jurisprudent" (Ph.D. dissertation, Rice University, 1972).

44. Williams, *Sam Houston*, 349-360; Donald P. Smith, ed., "Civil War Letters of Sam Houston," *SHQ* 81 (April 1978): 424.

45. Frank H. Smyrl, "Texans in the Union Army, 1861-1865," *SHQ* 65 (October 1961): 234-243; Richard N. Current, *Lincoln's Loyalists: Union Soldiers from the Confederacy* (Boston: Northeastern University Press, 1992), 95-101;

Ronald N. Gray, "Edmund J. Davis: Radical Republican and Reconstruction Governor of Texas" (Ph.D. dissertation, Texas Tech University, 1976), 31-40. For the experiences of an enlisted man in the First Texas Cavalry (Union) see August Santleben, *A Texas Pioneer: Early Staging and Overland Freighting Days on the Frontiers of Texas and Mexico* (New York: Neale Publishing, 1910), 35-40.

46. Vicki Betts, "'Private and Amateur Hangings': The Lynching of W. W. Montgomery, March 15, 1863," *SHQ* 88 (October 1984): 145-166; Gray, "Edmund J. Davis," 41-46.

47. James Marten, "John L. Haynes: A Southern Dissenter in Texas," *Southern Studies*, New Series, I (Fall 1990): 257-279; Jerry Don Thompson, *Vaqueros in Blue and Gray* (Austin: Presidial Press, 1976), 85-88; Jerry D. Thompson, *Mexican Texans in the Union Army* (El Paso: Texas Western Press, 1986), 12-17; Smyrl, "Texans in the Union Army, 1861-1865," 243-244.

48. Thompson, *Vaqueros in Blue and Gray*, 71-79; Thompson, *Mexican Texans in the Union Army*, 19-20, 24-28; Tilley, ed., *Federals on the Frontier*, 349-350; Jerry Don Thompson, "Mutiny and Desertion on the Rio Grande: The Strange Saga of Captain Adrian J. Vidal," *Military History of Texas and the Southwest* 12, no. 3 (1975): 160-167.

49. John L. Waller, *Colossal Hamilton of Texas: A Biography of Andrew Jackson Hamilton* (El Paso: Texas Western Press, 1968), 34-58; Current, *Lincoln's Loyalists*, 95-100; Marten, *Texas Divided*, 66-68.

50. Elliott, "Union Sentiment in Texas, 1861-1865," 450; James Marten, "Slaves and Rebels: The Peculiar Institution in Texas, 1861-1865," *ETHJ* 28 (Spring 1990): 29-36.

51. Jordan, *German Seed in Texas Soil*, 182-185; Ella Lonn, *Foreigners in the Confederacy* (Chapel Hill: University of North Carolina Press, 1940), 123-126, 193-194, 500-501. See also Robert W. Shook "German Unionism in Texas During the Civil War and Reconstruction" (M. A. thesis, North Texas State University, 1957).

52. Alwyn Barr, "Records of the Confederate Military Commission in San Antonio, July 2 - October 10, 1862," *SHQ* 70 (July 1966): 93-95. On October 10, 1862, Hebert rescinded the order for martial law at the insistence of President Davis.

53. The best account of the affair is Robert W. Shook, "The Battle of the Nueces, August 10, 1862," *SHQ* 66 (July 1962): 31-42. See also *Official Records*, 9:614-615; Guido E. Ransleben, *A Hundred Years of Comfort in Texas* (San Antonio: Naylor Press, 1954), 87-89, 92-93, 114; and Phillip Rutherford, "Defying the State of Texas," *Civil War Times Illustrated* 18 (April 1979): 16-21.

54. There are various accounts of the "great hanging" at Gainesville. One of the earliest was by George Washington Diamond, a newspaper editor and publisher from Henderson. Although not a participant in the events, Diamond came to Gainesville soon after to visit his brother, James Diamond, who had assisted in the arrests of Cooke County Unionists. George Diamond started compiling his account of the affair soon thereafter but did not complete the work until the 1870s. It was edited by Sam Acheson, long-time member of the editorial staff of the *Dallas Morning News*, and Julie Ann Hudson O'Connell, great, great-grand-daughter of George Washington Diamond, and published in the *Southwestern Historical Quarterly* 66 (January 1963): 331-414. Thomas Barrett, physician, Dis-

ciples of Christ minister, and one of the twelve jurors of the citizens' court, wrote an account of the affair in 1885. His narrative was privately published but later was reprinted by the Texas State Historical Association: *The Great Hanging at Gainesville* (Austin, 1961). For an account written by a son of one of those hanged, see L. D. Clark, ed., *Civil War Recollections of James Lemuel Clark, Including Previously Unpublished Material on the Great Hanging at Gainesville, Texas, in October 1862* (College Station: Texas A&M University Press, 1984), esp. 21-45, 94-112. Recent accounts are James Smallwood, "Disaffection in Confederate Texas: The Great Hanging at Gainesville," *Civil War History* 22 (December 1976): 349-360; Phillip Rutherford, "The Great Gainesville Hanging," *Civil War Times Illustrated* 17 (April 1978): 12-20; Pete A. Y. Gunter, "The Great Gainesville Hanging, October 1862," *Blue & Gray Magazine* 3 (April-May 1986): 48-55; and Richard B. McCaslin, *Tainted Breeze: The Great Hanging at Gainesville, Texas, 1862* (Baton Rouge: Louisiana State University Press, 1994). The McCaslin work, a thoroughly documented and well-researched volume, is a complete and objective account not only of the hanging but also of the Unionist sentiment in North Texas.

55. McCaslin, *Tainted Breeze*, 95-97; Smallwood, "Disaffection in Confederate Texas," 357; Marten, *Texas Divided*, 104.

56. Richard B. McCaslin, "Wheat Growers in the Cotton Confederacy: The Suppression of Dissent in Collin County, Texas, During the Civil War," *SHQ* 96 (April 1993): 535-536; Albert Castel, *William Clarke Quantrill: His Life and Times* (New York: Frederick Fell, Inc., Publishers, 1962), 157-168; Albert Castel, "Quantrill in Texas," *Civil War Times Illustrated* 11 (June 1972): 20-27; Lary C. Rampp, "William C. Quantrill's Civil War Activities in Texas," *Texas Military History* 8, no. 4 (1970): 224-226; Smith, *Frontier Defense in the Civil War*, 79-80, 110-111; Weddle, *Plow-Horse Cavalry*, 97-100.

57. Oates, ed., *Rip Ford's Texas*, 332-333.

58. See John Warren Hunter, "Heel-Fly Time in Texas: A Story of the Civil War Period," *Frontier Times* 1 (April 1924): 33-48, (May 1924): 33-48, (June 1924): 33-47; and Gra'Delle Duncan, *Texas Tough: Dangerous Men in Dangerous Times* (Austin: Eakin Press, 1990), 45-50.

59. Ella Lonn, *Desertion During the Civil War* (1928; reprint, Gloucester, MA: Peter Smith, 1966), 71, 231; Oates, ed., *Rip Ford's Texas*, 337-338; *Houston Tri-Weekly Telegraph*, December 21, 1864; Francis E. Abernethy, ed., *Tales from the Big Thicket* (Austin: University of Texas Press, 1966), 75-78; Campbell and Lynn Loughmiller, eds., *Big Thicket Legacy* (Austin: University of Texas Press, 1977), 69-72; Robert L. Schaadt and Clyde A. See, eds., *The History of Hardin County, Texas* (Dallas: Hardin County Historical Commission, 1991), 21-22.

60. Marten, *Texas Divided*, 102-103; Boyd W. Johnson, "Cullen Montgomery Baker: The Arkansas-Texas Desperado," *Arkansas Historical Quarterly* 25 (Autumn 1966): 229-239; *Handbook of Texas*, 1:98.

61. William E. Sawyer, "Martin Hart, Civil War Guerrilla," *Texas Military History* 3 (Fall 1963): 146-153; William E. Sawyer, "The Martin Hart Conspiracy," *Arkansas Historical Quarterly* 23 (Summer 1964): 154-165; J. S. Duncan, "Martin Hart, Civil War Guerrilla: Addenda," *Military History of Texas and the Southwest* 11, no. 2 (1973): 137-142.

62. Wallace, *Texas in Turmoil*, 138; *Official Records*, Series III, 4:53; *Diary of*

E. S. Dodd, Co. D., Terry's Texas Rangers & An Account of His Hanging As A Confederate Spy (Austin: Ranger Press, 1979); Giles, *Terry's Rangers*, 78.

63. Dwayne Holman and Henry Keatts, "The Coldest Day: The Activities and Execution of a Confederate Boy Spy — David O. Dodd," *Military History of Texas and the Southwest* 9, no. 4 (1971): 281-288; LeRoy H. Fischer, "David O. Dodd: Folk Hero of Confederate Arkansas," *Arkansas Historical Quarterly* 37 (Summer 1978): 130-146; W. C. Parham, "David O. Dodd: The Nathan Hale of Arkansas," *Publications of Arkansas Historical Association* (1908), 2:531-535.

64. Robert W. Delaney, "Matamoros, Port for Texas During the Civil War," *SHQ* 58 (April 1955): 473-475; Mitchell Smith, "The 'Neutral' Matamoros Trade, 1861-1865," *Southwest Review* 37 (Autumn 1952): 319-324. The most complete account of the trade through Matamoros is James W. Daddysman, *The Matamoros Trade: Confederate Commerce, Diplomacy, and Intrigue* (Newark, DE: University of Deleware Press, 1984).

65. Tyler, "Cotton on the Border, 1861-1865," 456-459; Delaney, "Matamoros," 473-480; J. Lee Stambaugh and Lillian J. Stambaugh, *The Lower Rio Grande Valley of Texas* (San Antonio: Naylor Co., 1954), 111-112.

66. Daddysman, *Matamoros Trade*, 106-112; Felgar, "Texas in the War for Southern Independence," 429; Tyler, "Cotton on the Border, 1861-1865," 460-462; Tom Lea, *The King Ranch*, 2 vols. (Boston: Little, Brown, and Company, 1957), 1:183-184; Judith F. Gentry, "White Gold: The Confederate Government and Cotton in Louisiana," *Louisiana History* 33 (Summer 1992): 233.

67. Ronnie C. Tyler, *Santiago Vidaurri and the Southern Confederacy* (Austin: Texas State Historical Association, 1973), 106-108; Tyler, "Cotton on the Border, 1861-1865," 462-463; John C. Rayburn and Virginia Kemp Rayburn, eds., *Century of Conflict, 1821-1913; Incidents in the Lives of William Neale and William A. Neale, Early Settlers in South Texas* (Waco: Texian Press, 1966), 83; Robert W. Glover, "The West Gulf Blockade, 1861-1865: An Evaluation" (Ph.D. dissertation, North Texas State University, 1974), 110-118.

68. L. Tuffly Ellis, "Maritime Commerce on the Far Western Gulf, 1861-1865," *SHQ* 77 (October 1973): 185-189; Daddysman, *Matamoros Trade*, 112-113.

69. Tyler, "Cotton on the Border, 1861-1865," 472-477; Ellis, "Maritime Commerce on the Far Western Gulf Coast, 1861-1865," 210-226; Peyton O. Abbott, "Business Travel Out of Texas During the Civil War: The Travel Diary of S. B. Brush, Pioneer Austin Merchant," *SHQ* 96 (October 1992): 259-271; Marilyn McAdams Sibley, "Charles Stillman: A Case Study of Entrepreneurship on the Rio Grande, 1861-1865," *ibid.*, 77 (October 1973): 227-240; Fredericka Meiners, "The Texas Border Cotton Trade, 1862-1863," *Civil War History* 23 (December 1977): 193-306.

70. Frank Owsley, *King Cotton Diplomacy* (2nd rev. ed., Chicago: University of Chicago Press, 1959), 229-267.

71. Marcus W. Price, "Ships That Tested the Blockade of the Gulf Ports, 1861-1865," *American Neptune* 11 (October 1951): 262-263; Ellis, "Maritime Commerce on the Far Western Gulf Coast, 1861-1865," 196-197; Glover, "The West Gulf Blockade, 1861-1865," 143-148, 234-235.

72. Hamilton Cochran, *Blockade Runners of the Confederacy* (Indianapolis: Bobbs-Merrill Company, 1958), 216-237; Henry Steele Commager, ed., *The Blue and the Gray: The Story of the Civil War As Told By Contemporaries*, 2 vols. (India-

napolis: Bobbs-Merrill Company, 1950), 1:387-388, 2:859-863. For Watson's full story, see his *Adventures of a Blockade Runner* (New York: Macmillan Company, 1892). Stephen R. Wise, *Lifeline of the Confederacy: Blockade Running During the Civil War* (Columbia, SC: University of South Carolina Press, 1988), 181-182, 272-275, lists only fifty-three arrivals of steam blockade runners in Texas ports, December 1861-June 1865. He shows only fifty-six steam blockade runners clearing Texas ports, 1862-1865.

73. Mary Elizabeth Massey, *Refugee Life in the Confederacy* (Baton Rouge: Louisiana State University Press, 1964), 6, 36, 38, 92-93; North, *Five Years in Texas*, 106; Fremantle, *Diary*, 51; Jefferson Davis Bragg, *Louisiana in the Confederacy* (Baton Rouge: Louisiana State University Press, 1941), 150-151, 219-220; Margaret Swett Henson and Deolece Parmelee, *The Cartwrights of San Augustine: Three Generations of Agrarian Entrepreneurs in Nineteenth-Century Texas* (Austin: Texas State Historical Association, 1993), 224.

74. Massey, *Refugee Life*, 90-92, 99, 123; Kate Stone, *Brokenburn: The Journal of Kate Stone, 1861-1868*, ed. John Q. Anderson (Baton Rouge: Louisiana State University Press, 1955), xx-xxiii, 237, 358.

75. Fremantle, *Diary*, 62; Jo Ella Powell Exley, ed., *Texas Tears and Texas Sunshine: Voices of Frontier Women* (College Station: Texas A&M University Press, 1985), 113; Felgar, "Texas in the Southern War for Independence," 389; Eliza McHatton-Ripley, *From Flag to Flag: A Woman's Adventures and Experiences in the South during the War, in Mexico, and in Cuba* (New York: D. Appleton & Co., 1896), 101.

76. McHatton-Ripley, *From Flag to Flag*, 101; Charles C. Nott, *Sketches in Prison Camps: A Contribution of Sketches of the War* (New York: Anson D. F. Randolph, 1865), 119-121; Amelia E. Barr, *All the Days of My Life: An Autobiography* (New York: D. Appleton & Co., 1917), 244.

77. Charles W. Ramsdell, *Behind the Lines in the Southern Confederacy* (Baton Rouge: Louisiana State University Press, 1944), 19, 70-71; Ella Lonn, *Salt as a Factor in the Confederacy* (1933; reprint, University, AL: University of Alabama Press, 1965), 13-15, 19-20, 29-30, 109; Vera Lea Dugas, "A Social and Economic History of Texas in the Civil War and Reconstruction Periods" (Ph.D. dissertation, University of Texas, 1963), 282; Felgar, "Texas in the War for Southern Independence," 411-415; Winsor, *Texas in the Confederacy*, 51-51; McHatton-Ripley, *From Flag to Flag*, 98.

78. *Clarksville Standard*, July 7, 1862; *Houston Tri-Weekly Telegraph*, January 11, 1865; *Galveston Weekly News*, September 24, 1862, January 27, 1864; Stone, *Brokenburn*, 332; John R. Hutto, "Living on Three Frontiers: Mrs. Martha Jane Conway," *WTHAYB* 25 (October 1949): 104-105; Sallie Haltom, "My Life in Tarrant County and Other Parts of Texas," *SHQ* 60 (July 1956): 102; Barr, *All the Days of My Life*, 243.

79. Dugas, "Social and Economic History," 286-287; Felgar, "Texas in the War for Southern Independence," 405-406; *Galveston Weekly News*, September 24, 1862; Hutto, "Living on Three Texas Frontiers," 104-105; Francis Butler Simkins and James Welch Patton, *The Women of the Confederacy* (Richmond: Garrett and Massie, Ind., 1936), 149-152.

80. William A. Albaugh III, *Tyler, Texas, C.S.A.* (Harrisburg, PA: Stackpole Co., 1958), 11-12, 20-26, 270-271; Winsor, *Texas in the Confederacy*, 41-43;

Dugas, "Social and Economic History," 272-281. Jefferson Nash, the founder of the first iron furnace in the state, offered to produce rifles, cannon, and shells at his Marion County facility but received no governmental encouragement. Nash did make some cannon balls for the army, but there is no record that rifles and cannons were made at the foundry. See Robert Lee Jones, "The First Iron Furnace in Texas," *SHQ* 63 (October 1959): 288-289.

81. Winsor, *Texas in the Confederacy*, 44; Dugas, "Social and Economic History of Texas," 299, 305; Richard D. Goff, *Confederate Supply* (Durham, NC: Duke University Press, 1969), 133; Nichols, *Confederate Quartermaster*, 88-89; Margaret Swett Henson, *History of Baytown* (Baytown, TX: Bay Heritage Society, 1986), 51; Evans, ed., *Confederate Military History*, 11:115-116; Garnett Cleveland, "The Confederate Naval Works at Goose Creek," *Touchstone* 9 (1990): 12-17.

82. Goff, *Confederate Supply*, 37; Frank E. Vandiver, "Texas and the Confederate Army's Meat Problem," *SHQ* 47 (January 1944): 225-233; Allan C. Ashcraft, "Confederate Beef Packing at Jefferson, Texas," *ibid.*, 68 (October 1964): 259-270.

83. Winsor, *Texas in the Confederacy*, 51; Felgar, "Texas in the War for Southern Independence," 463; McHatton-Ripley, *From Flag to Flag*, 102; Frank E. Vandiver, ed., "Letters from the Confederate Medical Service in Texas, 1863-1865," *SHQ* 55 (April 1952): 469; George C. Rable, *Civil Wars: Women and the Crisis of Southern Nationalism* (Urbana: University of Illinois Press, 1989), 98-99.

84. William Frank Zornow, "Texas State Aid for Indigent Soldiers, 1861-1865," *Mid America* 37 (July 1955): 171-175; Ashcraft, "Texas: 1860-1866," 142-143, 232; Rable, *Civil Wars*, 103-106; Warner, "Legislative History of Texas," 102-103.

85. Exley, ed., *Texas Tears and Texas Sunshine*, 130-137; Elizabeth Silverthorne, *Plantation Life in Texas* (College Station: Texas A&M University Press, 1986), 198; Abigail Curlee Holbrook, "A Glimpse of Life on Antebellum Slave Plantations in Texas," *SHQ* 76 (April 1973): 368; Rable, *Civil Wars*, 113-115.

86. Katherine G. Goodwin, "'A Woman's Curiosity': Martha Gaffney and Cotton Planting on the Texas Frontier," *ETHJ* 24 (Fall 1986): 4-17; Judith N. McArthur, "Myth, Reality, and Anomaly: The Complex World of Rebecca Hagerty," *ibid.*, 24 (Fall 1986): 18-32; Joleene Maddox Snider, "Sarah Devereux: A Study in Southern Femininity," *SHQ* 97 (January 1994): 498-502; David Gracy II, "Mildred Satterwhite Littlefield," in Evelyn Carrington, ed., *Women in Early Texas* (Austin: Pemberton Press, 1976), 163-167.

87. Alwyn Barr, "Revolutionary Changes in Civil War Texas," in *The Texas Heritage*, eds. Ben Procter and Archie P. McDonald (St. Louis: Forum Press, 1980), 89-90; Marshall *Texas Republican*, January 4, February 1 and 22, 1862; Silverthorne, *Plantation Life*, 198-199; Mary Elizabeth Massey, *Bonnet Brigades* (New York: Alfred A. Knopf, 1966), 79, 108; Annie Doom Pickrell, *Pioneer Women in Texas* (Austin: E. L. Steck, 1929), 202; Winegarten, *Texas Women*, 28.

88. Campbell, *A Southern Community in Crisis*, 225-241; James Wilson Nichols, *Now You Hear My Horn: The Journal of James Wilson Nichols*, ed. Catherine W. McDowell (Austin: University of Texas Press, 1968), 151-154; Exley, *Texas Tears and Texas Sunshine*, 146-147; Davis Bitton, ed., *Reminiscences and Civil War Letters of Levi Lamoni Wight: Life in a Mormon Splinter Colony on*

the Texas Frontier (Salt Lake City: University of Utah Press, 1970), 142-143, 158-160; Mary D. Farrell and Elizabeth Silverthorne, *First Ladies of Texas: A History* (Belton: Stillhouse Hollow Publishers, 1976), 130-131, 144-145; Seymour Connor, ed., *Dear America: Some Letters of Orange Cicero and Mary America (Aiken) Connor* (Austin: Pemberton Press, 1971), 39-40, 53-54, 73-76, 87.

89. Simkins and Patton, *Women of the Confederacy*, 163; Lizzie to Will Neblett, August 13 and 18, November 4, 1863, Lizzie Neblett Papers, cited in Marten, *Texas Divided*, 111-112; Marten, "Slaves and Rebels," 32; Drew Giplin Faust, "Trying to Do a Man's Business; Gender Violence and Slave Management in Civil War Texas," in *Southern Stories: Slaveholders in Peace and War* (Columbia: University of Missouri Press, 1992), 174-192.

90. Marten, *Texas Divided*, 109; Stone, *Brokenburn*, 298.

91. Campbell, *An Empire for Slavery*, 231-233, 243-244; Moneyhon, *Impact of the Civil War and Reconstruction on Arkansas*, 134. The increased number of slaves did cause some apprehension about slave rebellions. See Cecil Harper, Jr., "Slavery Without Cotton: Hunt County, Texas, 1846-1864," *SHQ* 88 (April 1985): 396-397.

92. Campbell, *An Empire for Slavery*, 247-248. See also Barr, "Revolutionary Changes in Civil War Texas," 86-87, and Silverthorne, *Plantation Life*, 201-203.

93. Campbell, *An Empire for Slavery*, 234-237.

94. *Ibid.*, 237-239; Meiners, "Texas Governorship, 1861-1865," 279-282; Felgar, "Texas in the War for Southern Independence," 279-286.

95. John A. Edwards, "Social and Cultural Activities of Texans During Civil War and Reconstruction, 1861-1873" (Ph.D. dissertation, Texas Tech University, 1985), 12-52, 253-261, 274-275, 287-289, 294-295.

96. *Ibid.*, 66-85, 100-104; Phelan, *A History of Early Methodism in Texas*, 464-465; Griggs, *Parson Henry Renfro*, 45-46, 68-69; *Handbook of Texas*, 1:145, 3:231; Robert Franklin Bunting Papers, University of Texas Archives; G. Clinton Prim, Jr., "Born Again in the Trenches: Revivals in the Army of Tennessee," *Tennessee Historical Quarterly* 43 (Fall 1984): 256; Paula Mitchell Marks, "The Ranger Reverend," *Civil War Times Illustrated* 24 (December 1985): 40-45; Donald E. Everett, ed., *Chaplain Davis and Hood's Texas Brigade* (San Antonio: Principia Press of Trinity University, 1962), xi-xiii, 20-23.

97. Edwards, "Social and Cultural Activities of Texans," 86-87, 126; David Marshall, "Texas Baptist Political Attitudes Under Four National Governments: 1835-1865" (M. A. thesis, Texas Tech University, 1986), 97-100. See also James W. Silver, *Confederate Morale and Church Propaganda* (Reprint, Gloucester, MA: Peter Smith, 1964), 49. For an example of denominational support (Baptist) of the Confederacy, see Frederick J. Dobney, "From Denominationlism to Nationalism in the Civil War," *Texana* 9 no. 4 (1971): 367-376.

98. Edwards, "Social and Cultural Activities of Texans," 182-184, 192-193, 246-247. Sylvia Hunt, "To Wed and to Teach: The Myth of the Single Teacher," in *Women and Texas History: Selected Essays*, ed., Fane Downs and Nancy Baker Jones (Austin: Texas State Historical Association, 1993), 128, indicates that Myra Belle Shirley, known later as Belle Starr, taught school near Dallas in 1863. Her biographer, Glenn Shirley, *Belle Starr and Her Times: The Literature, The Facts, and the Legends* (Norman: University of Oklahoma Press, 1982), makes no refer-

ence to her school teaching. He does state (66), that she was a student in a school near Dallas. Belle, or Myra Belle, was well educated for the times, having attended a classical preparatory school earlier in her native Carthage, Missouri. See Winegarten, *Texas Women*, 50, and Shirley, *Belle Starr*, 38.

99. For examples of other aspects of life on the Texas home front, see Tony E. Duty, "The Home Front: McLennan County in the Civil War," *Texana* 12 no. 3 (1974): 197-238; Ronald B. Jager, "Houston, Texas Fights the Civil War," *ibid.*, 11, no. 1 (1973): 30-51; Robert W. Williams and Ralph A. Wooster, eds., "Life in Civil War Central Texas: Letters from Mr. and Mrs. Thomas Affleck to Private Dunbar Affleck," *ibid.*, 7 (Summer 1964): 146-162; Ralph A. Wooster and Robert Wooster, "A People at War: East Texans During the Civil War," *ETHJ* 28 (Spring 1990): 3-16; Jack Stoltz, "Kaufman County in the Civil War," *ibid.*, 37-44; Helen Spanhanks, "Marshall and the Civil War," *Touchstone* 1 (1982): 40-45; Camilla Davis Trammell, *Seven Pines: Its Occupants and Their Letters, 1825-1872* (Houston: distributed by Southern Methodist University Press, 1986).

CHAPTER FIVE

1. Smith, *Frontier Defense in the Civil War*, 83-86; D. S. Howell, "Along the Texas Frontier During the Civil War," *WTHAYB* 13 (October 1937): 85-86; David Paul Smith, "Frontier Defense and the Cooke County Raid, 1863," *ibid.*, 64 (October 1988): 39-41; Thompson, *Vaqueros in Blue & Gray*, 103; Briscoe, *City by the Sea*, 232-233; Thompson, *Mexican Texans in the Union Army*, 21-22; McIntyre, *Federals on the Frontier*, 283-286. For an interesting account of the Union occupation of Brownsville, see James Marten, "For the Army, The People, and Abraham Lincoln: A Yankee Newspaper in Occupied Texas," *Civil War History* 39 (June 1993): 126-147.

2. Minetta Altgeld Goyne, ed., *Lone Star and Double Eagle: Civil War Letters of a German-Texas Family* (Fort Worth: Texas Christian University Press, 1982), 115-116; Dunbar Affleck to Mr. and Mrs. Thomas Affleck, December 30, 1863, in I. D. Affleck Letters, originals in possession of Affleck family, Galveston, TX; Oates, "Texas Under the Confederates," 206; James A. Creighton, *Narrative History of Brazoria County* (Waco: Texian Press, 1975), 244-245; *Official Records*, Pt. 2, 34: 931-932; Sifakis, *Compendium of Confederate Armies: Texas*, 38, 108-109, 110-111.

3. Barr, "Texas Coastal Defense, 1861-1865," 28-29; Fitzhugh, "Saluria, Fort Esperanza, and Military Operations on the Texas Coast, 1861-1864," 99-100; Oates, "Texas Under the Confederates," 206.

4. Ford himself claimed the rank of Confederate colonel throughout the war. Hebert, Magruder, and later John G. Walker, Confederate commanders of the Texas district, all recognized him as such. See Oates, ed., *Rip Ford's Texas*, 346n and W. J. Hughes, *Rebellious Ranger: Rip Ford and the Old Southwest* (Norman: University of Oklahoma Press, 1964), 205-212.

5. *Official Records*, Pt. 1, 34:647-649; Oates, ed., *Rip Ford's Texas*, 355-357; Jerry Don Thompson, "A Stand Along the Border: Santos Benavides and the Battle for Laredo," *Civil War Times Illustrated*, 19 (August 1980): 26-33; Thompson, *Vaqueros in Blue & Gray*, 107-110; Thompson, *Sabers on the Rio Grande*, 211-213; Thompson, *Mexican Texans in the Union Army*, 23-24; Joseph B. Wilkinson, *Laredo and the Rio Grande Frontier* (Austin: Jenkins Publishing Company, 1975), 295-296.

6. Oates, ed., *Rip Ford's Texas*, 362-363; Hughes, *Rebellious Ranger*, 220-221; *Official Records*, Pt. 1, 34:1054-1056.

7. Oates, ed., *Rip Ford's Texas*, 363-366; Hughes, *Rebellious Ranger*, 222-224.

8. T. R. Fehrenbach, *Lone Star: A History of Texas and the Texans* (New York: Macmillan Company, 1968), 385-387; Stambaugh, *Lower Rio Grande Valley of Texas*, 120; Charles W. Goldfinch, "Juan Cortina, 1842-1892: A Re-Appraisal," in *Juan N. Cortina: Two Interpretations* (New York: Arno Press, 1974), 51-52. For more on Cortina, see Jerry D. Thompson, ed., *Juan Cortina and the Texas-New Mexico Frontier* (El Paso: Texas Western Press, 1994).

9. Oates, ed., *Rip Ford's Texas*, 375-382; Hughes, *Rebellious Ranger*, 227-230.

10. Ludwell H. Johnson, *Red River Campaign: Politics and Cotton in the Civil War* (Baltimore: Johns Hopkins Press, 1958), 35-47; Carl P. Tyson, "Highway of War," *Red River Historical Review* 3 (Summer 1978): 28-56.

11. Although there were many stories and rumors concerning Banks and cotton speculators, Ludwell Johnson, *Red River Campaign*, 55-78, argues there is no evidence that Banks personally profited from the cotton trade. See also Kerby, *Kirby Smith's Confederacy*, 284-285; Fred Harvey Harrington, *Fighting Politician: Major General N. P. Banks* (Philadelphia: University of Pennsylvania Press, 1948), 160-162; and Norman D. Brown, ed., *Journey to Pleasant Hill: The Civil War Letters of Captain Elijah P. Petty, Walker's Texas Division, C.S.A.* (San Antonio: Institute of Texas Cultures, 1982), 371-372.

12. *Official Records*, Pt. 1, 34:194-196; Johnson, *Red River Campaign*, 79-87; Josephy, *Civil War in American West*, 191-194.

13. *Official Records*, Pt. 2, 34:1026-1027; Kerby, *Kirby Smith's Confederacy*, 288-289; Josephy, *Civil War in American West*, 194; Barr, *Polignac's Texas Brigade*, 21-30, 38-39; Fredericka Meiners, "Hamilton P. Bee in the Red River Campaign," *SHQ* 78 (July 1974): 23-24. Carl L. Duaine, *The Dead Men Wore Boots: An Account of the 32nd Texas Volunteer Cavalry, C.S.A.* (Austin: San Felipe Press, 1966), 84-86, provides a listing of all Texas units involved in the Red River campaign.

14. In his report of the loss of DeRussy, General Walker was highly critical of the design of the fort and "the wretched judgment displayed in the selection of the position." *Official Records*, Pt.1, 34:602. See also Blessington, *Campaigns of Walker's Texas Division*, 167-174; Richard Taylor, *Destruction and Reconstruction: Personal Experiences of the Late War*, ed. Richard B. Harwell (New York: Longmans, Green, and Company, 1955), 186-187.

15. Taylor, *Destruction and Reconstruction*, 190-194; Parrish, *Richard Taylor*, 335-338; Edmund Kirby Smith, "The Defense of the Red River," *Battles & Leaders*, 4:369-371.

16. Taylor, *Destruction and Reconstruction*, 194-195; Josephy, *Civil War in the American West*, 197-200; Johnson, *Red River Campaign*, 124-133; Parrish, *Richard Taylor*, 341-343.

17. Brown, ed., *Journey to Pleasant Hill*, 391-392; Arthur W. Bergeron, ed., *Reminiscences of Major Silas T. Grisamore, C.S.A.* (Baton Rouge: Louisiana State University Press, 1993), 145-149; John W. Spencer, *Terrell's Texas Cavalry* (Burnet, TX: Eakin Press, 1982), 14-16; Johnson, *Red River Campaign*, 132-133; Stanley S. McGowen, "Augustus Buchel: A Forgotten Texas Patriot," *Military History of the West* 25 (Spring 1995): 14–17.

18. *Official Records*, Pt. 1, 34:273-274, 392, 421-422, 564-565; Noel, *A Campaign From Santa Fe to the Mississippi*, 77-79; Rebecca W. Smith and Marion Mullins, eds., "The Diary of H. C. Medford, Confederate Soldier, 1864," *SHQ* 34 (January 1931): 216-219; Debray, *Debray's Texas Cavalry*, 18-19; Blessington, *Campaigns of Walker's Texas Division*, 135-141; Max S. Lale, "New Light on the Battle of Mansfield," *ETHJ* 25 (Fall 1987): 34-41; Max S. Lale, "For Lack of A Nail . . .," *ibid.*, 30 (Spring 1992): 39.

19. Taylor, *Destruction and Reconstruction*, 196-198; Brown, ed., *Journey to Pleasant Hill*, 394-398; Barr, *Polignac's Brigade*, 39-40; Weddle, *Plow-Horse Cavalry*, 115-119; William Arceneaux, *Acadian General: Alfred Mouton and the Civil War* (Lafayette, LA: Center for Louisiana Studies, University of Southwest Louisiana, 1981), 130-133.

20. Parrish, *Richard Taylor*, 354; Blessington, *Campaigns of Walker's Texas Division*, 193-194.

21. Johnson, *Red River Campaign*, 146-152; Brown, ed., *Journey to Pleasant Hill*, 399.

22. Parrish, *Richard Taylor*, 355-361; Meiners, "Hamilton P. Bee," 28-39; Evans, ed., *Confederate Military History*, 11:205-206; Spencer, *Terrell's Texas Cavalry*, 38-39; Yeary, comp., *Reminiscences of the Boys in Gray*, 361-362.

23. Blessington, *Campaigns of Walker's Texas Division*, 193-197; Noel, *Campaign From Santa Fe to the Mississippi*, 79-81; Taylor, *Destruction and Reconstruction*, 200-205; Johnson, *Red River Campaign*, 155-162; Alwyn Barr, ed., "The Civil War Diary of James Allen Hamilton, 1861-1864," *Texana* 2 (Summer 1964): 142; Thomas W. Cutrer, "'An Experience in Soldier's Life': The Civil War Letters of Volney Ellis, Adjutant, Twelfth Texas Infantry, Walker's Texas Division, C.S.A.," *Military History of the Southwest* 22 (Fall 1992): 154-155; Jane Harris Johansson and David H. Johansson, "Two 'Lost' Battle Reports: Horace Randal's and Joseph L. Brent's Reports of the Battles of Mansfield and Pleasant Hill, 8 and 9 April 1864," *Military History of the West* 23 (Fall 1993): 169-180.

24. Johnson, *Red River Campaign*, 168-169; Alwyn Barr, "Texas Losses in the Red River Campaign, 1864," *Texas Military History* 3 (Summer 1963): 104-105.

25. Taylor, *Destruction and Reconstruction*, 213-214; Joseph Howard Parks, *General Edmund Kirby Smith, C.S.A.* (Baton Rouge: Louisiana State University Press, 1954), 391-396; Smith, "Defense of the Red River," *Battles & Leaders*, 4:369-372.

26. The Federals later charged the Confederates with killing wounded black soldiers. Anne J. Bailey, "Was There a Massacre at Poison Spring?" *Military History of the Southwest* 20 (Fall 1990): 168, states that "all the evidence suggests that Confederates executed black soldiers after the battle." Albert Castel, *General Sterling Price and the Civil War in the West*, 177, says, "Confederates by their own admission showed Negroes no quarter . . ." For more on the Poison Spring affair, see *Official Records*, Pt. 1, 34:816-818; Edwin C. Bearss, *Steele's Retreat from Camden and the Battle of Jenkins' Ferry* (Little Rock: Arkansas Civil War Centennial Commission, 1967), 15-41; Wallace, *Charles DeMorse*, 149-150; Don Richards, "The Battle of Poison Spring," *Arkansas Historical Quarterly* 18 (Winter 1959): 330-385; Louise Horton, *Samuel Bell Maxey: A Biography* (Austin: University of Texas Press, 1974), 37-38; John Waugh, *Sam Bell Maxey*, 56-59.

27. *Official Records*, Pt. 1, 34:816-818; Johnson, *Red River Campaign*, 193-

202 (quotation, 197); Bearss, *Steele's Retreat from Camden*, 114-169; Blessington, *Campaigns of Walker's Texas Division*, 249-255; Castel, *General Sterling Price*, 181-183; Daniel E. Sutherland, "1864: 'A Strange and Wild Time'," in *Rugged and Sublime: The Civil War in Arkansas*, 120-123.

28. Johnson, *Red River Campaign*, 203-205; Blessington, *Campaigns of Walker's Texas Division*, 254-260.

29. Bailey, *Between the Enemy and Texas*, 170-178; Faulk, *General Tom Green*, 62; Winters, *Civil War in Louisiana*, 358-359; Gallaway, *Ragged Rebel*, 90-101; Alwyn Barr, "The Battle of Blair's Landing," *Louisiana Studies* 2 (Winter 1963): 204-212; Lester N. Fitzhugh, "Texas Forces in the Red River Campaign, March- May 1864," *Texas Military History* 3 (Spring 1963): 20.

30. Blessington, *Campaigns of Walker's Texas Division*, 184-185; Taylor, *Destruction and Reconstruction*, 216; David C. Humphrey, "A 'Very Muddy and Conflicting' View: The Civil War as Seen from Austin, Texas," *SHQ* 94 (January 1991): 408-409; Milbourn, "Brigadier General Thomas Green of Texas," 9-10.

31. Josephy, *Civil War in American West*, 217; Johnson, *Red River Campaign*, 236-241; Parrish, *Richard Taylor*, 383-384; Barr, *Polignac's Texas Brigade*, 42-43.

32. Parrish, *Richard Taylor*, 375-376; Taylor, *Destruction and Reconstruction*, 218-220; Josephy, *Civil War in American West*, 217-218; Meiners, "Hamilton P. Bee," 33-37. Wharton, a major general, had achieved success in the Army of Tennessee. After a misunderstanding between Wharton and Joe Wheeler over a letter written by Wharton, the Texan requested transfer to the Trans Mississippi. Jeffries, *Terry's Rangers*, 82-83.

33. Meiners, "Hamilton P. Bee," 37-38; Josephy, *Civil War in American West*, 218; Bailey, *Between the Enemy and Texas*, 182-184; Alwyn Barr, ed., "William T. Mechling Journal of the Red River Campaign, April 7- May 10, 1864," *Texana* 1 (Fall 1963): 373-374.

34. Meiners, "Hamilton P. Bee," 39-44; Parrish, *Richard Taylor*, 377-379; Taylor, *Destruction and Reconstruction*, 220-221. Ludwell Johnson, *Red River Campaign*, 233-234, criticizes Bee for errors in judgment but points out that even if Bee had conducted "a letter perfect defense," the Federals would still have been able to force a crossing because of their superior manpower.

35. Barr, *Polignac's Texas Brigade*, 43-44; Gallaway, *Ragged Rebel*, 108-112; Bailey, *Between the Enemy and Texas*, 184-185.

36. Johnson, *Red River Campaign*, 273, describes the scene at Mansura when the two massed armies faced each other as "strikingly beautiful." With 6,000 men Taylor stood in front of a Union force of 18,000 before withdrawing from the field. See also Noel, *A Campaign from Santa Fe to the Mississippi*, 88-89; *Official Records*, Pt. 1, 34:593; P. D. Browne, "Captain T. D. Nettles and the Valverde Battery," *Texana* 2 (Spring 1964): 15; Alwyn Barr, "Confederate Artillery in Western Louisiana," *Louisiana History* 5 (Winter 1964): 69-70.

37. Gallaway, *Ragged Rebel*, 115-123; Bailey, *Between the Enemy and Texas*, 186-190; Bergeron, ed., *Reminiscences of Major Silas T. Grisamore*, 157-159; Edwin C. Bearss, *A Louisiana Confederate: Diary of Felix Pierre Porce* (Natchitoches, LA: Louisiana Studies Institute, 1972), 122-124.

38. Barr, "Texas Losses in the Red River Campaign," 103-110; Johnson, *Red River Campaign*, 278; Duaine, *The Dead Men Wore Boots*, 87-88.

39. F. Lee Lawrence and Robert W. Glover, *Camp Ford, C.S.A.: The Story of*

Union Prisoners in Texas (Austin: Texas Civil War Committee, 1964), 3-9; Robert W. Glover and Randal B. Gilbert, "Camp Ford, Tyler, Texas — The Largest Confederate Prison Camp West of the Mississippi River," *Chronicles of Smith County* 28 (Winter 1989): 16-24; Leon Mitchell, Jr., "Camp Ford: Confederate Military Prison," *SHQ* 66 (July 1962): 1-2; *Official Records*, Series II, 7:208-210.

40. McPherson, *Ordeal by Fire*, 451; Lawrence and Glover, *Camp Ford*, 9-21, 72-73; Mitchell, "Camp Ford," 3-6, 11-13; Glover and Gilbert, "Camp Ford, Tyler, Texas," 24-32. For views of Camp Ford by inmates, see Charles C. Nott, *Sketches in Prison Camps: A Continuation of Sketches of the War* (New York: Amon D. F. Randolph, 1865), 132-150; Gary Wilson, "The Ordeal of William H. Cowdin and the Officers of the Forty-Second Massachusetts Regiment: Union Prisoners in Texas," *ETHJ* 23 (Spring 1985): 16-26; Gary E. Wilson, ed., "Diary of a Union Prisoner in Texas," *Louisiana Studies* 23 (Spring 1984): 103-119; David G. MacLean, ed., *Prisoner of the Rebels in Texas: The Civil War Narrative of Aaron T. Sutton, Corporal, 83rd Ohio Volunteer Infantry* (Decatur, IN: Americana Books, 1978), 11-28; Arthur E. Gilligan, "Ten Weeks in Texas as a Prisoner of War," in B. P. Gallaway, ed., *Texas, The Dark Corner of the Confederacy* (3rd ed., Lincoln: University of Nebraska Press, 1994), 192-204. For the view of a Confederate prison guard, see W. W. Heartsill, *Fourteen Hundred and 91 Days in the Confederate Army*, 195-210.

41. At least one prisoner, Cpl. Aaron T. Sutton of the 83rd Ohio Infantry, believed Camp Groce had more comforts than Camp Ford. MacLean, ed., *Prisoner of the Rebels in Texas*, 47. See also Leon Mitchell, Jr., "Camp Groce: Confederate Military Prison," *SHQ* 67 (July 1963): 16-18, 20; Ashcraft, "Texas: 1860-1866," 127; Nott, *Sketches of Prison Camps*, 94-118. Winsor, *Texas in the Confederacy*, 216, lists, in addition to Ford and Groce, prisoner of war camps at Brackettville (Fort Clark), Camp Verde (Prison Town), Houston, Rusk, San Antonio (Camp Van Dorn), and Shiner (Lavaca County).

42. Alwyn Barr, "The Battle of Calcasieu Pass," *SHQ* 66 (July 1962): 58-67; W. T. Block, "Calcasieu Pass, Victory, Heroism 'Equal Dowling's'," *ETHJ* 9 (Fall 1971): 139-144; Block, "Swamp Angels," *ibid.*, 30 (Spring 1992): 52-53. Creuzbaur's Battery was also known as "Creuzbaur's-Welhausen's Texas Battery." Sifakis, *Compendium of Confederate Armies: Texas*, 16. For more on the battery, see Paul C. Boethal, *The Big Guns of Fayette* (Austin: Von Boeckmann-Jones, 1965).

43. Kerby, *Kirby Smith's Confederacy*, 324-329; Barr, *Polignac's Texas Brigade*, 35-36; Parks, *General Edmund Kirby Smith*, 420-428; Bergeron, ed., *Civil War Reminiscences of Major Silas T. Grisamore*, 164-165.

44. In a reorganization of the Trans Mississippi Department, Magruder was sent to Arkansas from Texas, John G. Walker was transferred from West Louisiana to Texas, and newly arrived Simon Bolivar Buckner assumed command of West Louisiana. Kerby, *Kirby Smith's Confederacy*, 334.

45. *Ibid.*, 331-333, 338; Robert W. Williams, Jr., and Ralph A. Wooster, eds., "With Wharton's Cavalry in Arkansas: The Civil War Letters of Private Isaac Dunbar Affleck," *Arkansas Historical Quarterly* 21 (Autumn 1962): 249-252; Barr, *Polignac's Texas Brigade*, 49-50.

46. *Official Records*, Pt. 1, 41:641-642, Pt. 3, 966-971; Bailey, *Between the Enemy and Texas*, 195-196, 311.

47. *Official Records*, Pt. 1, 41:625-640; Kerby, *Kirby Smith's Confederacy*,

337-352; Josephy, *Civil War in American West*, 378-385. Governor Reynolds, formerly an ally of Sterling Price, was furious over Price's management of the campaign. In an account published in the Marshall *Texas Republican*, the Missouri governor denounced Price and demanded his resignation. For more on Price's raid, see Castel, *General Sterling Price*, 200-255; Oates, *Confederate Cavalry West of the River*, 140-145; and Norman Potter Morrow, "Price's Missouri Expedition, 1864" (M. A. thesis, University of Texas, 1949).

48. *Official Records*, Pt. 1, 41:681, 683, 693. Anne Bailey, *Between the Enemy and Texas*, 311, points out that Pratt's tombstone in Jefferson, Texas, states that he died of wounds received on October 26, 1864.

49. Kerby, *Kirby Smith's Confederacy*, 352-355. For the battle of Cabin Creek, see Marvin J. Hancock, "The Second Battle of Cabin Creek, 1864," *Chronicles of Oklahoma* 39 (Winter 1961): 414-426; Horton, *Samuel Bell Maxey*, 40-41; Abel, *American Indian in the Civil War, 1862-1865*, 332-333; Frank Cunningham, *General Stand Watie's Confederate Indians* (San Antonio: Naylor Company, 1959), 152-160; Waugh, *Sam Bell Maxey and The Confederate Indians*, 71–80.

50. Kerby, *Kirby Smith's Confederacy*, 361; Barr, *Polignac's Texas Brigade*, 51-52; Bailey, *Between the Enemy and Texas*, 199-200.

51. Smith, *Frontier Defense in the Civil War*, 64-65, 112-128; McCaslin, *Tainted Breeze*, 140-146; Richard B. McCaslin, "Dark Corner of the Confederacy: James G. Bourland and the Border Regiment," *Military History of the West* 24 (Spring 1994):57-70.

52. Smith, *Frontier Defense in the Civil War*, 131-134; David P. Smith, "The Elm Creek Raid, 1864: State and Confederate Defense and Response," *Military History of the Southwest* 19 (Fall 1989): 121-136; Kenneth Neighbours, "Elm Creek Raid in Young County, 1864," *WTHAYB* 40 (October 1964): 83-89; Barbara A. Neal Ledbetter, *Fort Belknap, Frontier Saga: Indians, Negroes, and Anglo Americans on the Texas Frontier* (Burnet, TX: Eakin Press, 1982), 111-121.

53. Smith, *Frontier Defense in the Civil War*, 134-135; Marilynne Howsley, "Forting Up on the Texas Frontier during the Civil War," *WTHAYB* 17 (October 1941): 71-76; J. R. Webb, "Chapters From the Frontier Life of Phin W. Reynolds," *ibid.*, 21 (October 1945): 115-117.

54. Smith, *Frontier Defense in the Civil War*, 135-138.

55. Simpson, *Lee's Grenadier Guard*, 384-388; Polley, *Hood's Texas Brigade*, 224-226; James Longstreet, *From Manassas to Appomattox: Memoirs of the Civil War in America* (Reprint; Bloomington: Indiana University Press, 1960), 517.

56. Polley, *Hood's Texas Brigade*, 226-227; Jerry D. Wert, *General James Longstreet: The Confederacy's Most Controversial Soldier* (New York: Simon & Schuster, 1993), 373-374; Gary R. Swanson and Timothy D. Johnson, "Conflict in East Tennessee: Generals Law, Jenkins, and Longstreet," *Civil War History* 31 (June 1985): 101-110.

57. Simpson, *Lee's Grenadier Guard*, 390-395; Douglas Southall Freeman, *Lee's Lieutenants*, 3 vols. (New York: Charles Scribner's Sons, 1942-1944), 3:344-356; Gordon Rhea, *The Battle of the Wilderness, May 5-6, 1864* (Baton Rouge: Louisiana State University Press, 1994), 283-298.

58. Robert Campbell, "Texans Always Move Them," in Commager, ed., *The Blue and the Gray*, 2:982-985; Rhea, *Battle of the Wilderness*, 299-302; Gary

Gallagher, ed., *Fighting for the Confederacy: The Personal Recollections of General Edward Porter Alexander* (Chapel Hill: University of North Carolina Press, 1989), 358. For a slightly different version of this affair see Edward Steeve, *The Wilderness Campaign* (Harrisburg, PA: Stackpole Company, 1960), 344-345, 351-352; and Noah Andre Trudeau, *Bloody Roads South: The Wilderness to Cold Harbor, May-June 1864* (Boston: Little, Brown, and Company, 1989), 92-93.

59. Simpson, *Lee's Grenadier Guard*, 398-400; Polley, *Hood's Texas Brigade*, 231-232; Rhea, *Battle of the Wilderness*, 302-306. Short biographical sketches of the four regimental commanders in the brigade may be found in Robert K. Krick, *Lee's Colonels: A Biographical Register of the Field Officers of the Army of Northern Virginia* (4th ed., revised; Dayton, OH: Morningside House, 1992), 44-45, 48, 74, 262.

60. Simpson, *Lee's Grenadier Guard*, 401. See also Gallagher, ed., *Fighting for the Confederacy*, 358; E. P. Alexander, *Military Memoirs of A Confederate* (Reprint; Bloomington: Indiana University Press, 1962), 504-507; Dayton Kelley, "The Texas Brigade at the Wilderness, May 6, 1864," *Texana* 11, no. 2 (1973):103-123; and Evander M. Law, "From the Wilderness to Cold Harbor," *Battles & Leaders*, 4: 125.

61. Simpson, *Lee's Grenadier Guard*, 401-404; Campbell, "Texans Always Move Them," 984-985.

62. Polley, *Hood's Texas Brigade*, 234-237; Wert, *General James Longstreet*, 385-389.

63. There is a good description of the battle of Spotsylvania by a member of Hood's Brigade in the Thomas L. McCarty Papers, May 10, 1864, University of Texas Archives. See also Hamilton, *History of Company M*, 58-59; *Official Records*, Pt. 2, 51:911; William D. Matter, *If It Takes All Summer: The Battle of Spotsylvania* (Chapel Hill: University of North Carolina Press, 1988), 154-155.

64. Grant lost over 7,000 men in less than thirty minutes of fighting. Total Confederate losses were approximately 1,500. Polley, *Hood's Texas Brigade*, 242-243; Gallagher, ed., *Fighting for the Confederacy*, 411-412; J. J. Cosgrove, "About the Attack at Cold Harbor," *Confederate Veteran* 20 (November 1912): 511.

65. Polley, *Hood's Texas Brigade*, 244-248; Simpson, *Lee's Grenadier Guard*, 422-430. For a map of the Richmond defenses showing the position of the Texas Brigade, see Richard J. Sommers, *Richmond Redeemed: The Siege of Petersburg* (Garden City, NY: Doubleday & Company, 1981), 24-25.

66. Sommers, *Richmond Redeemed*, 28-30, 31-34, 45-47, 61-62; Simpson, *Lee's Grenadier Guard*, 438-442; Douglas Southall Freeman, *R. E. Lee*, 4 vols. (New York: Scribner's Sons, 1936), 3: 509n; Gallagher, ed., *Fighting for the Confederacy*, 483-484.

67. Simpson, *Lee's Grenadier Guard*, 445-457.

68. The battery is often referred to as the Good-Douglas Battery as Capt. John J. Good of Dallas originally commanded the unit. Good was wounded at Pea Ridge and was then appointed presiding judge of the Confederate military courts of Mississippi, Alabama, and Georgia. Capt. James P. Douglas, principal of the Tyler Male Academcy and an editor and proprietor of the Tyler *Reporter*, succeeded Good in command. *Handbook of Texas*, 1:516, 708; Douglas, ed., *Douglas's Texas Battery, C.S.A.*, vii-viii, 87-88; *Official Records*, Pt. 3, 38:638-644; McMurry, *John Bell Hood*, 79-99; Hood, *Advance and Retreat*, 65-68.

69. Granbury's Brigade consisted of the Sixth Texas Infantry and Fifteenth Texas Cavalry (dismounted) consolidated, the Seventh Texas Infantry, the Tenth Texas Infantry, the Seventeenth and Eighteenth Texas Cavalry (dismounted) consolidated, and the Twenty-fourth and Twenty-fifth Texas Cavalry (dismounted) consolidated. *Official Records*, Pt. 3, 38:638-644, 686-687; Brown, ed., *One of Cleburne's Command*, 82-88; Harold B. Simpson, ed., *The Bugle Blows Softly: The Confederate Diary of Benjamin M. Seaton* (Waco: Texian Press, 1965), 49-53; Albert Castel, *Decision in the West: The Atlanta Campaign of 1864* (Lawrence: University Press of Kansas, 1992), 134-135, 229-241; McCaffrey, *This Band of Heroes*, 101-111.

70. McCaffrey, *This Band of Heroes*, 111-113; Castel, *Decision in the West*, 299-319; Brown, ed., *One of Cleburne's Command*, 97-98; Spurlin, ed., *Civil War Diary of Charles A. Leuschner*, 40.

71. The Ninth Texas Infantry, Tenth Texas Cavalry (dismounted), Fourteenth Texas Cavalry (dismounted), and Thirty-second Texas Cavalry (dismounted) were the Texas regiments in Ector's Brigade. McClure, ed., *Confederate From East Texas*, 27-28; Castel, *Decision in the West*, 204-205; Evans, ed., *Confederate Military History*, 11:185; William R. Scaife, *The Campaign for Atlanta* (Atlanta: privately published, 1990), 40-42.

72. Barron, *Lone Star Defenders*, 172-198; Kerr, ed., *Fighting With Ross' Texas Cavalry Brigade*, 108-115, 134-136; Hale, *Third Texas Cavalry*, 201-229; Benner, *Sul Ross*, 96-104; Perry Wayne Shelton, comp., *Personal Civil War Letters of General Lawrence Sullivan Ross* (Austin: W. M. Morrison, 1994), 65-66.

73. Wright and Simpson, eds., *Texas in the War, 1861-1865*, 81, 95, 114; Harry M. Henderson, *Texas in the Confederacy* (San Antonio: Naylor, 1955), 101-105; C. C. Jeffries, "The Character of Terry's Texas Rangers," *SHQ* 64 (April 1961): 456-462.

74. Evans, ed., *Confederate Military History*, 11:182-188; Jeffries, *Terry's Rangers*, 91-93; Giles, *Terry's Texas Rangers*, 81-82.

75. Wright and Simpson, eds., *Texas in the War, 1861-1865*, 114-115; McCaslin, *Tainted Breeze*, 47-48, 84-85; McCaslin, "Conditional Confederates: The Eleventh Texas Cavalry West of the Mississippi River," 87-99; Steve Peters, "Murder of Colonel Joseph M. Bounds, Eleventh Texas Cavalry, Young's Regiment, C.S.A.," *Texana* 12, no. 1 (1974): 56-60; McDonough, *Stones River*, 90, 253.

76. For more on the removal and controversy surrounding it see Thomas Lawrence Connelly, *Autumn of Glory: The Army of Tennessee, 1862-1865* (Baton Rouge: Louisiana State University Press, 1971), 391-426; Steven E. Woodworth, *Jefferson Davis and His Generals: The Failure of Confederate Command in the West* (Lawrence: University Press of Kansas, 1990), 282-285; Castel, *Decision in the West*, 352-365; Goree, ed., *Thomas Jewett Goree Letters*, 228-229, 237-238.

77. Brown, ed., *One of Cleburne's Command*, 106, 159; Bill O'Neal, ed., "The Civil War Memoirs of Samuel Alonzo Cooke," *SHQ* 74 (April 1971): 543; William C. Billingsley, ed., "'Such Is War': The Confederate Memoirs of Newton Asbury Keen," *Texas Military History* 7 (Summer 1968): 104-105; Douglas, ed., *Douglas's Texas Battery*, 114. For additional commentary on Johnston's removal and Hood's appointment, see Richard M. McMurry, "Confederate Morale in the Atlanta Campaign of 1864," *Georgia Historical Quarterly* 54 (Summer 1970): 226-243; Daniel, *Soldiering in the Army of Tennessee*, 140-147; Douglas John Cater, *As*

It Was: Reminiscences of a Soldier of the Third Texas Cavalry and the Nineteenth Louisiana Infantry (Austin: State House Press, 1990), 185; Kerr, ed., *Fighting with Ross' Texas Cavalry Brigade*, 158; and Spurlin, ed., *Civil War Diary of Charles A. Leuschner*, 43.

78. *Official Records*, Pt.3, 38:746, 748-754; Turner, "Jim Turner, Co. G, 6th Texas Infantry," 173-175; McCaffrey, *This Band of Heroes*, 114-120; Brown, ed., *One of Cleburne's Command*, 108-110. Irving Buck, an officer on Cleburne's staff, said that Cleburne spoke of the fighting on July 21 as the "bitterest" of his life. Buck, ed., *Cleburne and His Command* (Reprint; 1908, Jackson, TN: McCowat-Mercer Press, 1959), 213-214.

79. *Official Records*, Pt. 3, 38:545-546, 564-568, 731-732, 747-754; McCaffrey, *This Band of Heroes*, 120-121; Brown, ed., *One of Cleburne's Command*, 110-115; Castel, *Decision in the West*, 385-414; Connelly, *Autumn of Glory*, 444-450; Spurlin, ed., *Civil War Diary of Charles A. Leuschner*, 44.

80. Ector's injury put an end to active field command, although he later took part in the defense of Mobile in the closing days of the war. Evans, ed., *Confederate Military History*, 11:185-186; McClure, ed., *Confederate From East Texas*, 28-29; Warner, *Generals in Gray*, 80-81, 348-349.

81. *Official Records*, 38:963-965; Scaife, *Campaign for Atlanta*, 72-74; Kerr, ed., *Fighting With Ross' Texas Cavalry Brigade*, 136-137, 160-162; Barron, *Lone Star Defenders*, 199-204; Hale, *Third Texas Cavalry*, 233-238; Byron H. Matthews, Jr., *The McCook-Stoneman Raid* (Philadelphia: Dorrance & Company, 1976), 93-106.

82. Hood, *Advance and Retreat*, 198-202; Tom Cutrer, ed., "'We Are Stern and Resolved': The Civil War Letters of John Wesley Rabb, Terry's Texas Rangers," *SHQ* 91 (October 1987): 220-222. The Eighth and Eleventh Texas Cavalry were part of Harrison's Brigade in the division commanded by Brig. Gen. William Y. C. Humes. Felix H. Robertson, son of Jerome B. Robertson who commanded Hood's Brigade, commanded a cavalry brigade consisting of the Third, Eighth, Tenth, and Twelfth Confederate and Fifth Georgia regiments, in John H. Kelly's division. See James H. Colgin, ed., "The Life Story of Brig. Gen. Felix Robertson," *Texana* 8 (Spring 1970): 154-182, and Felix Robertson, "On Wheeler's Last Raid in Middle Tennessee," *Confederate Veteran* 30 (September 1922): 334-335; Jeffries, *Terry's Rangers*, 95-99.

83. McMurry, *John Bell Hood*, 145. Most historians believe Wheeler's raid was a failure. See Woodworth, *Jefferson Davis and His Generals*, 288-289; Lewis A. Lawson, *Wheeler's Last Raid* (Greenwood, FL: Penkevill Publishing Company, 1986), 1; and John P. Dyer, *Fightin' Joe Wheeler* (Baton Rouge: Louisiana State University, 1941), 196.

84. *Official Records* Pt. 2, 38:826; Stephen Z. Starr, *The Union Cavalry in the Civil War*, 3 vols. (Baton Rouge: Louisiana State University Press, 1985), 3:474-481; Benner, *Sul Ross*, 106; Hale, *Third Texas Cavalry*, 238-244; Barron, *Lone Star Defenders*, 239-242. One of those captured was Pvt. Newton Keen of the Sixth Texas Cavalry. For his experiences as a prisoner of war, see Billingsley, ed., "Such Is War," Pt. 4, 176-179.

85. McCaffrey, *This Band of Heroes*, 123-125; Hood, *Advance and Retreat*, 204-210; Brown, ed., *One of Cleburne's Command*, 123-130; Spurlin, ed., *Civil War Diary of Charles A. Leuschner*, 46-47; Castel, *Decision in the West*, 475-534.

86. As noted earlier, Young spent the rest of the war in the Union prison at Johnson's Island. Col. C. R. Earp of the Tenth Texas Cavalry assumed temporary command of Ector's Brigade following Young's capture. Evans, ed., *Confederate Military History*, 11:188-189; Wright and Simpson, *Texas in the War, 1861-1865,"* 97-98; Jon Harrison, "Tenth Texas Cavalry, C.S.A.," *Military History of Texas and the Southwest* 12, no. 3 (1975): 173-178; McClure, ed., *Confederate From East Texas*, 229; Fred E. Brown, "The Battle of Allatoona," *Civil War History* 6 (September 1960): 277-297.

87. Hood, *Advance and Retreat*, 257-269; McMurry, *John Bell Hood*, 159-165; Thomas Robson Hay, *Hood's Tennessee Campaign* (New York: Walter Neale, 1929), 19-21, 27-29. At least one Texas soldier, Wiley F. Donathan, approved of Hood's plan. In October 1864 he wrote his sister that "our prospects were never brighter; for a great change has been wrought within the last two weeks." Wiley F. Donathan Family Correspondence, Archives Division, Texas State Library, Austin, Texas.

88. *Official Records*, Pt. 1, 45:684-685, 707-708; McCaffrey, *This Band of Heroes*, 134-139; Douglas, ed., *Douglas's Texas Battery*, 150; Brown, ed., *One of Cleburne's Command*, 147-151; James Lee McDonough and Thomas L. Connelly, *Five Tragic Hours: The Battle of Franklin* (Knoxville: University of Tennessee Press, 1983), 92-168; Wiley Sword, *The Confederacy's Last Hurrah: Spring Hill, Franklin & Nashville* (Lawrence: University of Kansas Press, 1992), 221-224; Daniel, *Soldiering in the Army of Tennessee*, 160; Evans, ed., *Confederate Military History*, 11:189-190; Anderson, ed., *Campaigning with Parsons' Texas Cavalry*, 152. Ector's Brigade was not involved in the battle of Franklin. The brigade had been sent to Florence, Alabama, as a guard for the supply train and had not rejoined the army. *Official Records*, Pt. 1, 45:708.

89. McMurry, *John Bell Hood*, 176-177.

90. *Official Records*, Pt. 1, 45:709-710; Shelby Foote, *The Civil War: A Narrative*, 3 vols. (New York: Random House, 1958-1974), 3:685-705; McCaffrey, *This Band of Heroes*, 141-147; McMurry, *John Bell Hood*, 177-179; Brown, ed., *One of Cleburne's Command*, 152-156; Stanley Horn, *The Decisive Battle of Nashville* (Baton Rouge: Louisiana State University Press, 1956), 92-96; Hay, *Hood's Tennessee Campaign*, 148-170; Sword, *The Confederacy's Last Hurrah*, 324-325, 364, 369-370.

91. *Official Records*, Pt. 1, 45:664-669, 679-680; Kerr, ed., *Fighting with Ross' Texas Cavalry Brigade*, 195-198; Brown, ed., *One of Cleburne's Command*, 156-160; Hale, *Third Texas Cavalry*, 263-266; McMurry, *John Bell Hood*, 189-192.

CHAPTER SIX

1. Douglas, ed., *Douglas's Texas Battery*, 153; Goyne, ed., *Lone Star and Double Eagle*, 158; Connor, ed., *Dear America*, 104, 106. A proposal similar to the one Connor mentioned was made by Col. Guy M. Bryan, Governor Murrah's representative to Kirby Smith's headquarters. See Meiners, "The Texas Governorship, 1861-1865," 373-375.

2. Barr, *All the Days of My Life*, 248-249.

3. J. Marvin Hunter, "The Battle of Dove Creek," *WTHAYB* 18 (October 1942): 74-78; William C. Pool, "The Battle of Dove Creek," *SHQ* 53 (April 1950):

367-376; Smith, *Frontier Defense in the Civil War*, 151-153; I. D. Ferguson, "The Battle of Dove Creek," *Frontier Times* 1 (June 1924): 24-31.

4. James K. Greer, ed., *Buck Barry: Texas Ranger and Frontiersman* (Reprint; Lincoln: University of Nebraska Press, 1984), 190-192; Smith, *Frontier Defense in the Civil War*, 153-154.

5. Hunter, "The Battle of Dove Creek," 78-80; Pool, "The Battle of Dove Creek," 379-381; Greer, ed., *Buck Barry*, 192-193.

6. Smith, *Frontier Defense in the Civil War*, 154-155; Rupert N. Richardson, *The Frontier of Northwest Texas, 1846 to 1876* (Glendale, CA: Arthur H. Clark Company, 1963), 248-249; Lucy A. Erath, ed., "Memoirs of Major George Bernard Erath," Part IV, *SHQ* 27 (October 1923): 160-169; Pool, "The Battle of Dove Creek," 385; Phillip Rutherford, "The Other Civil War: Disaster at Dove Creek," *Civil War Times Illustrated* 22 (April 1983): 20-25.

7. Smith, *Frontier Defense in the Civil War*, 139-141, 164-166; Floyd F. Ewing, "Unionist Sentiment on the Northwest Texas Frontier," *WTHAYB* 33 (October 1957): 68-69.

8. Only the *Syren*, a blockade runner at Charleston, was more successful than the *Denbigh*. The *Syren* was captured near Charleston on February 18, 1865. Wise, *Lifeline of the Confederacy*, 176, 219, 296, 323; Glover, "West Gulf Blockade," 207-208, 233-240. For the experiences of one blockade runner who visited Galveston late in the war, see Thomas E. Taylor, *Running the Blockade: A Personal Narrative of Adventures, Risks, and Escapes During the American Civil War* (New York: Charles Scribner's Sons, 1896), 148-158.

9. Wise, *Lifeline of the Confederacy*, 219-220, 275, 308.

10. *Official Records*, Pt. 1, 48:1448, Pt. 2, 458-463; Oates, ed., *Rip Ford's Texas*, 386-389; Stephen B. Oates, "John S. 'Rip' Ford: Prudent Cavalryman, C.S.A.," *SHQ* 64 (January 1961): 310; Hughes, *Rebellious Ranger*, 232-236.

11. *Proceedings of the Second Confederate Congress, Second Session, December 15, 1864–March 18, 1865*, ed. Frank E. Vandiver, *Southern Historical Society Papers*, (Richmond: Virginia Historical Society, 1959), 52:283, 297, 300-306; King, *Louis T. Wigfall*, 210-211. For more on the Wigfall-Johnston relationship, see Craig L. Symonds, *Joseph E. Johnston: A Civil War Biography* (New York: W. W. Norton & Co., 1992), 176–182, 222–226, 341–343, 385.

12. Evans, ed., *Confederate Military History*, 11: 192-193; *Official Records*, Pt. 2, 11:1184-1188, 1218; McClure, ed., *Confederate From East Texas*, 32-33; Kerr, ed., *Fighting With Ross' Texas Cavalry Brigade*, 202-203; Arthur W. Bergeron, Jr., *Confederate Mobile* (Jackson: University of Mississippi Press, 1991), 173, 181-182, 184; Chester G. Hearn, *Mobile Bay and the Mobile Campaign: The Last Great Battles in the Civil War* (Jefferson, NC: McFarland & Company, 1993), 176, 188-189; Spurlin, ed., *Civil War Diary of Charles A. Leuschner*, 57-58; Cater, *As It Was*, 208-210; McCaffrey, *This Band of Heroes*, 151-153.

13. Fletcher, *Rebel Private, Front and Rear*, 144; Wade Hampton, "The Battle of Bentonville," *Battles & Leaders*, 4:700-705; Jay Luvaas, "Bentonville — Johnston's Last Stand," *North Carolina Historical Review* 33 (July 1956): 332-358; Joseph Glatthaar, *The March to the Sea and Beyond: Sherman's Troops in the Savannah and Carolinas Campaigns* (New York: New York University Press, 1988), 167-172; Jeffries, *Terry's Rangers*, 123-126; Barrett, *Civil War in North Carolina*, 338-339; Darst, "Robert Hodges, Jr.: Confederate Soldier," 39-40.

14. *Proceedings of the Second Confederate Congress, Second Session*, 176, 257-258; King, "Political Career of Williamson Simpson Oldham," 130-131.

15. *Ibid.*, 325, 329-330. For the full story of the debates, see Robert F. Durden, *The Gray and the Black: The Confederate Debates on Emancipation* (Baton Rouge: Louisiana State University Press, 1972).

16. *Proceedings of the Second Confederate Congress, Second Session*, 181-183, 337-338, 362-363, 365, 377, 383, 387, 452-457, 464-465; King, *Louis T. Wigfall*, 205-208.

17. Texas' other representative, Simpson Morgan, died in Monticello, Arkansas, in December 1864. Jon Wakelyn, *Biographical Directory of the Confederacy* (Westport, CT: Greenwood Press, 1977), 326; *Journal of the Congress of Confederate States of America, 1861-1865*, 7 vols. (Washington: Government Printing Office, 1904-1905), 2:612; *Proceedings of the Second Confederate Congress, Second Session*, 331, 465, 470; Yearns, *Confederate Congress*, 97-98.

18. Gallagher, ed., *Fighting for the Confederacy*, 513-515; Freeman, *Lee's Lieutenants*, 3:644-682; Wert, *General James Longstreet*, 398-399.

19. Polley, *Hood's Texas Brigade*, 274-277; Simpson, *Lee's Grenadier Guard*, 459-464. Col. Robert M. Powell was commanding the Fifth Texas Cavalry of Hood's Brigade when wounded and captured at Gettysburg. When he was exchanged in March 1865, he succeeded Col. Frederick S. Bass (whom he outranked) as the last commander of the Texas Brigade. *Ibid.*, 459-460 fn; Wright and Simpson, *Texas in the War, 1861-1865*, 19, 103, 213; Krick, *Lee's Colonels*, 308-309.

20. Simpson, *Lee's Grenadier Guard*, 464-465; Polley, *Hood's Texas Brigade*, 277-278.

21. Harold B. Simpson, "Hood's Brigade at Appomattox," *Texana* 3 (Spring 1965): 1-19; Simpson, *Lee's Grenadier Guard*, 468-469; Hamilton, *History of Company M*, 69. The total figures given here include members of the Third Arkansas, which was part of the brigade. Simpson, "East Texas Companies in Hood's Brigade," *ETHJ* 3 (March 1965): 13, states that 4,500 Texans had been in the brigade and that only 476 were present to surrender. Polley, *Hood's Texas Brigade*, 278, lists 557 members of the brigade (including Arkansans) at Appomattox.

22. Warner, *Generals in Gray*, 264-265; Wakelyn, *Biographical Directory of the Confederacy*, 374; Freeman, *Lee's Lieutenants*, 3:737, 764-765; Harold B. Simpson, "West Pointers in the Texas Confederate Army," *Texas Military History* 6 (Spring 1962): 82-83; Noah Andre Trudeau, *Out of the Storm: The End of the Civil War, April-June 1865* (Boston: Little, Brown, and Company, 1994), 31, 40, 104-105.

23. Simpson, *Lee's Grenadier Guard*, 469-472; Hamilton, *History of Company M*, 69-71.

24. Reagan, *Memoirs*, 209-231; Lubbock, *Six Decades in Texas*, 567-577; William C. Davis, *Jefferson Davis: The Man and His Hour* (New York: Harper Collins, 1991), 633-659.

25. McCaffrey, *This Band of Heroes*, 156, states that 440 Texans from Granbury's Brigade signed paroles; this of over 1,100 men who had served in the brigade. Simpson, *Lee's Grenadier Guard*, 472-473; Hamilton, *History of Company M*, 69-76; Fletcher, *Rebel Private, Front and Rear*, 146-158; Brown, ed., *One of Cleburne's Command*, 172-186.

26. Noah Andre Trudeau, *Out of the Storm*, 10-11, 205-207, 342-346, traces Oldham's journey from Richmond to Texas. Trudeau bases his account on

Oldham's manuscript "Last Days of the Confederacy," in the Barker History Center, the University of Texas at Austin.

27. For conditions in Texas in the spring of 1865, see Ashcraft, "Texas: 1860-1866," 238-246; and Trammell, *Seven Pines*, 207-209. Col. George W. Baylor commanded a cavalry battalion under Wharton in the Red River campaign. He was angry at Wharton for placing himself and his troops under an officer Baylor considered inferior. After an exchange of words with Wharton, Baylor pulled a pistol and shot Wharton. The episode is described in Young, *To the Tyrants Never Yield*, 183-185 and in Jeffries, *Terry's Rangers*, 83-85. For more on the two men see John L. Waller, "Colonel George Wythe Baylor," *Southwestern Social Science Quarterly* 24 (June 1943): 23-35; William Wharton Groce, "Major General John A. Wharton," *SHQ* 19 (January 1916): 271-278.

28. *Official Records*, Pt. 2, 48:1282-1285; Yearns, ed., *Confederate Governors*, 214; George Lee Robertson to Julia, May 8, 1865, Robertson Papers, University of Texas Archives; Heartsill, *Fourteen Hundred and 91 Days*, 239; William W. White, "The Disintegration of An Army: Confederate Forces in Texas, April-June 1865," *ETHJ* 26 (Fall 1988): 41-42; Emory Thomas, "Rebel Nationalism: E. H. Cushing and the Confederate Experience," *SHQ* 73 (January 1970): 349.

29. Weddle, *Plow-Horse Cavalry*, 158; Yearns, ed., *Confederate Governors*, 106, 215; Charles W. Ramsdell, *Reconstruction in Texas* (New York: Columbia University Press, 1910), 30-31; Meiners, "Texas Governorship, 1861-1865," 376-377.

30. Kerby, *Kirby Smith's Confederacy*, 418-419; Parks, *Kirby Smith*, 645-647.

31. *Official Records*, Vol. Pt. 1, 48:265-268. Ford's report is found in Evans, ed., *Confederate Military History*, 11:125-129. See also Oates, ed., *Rip Ford's Texas*, 389-393; Oates, "John S. 'Rip' Ford," 310-314; W. H. Carrington, "Last Battle of the War, May 13th, 1865," in John Henry Brown, *History of Texas, From 1685 to 1892*, 2 vols. (St. Louis: L. E. Daniell, Publisher, 1893), 2:431-436; Trudeau, *Out of the Storm*, 298-310; Hughes, *Rebellious Ranger*, 237-240.

32. Oates, ed., *Rip Ford's Texas*, 396-402; Kerby, *Kirby Smith's Confederacy*, 419-420; Hughes, *Rebellious Ranger*, 241-243.

33. Charles W. Ramsdell, "Texas From the Fall of the Confederacy to the Beginning of Reconstruction," *Quarterly of Texas State Historical Association* 11 (January 1908): 205-207; White, "The Disintegration of An Army," 43-45; Philip Graham, ed., "Texas Memoirs of Amelia Barr," *SHQ* 69 (April 1966): 488-489.

34. Ramsdell, *Reconstruction in Texas*, 36-39; Ashcraft, "Texas: 1860-1866," 254-255.

35. Kerby, *Kirby Smith's Confederacy*, 425-426; Parks, *Kirby Smith*, 475-478. Edmund J. Davis, prominent Texas Unionist and a brigadier general in Federal service, represented General Canby in the Galveston signing. After securing Smith's signature, Davis took the surrender documents to Canby in New Orleans. Gray, "Edmund J. Davis," 69-70.

36. Kerby, *Kirby Smith's Confederacy*, 427-428; Ashcraft, "Texas: 1860-1866," 257-259; Alexander W. Terrell, *From Texas to Mexico and the Court of Maximilian* (Dallas: Book Club of Texas, 1933), 3-10; William W. White, *The Confederate Veteran* (Tuscaloosa, AL: Confederate Publishing Company, 1962), 61-64; William C. Griggs, *The Elusive Eden: Frank McMullan's Confederate Colony in Brazil* (Austin: University of Texas Press, 1967); Laurence F. Hill, *The Confeder-*

ate Exodus to Latin America (Austin: Texas State Historical Association, 1961); Carl Coke Rister, "Carlota, A Confederate Colony in Mexico," *Journal of Southern History* 11 (February 1945): 33-50; Andrew F. Rolle, *The Lost Cause: The Confederate Exodus to Mexico* (Norman: University of Oklahoma Press, 1965); W. C. Nunn, *Escape From Reconstruction* (Fort Worth: Texas Christian University Press, 1956); Bell I. Wiley, "Confederate Exiles in Brazil," *Civil War Times Illustrated* 15 (January 1977): 22-23.

37. Robert W. Shook, "Federal Occupation and Administration of Texas, 1865-1870" (Ph.D. dissertation, North Texas State University, 1970), 76-78; William C. Richter, *The Army in Texas During Reconstruction* (College Station: Texas A & M University Press, 1987), 11-16.

38. Waller, *Colossal Hamilton of Texas*, 60-64; Richter, *Army in Texas During Reconstruction*, 21-23.

CHAPTER SEVEN

1. James M. McPherson, *Battle Cry of Freedom: The Civil War Era* (New York: Oxford University Press, 1988), 306-307, 485, 854. In a more recent work, *What They Fought For, 1861-1865* (Baton Rouge: Louisiana State University Press, 1994), 17, McPherson states that eleven to twelve percent of all Confederate soldiers were killed or mortally wounded in action. See also Richard H. Shryock, "A Medical Perspective on the Civil War," *American Quarterly* 14 (Summer 1962): 161-173.

Texas figures given here are based upon the estimated 88,000 number for enlistments given by Stephen B. Oates, "Texas Under the Secessionists," 187. Texas battle casualties may have been less than in some other states, as many Texans served in frontier units which saw less combat than those in armies east of the Mississippi River.

2. *Handbook of Texas*, 1:823, 2:89-90, 148; Warner, *Generals in Gray*, 117-118, 139-140, 270-271, 331-332; Wright and Simpson, *Texas in the War*, 98-99.

3. For his letter to the people of Texas, August 11, 1865, see Reagan, *Memoirs*, 286-295.

4. *Handbook of Texas*, 2:444; Procter, *Not Without Honor*, 176-301.

5. Simpson and Wright, *Texas in the War*, 59-60, lists all Confederate veterans who represented Texas in Congress. Several of these veterans came to Texas after the war. Maxey was appointed major general by Kirby Smith, but the appointment was never approved by President Davis. *Ibid.*, 86-102, 107-108; *Handbook of Texas*, 1:924, 2:150, 299-300; Warner, *Generals in Gray*, 59-60, 216; Claude H. Hall, "The Fabulous Tom Ochiltree: Promoter, Politician, and Raconteur," *SHQ* 71 (January 1968): 347-376; Alwyn Barr, "The Making of a Secessionist: The Antebellum Career of Roger Q. Mills," *ibid.*, 79 (October 1975): 129-144.

6. *Handbook of Texas*, 1:856-857, 2:200-201, 778, 3:182; Simpson and Wright, *Texas in the War*, 79, 113, 155-158; Elliott, *Leathercoat*, 235-249, 293-294.

7. *Handbook of Texas*, 1:856-857, 891-892, 2:506-507; Simpson and Wright, *Texas in the War*, 104-106, 108, 157-158; Dudley G. Wooten, "The Life and Services of Oran Milo Roberts," *Quarterly of the Texas State Historical Association* 2 (July 1898): 15-20; Lelia Bailey, "The Life and Public Career of O. M. Roberts" (Ph.D. dissertation, University of Texas, 1932); Jean Sutherlin Duncan, *Richard Bennett Hubbard: Texas Politician and Diplomat* (College Station: priv. pub.,

1972); Jean S. Duncan, "An East Texas [sic.] At An Oriental Court: Richard Bennett Hubbard, Minister to Japan, 1885-1889," *ETHJ* 16 (Fall 1978): 29-34; Martha Ann Turner, *Richard Bennett Hubbard: An American Life* (Austin: Shoal Creek Publisher, 1979).

8. *Handbook of Texas*, 1:443, 822-823; Simpson and Wright, *Texas in the War*, 82, 108.

9. *Handbook of Texas*, 1:354; Yearns, ed., *Confederate Governors*, 199; Tinsie Larson, "Edward Clark," in W. C. Nunn, ed., *Ten Texans in Gray* (Hillsboro: Hill Junior College Press, 1968), 30-32.

10. *Handbook of Texas*, 2:89; Yearns, ed., *Confederate Governors*, 208; Leann Cox Adams, "Francis R. Lubbock," in *Ten Texans in Gray*, 95-98; Lubbock, *Six Decades in Texas*, 578-643.

11. *Handbook of Texas*, 1:326-327, 2:251; Benny E. Deusen, "Pendleton Murrah," in *Ten Texans in Gray*, 133-134; Yearns, ed., *Confederate Governors*, 215; Margaret S. Henson and Kevin Ladd, *Chambers County: A Pictorial History* (Norfolk, VA: Denning Company, Publishers, 1988), 68; Jewel Horace Harry, *A History of Chambers County* (Dallas: Chambers County Historical Committee, 1981), 53.

12. *Handbook of Texas*, 2:311, 906-907; Warner, *Generals in Gray*, 336-337; Walther, *The Fire-Eaters*, 190-191; Trudeau, *Out of the Storm*, 384-385; King, *Louis T. Wigfall*, 220-231; King, "Political Career of Williamson Simpson Oldham," 132-133.

13. John H. Reagan was the other Texas representative in the Provisional Congress. *Handbook of Texas*, 1:733, 735, 2:871, 3:1087; Wright and Simpson, *Texas in the War*, 94-95, 108.

14. Wakelyn, *Biographical Directory of the Confederacy*, 93-94, 159, 208, 227, 381, 439, 450; *Handbook of Texas*, 1:124, 206, 464-465, 714, 723-724, 809, 2:594; Thompson, *Colonel John R. Baylor*, 93-97.

15. The list of Texas general officers is taken from Wright and Simpson, *Texas in the War*, 3-18. It is at slight variance with the biographical sketches in Warner, *Generals in Gray*. Warner does not include A. P. Bagby, Xavier B. Debray, Wilburn H. King, Hinche P. Mabry, Horace Randal, and Alexander W. Terrell in his list. He does note that Bagby, Debray, King, Randal, and Terrell were assigned as general officers in the Trans Mississippi Department, but not appointed by President Davis. *Ibid.*, 351-352. Warner makes no mention of Hinche P. Mabry of Jefferson, described by Wright and Simpson, 86, as "promoted to brigadier general by E. Kirby Smith sometime in 1864 but . . . never confirmed by Jefferson Davis or the Confederate Senate." Wright and Simpson do not enumerate James P. Major, a native of Missouri who commanded a Texas cavalry brigade in Louisiana, as a Texan, but he is included in the list of Texas general officers in Richard M. McMurry, *Two Great Rebel Armies: An Essay in Confederate Military History* (Chapel Hill: University of North Carolina Press, 1989), 163-164. Neither Wright and Simpson nor McMurry lists Brig. Gen. Adam Rankin Johnson, who served as commander of the Tenth Kentucky Cavalry, as a Texan, although Johnson resided in Texas seven years before the war, returned to Texas after the war, and was later buried in the Texas State Cemetery. For more on Johnson, see his 1904 memoirs, reprinted by the State House Press of Austin, *The Partisan Rangers of the Confederate States Army* (1995).

16. Readers of the early editions of Mary Boykin Chesnut's *Diary from Dixie*, or *Mary Chesnut's Civil War*, edited by C. Van Woodward (New Haven: Yale University Press, 1981), are aware that the engagement of Hood and Sally Buchanan ("Buck") Preston was the talk of Richmond society during the war. When the war ended, however, the two went their separate ways, she marrying her former fiance, Rollins Lowndes, and he marrying Anna Maria Hennen. According to one Hood biographer, John P. Dyer, *The Gallant Hood*, 308, there was no spectacular quarrel between "Buck" and Hood; instead, "the romance just played out." For Hood's later years, see Dyer, 304-311; McMurry, *John Bell Hood*, 189-203; Sword, *The Confederacy's Last Hurrah*, 434-439.

17. Warner, *Generals in Gray*, 264-265; Wright and Simpson, *Texas in the War*, 92.

18. *Handbook of Texas*, 1:541, 779-780; Warner, *Generals in Gray*, 80-81, 126-127; Wright and Simpson, *Texas in the War*, 77, 81.

19. *Ibid.*, 93-94; *Handbook of Texas*, 1:725, 3:963. See his account *From Texas to Mexico and the Court of Maximilian* (Dallas: Book Club of Texas, 1933); and Charles K. Chamberlain, "Alexander Watkins Terrell, Citizen, Statesman" (Ph.D. dissertation, University of Texas, 1956).

20. *Handbook of Texas*, 1:960, 2:106-107; Wright and Simpson, *Texas in the War*, 85, 88, 93; Warner, *Generals in Gray*, 201, 289-290. For Steele's role with the Rangers, see Walter Prescott Webb, *The Texas Rangers: A Century of Frontier Defense* (New York: Houghton Mifflin, 1935), 236, 238-239, 284-285, 291-292, 327, 331, 374, 377.

21. For reasons not apparent, Felix Robertson's appointment as brigadier general was never confirmed by the Confederate Senate. *Handbook of Texas*, 1:669-670, 2:487, 3:609-610; Wright and Simpson, *Texas in the War*, 77-78, 88-89, 89-91; Warner, *Generals in Gray*, 96, 219, 260-262; Harold B. Simpson, *Hood's Texas Brigade in Reunion and Memory* (Hillsboro: Hill Junior College Press, 1974) 15-16, 160-165, 231. Trudeau, *Out of the Storm*, 396, says Robertson was ninety-nine at the time of death but both Warner, *Generals in Gray*, 210, and *Handbook of Texas*, 2:487, give March 9, 1839, as the date of birth. His date of appointment to West Point was 1857.

22. *Handbook of Texas*, 1:730, 900; Wright and Simpson, *Texas in the War*, 75, 94, 95; Warner, *Generals in Gray*, 118, 326-327, 333-334.

23. *Handbook of Texas*, 1:94, 135-136, 2:24-25; Wright and Simpson, *Texas in the War*, 75-76, 85-86; Warner, *Generals in Gray*, 24-25, 173-174.

24. Hugh Young, "Two Texas Patriots," *SHQ* 44 (July 1940): 27-32; *Handbook of Texas*, 1:94, 2:948; Wright and Simpson, *Texas in the War*, 75, 97-98; Warner, *Generals in Gray*, 348-349.

25. Oates, ed., *Rip Ford's Texas*, 401-435; Hughes, *Rebellious Ranger*, 245-271. For an interesting sidelight on Colonel Ford's role in organizing the Texas State Historical Association, see Bride Nell Taylor, "The Beginnings of the Texas State Historical Association," *SHQ* 33 (July 1919): 4-6, and Dorman Winfrey, *Seventy-five Years of Texas History: The Texas State Historical Association, 1897-1972* (Austin: Pemberton Publishing Company, 1975), 3-4.

26. Wakelyn, *Biographical Directory of the Confederacy*, 305-306; Warner, *Generals in Gray*, 207-208; Rolle, *The Lost Cause*, 88-89, 120n, 195; J. Fred Rippy, "Mexican Projects of the Confederates," *SHQ* 22 (April 1919): 316-317.

27. Parks, *Edmund Kirby Smith*, 481-509; Warner, *Generals in Gray*, 279-280; William B. Hesseltine, *Confederate Leaders in the New South* (Baton Rouge: Louisiana State University Press, 1950), 83-84.

28. Parrish, *Richard Taylor*, 447-496; Richard Harwell, "Introduction," *Destruction and Reconstruction: Personal Experiences of the Late War* (1879, reprint; New York: Longmans, Green, and Company, 1955), xiii-xxxii.

29. William B. Hesseltine and Hazel C. Wolf, *The Blue and the Gray on the Nile* (Chicago: University of Chicago Press, 1961), 19-20, 43, 65-69, 80, 113-114; *Handbook of Texas*, 1:608; Warner, *Generals in Gray*, 276-277.

30. Warner, *Generals in Gray*, 319-320; *Handbook of Texas*, 3:1075-1076; Rolle, *The Lost Cause*, 188; Alfred J. Hanna and Kathryn A. Hanna, *Confederate Exiles in Venezuela* (Tuscaloosa, AL: Confederate Publishing Company, 1960), 22-24, 44, 79.

31. Wakelyn, *Biographical Directory of the Confederacy*, 387; Welsh, *Medical Histories of Confederate Generals*, 198; Warner, *Generals in Gray*, 279.

32. *Ibid.*, 241-242; *Handbook of Texas*, 3:742; Barr, *Polignac's Texas Brigade*, 54.

33. Warner, *Generals in Gray*, 209-210; *Handbook of Texas*, 3:564.

34. *Ibid.*, 1:792; Warner, *Generals in Gray*, 131-132; Wakelyn, *Biographical Directory of the Confederacy*, 224-225.

35. Kenneth L. Stewart and Arnoldo De Leon, *Not Room Enough: Mexicans, Anglos, and Socioeconomic Change in Texas, 1850-1900* (Albuquerque: University of New Mexico Press, 1993), 47-48, describe Benavides as an "accomodationist," who, like Jose Antonio Navarro, formed coalitions with Anglo newcomers that transcended ethnic differences. For more on Benavides, see John Denny Riley, "Santos Benavides: His Influence on the Lower Rio Grande, 1823-1891" (Ph.D. dissertation, Texas Christian University, 1976).

36. Silverthorne, *Ashbel Smith of Texas*, 169-233.

37. Wallace, *Charles DeMorse*, 154-237; Wright and Simpson, *Texas in the War*, 119-120; *Handbook of Texas*, 1:489.

38. George P. Garrison, "Guy Morrison Bryan," *Quarterly of the Texas State Historical Association* 5 (October 1901): 133-136; *Handbook of Texas*, 1:293.

39. Muir, "Dick Dowling and the Battle of Sabine Pass," 423-428.

40. Waller, "Colonel George Wythe Baylor," 26-35; Wright and Simpson, *Texas in the War*, 84-85; Webb, *Texas Rangers*, 395-408, 454.

41. Bailey, *Between Texas and the Enemy*, 206; Bailey, *Texans in the Confederate Cavalry*, 48; Simpson and Wright, *Texas in the War*, 115.

42. Day, "Leon Smith," 43-46.

43. Douglas, ed., *Douglas's Texas Battery, C.S.A.*, ix-x; Wright and Simpson, *Texas in the War*, 132; *Handbook of Texas*, 1:516.

44. Brown, ed., *One of Cleburne's Command*, xix-xxv.

45. Gallaway, *The Ragged Rebel*, 132-135.

46. Wiley, ed., *Fourteen Hundred and 91 Days*, xxiii-xxiv; *Handbook of Texas*, 1:791-792.

47. Fletcher, *Rebel Private, Front and Rear*, x, 158.

48. Anderson, ed., *Brokenburn*, xxvii-xxviii.

49. Barr, *All the Days of My Life: An Autobiography* (New York: D. Appleton and Company, 1917); *Handbook of Texas*, 1:112-113; Paul Adams, "Amelia Barr in

Texas, 1856-1868," *SHQ* 49 (January 1946): 361-373; Philip Graham, ed., "Texas Memoirs of Amelia E. Barr," *ibid.,* 69 (April 1966): 473-498.

50. Snider, "Sarah Devereux," 500-507; McArthur, "Rebecca Hagerty," 28-29.

51. Faust, "Trying to Do a Man's Business," 192.

52. Ralph A. Wooster, "Wealthy Texans, 1870," *SHQ* 74 (July 1970): 25-26, 33; Stambaugh and Stambaugh, *Lower Rio Grande Valley of Texas*, 144-145; Lea, *The King Ranch*, 185-186.

53. Marten, *Texas Divided*, 33-52, 131-135; Wooster, "Ben Epperson," 34-38; O. M. Roberts, "The Experiences of an Unrecognized Senator," *SHQ* 12 (October 1908): 97-119; *Handbook of Texas*, 1:104; Carl H. Moneyhon, *Republicanism in Reconstruction Texas* (Austin: University of Texas Press, 1980), 28-29, 43-47; John Henry Brown, *Indian Wars and Pioneers of Texas* (Austin: L. E. Daniell Publisher, 1880), 376-377.

54. Marten, *Texas Divided*, 128-130, 138-144, 147-148; Moneyhon, *Republicanism in Reconstruction Texas*, 82-83, 117-120; Waller, *Colossal Hamilton*, 59-77; Griffin, "Connecticut Yankee in Texas," 257-272.

55. Gray, "Edmund J. Davis," 150-358; Moneyhon, *Republicanism in Reconstruction Texas*, 84-85, 99-110, 112-126.

56. Marten, *Texas Divided*, 141, 149-150, 175-176; Moneyhon, *Republicanism in Reconstruction Texas*, 67, 98, 115-117, 121-122, 154, 169.

57. According to Richard Moore, "A Smuggler's Exile: S. M. Swenson Flees Texas," *ETHJ* 25 (Spring 1987): 27, Swenson tried unsuccessfully to get back into Texas in Autumn 1864, but only to arrange shipment of cotton from the state. Marten, *Texas Divided*, 176; *Handbook of Texas*, 2:687-689.

58. Andrew Forest Muir, "William Marsh Rice, Houstonian," *ETHJ* 2 (Spring 1964): 32-39; Muir, "Murder on Madison Avenue: The Rice Case Revisited," *Southwest Review* 44 (Winter 1959): 1-9; Muir, *William Marsh Rice and His Institute: A Biographical Study*, ed. Sylvia Stallings Morris, *Rice University Studies* 58, no. 2 (1972); Steven Storm, "Cotton and Profits Across the Border: William Marsh Rice in Mexico, 1863-1865," *Houston Review* 8, no. 2 (1986): 89-96.

59. Smithwick, *Evolution of a State*, 263.

Bibliography

Primary Sources

Manuscripts

Affleck, I. D. Letters. In possession of Affleck family. Galveston, Texas.

Brightman, John Claver. Papers, 1859–1865. Archives, University of Texas. Austin, Texas.

Brown, John E. Letters, 1861–1864. Archives, University of Texas. Austin, Texas.

Bryan, James Perry. Papers. Archives, University of Texas. Austin, Texas.

Bunting, Robert Franklin. Papers. Archives, University of Texas. Austin, Texas.

Carothers, Duncan C. Papers. Archives, Texas State Library. Austin, Texas.

Crockett, Edward R. Diary of Events During the Civil War. Archives, University of Texas. Austin, Texas.

Donathan, Wiley F. Family Correspondence. Archives, Texas State Library. Austin, Texas.

Erskine, Andrew N. Papers, 1845–1862. Archives, University of Texas. Austin, Texas.

Executive Record Book, No. 81. Archives, Texas State Library, Austin, Texas.

Farrow, Sam W. Papers, 1862–1865. Archives, University of Texas. Austin, Texas.

Fisher, George. Papers, 1861–1865. Archives, University of Texas. Austin, Texas.

Fogle, Andrew J. Papers, 1862–1865. Archives, University of Texas. Austin, Texas.

Governors' Letters. Archives, Texas State Library. Austin, Texas.

Guess, George W. Letters, 1861–1865. Archives, University of Texas. Austin, Texas.

Hanks, O. T. "History of B. F. Benton's Company, or Account of Civil War Experiences," Reminiscences, 1861–1862. Archives, University of Texas. Austin, Texas.

Hill, John W. Papers, 1861–1866. Archives, University of Texas. Austin, Texas.

Hopkins, Desmond Pulaski Hopkins. Papers, 1855–1873. Archives, University of Texas. Austin, Texas.

Howell, W. Randolph. Papers. Archives, University of Texas. Austin, Texas.

Kuykendall, James H. Collection. Archives, University of Texas. Austin, Texas.

McCarty, Thomas L. Papers, 1864–1865. Archives, University of Texas. Austin, Texas.

Minor, Mary J. Letters, 1863–1864. Archives, University of Texas. Austin, Texas.

Neblett, Lizzie Scott. Papers, 1849–1928. Archives, University of Texas. Austin, Texas.

Oden, William M. Papers, 1856–1864. Archives, University of Texas. Austin, Texas.

Rabb, Mary. Family Papers, 1823–1922. Archives, University of Texas. Austin, Texas.

Reding, James. Family Papers, 1837–1910. Archives, University of Texas. Austin, Texas.

Robertson, George L. Papers, 1839–1869. Archives, University of Texas. Austin, Texas.

Rogers, William P. Papers, 1846–1862. Archives, University of Texas. Austin, Texas.

Sweargen, R. M. "Four Years in the Confederate army; or, My part of the great rebellion . . ." Manuscript. Archives, University of Texas. Austin, Texas.

Templeton, John A. Papers, 1861–1868. Archives, University of Texas. Austin, Texas.

Whatley, William J. Letters, 1862–1866. Archives, University of Texas. Austin, Texas.

Books

Alberts, Don, ed. *Rebels on the Rio Grande: The Civil War Journal of A. B. Peticolas.* Albuquerque: Merit Press, 1993.

Alexander, E. P. *Military Memoirs of a Confederate.* Reprint. Bloomington: Indiana University Press, 1962.

Anderson, John Q., ed. *Campaigning with Parsons' Cavalry Brigade, CSA: The War Journals and Letters of the Four Orr Brothers, 12th Texas Cavalry Regiment.* Hillsboro: Hill Junior College Press, 1967.

———. *Brokenburn: The Journal of Kate Stone, 1861–1868.* Baton Rouge: Louisiana State University Press, 1955.

Barr, Alwyn, ed. *Charles Porter's Account of the Confederate Attempt to Seize Arizona and New Mexico.* Austin: Pemberton Press, 1964.

Barr, Amelia. *All the Days of My Life: An Autobiography.* New York: D. Appleton and Company, 1917.

Barrett, Thomas. *The Great Hanging at Gainesville, Cooke County, Texas, October A.D. 1862.* Reprint. Austin: Texas State Historical Association, 1961.

Barron, S. B. *The Lone Star Defenders: A Chronicle of the Third Texas Cavalry, Ross' Brigade.* New York: Neale Publishing Company, 1908.

Barziza, Decimus et Ultimus. *The Adventures of a Prisoner of War, 1863–1864.* Ed. R. Henderson Shuffler. Austin: University of Texas Press, 1964.

Bearss, Edwin, ed. *A Louisiana Confederate: Diary of Felix Pierre Poche.* Natchitoches: Louisiana Studies Institute, Northwestern State University, 1972.

Bergeron, Arthur W., ed. *Reminiscences of Major Silas T. Grisamore, C.S.A.* Baton Rouge: Louisiana State University Press, 1993.

Bitton, Davis, ed. *Reminiscences and Civil War Letters of Levi Lamoni Wight: Life in a Mormon Splinter Colony on the Texas Frontier.* Salt Lake City: University of Utah Press, 1970.

Blessington, J. P. *The Campaigns of Walker's Texas Division.* Reprint. Austin: State House Press, 1994.

Brown, Norman, ed. *Journey to Pleasant Hill: The Civil War Letters of Captain Elijah P. Petty, Walker's Division,C.S.A.* San Antonio: Institute of Texan Cultures, 1982.

————, ed. *One of Cleburne's Command: The Civil War Reminiscences and Diary of Captain Samuel T. Foster, Granbury's Texas Brigade, C.S.A.* Austin: University of Texas Press, 1980.

Bureau of the Census. *Agriculture of the United States in 1860; Compiled from Original Returns of the Eighth Census* (Washington: Government Printing Office, 1864).

————. *Population of the United States in 1860; Compiled from Original Returns of the Eighth Census* (Washington: Government Printing Office, 1864).

Cater, Douglas John. *As It Was: Reminiscences of a Soldier of the Third Texas Cavalry and the Nineteenth Louisiana Infantry.* Reprint. Austin: State House Press, 1990.

Clark, L. D., ed. *Civil War Recollections of James Lemuel Clark, Including Previously Unpublished Material on the Great Hanging at Gainesville, Texas, in October 1862.* College Station: Texas A&M University Press, 1984.

Commager, Henry Steele, ed. *The Blue and the Gray: The Story of the Civil War As Told By Participants.* 2 vols. Indianapolis: Bobbs–Merrill Company, 1950.

Connor, Seymour V., ed. *Dear America: Some Letters of Orange Cicero and Mary America.* Austin: Pemberton Press, 1971.

Day, James M., ed. *Senate Journal of the Ninth Legislature of the State of Texas, November 4, 1861 – January 14, 1862.* Austin: Texas State Library, 1963.

De Boer, Marvin, comp. *Destiny By Choice: The Inaugural Addresses of the Governors of Texas.* Fayetteville: University of Arkansas Press, 1992.

DeBow, James D. B., comp. *Statistical View of the Seventh Census.* Washington: Government Printing Office, 1854.

Debray, X. B. *A Sketch of Debray's (26th) Regiment of Texas Cavalry.* Austin: Von Boeckmann, 1884.

Diary of E. S. Dodd, Co. D, Terry's Texas Rangers & An Account of His Hanging As A Confederate Spy. Austin: Ranger Press, 1979.

Douglas, Lucia Rutherford, ed. *Douglas's Texas Battery, C.S.A.* Waco: Smith County Historical Society, 1966.

Everett, Donald E., ed. *Chaplain Davis and Hood's Texas Brigade.* San Antonio: Principia Press of Trinity University, 1962.

Fisher, George Adams. *The Yankee Conscript; Or, Eighteen Months in Dixie.* Philadelphia: J. W. Doughaday, Publisher, 1864.

Fitzhugh, Lester Newton, ed. *Cannon Smoke: The Letters of Captain John J. Good, Good–Douglas Texas Battery, C.S.A.* Hillsboro: Hill Junior College Press, 1971.

Fletcher, William A. *Rebel Private, Front and Rear.* Reprint. Washington: Zenger Publishing Company, 1985.

Ford, John Salmon. *Rip Ford's Texas.* ed. Stephen B. Oates. Austin: University of Texas Press, 1963.

Fremantle, Arthur James L. *The Fremantle Diary: Being the Journal of Lieutenant Colonel Arthur James Lyon Fremantle, Coldstream Guards, on His Three Months in the Southern States*. ed. Walter Lord. Reprint. Boston: Little, Brown, 1954.

Gallagher, Gary, ed. *Fighting for the Confederacy: The Personal Recollections of General Edward Porter Alexander*. Chapel Hill: University of North Carolina Press, 1989.

Gallaway, B. P., ed. and comp. *Texas: The Dark Corner of the Confederacy: Contemporary Accounts of the Lone Star State in the Civil War*. 3rd. ed. Lincoln: University of Nebraska Press, 1994.

Glover, Robert W., ed. *"Tyler to Sharpsburg": The War Letters of Robert H. and William H. Gaston, Company H, First Texas Infantry Regiment, Hood's Texas Brigade*. Waco: Morrison, 1960.

Goree, Langston James, V, ed. *The Thomas Jewett Goree Letters*, Vol. I. Bryan: Family History Foundation, 1981.

Goyne, Minetta Altgeld, ed. *Lone Star and Double Eagle: Civil Letters of a German–Texas Family*. Fort Worth: Texas Christian University Press, 1982.

Graber, Henry W. *The Life Record of H. W. Graber, a Terry Ranger, 1861–1865*. Reprint. Austin: State House Press, 1987.

Greer, James K., ed. *Buck Barry: Texas Ranger and Frontiersman*. Reprint. Lincoln: University of Nebraska Press, 1984.

Hamilton, D. H. *History of Company M, First Texas Volunteer Infantry: Hood's Brigade*. Waco: W. M. Morrison, 1962.

Heartsill, William W. *Fourteen Hundred and 90 Days in the Confederate Army; or, Camp Life, Day by Day, of the W. P. Lane Rangers from April 19, 1861, to May 20, 1865*. Ed. Bell I. Wiley. Reprint. Jackson, TN: McCowat–Mercer Press, 1954.

Hood, John Bell. *Advance and Retreat: Personal Experiences in the United States and Confederate States Armies*. New Orleans: G. T. Beauregard, Published for Hood Orphan Memorial Fund, 1880.

Ingram, Henry, ed. and comp. *Civil War Letters of George W. and Martha Ingram, 1861–1865*. College Station: Texas A&M University Press, 1973.

Johnson, Adam Rankin. *The Partisan Rangers of the Confederate States Army: Memoirs of General Adam R. Johnson*. Reprint. Austin: State House Press, 1995.

Journal of the Congress of the Confederate States of America, 1861–1865. 7 vols. Washington: Government Printing Office, 1904–1905.

Kerr, Homer L., ed. *Fighting With Ross' Texas Cavalry Brigade, C.S.A.: The Diary of George L. Griscom, Adjutant, 9th Texas Cavalry Regiment*. Hillsboro: Hill Junior College Press, 1976.

Lane, Walter P. *The Adventures and Recollections of General Walter P. Lane, A San Jacinto Veteran, Containing Sketches of the Texan, Mexican, and Late Wars, with Several Indian Fights Thrown In*. Reprint. Austin: Pemberton Press, 1970.

Laswell, Mary, ed. *Rags and Hope: The Recollections of Val C. Giles, Four Years with Hood's Brigade, Fourth Texas Infantry*. New York: Coward–McCann, Inc., 1961.

Longstreet, James. *From Manassas to Appomattox: Memoirs of the Civil War in America*. Reprint. Bloomington: Indiana University Press, 1960.

Lubbock, Francis R. *Six Decades in Texas, or Memoirs of Francis R. Lubbock, Governor of Texas in War Time, 1861–1863.* Ed. C. W. Raines. Austin: Ben C. Jones & Co., 1900.

MacLean, David G., ed. *Prisoner of the Rebels in Texas: The Civil War Narrative of Aaron T. Sutton, Corporal, 83rd Ohio Volunteer Infantry.* Decatur, IN: Americana Books, 1978.

McClure, Judy Watson, ed. *Confederate From East Texas: The Civil War Letters of James Monroe Watson.* Quanah: Nortex Press, 1976.

McDowell, Catherine W., ed. *Now You Hear My Horn: The Journal of James Wilson Nichols.* Austin: University of Texas Press, 1968.

McHatton–Ripley, Eliza. *From Flag to Flag: A Woman's Adventures and Experiences in the South During the War, in Mexico, and in Cuba.* New York: D. Appleton & Co., 1896.

McKee, Major James Cooper. *Narrative of the Surrender of a Command of U. S. Forces at Fort Fillmore, New Mexico, in July, A. D., 1861, with Related Reports by John R. Baylor, C.S.A. & Others.* Reprint. Houston: Stagecoach Press, 1960.

Noel, Theophilus. *A Campaign From Santa Fe to the Mississippi: Being a History of the Old Sibley Brigade.* Shreveport: News Printing Establishment, 1865.

North, Thomas. *Five Years in Texas; or, What You Did Not Hear During the War from January, 1861, to January, 1866.* Cincinnati: Elm Street Printing Company, 1871.

Nott, Charles C. *Sketches in Prison Camps: A Continuation of Sketches of the War.* New York: Anson D. F. Randolph, 1865.

Official Records of the Union and Confederate Navies in the *War of Rebellion.* 30 vols. Washington: Government Printing Office, 1894–1922.

Proceedings of the Second Confederate Congress, Second Session, December 15, 1864 – March 18, 1865. Ed. Frank E. Vandiver. *Southern Historical Society Papers,* Vol. 52. Richmond: Virginia Historical Society, 1959.

Rayburn, John C., and Virginia Kemp, eds. *Century of Conflict, 1821–1913: Incidents in the Lives of William Neale and William A. Neale, Early Settlers in South Texas.* Waco: Waco: Texian Press, 1966.

Reagan, John H. *Memoirs, With Special Reference to Secession and the Civil War.* Ed. Walter F. McCaleb. New York: Neale Publishing Company, 1906.

Rugeley, H. J. H., ed. *Batchelor–Turner Letters, 1861–1864, Written by Two of Terry's Texas Rangers.* Austin: Steck Company, 1961.

Santleben, August. *A Texas Pioneer: Early Staging and Overland Freighting Days on the Frontiers of Texas and Mexico.* New York: Neale Publishing Company, 1910.

Semmes, Raphael. *Memoirs of Service Afloat, During the War Between the States.* Baltimore: Kelly, Piet, and Co., 1869.

Shelton, Perry Wayne, comp. *Personal Civil War Letters of General Lawrence Sullivan Ross.* Austin: W. M. Morrison, 1994.

Simpson, Harold B., ed. *The Bugle Softly Blows: The Confederate Diary of Benjamin M. Seaton.* Waco: Texian Press, 1965.

———. *Touched with Valor: The Civil War Papers and Casualty Reports of Hood's Texas Brigade.* Hillsboro: Hill Junior College Press, 1964.

Smith, Ralph J. *Reminiscences of the Civil War and Other Sketches.* Reprint. Waco: W. M. Morrison Company, 1962.

Smithwick, Noah. *The Evolution of A State, or Recollections of Old Texas Days.* Reprint. Austin: Texas State Historical Association, 1983.

Sparks, A. W. *The War Between the States, As I Saw It.* Tyler: Lee and Burnett, Printers, 1901.

Sprague, J. T. *The Treachery in Texas, the Secession of Texas, and the Arrest of the United States Officers and Soldiers Serving in Texas.* New York: New York Historical Society, 1862.

Spurlin, Charles D., ed. *The Civil War Diary of Charles A. Leuschner.* Austin: Eakin Press, 1992.

————. *West of the Mississippi with Waller's 13th Texas Cavalry Battalion, CSA.* Hillsboro: Hill Junior College Press, 1971.

Taylor, Richard. *Destruction and Reconstruction: Personal Experiences of the Late War.* Reprint. Ed. Richard Harwell New York: Longmans, Green, and Company, 1955.

Taylor, Thomas E. *Running the Blockade: A Personal Narrative of Adventures, Risks, and Escapes During the American Civil War.* New York: Charles L. Scribner's Sons, 1896.

Terrell, Alexander W. *From Texas to Mexico and the Court of Maximilian.* Dallas: Book Club of Texs, 1933.

Thompson, Jerry D., ed. *From Desert to Bayou: The Civil War Journal and Sketches of Morgan Wolfe Merrick.* San Antonio: Daughters of the Republic of Texas Library, 1991.

————. *Juan Cortina and the Texas–Mexico Frontier, 1859– 1877.* El Paso: Texas Western Press, 1994.

————. *Westward the Texans: The Civil War Journal of Private William Howell.* El Paso: Texas Western Press, 1990.

Tilley, Nannie M., ed. *Federals on the Frontier: The Diary of Benjamin F. McIntyre, 1862–1864.* Austin: University of Texas Press, 1963.

The War of the Rebellion: A Compilation of the Official Records of the Union and Confederate Armies. 128 vols. Washington: Government Printing Office, 1880–1901.

Watson, William. *The Adventures of a Blockade Runner; Or, Trade in Time of War.* New York: Macmillan Company, 1892.

Williams, Amelia W., and Eugene C. Barker, eds. *The Writings of Sam Houston.* 8 vols. Austin: University of Texas Press, 1928–1943.

Winkler, E. W., ed. *Journal of the Secession Convention, 1861.* Austin: Austin Printing Company, 1912.

Woodward, C. Vann, ed. *Mary Chesnut's Civil War.* New Haven: Yale University Press, 1981.

Yeary, Mamie, comp. *Reminiscences of the Boys in Gray, 1861–1865.* Dallas: Smith & Lamar, 1912.

Articles and Parts of Books

Abbott, Peyton O., ed. "Business Travel Out of Texas During the Civil War: The Travel Diary of S. B. Brush, Pioneer Austin Merchant." *SHQ* 96 (October 1992): 259–271.

Acheson, Sam, and Julie Ann Hudson O'Connell, eds. "George Washington Diamond's Account of the Great Hanging at Gainesville, 1862." *SHQ* 66 (January 1963): 331–414.

Bailey, W. "The Star Company of Ector's Texas Brigade." *Confederate Veteran* 22 (1914): 404–405.

Barr, Alwyn, ed. "The Civil War Diary of James Allen Hamilton, 1861–1864." *Texana* 2 (Summer 1964): 132–145.

———. "William T. Mechling Journal of the Red River Campaign, April 7– May 10, 1864." *Texana* 1 (Fall 1963): 363–379.

———. "Records of the Confederate Military Commission in San Antonio, July 2–October 10, 1862." *SHQ* 70 (July–April 1966–1967): 93–109, 289–313, 623–644; 71 (October 1967): 247–277; 73 (July–October 1969): 83–104, 243–274.

Billingsley, William C., ed. "'Such Is War': The Confederate Memoirs of Newton Ashbury Keen." *Texas Military History* 6 (Winter 1967): 239–253; 7 (Spring– Fall 1968): 44–70, 103– 119, 176–194.

Blackburn, J. K. P. "Reminiscences of the Terry Rangers." *SHQ* 22 (July–October 1918): 38–77, 143–179.

Campbell, Robert. "Texans Always Move Them," in Henry S. Commager, ed. *The Blue and the Gray*. 2 vols. Indianapolis: Bobbs–Merrill Company, 1950.

Carrington, W. H. "Last Battle of the War, May 13th, 1865," in John Henry Brown. *History of Texas, From 1685 to 1892*. 2 vols. St. Louis: L. E. Daniell, Publisher, 1893, 2:431– 436.

Coffman, Edward, ed. "Ben McCulloch Letters." *SHQ* 60 (July 1956): 118–122.

Cosgrove, J. H. "About the Attack at Cold Harbor." *Confederate Veteran* 20 (November 1912): 511.

Cox, C. C., II. "Reminiscences of C. C. Cox, II." *SHQ* 6 (January 1903): 204–235.

Cutherson, Gilbert, ed. "Coller of the Sixth Texas: Correspondence of a Texas Infantry Man, 1861–1864." *Military History of Texas and the Southwest* 9, no. 2 (1973): 129–136.

Cutrer, Thomas W., ed. "'An Experience in Soldier's Life': The Civil War Letters of Volney Ellis, Adjutant, Twelfth Texas Infantry, Walker's Texas Division, C.S.A." *Military History of the Southwest* 22 (Fall 1992): 109–172.

———. "'Bully for Flournoy's Regiment, We Are Some Pumkins, You'll Bet': The Civil War Letters of Virgil Sullivan Rabb, Captain, Company 'I,' Sixteenth Texas Infantry, C.S.A." *Military History of the Southwest* 19 (Fall 1989): 161–190; 20 (Spring 1990): 61–96.

———. "'We Are Stern and Resolved': The Civil War Letters of John Wesley Rabb, Terry's Texas Rangers." *SHQ* 91 (October 1987): 185–226.

Darrow, Caroline Baldwin. "Recollections of the Twiggs Surrender," in *Battles & Leaders of the Civil War*. 4 vols. Reprint. New York: Thomas Yoseloff, 1956. 1:33–39.

Delaney, Norman, ed. "The Diary and Memoirs of Marshall Samuel Pierson,

Company C, 17th Regt., Texas Cavalry." *Military History of Texas and the Southwest* 13, no. 3 (1976): 23–38.

Dempster, Ann Lee (Clark), and Homer L. Kerr, eds. "Civil War Letters of William L. Edwards, A Soldier in Hood's Texas Brigade." *Texas Military History* 7 (Spring 1968): 5–26.

Duncan, John Thomas, ed. "Some Civil War Letters of D. Port Smythe." *WTHAYB* 37 (October 1961): 147–176.

Erath, Lucy A., ed. "Memoirs of Major George Bernard Erath." *SHQ* 27 (October 1923): 140–163.

Estill, Mary S., ed. "Diary of a Confederate Congressman [Franklin Sexton], 1862–1863." *SHQ* 38 (April 1935): 270–301, and 29 (July 1935): 33–65.

Evans, A. W. "Canby at Valverde," in *Battles & Leaders*, 2:699–700.

Faulkner, Walter A., ed. "With Sibley in New Mexico: The Journal of William Henry Smith." *WTHAYB* 27 (October 1951): 111–142.

Foster, Samuel C. "We Are Prisoners of War: A Texan's Account of the Capture of Fort Hindman." *Civil War Times Illustrated* 16 (May 1977): 24–34.

Glover, Robert W., ed. "War Letters of a Texas Conscript in Arkansas." *Arkansas Historical Quarterly* 20 (Winter 1961): 354–387.

Gracy, David, II, ed. "New Mexico Campaign Letters of Frank Starr, 1861–1862." *Texas Military History* 4 (Fall 1964): 169–188.

———. "With Danger and Honor: George W. Littlefield, 1861– 1864." *Texana* 1 (Winter 1963): 1–19; (Spring 1964): 120–152.

Graham, Philip, ed. "Texas Memoirs of Amelia E. Barr." *SHQ* 69 (April 1966): 473–498.

Haas, Oscar, trans. "The Diary of Julius Giesecke, 1861–1862." *Texas Military History* 3 (Winter 1963): 228–242.

———. "The Diary of Julius Giesecke, 1863–1865." *Texas Military History* 4 (Spring 1964): 27–54.

Hall, Martin H., ed. "An Appraisal of the 1862 New Mexico Campaign: A Confederate Officer's Letter to Nacogdoches." *New Mexico Historical Review* 51 (October 1976): 329–335.

Haltom, Sallie. "My Life in Tarrant County and Other Parts of Texas." *SHQ* 60 (July 1956): 100–105.

Hamby, William R. "Hood's Texas Brigade at Sharpsburg." *Confederate Veteran* 16 (January 1908): 19–22.

Hampton, Wade. "The Battle of Bentonville," in *Battles & Leaders*, 4:700–705.

Harrison, Jon, ed. "The Confederate Letters of John Simmons." *Chronicles of Smith County, Texas* 14 (Summer 1975): 25–27.

Hogan, George H. "Parsons' Brigade of Texas Cavalry." *Confederate Veteran* 33 (January 1925): 17–20.

Hogg, Tom. "Reminiscences of the War: The Last Day at Corinth." Ed. Robert C. Cotner. *ETHJ* 20 (Spring 1982): 48–53.

Houston, Sam, Jr. "Shiloh Shadows." *SHQ* 34 (April 1931): 329–333.

Humphrey, David C., ed. "A 'Very Muddy and Conflicting' View: The Civil War as Seen from Austin, Texas." *SHQ* 94 (January 1991): 389–414.

Johansson, Jean Harris, and David H. Johansson, eds. "Two 'Lost' Battle Reports: Horace Randal's and Joseph L. Brent's Reports of the Battles of Mansfield and Pleasant Hill, 8 and 9 April 1864." *Military History of the West* 23 (Fall 1993): 169–180.

Keith, K. D. "The Memoirs of Captain Kosciuszko D. Keith." *Texas Gulf Historical and Biographical Record* 10 (November 1974): 41–64.

Lackner, Edgar E., ed. "Civil War Diaries of Edwin F. Stanton, U. S. A., and William Quensell, C.S.A.: 'Yank and Reb' Under One Cover." *ETHJ* 18 (Fall 1980): 25–59.

Lale, Max S., ed. "For Lack of a Nail . . ." *ETHJ* 30 (Spring 1992): 34–43.

———. "The Boy–Bugler of the Third Texas Cavalry: The A. B. Blocker Narrative." *ETHJ* 14, no. 2–4 (1976): 71–92, 147–168, 215–228; 15, no. 1 (1977): 21–34.

Law, Evander M. "From the Wilderness to Cold Harbor," in *Battles & Leaders*, 4:118–144.

Marsh, Bryan. "The Confederate Letters of Bryan Marsh." *Chronicles of Smith County, Texas* 14 (Winter 1975): 9–30, 43–55.

Marten, James, ed. "The Diary of Thomas H. DuVal: The Civil War in Austin, Texas, February 26 to October 9, 1863." *SHQ* 94 (January 1991): 435–457.

Maye, Walter H., ed. "The Vicksburg Diary of M. K. Simons, 1863." *Texas Military History* 5 (Spring 1965): 21–38.

McArthur, Judith N., ed. "'Those Texians Are Number One Men': A New Confederate Account of the Affair at Lee's House, Virginia." *SHQ* 95 (April 1992): 488–496.

Mills, Roger Q. "A Texan at Wilson's Creek." *Civil War Times Illustrated* 17 (January 1979): 46–47.

Moore, John C. "Shiloh Issue Again." *Confederate Veteran* 10 (July 1902): 316–317.

O'Neal, Bill, ed. "The Civil War Memoirs of Samuel Alonzo Cooke." *SHQ* 74 (April 1971): 535–548.

Pace, Eleanor Damon, ed. "The Diary and Letters of William P. Rogers." *SHQ* 32 (April 1929): 259–299.

Pollard, Charleen Plumly, ed. "Civil War Letters of George W. Allen." *SHQ* 83 (July 1979): 46–52.

Polley, J. B. "Texans in the Battle of the Wilderness." *Confederate Veteran* 5 (June 1897): 290–291.

Purifoy, John. "Battle of Gettysburg." *Confederate Veteran* 31 (July–November 1923): 252–253, 416–418.

Ragan, Cooper K., ed. "The Diary of Captain George W. O'Brien." *SHQ* 67 (July 1963 – January 1964): 28–54, 235–246, 414–433.

Ray, Johnette Highsmith, ed. "Civil War Letters from Parsons' Cavalry Brigade." *SHQ* 69 (October 1965): 210–223.

Reagan, John H. "A Conversation with Governor Houston." *Quarterly of the Texas State Historical Association* 3 (April 1900): 279–281.

Roberts, O. M. "The Experiences of an Unrecognized Senator." *SHQ* 12 (October 1908): 87–147.

Robertson, Felix. "On Wheeler's Last Raid in Middle Tennessee." *Confederate Veteran* 30 (September 1922): 334–335.

Smith, David P., ed. "Civil War Letters of Sam Houston." *SHQ* 81 (April 1978): 417–426.

Smith, Edmund Kirby. "The Defense of the Red River," in *Battles & Leaders*, 4: 369–374.

Smith, Rebecca W., and Marion Mullins, eds. "The Diary of H. C. Medford, Confederate Soldier." *SHQ* 34 (October 1930–January 1931): 106–140, 203–230.

Snead, Thomas L. "The Conquest of Arkansas," in *Battles & Leaders*, 3:441–458.

Strom, Steven, ed. "Cotton and Profits Across the Border: William Marsh Rice in Mexico, 1863–1865." *Houston Review* 8 (1986): 89–96.

Tate, Michael L., ed. "A Johnny Reb in Sibley's New Mexico Campaign: Reminiscences of Pvt. Henry C. Wright, 1861–1862." *ETHJ* 25 (Fall 1987): 20–33; 26 (Spring–Fall 1988): 23–35, 48–60.

Teel, T. T. "Sibley's New Mexico Campaign — Its Objects and the Cause of Its Failure," in *Battles & Leaders*, 2:700.

Turner, Jim. "Jim Turner, Co. G, 6th Texas Infantry, C.S.A. From 1861 to 1865." *Texana* 12, no. 2 (1974): 149–178.

Vandiver, Frank E., ed. "Letters from the Confederate Medical Service in Texas, 1863–1865." *SHQ* 55 (January – April 1952): 378–393, 459–474.

Wheeler, Joseph. "Bragg's Invasion of Kentucky." *Battles & Leaders*, 3:1–25.

Williams, Robert W., and Ralph A. Wooster, eds. "Life in Civil War Central Texas: Letters from Mr. and Mrs. Thomas Affleck to Private Dunbar Affleck." *Texana* 7 (Summer 1969): 146–162.

———. "With Wharton's Cavalry in Arkansas: The Civil War Letters of Private Isaac Dunbar Affleck." *Arkansas Historical Quarterly* 21 (Autumn 1962): 247–268.

———. "With Terry's Texas Rangers: Letters of Dunbar Affleck." *Civil War History* 9 (September 1963): 299–319.

Wilson, Gary, ed. "Diary of a Union Prisoner in Texas." *Southern Studies* 23 (Spring 1988): 103–119.

Wise, Joe R., ed. "The Letters of Lt. Flavius W. Perry, 17th Texas Cavalry, 1862–1863." *Military History of Texas and the Southwest* 13, no. 2 (1976): 11–37.

Newspapers

Austin *Texas State Gazette*, February 9, March 30, June 22, 1861.

Bellville Countryman, July 17, 1861.

Clarksville Standard, July 7 and 20, 1862.

Dallas Herald, January 30, 1861.

Galveston Weekly News, September 24 and October 15, 1862; January 27, 1864.

Houston Tri–Weekly Telegraph, December 21, 1864.

Marshall *Texas Republican*, April 27 and June 1, 1861; January 4, February 1 and 22, 1862.

Port Arthur News, July 1, 1923.

Secondary Sources

Books

Abel, Annie H. *The American Indian as a Participant in the Civil War.* Reprint. Lincoln: University of Nebraska Press, 1992.

———. *The American Indian as a Slaveholder and Secessionist.* Reprint. Lincoln: University of Nebraska Press, 1992.

Abernethy, Francis E., ed. *Tales from the Big Thicket*. Austin: University of Texas Press, 1966.

Albaugh, William A., III. *Tyler, Texas, C.S.A.* Harrisburg: Stackpole Company, 1958.

Alexander, Thomas B., and Richard E. Beringer. *The Anatomy of* the Confederate Congress: A Study of the Influences of Member Characteristics on Legislative Voting Behavior, 1861–1865. Nashville: Vanderbilt University Press, 1972.

Anderson, John Q. *A Texas Surgeon in the C.S.A.* Tuscaloosa: Confederate Publishing Company, 1957.

Arceneaux, William. *Acadian General: Alfred Mouton and the Civil War*. Lafayette: Center for Louisiana Studies, University of Southwestern Louisiana, 1981.

Ashcraft, Allan C. *Texas in the Civil War: A Resume History*. Austin: Texas Civil War Centennial Commission, 1962.

Bailey, Anne J. *Between the Enemy and Texas: Parsons's Texas Cavalry Brigade in the Civil War*. Fort Worth: Texas Christian University, 1989.

———. *Texans in the Confederate Cavalry*. Fort Worth: Ryan Place Publishers, 1995.

Barr, Alwyn. *Polignac's Texas Brigade*. Houston: Texas Gulf Coast Historical Association Publication Series, 1964.

Barrett, John G. *The Civil War in North Carolina*. Chapel Hill: University of North Carolina Press, 1963.

Bearss, Edwin C. *Steele's Retreat From Camden and the Battle of Jenkins' Ferry*. Little Rock: Arkansas Civil War Centennial Commission, 1967.

Benner, Judith Ann. *Sul Ross: Soldier, Statesman, and Educator*. College Station: Texas A&M University Press, 1983.

Bergeron, Arthur W., Jr. *Confederate Mobile*. Jackson: University Press of Mississippi, 1991.

Biesele, Rudolph L. *The History of the German Settlements in Texas, 1831–1861*. Austin: priv. publ., 1930.

Block, W. T. *A History of Jefferson County, Texas From Wilderness to Reconstruction*. Nederland: Nederland Printing, 1976.

Boethal, Paul C. *The Big Guns of Fayette*. Austin: Von Boeckmann-Jones, 1965.

Bowden, J. J. *The Exodus of Federal Forces from Texas, 1861*. Austin: Eakin Press, 1986.

Bradlee, Francis B. C. *Blockade Running During the Civil War and the Effect of Land and Water Transportation on the Confederacy*. Philadelphia: Porcupine Press, 1925.

Bragg, Jefferson D. *Louisiana in the Confederacy*. Baton Rouge: Louisiana State University Press, 1941.

Brasseaux, Carl A. *Acadian to Cajun: Transformation of a People, 1803–1877*. Jackson: University Press of Mississippi, 1992.

Briscoe, Eugenia R. *City by the Sea: A History of Corpus Christi, Texas, 1519–1875*. New York: Vantage Press, 1985.

Brown, John Henry. *Indian Wars and Pioneers of Texas*. Austin: L. E. Daniell Publisher, 1880.

———. *History of Texas, From 1685 to 1892*. 2 vols. St. Louis: L. E. Daniell Publisher, 1893.

Buck, Irving. *Cleburne and His Command*. Reprint. Jackson, TN: McCowat–Mercer Press, 1959.

Buenger, Walter L. *Secession and the Union in Texas*. Austin: University of Texas Press, 1984.

Burnham, W. Dean. *Presidential Ballots, 1836–1892*. Baltimore: Johns Hopkins University Press, 1955.

Campbell, Randolph B. *An Empire for Slavery: The Peculiar Institution in Texas, 1821–1865*. Baton Rouge: Louisiana State University Press, 1989.

———. *A Southern Community in Crisis: Harrison County, Texas, 1850–1880*. Austin: Texas State Historical Asssociation, 1983.

———. *Sam Houston and the American Southwest*. New York: Harper Collins Publishers, 1993.

Campbell, Randolph, and Richard G. Lowe. *Wealth and Power in Antebellum Texas*. College Station: Texas A&M University Press, 1977.

Carrington, Evelyn M., ed. *Women in Early Texas*. Austin: Pemberton Press, 1976.

Carter, Samuel, III. *The Final Fortress: The Campaign for Vicksburg, 1862–1863*. New York: St. Martin's Press, 1980.

Castel, Albert. *Decision in the West: The Atlanta Campaign of 1864*. Lawrence: University Press of Kansas, 1992.

———. *General Sterling Price and the Civil War in the West*. Baton Rouge: Louisiana State University Press, 1968.

———. *William Clark Quantrill: His Life and Times*. New York: Frederick Fell, Inc., Publisher, 1962.

Chance, Joseph. *The Second Texas Infantry: From Shiloh to Vicksburg*. Austin: Eakin Press, 1984.

Christ, Mark K., ed., *Rugged and Sublime: The Civil War in Arkansas*. Fayetteville: University of Arkansas Press, 1994.

Cochran, Hamilton. *Blockade Runners of the Confederacy*. Indianapolis: Bobbs–Merrill Company, 1958.

Coddington, Edwin B. *The Gettysburg Campaign: A Study in Command*. New York: Charles Scribner's Sons, 1968.

Colton, Roy C. *The Civil War in the Western Territories*. Norman: University of Oklahoma Press, 1959.

Connelly, Thomas L. *Autumn of Glory: The Army of Tennessee, 1862–1865*. Baton Rouge: Louisiana State University Press, 1971.

Cooling, Benjamin Franklin. *Forts Henry and Donelson: The Key to the Confederate Heartland*. Knoxville: University of Tennessee Press, 1987.

Cozzens, Peter. *No Better Place to Die: The Battle of Stone's River*. Urbana: University of Illinois Press, 1991.

———. *This Terrible Sound: The Battle of Chickamauga*. Urbana: University of Illinois Press, 1992.

Creighton, James A. *A Narrative History of Brazoria County*. Waco: Texian Press, 1975.

Cunningham, Edward. *The Port Hudson Campaign, 1862–1863*. Baton Rouge: Louisiana State University Press, 1963.

Cunningham, Frank. *General Stand Watie's Confederate Indians*. San Antonio: Naylor Company, 1959.

Current, Richard N. *Lincoln's Loyalists: Union Soldiers from the Confederacy.* Boston: Northeastern University Press, 1992.

Cutrer, Thomas W. *Ben McCulloch and the Frontier Military Tradition.* Chapel Hill: University of North Carolina Press, 1993.

Daddysman, James W. *The Matamoros Trade: Confederate Commerce, Diplomacy, and Intrigue.* Newark, DE: University of Delaware Press, 1984.

Daniel, Larry J. *Soldiering in the Army of Tennessee.* Chapel Hill: University of North Carolina Press, 1991.

Davis, William C. *Jefferson Davis: The Man and His Hour.* New York: Harper Collins, 1991.

De Bruhl, Marshall. *Sword of San Jacinto: A Life of Sam Houston.* New York: Random House, 1993.

Dougan, Michael B. *Confederate Arkansas: The People and Policies of a Frontier State in Wartime.* University, AL.: University of Alabama Press, 1976.

Duaine, Carl L. *The Dead Men Wore Boots: An Account of the 32nd Texas Volunteer Cavalry, CSA.* Austin: San Felipe Press, 1966.

Duncan, Gra'Delle. *Texas Tough: Dangerous Men in Dangerous Times.* Austin: Eakin Press, 1990.

Duncan, Jean Sutherlin. *Richard Bennett Hubbard: Texas Politician and Diplomat.* College Station: priv. publ., 1972.

Durden, Robert F. *The Gray and the Black: The Confederate Debate on Emancipation.* Baton Rouge: Louisiana State University Press, 1972.

Dyer, John P. *The Gallant Hood.* Indianapolis: Bobbs–Merrill Company, 1950.

Elliott, Claude. *Leathercoat: The Life History of a Texas Patriot.* San Antonio: Standard Printing Company, 1938.

Evans, Clement. *Confederate Military History.* 12 vols. Atlanta: Confederate Publishing Company, 1899.

Exley, Jo Ella Powell, ed. *Texas Tears and Texas Sunshine: Voices of Frontier Women.* College Station: Texas A&M University Press, 1985.

Farrell, Mary D., and Elizabeth Silverthorne. *First Ladies of Texas: A History.* Belton: Stillhouse Hollow Publishers, 1976.

Faulk, J. J. *History of Henderson County, Texas.* Athens: Athens Publishing Company, 1929.

Faulk, Odie. *General Tom Green: Fightin' Texan.* Waco: Texian Press, 1963.

Fehrenbach, T. R. *Lone Star: A History of Texas and the Texans.* New York: Macmillan Company, 1968.

Felmly, Bradford K. *Suffering in Silence: 28th Texas Cavalry, CSA, Regimental History.* Quanah, TX: Nortex Press, 1975.

Fitzhugh, Lester N., comp. *Texas Batteries, Battalions, Regiments, Commanders and Field Officers, Confederate States Army, 1861–1865.* Midlothian: Mirror Press, 1959.

Foote, Shelby. *The Civil War: A Narrative.* 3 vols. New York: Random House, 1958–1974.

Fornell, Earl W. *The Galveston Era: The Texas Crescent on the Eve of Secession.* Austin: University of Texas Press, 1961.

Fowler, John. *James P. Newcomb: Texas Journalist and Political Leader.* Austin: Department of Journalism, University of Texas, 1976.

Franklin, Robert M. *Battle of Galveston, January 1, 1863*. Reprint. Galveston: San Luis Press, 1975.

Freeman, Douglas S. *Lee's Lieutenants: A Study in Command*. 3 vols. Charles Scribner's Sons, 1942–1944.

———. *R. E. Lee: A Biography*. 4 vols. New York: Charles Scribner's Sons, 1936.

Friend, Llerena. *Sam Houston: The Great Designer*. Austin: University of Texas Press, 1954.

Gallaway, B. P. *The Ragged Rebel: A Common Soldier in W. H. Parsons' Texas Cavalry, 1861–1865*. Austin: University of Texas Press, 1988.

Giles, L. B. *Terry's Rangers*. Austin: Pemberton Press, 1967.

Glatthaar, Joseph. *The March to the Sea and Beyond: Sherman's Troops in the Savannah and Carolinas Campaign*. New York: New York University Press, 1986.

———. *Forged in Battle: The Civil War Alliance of Black Soldiers and White Officers*. New York: Free Press, 1990.

Goff, Richard D. *Confederate Supply*. Durham: Duke University Press, 1969.

Goldfinch, Charles W. *Juan Cortina, 1824–1892: A Re–Appraisal*. New York: Arno Press, 1974.

Griggs, William Clark. *Parson Henry Renfro: Free Thinking on the Texas Frontier*. Austin: University of Texas Press, 1994.

———. *The Elusive Eden: Frank McMullan's Confederate Colony in Brazil*. Austin: University of Texas Press, 1987.

Hale, Douglas. *The Third Texas Cavalry in the Civil War*. Norman: University of Oklahoma Press, 1993.

Hall, Martin H. *Sibley's New Mexico Campaign*. Austin: University of Texas Press, 1960.

———. *The Confederate Army of New Mexico*. Austin: Presidial Press, 1978.

Hanna, Kathryn A. *Confederate Exiles in Venezuela*. Tuscaloosa, AL: Confederate Publishing Company, 1960.

Harrington, Fred Harvey. *Fighting Politician: Major General N. P. Banks*. Philadelphia: University of Pennsylvania Press, 1948.

Harry, Jewel H. *A History of Chambers County*. Dallas: Chambers County Historical Committee, 1981.

Hartje, Robert G. *Van Dorn: The Life and Times of a Confederate General*. Nashville: Vanderbilt University Press, 1967.

Hattaway, Herman. *General Stephen D. Lee*. Jackson: University Press of Mississippi, 1976.

Hay, Thomas R. *Hood's Tennessee Campaign*. New York: Walter Neale, 1929.

Hearn, Chester G. *Mobile Bay and the Mobile Campaign: The Last Great Battles in the Civil War*. Jefferson, NC: McFarland & Company, Inc., 1983.

Henderson, Harry M. *Texas in the Confederacy*. San Antonio: Naylor Company, 1955.

Hennessy, John J. *Return to Bull Run: The Campaign and Battle of Second Manassas*. New York: Simon & Schuster, 1991.

Henson, Margaret Swett. *History of Baytown*. Baytown: Bay Heritage Society, 1986.

Henson, Margaret Swett, and Kevin Ladd. *Chambers County: A Pictorial History*. Norfolk, VA: Denning Company, 1988.

Henson, Margaret Swett, and Deolece Parmelee. *The Cartwrights of San Augustine: Three Generations of Agricultural Entrepreneurs in Nineteenth-Century Texas.* Austin: Texas State Historical Association, 1993.

Hesseltine, William B. *Confederate Leaders in the New South.* Baton Rouge: Louisiana State University Press, 1950.

Hesseltine, William B., and Hazel C. Wolf. *The Blue and Gray on the Nile.* Chicago: University of Chicago Press, 1961.

Hewitt, Lawrence Lee. *Port Hudson: Confederate Bastion on the Mississippi.* Baton Rouge: Louisiana State University Press, 1987.

Heyman, Max L., Jr. *Prudent Soldier: A Biography of Major General E. R. S. Canby, 1817–1873.* Glendale, CA: Arthur H. Clark Company, 1959.

Hill, Lawrence F. *The Confederate Exodus to Latin America.* Austin: Texas State Historical Association, 1961.

Horn, Stanley. *The Decisive Battle of Nashville.* Baton Rouge: Louisiana State University Press, 1956.

Horton, Louise. *Samuel Bell Maxey: A Biography.* Austin: University of Texas Press, 1974.

Hughes, W. J. *Rebellious Ranger: Rip Ford and the Old Southwest.* Norman: University of Oklahoma Press, 1964.

Irby, James A. *Backdoor at Bagdad: The Civil War on the Rio Grande.* El Paso: Texas Western Press, 1977.

James, Marquis. *The Raven: A Biography of Sam Houston.* Indianapolis: Bobbs–Merrill, Inc., 1919.

Jeffries, C. C. *Terry's Rangers.* New York: Vantage Press, 1961.

Johnson, Ludwell H. *Red River Campaign: Politics and Cotton in the Civil War.* Baltimore: Johns Hopkins Press, 1958.

Johnston, William Preston. *The Life of Gen. Albert Sidney Johnston.* New York: Appleton and Company, 1879.

Jones, Virgil Carrington. *The Civil War at Sea.* 3 vols. New York: Holt, Rinehart, Winston, 1961.

Jordan, Terry G. *German Seed in Texas Soil: Immigrant Farmers in Nineteenth Century Texas.* Austin: University of Texas Press, 1966.

Josephy, Alvin M., Jr. *The Civil War in the American West.* New York: Alfred A. Knopf, 1991.

Kerby, Robert L. *Kirby Smith's Confederacy: The Trans–Mississippi South, 1863–1865.* New York: Columbia University Press, 1972.

King, Alvy L. *Louis T. Wigfall, Southern Fire–eater.* Baton Rouge: Lousiana State University Press, 1970.

Krick, Robert K. *Lee's Colonels: A Biographical Register of the Field Officers of the Army of Northern Virginia.* 4th ed., revised. Dayton, OH: Morningside House, Inc., 1992.

Lawrence, F. Lee, and Robert W. Glover. *Camp Ford, C.S.A.: The Story of Union Prisoners in Texas.* Austin: Texas Civil War Centennial Committee, 1964.

Lawson, Lewis A. *Wheeler's Last Raid.* Greenwood, FL: Pendevill Publishing Company, 1986.

Lea, Tom. *The King Ranch.* 2 vols. Boston: Little, Brown, 1957.

Ledbetter, Barbara A. Neal. *Fort Belknap, Frontier Saga: Indians, Negroes, and Anglo Americans on the Texas Frontier.* Austin: Eakin Press, 1987.

Lee, Charles Robert, Jr. *The Confederate Constitutions*. Chapel Hill: University of North Carolina Press, 1963.

Livermore, Thomas L. *Numbers & Losses in the Civil War in America, 1861–65*. Reprint. Bloomington: Indiana University Press, 1957.

Lonn, Ella. *Desertion During the Civil War*. Reprint. Gloucester, MA: Peter Smith, 1968.

———. *Foreigners in the Confederacy*. Chapel Hill: University of North Carolina Press, 1940.

———. *Salt as a Factor in the Confederacy*. Reprint. University, AL: University of Alabama Press, 1965.

Loughmiller, Campbell, and Lynn Loughmiller, eds. *Big Thicket Legacy*. Austin: University of Texas Press, 1977.

Lowe, Richard, and Randolph Campbell. *Planters and Plain Folk: Agriculture in Antebellum Texas*. Dallas: Southern Methodist University Press, 1987.

Marks, Paula Mitchell. *Turn Your Eyes Toward Texas: Pioneers Sam and Mary Maverick*. College Station: Texas A&M University Press, 1989.

Marten, James. *Texas Divided: Loyalty and Dissent in the Lone Star State*. Lexington: University Presses of Kentucky, 1990.

Mathews, Byron H., Jr., *The McCook–Stoneman Raid*. Philadelphia: Dorrance & Company, 1976.

Matter, William D. *If It Takes All Summer: The Battle of Spotsylvania*. Chapel Hill: University of North Carolina Press, 1988.

Massey, Mary Elizabeth. *Bonnet Brigades*. New York: Alfred A. Knopf, 1966.

———. *Refugee Life in the Confederacy*. Baton Rouge: Louisiana State University Press, 1964.

McCaffrey, James M. *This Band of Heroes: Granbury's Texas Brigade, C.S.A.* Austin: Eakin Press, 1985.

McCaslin, Richard B. *Tainted Breeze: The Great Hanging at Gainesville, Texas*. Baton Rouge: Louisiana State University Press, 1994.

McComb, David G. *Galveston: A History*. Austin: University of Texas Press, 1986.

McDonald, Archie P., ed. *A Nation of Soveriegn States: Secession and War in the Confederacy*. Murfreesboro, TN: Southern Heritage Press, 1994.

McDonough, James Lee. *Chattanooga — A Death Grip on the Confederacy*. Knoxville: University of Tennessee Press, 1984.

———. *Shiloh — in Hell before Night*. Knoxville: University of Tennessee Press, 1977.

———. *Stone's River — Bloody Winter in Tennessee*. Knoxville: University of Tennessee Press, 1980.

———. *War in Kentucky: From Shiloh to Perryville*. Knoxville: University of Tennessee Press, 1994.

McDonough, James Lee, and Thomas L. Connelly. *Five Tragic Hours: The Battle of Franklin*. Knoxville: University of Tennessee Press, 1983.

McMurry, Richard M. *John Bell Hood and the War for Southern Independence*. Lexington: University Press of Kentucky, 1993.

———. *Two Great Rebel Armies: An Essay in Confederate Military History*. Chapel Hill: University of North Carolina Press, 1989.

McPherson, James M. *Battle Cry of Freedom: The Civil War Era.* New York: Oxford University Press, 1988.

———. *Ordeal By Fire: The Civil War and Reconstruction.* New York: Alfred A. Knopf, 1982.

———. *What They Fought For, 1861–1865.* Baton Rouge: Louisiana State University Press, 1994.

McWhiney, Grady. *Braxton Bragg and Confederate Defeat.* New York: Columbia University Press, 1969.

Moneyhon, Carl H. *Republicanism in Reconstruction Texas.* Austin: University of Texas Press, 1980.

———. *The Impact of the Civil War and Reconstruction on Arkansas: Persistence in the Midst of Ruin.* Baton Rouge: Louisiana State University Press, 1994.

Moore, Albert. *Conscription and Conflict in the Confederacy.* New York: Macmillan Company, 1924.

Muir, Andrew Forest. *William Marsh Rice and His Institute: A Biographical Study.* Ed. Sylvia Stallings Morris. *Rice University Studies* 58, no. 2 (1972).

Nichols, James L. *The Confederate Quartermaster in the Trans–Mississippi.* Austin: University of Texas Press, 1964.

Nueces County Historical Society. *The History of Nueces County.* Austin: Jenkins Publishing Company, 1972.

Nunn, W. C., ed. *Ten Texans in Gray.* Hillsboro: Hill Junior College Press, 1961.

Oates, Stephen B. *Confederate Cavalry West of the River.* Austin: University of Texas Press, 1961.

Parks, Joseph H. *General Edmund Kirby Smith, C.S.A.* Baton Rouge: Louisiana State University Press, 1954.

Parrish, T. Michael. *Richard Taylor: Prince of Dixie.* Chapel Hill: University of North Carolina Press, 1992.

Phelan, Macum. *A History of Early Methodism in Texas, 1817–1866.* Nashville: Cokesbury Press, 1924.

Pickrell, Annie Doom. *Pioneer Women in Texas.* Austin: E. L. Steck, 1929.

Polley, J. B. *Hood's Texas Brigade: Its Marches, Its Battles, Its Achievements.* New York: Neale Publishing Company, 1910.

Priest, John Michael. *Antietam: The Soldiers' Battle.* New York: Oxford University Press, 1989.

Procter, Ben H. *Not Without Honor: The Life of John H. Reagan.* Austin: University of Texas Press, 1962.

Rable, George C. *Civil Wars: Women and the Crisis of Southern Nationalism.* Urbana: University of Illinois Press, 1989.

———. *The Confederate Republic: A Revolution Against Politics.* Chapel Hill: University of North Carolina Press, 1994.

Rampp, Lary C., and Donald L. Rampp. *The Civil War in Indian Territory.* Austin: Presidial Press, 1975.

Ramsdell, Charles W. *Behind the Lines in the Southern Confederacy.* Baton Rouge: Louisiana State University Press, 1944.

———. *Reconstruction in Texas.* New York: Columbia University Press, 1910.

Randall, James G., and David Donald. *The Civil War and Reconstruction.* 2nd ed., rev. Lexington, MA: D. C. Heath, 1969.

Ransleben, Guido E. *A Hundred Years of Comfort in Texas*. San Antonio: Naylor Press, 1954.

Reynolds, Donald E. *Editors Make War: Southern Newspapers in the Secession Crisis*. Nashville: Vanderbilt University Press, 1970.

Rhea, Gordon C. *The Battle of the Wilderness, May 5–6, 1864*. Baton Rouge: Louisiana State University Press, 1994.

Richardson, Rupert N. *The Frontier of Northeast Texas, 1846 to 1876*. Glendale, CA: Arthur H. Clark Company, 1963.

Richter, William C. *The Army in Texas During Reconstruction*. College Station: Texas A&M University Press, 1987.

Rister, Carl Coke. *Robert E. Lee in Texas*. Norman: University of Oklahoma Press, 1946.

Roland, Charles P. *Albert Sidney Johnston: Soldier of Three Republics*. Austin: University of Texas Press, 1964.

Rolle, Andrew F. *The Lost Cause: The Confederate Exodus to Mexico*. Norman: University of Oklahoma Press, 1965.

Rose, Victor M. *The Life and Services of Gen. Ben McCulloch*. Reprint. Austin: Steck Company, 1958.

Scaife, William R. *The Campaign for Atlanta:* Atlanta: priv. publ., 1990.

Schaadt, Robert L., and Clyde A. See, eds. *The History of Hardin County, Texas*. Dallas: Hardin County Historical Commission, 1991.

Scharf, J. Thomas. *History of the Confederate States Navy From Its Organization to the Surrender of Its Last Vessel*. New York: Rogers & Sherwood, 1887.

Sears, Stephen. *Landscape Turned Red: The Battle of Antietam*. New Haven and New York: Ticknor & Fields, 1983.

———. *To the Gates of Richmond: The Peninsula Campaign*. New York: Ticknor & Fields, 1992.

Shea, William L., and Earl J. Hess. *Pea Ridge: Civil War Campaign in the West*. Chapel Hill: University of North Carolina Press, 1992.

Shirley, Glenn. *Belle Starr and Her Times: The Literature, the Facts, and the Legends*. Norman: University of Oklahoma Press, 1982.

Sifakis, Stewart. *Compendium of the Confederate Armies: Texas*. New York: Facts on File, 1995.

Silver, James W. *Confederate Morale and Church Propaganda*. Reprint. Gloucester, MA: Peter Smith, 1964.

Silverthorne, Elizabeth. *Ashbel Smith of Texas: Pioneer, Patriot, Statesman, 1805–1886*. College Station: Texas A&M University Press, 1982.

———. *Plantation Life in Texas*. College Station: Texas A&M University Press, 1986.

Simkins, Francis B., and James Welch Patton. *The Women of the Confederacy*. Richmond: Garrett and Massie, 1936.

Simpson, Harold B. *Gaines Mill to Appomattox: Waco and McLennan County in Hood's Texas Brigade*. Waco: Texian Press, 1963.

———. *Hood's Texas Brigade in Poetry and Song*. Waco: Texian Press, 1968.

———. *Hood's Texas Brigade: Lee's Grenadier Guard*. Waco: Texian Press, 1970.

———. *Hood's Texas Brigade in Reunion and Memory*. Waco: Texian Press, 1974.

———. *Hood's Texas Brigade: A Compendium*. Waco: Texian Press, 1977.

Smith, David Paul. *Frontier Defense in the Civil War: Texas' Rangers and Rebels.* College Station: Texas A&M University Press, 1992.

Sommers, Richard J. *Richmond Redeemed: The Siege of Petersburg.* Garden City: Doubleday & Company, 1981.

Spencer, John. *From Corsicana to Appomattox: The Story of the Corsicana Invincibles and the Navarro Rifles.* Corsicana: The Texan Press, 1984.

———. *Terrell's Texas Cavalry.* Burnet, TX: Eakin Press, 1982.

Stambaugh, J. Lee, and Lillian J. Stambaugh. *The Lower Rio Grande Valley of Texas.* San Antonio: Naylor Company, 1954.

Starr, Stephen Z. *The Union Cavalry in the Civil War.* 3 vols. Baton Rouge: Louisiana State University Press, 1979–1985.

Steere, Edward. *The Wilderness Campaign.* Harrisburg, PA: Stackpole Company, 1960.

Stephens, Robert W. *August Buchel: Texan Soldier of Fortune.* Dallas, priv. publ., 1970.

Stewart, Kenneth L., and Arnoldo De Leon. *Not Room Enough: Mexicans, Anglos, and Socioeconomic Change in Texas, 1850–1900.* Albuquerque: University of New Mexico Press, 1993.

Sumrall, Alan K. *Battle Flags of Texans in the Confederacy.* Austin: Eakin Press, 1995.

Sword, Wiley. *Shiloh: Bloody April.* New York: William Morrow & Company, 1974.

———. *The Confederacy's Last Hurrah: Spring Hill, Franklin, & Nashville.* Lawrence: University of Kansas Press, 1992.

Symonds, Craig L. *Joseph E. Johnston: A Civil War Biography.* New York: W. W. Norton & Co., 1992.

Taylor, John M. *Bloody Valverde: A Civil War Battle on the Rio Grande, February 21, 1862.* Albuquerque: University of New Mexico Press, 1995.

Thompson, Jerry Don. *Colonel John Robert Baylor: Texas Indian Fighter and Confederate Soldier.* Hillsboro: Hill Junior College Press, 1971.

———. *Henry Hopkins Sibley, Confederate General of the West.* Natchitoches: Northwestern University Press, 1978.

———. *Mexican Texans in the Union Army.* El Paso: Texas Western Press, 1986.

———. *Sabers on the Rio Grande.* Austin: Presidial Press, 1974.

———. *Vaqueros in Blue & Gray.* Austin: Presidial Press, 1976.

Timmons, W. H. *El Paso: A Borderlands History.* El Paso: Texas Western Press, 1990.

Tolbert, Frank X. *Dick Dowling at Sabine Pass.* New York: McGraw-Hill, 1962.

Trammell, Camilla Davis. *Seven Pines: Its Occupants and Their Letters, 1825–1872.* Houston: Distributed by Southern Methodist University Press, 1986.

Trudeau, Noah Andre. *Bloody Roads South: The Wilderness to Cold Harbor, May–June 1864.* Boston: Little, Brown and Company, 1989.

———. *Out of the Storm: The End of the Civil War, April–June 1865.* Boston: Little, Brown, and Company, 1994.

Tucker, Glenn. *Chickamauga: Bloody Battle in the West.* Indianapolis: Bobbs-Merrill Company Publishers, 1961.

Turner, Martha Anne. *Richard Bennett Hubbard: An American Life.* Austin: Shoal Creek Publisher, 1979.

Tyler, Ronnie C. *Santiago Vidaurri and the Southern Confederacy*. Austin: Texas State Historical Association, 1973.

Wakelyn, Jon. *Biographical Directory of the Confederacy*. Westport, CT: Green-wood Press, 1977.

Wallace, Ernest. *Charles DeMorse: Pioneer Statesman and Father of Texas Journalism*. Lubbock: Texas Tech Press, 1943.

———. *Texas in Turmoil*. Austin: Steck-Vaughn, 1965.

Waller, John L. *Colossal Hamilton of Texas: A Biography of Andrew Jackson Hamilton*. El Paso: Texas Western Press, 1968.

Walther, Eric H. *The Fire-Eaters*. Baton Rouge: Louisiana State University Press, 1992.

Warner, Erza. *Generals in Blue: Lives of Union Commanders*. Baton Rouge: Louisiana State University Press, 1964.

———. *Generals in Gray: Lives of Confederate Commanders*. Baton Rouge: Louisiana State University Press, 1959.

Warner, Erza, and W. Buck Yearns. *Biographical Register of the Confederate Congress*. Baton Rouge: Louisiana State University Press, 1975.

Waugh, John C. *Sam Bell Maxey and the Confederate Indians*. Fort Worth: Ryan Place Publishers, 1995.

Webb, Walter P. *The Texas Rangers: A Century of Frontier Defense*. New York: Houghton Mifflin, 1935.

Webb, Walter P., H. Bailey Carroll, and Eldon Branda, eds. *The Handbook of Texas*. 3 vols. Austin: Texas State Historical Association, 1952, 1976.

Weddle, Robert S. *Plow–Horse Cavalry: The Caney Creek Boys of the Thirty–fourth Texas*. Austin: Madrona Press, 1974.

Welsh, Jack D. *Medical Histories of Confederate Generals*. Kent, OH: Kent State University Press, 1995.

Wert, Jerry D. *General James Longstreet: The Confederacy's Most Controversial Soldier*. New York: Simon & Schuster, 1993.

Whitford, William C. *Colorado Volunteers in the Civil War: The New Mexico Campaign in 1862*. Reprint. Glorieta, NM: Rio Grande Press, 1971.

Wilkinson, Joseph B. *Laredo and the Rio Grande Frontier*. Austin: Jenkins Publishing Company, 1975.

Williams, John Hoyt. *Sam Houston: A Biography of the Father of Texas*. New York: Simon and Schuster, 1993.

Winegarten, Ruthe. *Texas Women: A Pictorial History from Indians to Astronauts*. Austin: Eakin Press, 1986.

Winfrey, Dorman. *Seventy–five Years of Texas History: The Texas State Historical Association, 1897–1972*. Austin: Pemberton Publishing Company, 1975.

Winsor, Bill. *Texas in the Confederacy: Military Installations, Economy, and People*. Hillsboro: Hill Junior College Press, 1978.

Winters, John D. *The Civil War in Louisiana*. Baton Rouge: Louisiana State University Press, 1963.

Wise, Stephen R. *Lifeline of the Confederacy: Blockade Running During the Civil War*. Columbia: University of South Carolina Press, 1988.

Wisehart, M. K. *Sam Houston: American Giant*. Washington: Luce Publishing, 1962.

Woodworth, Steven E. *Jefferson Davis and His Generals: The Failure of Confederate Command in the West*. Lawrence: University Press of Kansas, 1990.

Wooster, Ralph A. *The Secession Conventions of the South*. Princeton: Princeton University Press, 1962.

Wooster, Robert. *Soldiers, Sutlers and Settlers: Garrison Life on the Texas Frontier*. College Station: Texas A&M University Press, 1987.

Wooten, Dudley G. *A Comprehensive History of Texas, 1685 to 1897*. 2 vols. Dallas: William G. Scarff, 1898.

Wright, Arthur A. *The Civil War in the Southwest*. Denver: Big Mountain Press, 1964.

Wright, Marcus J., comp. *Texas in the War, 1861–1865*. Ed. Harold B. Simpson. Hillsboro: Hill Junior College Press, 1965.

Yearns, W. Buck, ed. *Confederate Governors*. Athens: University of Georgia Press, 1985.

———. *The Confederate Congress*. Athens: University of Georgia Press, 1960.

Young, Kevin. *To the Tyrants Never Yield: A Texas Civil War Sampler*. Plano: Wordware Publishing Inc., 1992.

Articles and Parts of Books

Adams, Paul. "Amelia Barr in Texas, 1856–1868." *SHQ* 49 (January 1946): 361–373.

Addington, Wendell G. "Slave Insurrections in Texas." *Journal of Negro History* 35 (October 1950): 408–434.

Alberts, Don E. "The Battle of Peralta." *New Mexico Historical Review* 63 (October 1983): 369–379.

Ashcraft, Allan C. "Confederate Beef Packing at Jefferson, Texas." *SHQ* 68 (October 1964): 259–270.

———. "The Union Occupation of the Lower Rio Grande in the Civil War." *Texas Military History* 8, no. 4 (1970): 13–26.

Avillo, Philip J., Jr. "John H. Reagan: Unionist or Secessionist?" *ETHJ* 13 (Spring 1975): 23–33.

Baggett, James Alex. "The Constitutional Union Party in Texas." *SHQ* 82 (January 1979): 233–264.

Bailey, Anne J. "A Texas Cavalry Raid: Reaction to Black Soldiers and Contrabands." *Civil War History* 35 (June 1989): 138–152.

———. "Henry McCulloch's Texans and the Defense of Arkansas in 1862." *Arkansas Historical Quarterly* 46 (Spring 1987): 46–59.

———. "Texans Invade Missouri: The Cape Giradeau Raid, 1863." *Missouri Historical Review* 84 (January 1990): 166–187.

———. "The Texas Cavalry's Race to Reinforce Arkansas Post, January 1863." *ETHJ* 28 (Spring 1990): 45–56.

———. "Was There a Massacre at Poison Spring?" *Military History of the Southwest* 20 (Fall 1990): 157–168.

Baker, Robin E., and Dale Baum. "The Texas Voter and the Crisis of the Union, 1859–1861." *Journal of Southern History* 53 (August 1987): 395–420.

Barr, Alwyn. "Confederate Artillery in Arkansas." *Arkansas Historical Quarterly* 22 (Autumn 1963): 238–272.

————. "Confederate Artillery in the Trans Mississippi." *Military Affairs* 27 (Summer 1963): 77–83.

————. "Confederate Artillery in Western Louisiana, 1862–1863." *Civil War History* 9 (March 1963): 74–85.

————. "Confederate Artillery in Western Louisiana, 1864." *Louisiana History* 5 (Winter 1964): 53–74.

————. "Revolutionary Changes in Civil War Texas," in *Texas Heritage*, ed. Ben Procter and Archie P. McDonald (St. Louis: Forum Press, 1980): 81–92.

————. "Sabine Pass, September 1863." *Texas Military History* 2 (February 1962): 17–22.

————. "Texas Coastal Defense, 1861–1865." *SHQ* 65 (July 1961): 1–31.

————. "Texas Confederate Artillery." *Texas Military History* 1 (August 1961): 1–12.

————. "Texas Losses in the Red River Campaign, 1864." *Texas Military History* 3 (Summer 1963): 103–110.

————, ed. "The Battle of Bayou Bourbeau, November 3, 1863: Colonel Oran M. Roberts' Report." *Louisiana History* 6 (Winter 1965): 83–91.

————. "The Battle of Blair's Landing." *Louisiana Studies* 2 (Winter 1963): 204–212.

————. "The Battle of Calcasieu Pass." *SHQ* 66 (July 1962): 58–67.

————. "The Making of a Secessionist: The Antebellum Career of Roger Q. Mills." *SHQ* 79 (October 1975): 129–144.

Baum, Dale. "Pinpointing Apparent Fraud in the 1861 Texas Secession Referendum." *Journal of Interdisciplinary History* 22 (Autumn 1991): 201–221.

Bearss, Edwin C. "The Battle of Pea Ridge." *Arkansas Historical Quarterly* 20 (Spring 1961): 74–94.

————. "The Battle of the Post of Arkansas." *Arkansas Historical Quarterly* 18 (Autumn 1959): 237–279.

Betts, Vicki. "'Private and Amateur Hangings'" The Lynching of W. W. Montgomery, March 15, 1863." *SHQ* 88 (October 1984): 145–166.

Block, W. T. "A Towering East Texas Pioneer: A Biographical Sketch of Colonel Albert Miller Lea." *ETHJ* 32 (Fall 1993): 23–33.

————. "Calcasieu Pass, Victory, Heroism 'Equal Dowling's'." *ETHJ* 9 (Fall 1971): 139–144.

————. "Fort Griffin Myths Exploded." *ETHJ* 9 (October 1971): 137–139.

————. "Legend of 2 Old Cannons." *ETHJ* 9 (October 1971): 147–149.

————. "Sabine Pass in the Civil War." *ETHJ* 9 (October 1971): 129–136.

————. "The Aftermath of Dowling's Victory: Military Activity in and Around Sabine Pass from September 1863 to Surrender." *Blue & Gray Magazine* 4 (September 1986): 54–60.

————. "The Civil War Comes to Jefferson County, Texas." *Blue & Gray Magazine* 4 (September 1986): 10–18.

————. "The Swamp Angels: A History of Spaight's 11th Battalion, Texas Volunteer, Confederate States Army." *ETHJ* 30 (Spring 1992): 44–57.

Bowen, Nancy Head. "A Political Labyrinth: Texas in the Civil War." *ETHJ* 11 (Fall 1973): 3–11.

Bridges, C. A. "The Knights of the Golden Circle: A Filibustering Fantasy." *SHQ* 44 (January 1941): 287–302.

Brown, Fred E. "The Battle of Allatoona." *Civil War History* 6 (September 1960): 277–297.

Brown, Russell. "An Old Woman with a Broomstick: General David E. Twiggs and the U.S. Surrender in Texas, 1861." *Military Affairs* 48 (April 1984): 57–61.

Brown, Walter L. "Pea Ridge: Gettysburg of the West." *Arkansas Historical Quarterly* 15 (Spring 1956): 3–16.

Browne, P. D. "Captain T. D. Nettles and the Valverde Battery." *Texana* 2 (Spring 1964): 1–23.

Buenger, Walter L. "Secession and the Texas German Community: Editor Lindheimer vs. Editor Flake." *SHQ* 82 (April 1979): 379–402.

———. "Secession Revisited: The Texas Experience." *Civil War History* 30 (December 1984): 293–315.

———. "Texas and the Riddle of Secession." *SHQ* 87 (October 1983): 151–182.

———. "Unionism on the Texas Frontier, 1859–1861." *Arizona and the West* 22 (Autumn 1980): 237–254.

Campbell, Randolph B. "George W. Whitmore: East Texas Unionist." *ETHJ* 28 (Spring 1990): 17–28.

Castel, Albert. "Quantrill in Texas." *Civil War Times Illustrated* 11 (June 1972): 20–27.

———. "Theophilus Holmes — Pallbearer of the Confederacy." *Civil War Times Illustrated* 15 (July 1977): 10–17.

Cleveland, Garnett. "The Confederate Naval Works at Goose Creek." *Touchstone* 9 (1990): 12–17.

Cole, A. C. "Lincoln's Election an Immediate Menace to Slavery in the States?" *American Historical Review* 36 (July 1931): 740–767.

Colquin, James. "The Life Story of Brig. Gen. Felix Robertson." *Texana* 8 (Spring 1970): 154–182.

Crook, Carland Elaine. "Benjamin Theron and French Designs in Texas During the Civil War." *SHQ* 68 (April 1965): 432–454.

Culberson, Charles. "General Sam Houston and Secession." *Scribner's Magazine* 39 (May 1906): 584–591.

Cullen, Joseph P. "The Battle of Gaines Mill." *Civil War Times Illustrated* 3 (April 1964): 11–17, 24.

Cumberland, Charles C. "The Confederate Loss and Recapture of Galveston, 1862–1863." *SHQ* 51 (October 1947): 109–130.

Darst, Maury. "Artillery Defenses of Galveston, 1863." *Military History of Texas and the Southwest* 12, no. 1 (1975): 63–67.

———. "Robert Hodges, Jr.: Confederate Soldier." *ETHJ* 9 (March 1971): 20–49.

Day, James M. "Leon Smith: Confederate Mariner." *ETHJ* 3 (March 1965): 34–49.

Delaney, Norman. "Corpus Christi — The Vicksburg of Texas." *Civil War Times Illustrated* 16 (July 1970): 4–9, 44–48.

Delaney, Robert W. "Matamoros, Port for Texas During the Civil War." *SHQ* 58 (April 1955): 473–487.

Dobney, Frederick J. "From Denominationalism to Nationalism in the Civil War." *Texana* 9, no. 4 (1971): 367–376.

Duncan, J. S. "Martin Hart, Civil War Guerrilla: Addenda." *Military History of Texas and the Southwest* 11, no. 2 (1973): 137–142.

Duncan, Jean S. "An East Texas *[sic.]* at an Oriental Court: Richard Bennett Hubbard, Minister to Japan, 1885–1889." *ETHJ* 16 (Fall 1978): 29–34.

Dunn, Roy Sylvan. "The KGC in Texas, 1860–1861." *SHQ* 70 (April 1967): 543–573.

Duty, Tony E. "The Home Front: McLennan County in the Civil War." *Texana* 12, no. 3 (1974): 197–238.

Edmonds, David C. "Surrender on the Bourbeux: Honorable Defeat or Incompetency Under Fire." *Louisiana History* 18 (Winter 1977): 63–86.

Elliott, Claude. "Union Sentiment in Texas, 1861–1865." *SHQ* 51 (April 1947): 449–477.

Ellis, L. Tuffly. "Maritime Commerce on the Far Western Gulf, 1861–1865." *SHQ* 77 (October 1973): 167–226.

Ewing, Floyd. "Origins of Unionist Sentiment on the West Texas Frontier." *WTHAYB* 32 (October 1956): 21–29.

———. "Unionist Sentiment on the Northwest Texas Frontier." *WTHAYB* 33 (October 1957): 58–70.

Faust, Drew Gilpin. "Trying to Do a Man's Business; Gender Violence and Slave Management in Civil War Texas," in Faust, *Southern Stories: Slaveholders in Peace and War* (Columbia: University of Missouri Press, 1992): 174–192.

Ferguson, I. D. "Battle of Dove Creek." *Frontier Times* 1 (June 1924): 24–31.

Fischer, LeRoy H. "David O. Dodd: Folk Hero of Confederate Arkansas." *Arkansas Historical Quarterly* 37 (Summer 1978): 130–146.

Fitzhugh, Lester N. "Saluria, Fort Esperanza, and Military Operations on the Texas Coast, 1861–1864." *SHQ* 61 (July 1957): 66–100.

———. "Texas Forces in the Red River Campaign, March–May 1864." *Texas Military History* 3 (Spring 1963): 15–22.

Frazier, Donald S. "Texans on the Teche: The Texas Brigade at the Battles of Bisland and Irish Bend, April 12–14, 1863." *Louisiana History* 32 (Fall 1991): 417–435.

Flynt, Wayne. "The Texas Legion at Vicksburg." *ETHJ* 17 (Spring 1979): 60–67.

Franks, Kenny A. "Operations Against Opothleyahola." *Military History of Texas and the Southwest* 10, no. 3 (1972): 187–196.

Gage, Larry J. "The Texas Road to Secession and War: John Marshall and the *Texas State Gazette*, 1860–1861." *SHQ* 62 (October 1958): 191–226.

Gallaway, B. P. "A Texas Farm Boy Enlists in the 12th Cavalry." *Texas Military History* 8, no. 2 (1970): 87–95.

Garrison, George P. "Guy Morrison Bryan." *Quarterly of the Texas State Historical Association* 5 (October 1901): 121–136.

Garrison, L. R. "Administrative Problems of the Confederate Post Office." *SHQ* 19 (October–January 1915–16): 111–141, 232–250.

Geise, William R. "Missouri's Confederate Capital at Marshall, Texas." *SHQ* 66 (October 1962): 193–207.

———. "The Confederate Northwest, May–August 1861: A Study of Organization and Command in the Trans–Mississippi West." *Military History of Texas and the Southwest* 13, no. 1 (1976): 11–20.

————. "Divided Command in the West, August–September 1861." *Military History of Texas and the Southwest* 13, no. 2 (1976): 47–54.

————. "Texas — The First Year of the War, April 1861–April 1862." *Military History of Texas and the Southwest* 13, no. 4 (1976): 19–43.

————. "Holmes, Arkansas, and the Defense of the Lower River, August 1862–February 1863." *Military History of Texas and the Southwest* 14, no. 4 (1977): 229–236.

Gentry, Judith F. "White Gold: The Confederate Government and Cotton in Louisiana." *Louisiana History* 33 (Summer 1992): 229–240.

Glover, Robert W., and Randal B. Gilbert. "Camp Ford, Tyler, Texas — The Largest Confederate Prison Camp West of the Mississippi River." *Chronicles of Smith County, Texas* 28 (Winter 1989): 16–36.

Goldberg, Mitchell S. "A Federal Raid into Galveston Harbor, November 7–8, 1861: What Really Happened?" *SHQ* 76 (July 1972): 58–70.

Goldblatt, Kenneth A. "The Confederate Capture of Arizona." *Texas Military History* 8, no. 2 (1970): 77–86.

Goodwin, Katherine G. "'A Woman's Curosity': Martha Gaffney and Cotton Planting on the Texas Frontier." *ETHJ* 24 (Fall 1986): 4–17.

Graham, Stanley S. "Campaign for New Mexico, 1861–1862." *Military History of Texas and the Southwest* 10, no. 1 (1972): 5–28.

Green, Michael Robert. "'. . . So Illy Provided . . .': Events Leading to the Creation of the Texas Military Board." *Military History of Texas and the Southwest* 10, no. 2 (1975): 115–125.

Gregory, Ival L. "The Battle of Prairie Grove, Arkansas, December 7, 1862." *Journal of the West* 19 (October 1980): 63–75.

Groce, William Wharton. "Major General John A. Wharton." *SHQ* 19 (January 1916): 271–278.

Gunn, Jack W. "Ben McCulloch: A Big Captain." *SHQ* 58 (July 1954): 1–18.

Gunter, Pete A. Y. "The Great Gainesville Hanging, October 1862. *Blue & Gray Magazine* 3 (April–May 1986): 48–55.

Hale, Douglas. "Life and Death Among the Lone Star Defenders: Cherokee County Boys in the Civil War." *ETHJ* 29 (Autumn 1991): 26–40.

————. "One Man's War: Captain Joseph H. Bruton, 1861–1865." *ETHJ* 20 (Fall 1982): 28–45.

————. "The Third Texas Cavalry: A Socioeconomic Profile of a Confederate Regiment." *Military History of Texas and the Southwest* 19 (Spring 1989): 1–26.

Hall, Claude H. "The Fabulous Tom Ochiltree: Promoter, Politician, and Raconteur." *SHQ* 71 (January 1968): 347–376.

Hall, Martin H. "Planter vs. Frontiersman: Conflict in Confederate Indian Policy," in *Essays on the American Civil War*, ed. William F. Holmes and Harold M. Hollingsworth (Austin: University of Texas at Arlington, 1968): 45–72.

————. "The Court–Martial of Arthur Pendleton Bagby." *ETHJ* 19 (Fall 1981): 60–67.

————. "The Formation of Sibley's Brigade and the March to New Mexico." *SHQ* 61 (January 1958): 383–405.

————. "The Skirmish at Mesilla." *Arizona and the West* 1 (Winter 1959): 343–351.

Hamilton, J. C. deRoulac. "Lincoln's Election an Immediate Menace to Slavery in the States?" *American Historical Review* 37 (July 1932): 700–711.

Hancock, Marvin J. "The Second Battle of Cabin Creek, 1864." *Chronicles of Oklahoma* 39 (Winter 1961): 414–426.

Hanson, Maynard J. "The Battle of Pea Ridge, Arkansas, March 6–8, 1862." *Journal of the West* 19 (October 1980): 39–50.

Harper, Cecil, Jr. "Slavery without Cotton: Hunt County, Texas, 1846–1864." *SHQ* 88 (April 1985): 386–405.

Harrison, Jon. "Tenth Texas Cavalry, C.S.A." *Military History of Texas and the Southwest* 12, no. 2–3 (1975): 93–107, 171–182.

Harrison, Lowell. "Perryville: Death on a Dry River." *Civil War Times Illustrated* 18 (May 1979): 4–9, 44–47.

Havins, T. R. "Administration of the Sequestration Act in the Confederate District Court for the Western District of Texas, 1862–1865." *SHQ* 43 (January 1940): 295–322.

Heidler, Jeanne T. "'Embarrassing Situation': David E. Twiggs and the Surrender of United States Forces in Texas, 1861." *Military History of the Southwest* 21 (Fall 1991): 157–172.

Hicks, Jimmie. "Texas and Separate Independence, 1860–1861." *ETHJ* 4 (October 1966): 85–106.

Holbrook, Abigail Curlee. "A Glimpse of Life on Antebellum Slave Plantations in Texas." *SHQ* 86 (April 1973): 361–383.

Holden, W. C. "Frontier Defense in Texas During the Civil War." *WTHAYB* 4 (June 1928): 16–31.

Holman, Dwayne, and Henry Keatts. "The Coldest Day: The Activities of a Confederate Boy Spy — David O. Dodd." *Military History of Texas and the Southwest* 9, no. 4 (1971): 281–288.

Horton, L. W. "General Sam Bell Maxey: His Defense of North Texas and the Indian Territory." *SHQ* 74 (April 1971): 507–524.

Howell D. S. "Along the Texas Frontier During the Civil War." *WTHAYB* 13 (October 1937): 82–95.

Howsley, Marilynne. "Forting Up on the Texas Frontier During the Civil War." *WTHAYB* 17 (October 1941): 71–76.

Hunt, Sylvia. "To Wed and to Teach: The Myth of the Single Teacher," in *Women and Texas History: Selected Essays,* ed. Fane Downs and Nancy Baker Jones (Austin: Texas State Historical Association, 1993): 127–142.

Hunter, J. Marvin. "The Battle of Dove Creek." *WTHAYB* 18 (October 1942): 74–87.

Hunter, John Warren. "Heel–Fly Time in Texas: Story of the Civil War Period." *Frontier Times* 1 (April 1924): 33–48; (May 1924): 33–48; (June 1924): 33–47.

Hutto, John R. "Living on Three Frontiers: Mrs. Martha Jane Conway." *WTHAYB* 25 (October 1949): 104–109.

Jager, Ronald B. "Houston, Texas Fights the Civil War." *Texana* 11, no. 1 (1973): 30–51.

Jeffries, C. C. "The Character of Terry's Texas Rangers." *SHQ* 64 (April 1961): 454–462.

Johnson, Boyd W. "Cullen Montgomery Baker: The Arkansas–Texas Desperado." *Arkansas Historical Quarterly* 25 (Autumn 1966): 229–239.

Jones, Allen W. "Military Events in Texas During the Civil War, 1861–1865." *SHQ* 64 (July 1960): 64–70.

Jones, Ernest. "The Battle of Sabine Pass, September 8, 1863." *Blue & Gray Magazine* 4 (September 1986): 19–24, 47–48, 50–53.

Jones, Robert L. "The First Iron Furnace in Texas." *SHQ* 63 (October 1959): 279–289.

Jones, Virgil C. "The Battle of Galveston Harbor." *Civil War Times Illustrated* 5 (February 1967): 28–38.

Jordan, Terry G. "A Century and Half of Ethnic Change in Texas, 1836–1986." *SHQ* 89 (April 1986): 385–422.

Kelley, Dayton. "The Texas Brigade at the Wilderness, May 6, 1864." *Texana* 11, no. 2 (1973): 103–123.

Kerr, Homer L. "Battle of Elkhorn: The Gettysburg of the Trans–Mississippi West," in *Essays on the American Civil War*, ed. William F. Holmes and Harold M. Hollingsworth (Austin: University of Texas at Arlington, 1968): 31–44.

King, Alma Dexta. "The Political Career of Williamson Simpson Oldham." *SHQ* 33 (October 1929): 112–131.

Lale, Max S. "New Light on the Battle of Mansfield." *ETHJ* 25 (Fall 1987): 34–41.

———. "Robert W. Loughery: Rebel Editor." *ETHJ* 21 (Spring 1983): 3–15.

Ledbetter, Bill. "Slave Unrest and White Panic: The Impact of Black Republicanism in Ante–Bellum Texas." *Texana* 10, no. 4 (1972): 335–350.

Logan, Robert, "The Battle of Prairie Grove." *Arkansas Historical Quarterly* 16 (Autumn 1957): 258–267.

Luvaas, Jay. "Bentonville — Johnston's Last Stand." *North Carolina Historical Review* 33 (July 1956): 332–358.

Maher, Edward R., Jr. "Sam Houston and Secession." *SHQ* 55 (April 1952): 448–458.

Marks, Paula Mitchell. "The Ranger Reverend." *Civil War Times Illustrated* 24 (December 1985): 40–45.

Marten, James. "A Wearying Experience: Texas Refugees in New Orleans, 1862–1865." *Louisiana History* 28 (February 1987): 343–356.

———. "For the Army, The People, and Abraham Lincoln: A Yankee Newspaper in Occupied Texas." *Civil War History* 39 (June 1993): 126–147.

———. "John L. Haynes: A Southern Dissenter in Texas." *Southern Studies*, New Series, 1 (Fall 1990): 257–279.

———. "Slaves and Rebels: The Peculiar Institution in Texas, 1861–1865." *ETHJ* 28 (Spring 1990): 29–36.

Martin, David P. "The *Harriet Lane*." *SHQ* 39 (July 1935): 15–20.

Martin, Howard N. "Texas Redskins in Confederate Gray." *SHQ* 70 (April 1967): 586–592.

McArthur, Henry S. "A Yank at Sabine Pass." *Civil War Times Illustrated* 12 (December 1973): 38–43.

McArthur, Judith N. "Myth, Reality, and Anomaly: The Complex World of Rebecca Hagerty." *ETHJ* 24 (Fall 1986): 18–32.

McCaslin, Richard B. "Conditional Confederates: The Eleventh Texas Cavalry West of the Mississippi River." *Military History of the Southwest* 21 (Spring 1991): 87–99.

———. "Dark Corner of the Confederacy: James G. Bourland and the Border Regiment." *Military History of the West* 24 (Spring 1994): 57–70.

———. "Wheat Growers in the Cotton Confederacy: The Suppression of Dissent in Collin County, Texas, During the Civil War." *SHQ* 96 (April 1993): 528–539.

McGowen, Stanley S. "Augustus Buchel: A Forgotten Texas Patriot," *Military History of the West* 25 (Spring 1995): 1–21.

McMurry, Richard M. "Confederate Morale in the Atlanta Campaign of 1864." *Georgia Historical Quarterly* 54 (Summer 1970): 226–243.

McWhiney, Grady. "Controversy in Kentucky: Braxton Bragg's Campaign of 1862." *Civil War History* 6 (March 1960): 5–42.

Meiners, Fredericka. "Hamilton P. Bee in the Red River Campaign." *SHQ* 78 (July 1974): 21–44.

———. "The Texas Border Cotton Trade, 1862–1863." *Civil War History* 23 (December 1977): 293–306.

Mering, John V. "Allies or Opponents? The Douglas Democrats and the Constitutional Unionists." *Southern Studies* 23 (Winter 1984): 376–385.

Michot, Stephen S. "In Relief of Port Hudson: Richard Taylor's 1863 Lafourche Offensive." *Military History of the West* 23 (Fall 1993): 103–134.

Milbourn, Curtis W. "Brigadier General Thomas Green of Texas." *ETHJ* 32 (Spring 1994): 3–11.

Miller, E. T. "The State Finances of Texas During the Civil War." *Quarterly of Texas State Historical Association* 14 (July 1910): 1–23.

Mitchell, Leon, Jr. "Camp Ford: Confederate Military Prison." *SHQ* 66 (July 1962): 1–16.

———. "Camp Groce: Confederate Military Prison." *SHQ* 67 (July 1963): 15–27.

Moore, Richard. "A Smuggler's Exile: S. M. Swenson Flees Texas." *ETHJ* 25 (Spring 1987): 23–29.

Moretta, John. "William Pitt Ballinger and the Travail of Texas Secession." *Houston Review* 11, no. 1 (1989): 3–26.

Muir, Andrew Forest. "Dick Dowling and the Battle of Sabine Pass." *Civil War History* 4 (December 1958): 399–428.

———. "Sam Houston and the Civil War." *Texana* 6 (Fall 1968): 282–287.

———. "Murder on Madison Avenue: The Rice Case Revisited." *Southwest Review* 44 (Winter 1959): 1–9.

———. "William Marsh Rice, Houstonian." *ETHJ* 2 (Spring 1964): 32–39.

Neighbours, Kenneth. "Elm Creek Raid in Young County, 1864." *WTHAYB* 40 (October 1964): 83–89.

Norton, Wesley. "The Methodist Episcopal Church and the Civil Disturbances in North Texas in 1859 and 1860." *SHQ* 68 (January 1965): 317–341.

Oates, Stephen B. "Cavalry Fight at Cane Hill." *Arkansas Historical Quarterly* 20 (Spring 1961): 65–73.

———. "John S. 'Rip' Ford: Prudent Cavalryman, C.S.A." *SHQ* 64 (January 1961): 289–314.

———. "Recruiting Confederate Cavalry in Texas." *SHQ* 69 (April 1961): 463–477.

———. "The Prairie Grove Campaign, 1862." *Arkansas Historical Quarterly* 19 (Summer 1960): 119–141.

————. "Texas Under the Secessionists." *SHQ* 67 (October 1963): 167–212.

Parham, W. C. "David O. Dodd: The Nathan Hale of Arkansas." *Publications of Arkansas Historical Association* 2 (1908): 531–535.

Paschal, George W. "The Last Years of Sam Houston." *Harper's New Monthly Magazine* 32 (December–May 1865–1866): 630–635.

Perrine, David P. "The Battle of Valverde, New Mexico Territory, February 21, 1862." *Journal of the West* 19 (October 1980): 26–38.

Peters, Steve. "Murder of Col. Joseph M. Bounds, Eleventh Texas Cavalry, C.S.A." *Texana* 12, no. 1 (1974): 56–60.

Pickens, Kel N. "The Battle of Wilson's Creek, Missouri, August 10, 1861." *Journal of the West* 19 (October 1980): 10–25.

Pool, William C. "The Battle of Dove Creek." *SHQ* 53 (April 1950): 367–385.

Price, Marcus W. "Ships That Tested the Blockade of the Gulf Ports, 1861–1865." *American Neptune* 11 (October 1951): 262–290; 12 (July 1952): 229–238; 13 (April 1953): 154–161; 15 (January 1955): 97–131.

Prim, C. Clinton, Jr. "Born Again in the Trenches: Revivals in the Army of Tennessee." *Tennessee Historical Quarterly* 43 (Fall 1984): 250–272.

Rampp, Lary C. "William C. Quantrill's Civil War Activities in Texas." *Texas Military History* 8, no. 4 (1970): 221–231.

Rampp, Lary C., and Donald L. Rampp. "The Civil War in Indian Territory." *Military History of Texas and the Southwest* 10, no. 1–2, 4: 29–42, 93–114, 249–272; 11, no. 2–4: 77–198, 173–195, 251–280.

————. "The Phillips Expedition: The Abortive Federal Invasion of Texas, January–February 1864." *Military History of Texas and the Southwest* 9, no. 1 (1971): 22–33.

Ramsdell, Charles W. "Last Hope of the Confederacy — John Tyler to Governor and Authorities of Texas." *Quarterly of Texas State Historical Association* 14 (October 1910): 129–145.

————. "Texas From the Fall of the Confederacy to the Beginning of Reconstruction." *Quarterly of Texas State Historical Association* 11 (January 1908): 199–219.

————. "The Frontier and Secession," in *Studies in Southern History Inscribed to William Archibald Dunning* (New York: Columbia University Press, 1914): 63–79.

————. "The Texas State Military Board, 1862–1865." *SHQ* 27 (April 1924): 253–275.

Randolph, Nowlin. "Judge William Pinckney Hill Aids the Confederate War Effort." *SHQ* 68 (July 1964): 14–28.

Reynolds, Donald E. "Reluctant Martyr: Anthony Bewley and the Texas Slave Insurrection Panic of 1860." *SHQ* 96 (January 1993): 345–361.

Richards, Don. "The Battle of Poison Spring." *Arkansas Historical Quarterly* 18 (Winter 1959): 330–385.

Richter, William L. "Devil Take Them All: Military Rule in Texas, 1862–1870." *Southern Studies* 25 (Spring 1986): 5–30.

Rippy, J. Fred. "Mexican Projects of the Confederates." *SHQ* 22 (April 1919): 291–317.

Rister, Carl Coke. "Carlota, A Confederate Colony in Mexico." *Journal of Southern History* 11 (February 1945): 33–50.

Roberts, O. M. "The Political, Legislative, and Judicial History of Texas For Its Fifty Years of Statehood, 1845–1895," in Dudley G. Wooten, *Comprehensive History of Texas, 1685–1897*, 2 vols. (Dallas: William G. Scarff, 1898): 2:7–325.

Rutherford, Phillip. "Defying the State of Texas." *Civil War Times Illustrated* 18 (April 1979): 16–21.

———. "The Great Gainesville Hanging." *Civil War Times Illustrated* 17 (April 1978): 12–20.

———. "The Other Civil War: Disaster at Dove Creek." *Civil War Times Illustrated* 22 (April 1983): 20–25.

Sandbo, Anna Irene. "Beginnings of the Secession Movement in Texas." *SHQ* 18 (July 1914): 41–73.

———. "First Session of the Secession Convention." *SHQ* 18 (October 1914): 162–194.

Sandefer, H. L., and Archie P. McDonald. "Sabine Pass: David and Goliath." *Texana* 7 (Fall 1969): 177–188.

Santee, J. F. "The Battle of La Glorieta Pass." *New Mexico Historical Review* 6 (January 1931): 66–75.

Sawyer, William E. "The Martin Hart Conspiracy." *Arkansas Historical Quarterly* 23 (Summer 1964): 154–165.

———. "Martin Hart, Civil War Guerrilla." *Texas Military History* 3 (Fall 1963): 146–153.

Schooner, Thomas. "Confederate Diplomacy and the Texas–Mexican Border, 1861–1865." *ETHJ* 11 (Spring 1973): 33–39.

Shea, William L. "The Confederate Defeat at Cache River." *Arkansas Historical Quarterly* 52 (Summer 1993): 129–155.

———. "The Road to Pea Ridge." *Arkansas Historical Quarterly* 52 (Autumn 1993): 205–222.

Shook, Robert W. "The Battle of the Nueces, August 10, 1862." *SHQ* 66 (July 1962): 31–42.

Sibley, Marilyn McAdams. "Charles Stillman: A Case Study of Entrepreneurship on the Rio Grande, 1861–1865." *SHQ* 78 (October 1973): 227–240.

Silverman, Jason H. "Confederate Ambitions for the Southwest: A New Perspective." *Red River Valley Historical Review* 4 (Winter 1979): 62–71.

Simmons, Laura. "Waul's Legion From Texas to Mississippi." *Texana* 7 (Spring 1969): 1–16.

Simpson, Harold B. "East Texas Companies in Hood's Brigade." *ETHJ* 3 (March 1965): 5–17.

———. "Foraging with Hood's Texas Brigade From Texas to Pennsylvania." *Texana* 1 (Summer 1963): 258–276.

———. "Hood's Brigade at Appomattox." *Texana* 3 (Spring 1965): 1–19.

———. "The Battle of Sabine Pass," in Seymour Connor, et. al., *Battles of Texas* (Waco: Texian Press, 1967): 137–169.

———. "The Recruiting, Training, and Camp Life of a Company of Hood's Brigade in Texas." *Texas Military History* 2 (August 1962): 171–192.

———. "West Pointers in the Texas Confederate Army." *Texas Military History* 6 (Spring 1967): 55–88.

Smallwood, James. "Disaffection in Confederate Texas: The Hanging at Gaines-ville." *Civil War History* 22 (December 1976): 349–360.

Smith, David P. "Conscription and Conflict on the Texas Frontier, 1863–1865." *Civil War History* 36 (September 1990): 250–261.

———. "Frontier Defense and the Cooke County Raid, 1863." *WTHAYB* 64 (October 1988): 30–43.

———. "The Elm Creek Raid, 1864: State and Confederate Defense and Re-sponse." *Military History of the Southwest* 19 (Fall 1989): 121–136.

Smith, Mitchell. "The 'Neutral' Matamoros Trade, 1861–1865." *Southwest Review* 37 (Autumn 1952): 319–324.

Smyrl, Frank H. "Texans in the Union Army, 1861–1865." *SHQ* 65 (October 1961): 234–250.

———. "Unionism in Texas, 1856–1861." *SHQ* 68 (October 1964): 172–195.

Snider, Joleene Maddox. "Sarah Devereux: A Study in Southern Femininity." *SHQ* 97 (January 1994): 479–508.

Somers, Dale A. "James P. Newcomb: The Making of a Radical." *SHQ* 72 (April 1969): 449–469.

Spanhanks, Helen. "Marshall and the Civil War." *Touchstone* 1 (1982): 40–45.

Stoltz, Jack. "Kaufman County in the Civil War." *ETHJ* 28 (Spring 1990): 37–44.

Stuart, Ben C. "Hamilton Stuart: Pioneer Editor." *SHQ* 21 (April 1918): 381–388.

Swanson, Gary R., and Timothy D. Johnson. "Conflict in East Tennessee: Gener-als Law, Jenkins, and Longstreet." *Civil War History* 31 (June 1985): 101–110.

Taylor, Bride Neill. "The Beginnings of the Texas State Historical Association." *SHQ* 33 (July 1929): 1–17.

Thomas, Emory. "Rebel Nationalism: E. H. Cushing and the Confederate Experi-ence." *SHQ* 73 (January 1970): 343–355.

Thompson, Jerry Don. "A Stand Along the Border: Santos Benavides and the Battle for Laredo." *Civil War Times Illustrated* 19 (August 1980): 26–33.

———. "Mexican Americans in the Civil War: The Battle of Valverde." *Texana* 10, no. 1 (1972): 1–19.

———. "Mutiny and Desertion on the Rio Grande: The Strange Saga of Captain Adrian J. Vidal." *Military History of Texas and the Southwest* 12, no. 3 (1975): 160–167.

Timmons, Joe T. "The Referendum in Texas on the Ordinance of Secession, Feb-ruary 23, 1861: The Vote." *ETHJ* 11 (Fall 1973): 12–28.

Trexler, H. A. "The *Harriet Lane* and the Blockade of Galveston." *SHQ* 35 (Octo-ber 1931): 109–123.

Tucker, Philip C., III. "The United States Gunboat *Harriet Lane*." *SHQ* (April 1918): 360–380.

Tyler, Ronnie C. "Cotton on the Border, 1861–1865." *SHQ* 73 (April 1970): 456–477.

Tyson, Carl P. "Highway of War." *Red River Historical Review* 3 (Summer 1978): 28–56.

Vandiver, Frank E. "Texas and the Confederate Army's Meat Problem." *SHQ* 47 (January 1944): 225–233.

Walker, Charles R. "Spaight's Battalion, C.S.A." *Texas Gulf Historical and Bio-graphical Record* 8 (November 1972): 22–38.

Waller, John L. "Colonel George Wythe Baylor." *Southwestern Social Science Quarterly* 24 (June 1943): 23–35.

Watford, W. H. "Confederate Western Ambitions." *SHQ* 44 (October 1940): 161–187.

Webb, J. R. "Chapters From the Frontier Life of Phin W. Reynolds." *WTHAYB* 21 (October 1945): 110–143.

Weinert, Richard P. "Confederate Border Troubles with Mexico." *Civil War Times Illustrated* 3 (October 1964): 36–43.

Westphall, David. "The Battle of Glorieta Pass: Its Importance in the Civil War." *New Mexico Historical Review* 44 (April 1969): 137–151.

Westwood, Howard C. "President Lincoln's Overture to Sam Houston." *SHQ* 88 (October 1984): 125–144.

White, William W. "The Disintegration of an Army: Confederate Forces in Texas, April–June 1865." *ETHJ* 26 (Fall 1988): 40–47.

———. "The Texas Slave Insurrection in 1860." *SHQ* 52 (January 1949): 259–285.

Wiley, Bell I. "Confederate Exiles in Brazil." *Civil War Times Illustrated* 15 (January 1977): 22–32.

Wilson, Gary. "The Ordeal of William H. Cowdin and the Officers of the Forty–Second Massachusetts Regiment: Union Prisoners in Texas." *ETHJ* 23 (Spring 1985): 16–26.

Winschel, Terrence J. "To Rescue Gibraltar: John Walker's Texas Division and its Expedition to Relieve Fort Vicksburg." *Civil War Regiments* 3, no. 3 (1994): 33–58.

Wooster, Ralph A. "An Analysis of the Membership of the Texas Secession Convention." *SHQ* 62 (January 1959): 322–335.

———. "Ben H. Epperson: East Texas Lawyer, Legislator, and Civic Leader." *ETHJ* 5 (March 1967): 29–42.

———. "Confederate Success at Perryville." *Register of the Kentucky Historical Society* 59 (October 1961): 318–323.

———. "The Texas Gulf Coast in the Civil War." *Texas Gulf Historical and Biographical Record* 1 (November 1965): 7–16.

———. "Wealthy Texans, 1860." *SHQ* 71 (October 1967): 163–180.

———. "Wealthy Texans, 1870." *SHQ* 74 (October 1970): 24–35.

———. "With the Confederate Cavalry in the West: The Civil War Experiences of Isaac Dunbar Affleck." *SHQ* 83 (July 1979): 1–28.

Wooster, Ralph A., and Robert Wooster. "A People at War: East Texans During the Civil War." *ETHJ* 28 (Spring 1990): 3–16.

———. "'Rarin' for a Fight': Texans in the Confederate Army." *SHQ* 84 (April 1981): 387–426.

Wooten, Dudley G. "The Life and Services of Oran Milo Roberts." *Quarterly of Texas State Historical Association* 2 (July 1898): 1–20.

Young, Hugh. "Two Texas Patriots." *SHQ* 44 (July 1910): 27–32.

Young, Jo. "The Battle of Sabine Pass." *SHQ* 52 (April 1949): 398–409.

Dissertations and Theses

Airey, Guy, Jr. "The Texas–Mexican Border, 1861–1866." M.A. thesis, Lamar University, 1971.

Ashcraft, Allan C. "Texas: 1860–1866. The Lone Star State in the Civil War." Ph.D. dissertation, Columbia University, 1960.

Bailey, Lelia. "The Life and Public Career of O. M. Roberts." Ph.D. dissertation, University of Texas, 1932.

Benjamin, Ronald Leon. "East Texas in the Civil War." M.A. thesis, Lamar State College of Technology, 1970.

Bowen, Nancy Head. "A Political Labyrinth: Texas in the Civil War — Questions in Continuity." Ph.D. dissertation, Rice University, 1974.

Buenger, Walter L., Jr. "Stilling the Voice of Reason: Texans and the Union, 1854–1861." Ph.D. dissertation, Rice University, 1979.

Chamberlain, Charles K. "Alexander W. Terrell, Citizen, Statesman." Ph.D. dissertation, University of Texas, 1956.

Cowling, Annie. "The Civil War Trade of the Lower Rio Grande Valley." M.A. thesis, University of Texas, 1926.

Dugas, Vera Lea. "A Social and Economic History of Texas in the Civil War and Reconstruction Periods." Ph.D. dissertation, University of Texas, 1963.

Edwards, John A. "Social and Cultural Activities of Texans During Civil War and Reconstruction, 1861–1873." Ph.D. dissertation, Texas Tech University, 1985.

Friend, Llerena B. "The Life of Thomas Jefferson Chambers." M.A. thesis, University of Texas, 1928.

Felgar, Robert P. "Texas in the War for Southern Independence, 1861–1865." Ph.D. dissertation, University of Texas, 1935.

Garner, Ruby. "Galveston during the Civil War." M.A. thesis, University of Texas, 1927.

Geise, William Royston. "The Confederate Military Forces in the Trans–Mississippi West, 1861–1865: A Study in Command." Ph.D. dissertation, University of Texas, 1974.

Glover, Robert W. "The West Gulf Blockade, 1861–1865: An Evaluation." Ph.D. dissertation, North Texas State University, 1974.

Gray, Ronald N. "Edmund J. Davis: Radical Republican and Reconstruction Governor of Texas." Ph.D. dissertation, Texas Tech University, 1976.

Griffin, Roger Allen. "Connecticut Yankee in Texas: A Biography of Elisha Marshall Pease." Ph.D. dissertation, University of Texas, 1973.

Heidler, Jeanne Twiggs. "The Military Career of David Emanuel Twiggs." Ph.D. dissertation, Auburn University, 1988.

Hering, Julia Lee. "The Secession Movement in Texas." M.A. thesis, University of Texas, 1933.

Hudson, Linda S. "Military Knights of the Golden Circle in Texas, 1854–1861." M.A. thesis, Stephen F. Austin State University, 1990.

Johansson, M. Jane Harris. "Peculiar Honor: A History of the 28th Texas Cavalry (dismounted), Walker's Texas Division, 1862–1865." Ph.D. dissertation, University of North Texas, 1993.

Ledbetter, Billy J. "Slavery, Fear, and Disunion in the Lone Star State: Texans' Attitudes toward Secession and the Union, 1846–1861." Ph.D. dissertation, North Texas State University, 1972.

Maberry, Robert T., Jr. "Texans in the Defense of the Confederate Northwest,

April 1861–April 1862." Ph.D. dissertation, Texas Christian University, 1992.

Maher, Edward R., Jr. "Secession in Texas." Ph.D. dissertation, Fordham University, 1960.

Marshall, David. "Texas Baptist Political Attitudes Under Four National Governments: 1835–1865." M.A. thesis, Texas Tech University, 1986.

Meiners, Fredericka Ann. "The Texas Governorship, 1861–1865: Biography of an Office." Ph.D. dissertation, Rice University, 1974.

Moretta, John A. "William Pitt Ballinger: Public Servant, Private Pragmatist." Ph.D. dissertation, Rice University, 1985.

Morrow, Norman Potter. "Price's Missouri Expedition, 1864." M.A. thesis, University of Texas, 1949.

Purcell, Allan R. "The History of the Texas Militia, 1835–1903." Ph.D. dissertation, University of Texas, 1981.

Riley, John Denny. "Santos Benavides: His Influence on the Lower Rio Grande, 1823–1891." Ph.D. dissertation, Texas Christian University, 1976.

Scarborough, Jane L. "George W. Paschal, Texas Unionist and Scalawag Jurisprudent." Ph.D. dissertation, Rice University, 1972.

Settles, Thomas M. "The Military Career of John Bankhead Magruder." Ph.D. dissertation, Texas Christian University, 1972.

Shook, Robert W. "Federal Occupation and Administration of Texas, 1865–1870." Ph.D. dissertation, North Texas State University, 1970.

———. "German Unionism in Texas During the Civil War and Reconstruction." M.A. thesis, North Texas State University, 1957.

Sinclair, Lonnie. "Crossroads of Conviction: A Study of the Texas Political Mind, 1856–1861." Ph.D. dissertation, Rice University, 1975.

Smyrl, Frank H. "Unionism, Abolitionism, and Vigilantism in Texas, 1856–1865." M.A. thesis, University of Texas, 1961.

Spell, Timothy D. "John Bankhead Magruder: Defender of the Texas Coast, 1863." M.A. thesis, Lamar University, 1981.

Thompson, Jerry Don. "Brigadier General Henry Hopkins Sibley and the American Military Tradition." D.A. dissertation, Carnegie–Mellon University, 1981.

Villemez, Clyde. "Presidential Elections in Texas from Statehood to Secession." M.A. thesis, Lamar State College of Technology, 1968.

Warner, James B. "A Legislative History of Texas During the Civil War." M.A. thesis, Lamar State College of Technology, 1971.

York, Teresa Kay. "'Piney Woods' Dissidence: Angelina County in the 1850s and the Secession Crisis." M.A. thesis, Stephen F. Austin State University, 1990.

Index